SMALL FIRMS, LARGE CONCERNS

General Editor
Professor Akira Kudo, Institute of Social Science, University of Tokyo

Series Adviser
Professor Mark Mason, Yale University

FUJI CONFERENCE SERIES III

SMALL FIRMS, LARGE CONCERNS

The Development of Small Business in Comparative Perspective

Edited by

KONOSUKE ODAKA

and

MINORU SAWAI

OXFORD

UNIVERSITY PRESS

OXFORD
UNIVERSITY PRESS

Great Clarendon Street, Oxford OX2 6DP

Oxford University Press is a department of the University of Oxford
and furthers the University's aim of excellence in research, scholarship,
and education by publishing worldwide in

Oxford New York

Athens Auckland Bangkok Bogotá Buenos Aires Calcutta
Cape Town Chennai Dar es Salaam Delhi Florence Hong Kong Istanbul
Karachi Kuala Lumpur Madrid Melbourne Mexico City Mumbai
Nairobi Paris São Paulo Singapore Taipei Tokyo Toronto Warsaw
and associated companies in Berlin Ibadan

Oxford is a registered trade mark of Oxford University Press

Published in the United States
by Oxford University Press Inc., New York

British Library Cataloguing in Publication Data
Data available

Library of Congress Cataloging in Publication Data
Data available

ISBN 0–19–829379–8

1 3 5 7 9 10 8 6 4 2

Typeset in Palatino
by Alliance Phototypesetters, Pondicherry
Printed in Great Britain
on acid-free paper by
Biddles Limited, Guildford and King's Lynn

ACKNOWLEDGEMENTS

The chapters that make up this book consist of papers that were delivered at the 24th International Conference on Business History, which took place from 5 to 8 January 1997 at the foot of Mt. Fuji. The International Conference on Business History has been held in Japan in January of every year since 1974, becoming known throughout the world as the 'Fuji Conference'. This annual conference has been made possible by the gracious co-operation of business historians from all parts of the world. The continued generous support of the Taniguchi Foundation made it possible to inaugurate a fifth conference series, running from January 1994 to January 1998. The Organizing Committee of the fifth series, chaired by Professor Akira Kudo, decided to direct attention towards production systems, business–government relationships, interfirm relationships, small business, and entrepreneurships, all of which have been focal points in recent discussion in the field of business history.

Konosuke Odaka and Minoru Sawai were entrusted with the work of organizing the fourth conference of the fifth series around a general topic relating to small business. In line with the wishes of the Organizing Committee, Odaka and Sawai set the theme for the conference as the 'Comparative Business History of Small Business'. This was the first time in the nearly quarter-century history of the International Conference to take up the theme of small business, which has been the focus of public attention in industrialized countries since the oil crisis of the early 1970s.

The financial support of the Taniguchi Foundation is also making it possible to publish the papers of the 24th International Conference. The editors, as well as the Organizing Committee, would like to express their deepest gratitude to the Taniguchi Foundation for its continuing sponsorship of the Conference. Professor Mark Mason kindly acted as adviser for the publication of the papers in the fifth series of the International Conference on Business History: his diligent support and expert advice greatly facilitated the publication of this book.

The papers in this book were revised in accordance with the discussion at the Conference, which was attended not only by the authors but also by the following distinguished commentators and guests: Masanao Kasai, Ryoichi Koda, Fumikatsu Kubo, Akira Kudo, Satoshi Matsumura, Keiichiro Nakagawa, Toshikatsu Nakajima, Kazuhiro Omori, Jun Sasaki, Takao Shiba, Satoshi Takada, Kazuo Wada, Toshihiro Wada, Hiroaki Yamazaki,

Tomomichi Yoshikawa, and Tsunehiko Yui. The editors would like to thank them for their active participation and valuable contributions.

International Conferences require much administrative and secretarial support, and such support was ably provided by the Conference staff: Katsunori Morita, Kazunori Sunagawa, and Nobuyuki Yabushita. As the interpreter, Brendon Hanna helped ensure smooth communications among the participants at the Conference. He also served as the English editor, and his diligent efforts have contributed greatly to the readability of the present volume.

At the Oxford University Press, David Musson expertly guided the editors and authors through the complexities of publishing—complexities eased by the careful editing of Leonie Hayler and Sarah Dobson. The generosity of all those listed here improved this book immeasurably. Last but not least, the editors would like to express their gratitude to the many business historians, not mentioned above, who have helped us in so many ways.

                                                                K.O.
                                                                M.S.

While this book was in the process of being printed, the editors learned of the sudden passing of Professor Yoshitaro Wakimura, the first president of the Business History Society of Japan, and Professor Jun Sakudo, a vice-chairman of the Organizing Committee for the Fuji Conference. On behalf of the Organizing Committee and the Business History Society of Japan, we wish to convey to the families of Professors Yoshitaro Wakimura and Jun Sakudo our sincere condolences. Memories of them and their lasting contributions to the development of business history and to mutual understanding among business historians will remain with us.

CONTENTS

LIST OF CONTRIBUTORS

TAKESHI ABE is Professor in the Graduate School of Economics at Osaka University.

AURELIO ALAIMO is Lecturer at the State Commercial High School, Castiglione dei Pepoli, Bologna.

MANSEL G. BLACKFORD is Professor in the Department of History at the Ohio State University.

KRIS INWOOD is Associate Professor in the Department of Economics at the University of Guelph.

MICHEL LESCURE is Professor in the Department of History at the University of Tours.

KONOSUKE ODAKA is Professor at the Institute of Economic Research at Hitotsubashi University.

C. F. PRATTEN is Senior Research Officer in the Department of Applied Economics at the University of Cambridge.

MINORU SAWAI is Professor in the Graduate School of Economics at Osaka University.

PHILIP SCRANTON is Kranzberg Professor of the History of Technology at the Georgia Institute of Technology.

JOHZEN TAKEUCHI is Professor in the School of Economics at Nagoya University.

ULRICH WENGENROTH is Professor at the Technische Universität, Munich.

LIST OF FIGURES

LIST OF TABLES

LIST OF MAPS

Introduction: Small Business in Historical Perspective

KONOSUKE ODAKA and MINORU SAWAI

The Concept of Small Business

Small business is a generic concept. Being the antonym of big business, its social significance becomes clearer when placed in the historical context where the latter first appeared in the world economy.

Big business became conspicuous in the US economy in the second half of the nineteenth century, especially after the 1890s when the wave of corporate mergers swept the country:

... it is during these closing years of the nineteenth century that one can first speak of the mass demand of a national urban market, a market brought into being by the railroads and by legal change, and sustained in effectiveness by rising per capita incomes.   (Bruchey 1980: 11)

Mass-production methods were then introduced after the turn of the century, as best exemplified by the phenomenal success of Ford's Model T, produced at the company's Highland Park plant beginning in 1913 (cf. Hounshell 1984: 9). As noted by Peter Drucker (1946/1960), Ford's method demonstrated for the first time that 'under conditions of modern technology, the maximum profit is obtained by maximising production at the minimum cost' (p. 220).

Mass production, characterized by 'the principle of power, accuracy, economy, system, continuity, speed, and repetition' (Ford 1950: 38)

... includes the factory as a logistic concept, division of labor as an organizational concept, the special-purpose machine tool as a technological concept, scientific management as an intellectual concept, and fabrication from interchangeable parts as a concept at once logistical, organizational, technological, and abstract.   (Mayr and Post 1981, p. xvi)

It is probably no coincidence that the 1900s and the 1910s were identified by W. W. Rostow (1960: 75–6) as the period of mass-consumption-come of-age in the USA. Relevant to the phenomenon was the thesis put forward by Alfred Chandler (1977: 486), according to which mass production was distinguished from its predecessors by its administrative co-ordination with mass distribution.

Big corporations almost immediately led to the evolution of operational hierarchical structures with the introduction of professional experts who facilitated smooth flows of information and decision-making, leading inevitably to bureaucratization as noted by Max Weber (1922). In order to meet the surge of new demand for management specialists, collegiate business schools were established in the USA beginning in the late nineteenth century.[1]

Along with the prosperity of big corporations, theories were propounded (albeit with some time lag) such as the separation of ownership and management by A. A. Berle and G. C. Means (1932), and monopolistic competition by Edward Chamberlin (1933) and Joan Robinson (1933). Another important development in the UK and the USA in the late nineteenth and the early twentieth centuries was of an entirely new type of labour organization, i.e. the general and industrial union, often accompanied by serious labour–management confrontations.

The establishment and the spread of big business was observed in other industrialized countries as well. Hardly an exception, Japan experienced the arrival of giant corporations around the First World War and thereafter (Hashimoto 1989, ch. 2). The formation of the 'zaibatsu', corporate groups jointly owned and operated by family clans, as well as their growing influence in the economy, also hit full stride in the 1910s and the 1920s.

Big corporations (particularly those in the USA) created so strong an impression at that time that one might have imagined they would eventually dominate all the important markets. The market-concentration ratio in the USA rose significantly from the end of the American Civil War until around 1905. However, it stopped increasing after 1905 for quite some time even well into the 1950s (Bain 1959: 201), since new products kept pouring in and the size of the markets—and therefore the volumes of economic transactions—continued to grow. The small-business sector indeed survived.

While its economic position is far less prominent in most sectors today, it retains a surprising degree of importance in the growing service sector and also serves as an adjunct to large manufacturing enterprises.   (Bruchey 1980: 1)

This was not the end of the story, of course. The economic history of the twentieth century has observed repeated surges of small, yet highly dynamic, venture firms, often clustering themselves in a special region to exploit locational externalities, as illustrated by those in the Silicon Valley in California in the 1980s and onward.

There has also been the development of interfirm linkages: loosely connected, tree-shaped networks of suppliers of speciality goods and services. The networks have drawn much attention since the 1970s in connection with the successful performance of the Japanese automobile industry, which relied extensively on networks of associated, smaller corporations for the supply of parts and components. Long-lasting trust relations were much praised as the source of flexible production, as well as of efficiency improvement (see, e.g. Smitka 1991), and the importance of networking was reinforced later by the extremely rapid adoption and popularization of information technology (see, e.g. Imai 1984).

Networking is an area where small firms have definite comparative advantages over big business. Each member of the network is an independent specialist in designing and/or manufacturing intermediate products, while being simultaneously integrated into a coherent group of co-operation led by the core leader at the centre, which generally serves as the designer-cum-assembler of the final product. The network could be characterized by a long-lasting relationship, as in the case of automobile production in Japan through the 1980s, but could very well consist of series of spot-type, relatively short-lived transactions.

There is yet another side to the story of small business. As industrialization spread from the West to the other parts of the world, a new variety of small firms has been brought in. Since industrialization in the follower countries has often been realized by transplanting physical capital embodied with Western technologies, it has often resulted in the emergence of economic dualism: the coexistence of relatively big firms equipped with imported, up-to-date production technology, with smaller, indigenous concerns typically operated by means of labour-intensive traditional technology.

Small business has sometimes been criticized for its economic 'vices': rat-race competition, the exploitation of employees through low wages, poor working conditions, paternalistic labour relations, and so on. In so far as small firms are characterized by the relatively labour-intensive choice of technology (as indeed was the case in Japan in the first half of the twentieth century), they contributed to society by enhancing the employment capabilities of the latter. For one thing, a small firm with indigenous technologies is often run as an owner-operated family business, which may be ruled by a behavioural principle that is distinct from that of profit maximization, e.g. output maximization. This may account for the presence of a mechanism which absorbs redundant labour, thus 'disguising' otherwise unemployed manpower resources (see, e.g., Georgescu-Roegen 1966, ch. 11 and Ishikawa 1967, ch. 3). In more practical terms this means some labour services are either unpaid or ignored in the cost accounting.

Small firms have also acted as a reservoir of traditional manual skills, which are not necessarily needed in big enterprises with high capital–labour ratios; this has been the case in Germany and, to a lesser extent, in Japan.

The Statistical Definition of Small Business

Statistical definitions of small business vary from one country to another. In the UK, for example, manufacturing enterprises with 200 or fewer employees are defined as small businesses, while the upper limit for 'smallness' is 300 employees in both Japan and Korea, or 500 in France, Germany, Italy, and the USA.[2]

The image of small size also shifts from time to time. In the official Japanese statistics before the First World War, for example, a production unit was defined as a 'factory' if it met the arbitrary criterion of having ten workers or more, and, if not, as a 'cottage industry'. This of course reflected a sense of judgement based on the prevailing scale of economic activities, and the upper bound of small scale subsequently rose. A 1937 survey by the Osaka Municipal Government, for instance, classified enterprises into three groups: those employing 100 operatives or more as 'big', 30 to 99 operatives as 'medium-sized', and fewer than 30 as 'small' (Osaka Shi 1940, 'Introduction').

The terminology for small business is equally haphazard. Whereas the term 'small business' is widely used, 'small' is often extended to 'small- and medium-sized'. By the same token, 'business' is frequently substituted for by 'company', 'concern', 'enterprise', 'firm', or even 'industry', depending on the preference of the author. No single phrase or definition has yet been universally agreed upon.

It is our belief that the issue of definition may be discussed more meaningfully if one gives up trying to fit rigid statistical rules to ever-changing reality, and adopts instead an organization-genesis (or developmental) point of view. Given the inherent characteristics of high heterogeneity, diversity and complexity (Sato 1996: 37), small business can be best understood when it is placed in its historical and regional context and viewed according to general, macro-economic conditions. For this reason, no uniform rule has been established in this volume to define exactly what small business is (or what it is not). Inasmuch as the concept refers to the opposite of big business it accentuates one commonality, i.e. the lack of economic power to control output and/or factor markets. For the purpose of this introductory chapter, the terms 'small business' and 'small- and medium-size company (SMC)' will be used interchangeably.

Small Business in Industrialized Europe and North America

The problem of definition set aside, statistical records demonstrate that Western Europe and North America abound with a surprisingly large number of small companies. An international comparison of small business conducted by S. Kato (1967) indicated that the number of manufacturing establishments with fewer than 100 employees comprised 98.2 per cent of the total in West Germany (1962), 99.4 per cent in Italy (1951), 97.6 per cent in Japan (1962), 83.8 per cent in the UK (1958), and 90.9 per cent in the USA

(1958). Correspondingly, the percentage figures of total employment working for manufacturing establishments with fewer than 100 employees were 42.5 (West Germany), 50.5 (Italy), 52.6 (Japan), 20.3 (UK), and 27.0 (USA).[3] Based on these and other findings, Kato suggests that the weight of small business is relatively light in the UK and the USA, much heavier in follower countries of industrialization such as Japan, with continental European nations falling somewhere in between (Kato 1967: 56–66).

The diversity of SMCs, as attested to by even a cursory observation of statistics such as those cited above, is essentially a reflection of the historical and geographical settings in which they were embedded.

Small business in the UK, for instance, has often been regarded as socially marginal and economically less efficient, making only minor contributions to the overall economy. As if to verify this view, the relative weight of SMCs (with, say, fewer than 200 employees) declined significantly from the inter-war to the post-war periods, both in terms of the number of establishments and of net output (Rothwell and Zegveld 1982: 12). Yet lively discussions have persisted in the UK expounding on reasons why small business could (and did) stand the test of history (e.g. Bolton 1972). Alfred Marshall (1919, chs. 3 and 4) typically ascribed the fact to: (a) never-ending genesis of small firms, (b) limit of scale economies, and (c) advantages uniquely enjoyed by small business. The proposition inspired the idea of the 'optimum firm' by Sir Austin Robinson (1935, ch. 2), asserting that large size was not necessarily optimal, and thus accounting for the survival of SMCs (cf. Takizawa 1974(1), 18–22).

Small business in the UK today displays relatively little differential in productivity and wages by size of enterprise, as compared to a country such as Japan (Rothwell and Zegveld 1982). What we observe in the UK, however, is the end result of a long historical process of industrial development, originating at the latest in the nineteenth century. In mid-nineteenth century England, by contrast, size differentials in wages and in labour efficiency were widely observable in a number of sectors. But this dualism retreated gradually, due in part to the adoption of social policies such as the Trade Board Act in 1909, and to the penetration of labour unions into sectors formerly dominated by the Sweating System and subcontracting (Toike 1971: 149–50).

There were many cases that demonstrated the vibrancy of small business in nineteenth- and twentieth-century North America, side by side with the overwhelming success stories of the American system of manufacture and, later on, of mass production. True, the largest manufacturing firms grew, in terms of employment size, from around 1,500 in 1880 to between 20,000 and 60,000 during the 1920s. It is worth remembering, however, that the average size of establishments in US manufacturing remained rather modest: 10.8 workers in 1880, 10.4 in 1900, and 31.4 even as late as 1920 (Gordon, Edwards, and Reich 1982: 133–4).[4]

As Philip Scranton (1991) has shown, growing emphasis on size in America, lasting for about half a century after 1880, should not obscure the other side of the coin—that there always flourished a kingdom of small business, the healthy world of custom- and batch-production systems. Although mostly unnoticed by students of big business, the striking achievements of mass manufacturing were often supported by batch firms. For example, 'The scientific instrumentation and conveyors basic to mass production were crafted by batch firms' (ibid. 32). In reality the two actors in industrialization, big and small firms, have been mutually complementary rather than contradictory.[5]

SMCs in the machine-tool industry are a case in point. Particularly influential in this regard were those in Cincinnati and in Vermont's 'precision valley' (Broel 1959 and Wing 1964). Tsutomu Hayasaka, a well-known Japanese engineer at Ikegai Ironworks, the oldest machine-tool builder in Japan, observed after his study of American machine-tool making in the 1930s that '. . . some small builders could produce parts of much superior quality than larger-scale companies' (Hayasaka 1964: 728), and, referring to small manufacturers of complete machine tools, that '. . . they could build high-quality machine tools by skilful combination of purchased parts and components. Herein lies a reason why such small firms can survive in the U.S. market' (ibid. 730). Hayasaka's observations suggest the existence of a network of highly competitive small firms, supporting and supplementing an intricate social division of labour.

On the other hand, the relative weight of small business in European countries such as former West Germany and Italy is clearly notable in contrast to the UK and the USA. This is partly attributable to the legacies in continental Europe of craft (or hand) industries (*artisanat* in French, *Handwerk* in German, and *artigianato* in Italian) (Kato 1967: 23–4). In Germany, for example, many small firms in the old craft industries (*altes Handwerk*) which were doomed to decline were able to transform themselves into new craft industries (*neuzeitliches Handwerk*). This process was described as that of 'easy in, and easy out' by Tadao Kiyonari (1965: 26–30).

Why were there so many old craft industries in the early years of Imperial Germany? Some say this was a result of incomplete dissolution of the peasantry, but others cite public policies as a possible reason which allowed trade associations to regulate excessive competition among craft industries and to restrain new entries to the market. In any event, during the decades following the collapse of Imperial Germany small enterprises continued to seize upon new business opportunities in such expanding areas as subcontracting, small-lot production of large items, repair work, and servicing. In an ever-changing economic climate, German craft industries have demonstrated vitality and high level of adaptability. In this manner the German SMCs have indeed acted as a flexible element in economic growth (see Chapter 5 of the present volume).

In 1973, the publication of Ernest Schumacher's painstaking study, *Small Is Beautiful*, helped recast the public's image of small business in contemporary industrialized societies through the newly proposed concept of 'intermediate technology'. About a decade afterwards, *The Second Industrial Divide* by Michael Piore and Charles Sabel (1984) examined the role of small business from an entirely new perspective, suggesting that small-lot production with the use of 'flexible specialization' is more suitable for certain major industrial products. The authors called attention to the vital importance of the social context in which technology has been selected, e.g. the political atmosphere and the community tradition in which small business has been nurtured. The book prompted a major paradigm shift in research on small business in Europe and North America, marking a starting point for a series of new studies on industrial organization.

A curious by-product of the hypothesis is that it has authenticated a new version of industrial dualism, this time focusing on the dichotomy between orthodox Fordism and flexible production, and yet reiterating the same basic tenet of old-time dualism between big and small. An important, unfinished task is to establish a well-grounded explanation of how and why flexible production came about.

The oil crisis of the early 1970s and the economic stagnation that followed prompted rising expectations toward the mysterious power of small business in industrialized countries, as if it could magically step in as a creator of new jobs, a 'seedbed' (or 'incubator') of new technology, a pool of dynamic new entrepreneurship free from rigid bureaucratic vices, and even provide the momentum for the revitalization of local communities. The enthusiasm with which *The Second Industrial Divide* was received partly reflected this socio-economic climate. However, it remains to be seen if small size is in fact superior to large scale in creating new job opportunities and promoting new technologies. In any event, the symbiosis between small and big businesses needs to be examined with a clear historical perspective.

Historical Significance of Small Business in Japan

In the early days of Japanese industrialization, the issue of small business was reckoned to be a question of 'indigenous' industries.[6] The Meiji Restoration (1868) inherited 'traditional' small production units descending directly from the previous regime. Shortly after the Restoration, they were joined by another class of small business which catered to freshly created markets of newly introduced goods and services. Four possible combinations resulted:

manufacturing new types of products using either (1) new, or (2) old technologies, and manufacturing traditional goods by either (3) new, or (4) old
methods.[7]

Until well into the 1880s and the 1890s, all of these firms, both new and
indigenous, were of rather limited scale. In fact, export-led components of
nineteenth-century development were comprised mostly of the products of
small business. It was only much later, especially after the Russo-Japanese
War of 1904–5, that big corporations came to represent modernity with the
help of borrowed technologies from the West. But even then the products of
the large-scale sectors seldom acquired international competitiveness, unless
they received subsidies (e.g. ocean transport) or extra political manœuvring
(e.g. Japanese direct investments in China). An intriguing question then, is
how the small firms could attain such strong comparative advantage and
prosper as export industries, acquiring foreign exchange to facilitate the
importation of highly needed raw materials and intermediate goods (i.e.
capital equipment).

Through the First World War, Japanese small-industry issues were often
discussed in a framework of the stage theory in the German, historical-
school tradition. After the war, the role of wholesale merchants in production, distribution, and financing was hotly debated, followed by intense
examination of the subcontracting system which emerged after the Great
Depression especially in metal fabrication and machine-building trades.
The studies uncovered the fact that opportunism often prevailed in both
parent (i.e. big) and subcontracting (small) firms during the 1930s, as they
were inclined to take only short-run perspectives. It was only after the inevitable collapse of the wartime expansion of subcontracting and the later
arrival of the high-speed growth era that mutually supporting, long-lasting
relationships began to develop between the two sides.

In the period after the Second World War, the issue of SMCs continued to
plague well-informed intellectuals and high-ranking government policy-
makers.[8] A case in point was the significant, long-sustained presence of
earnings differentials by size of establishment, which was interpreted by
some as convincing evidence of economic exploitation of SMCs by big
firms.[9] Small firms could not, after all, be anything but an underdog.

But the tide changed around the mid-point of the era of high-speed
growth, as many SMCs began to record outstanding economic performance
by means of improvements in production efficiency, transformations of
managerial practices, introduction of new technologies, etc. Some SMCs,
typically those in the machinery industry, banded together to form an association of parts and components suppliers to a specific assembler, where each
member was expected to (and in fact did) act as an organic component of the
vertical network. At the same time, SMCs maintained mutual, horizontal
linkages by forming industrial associations, which functioned not only as
a medium of information exchange but also as a sounding-board of the

industry's requests, resolutions, technical information, etc. to government bureaucrats.

During the high-speed growth period, contributions by SMCs to the dramatic improvements in international competitiveness cannot be denied. A number of successful companies (such as Sony and Honda) began to grow in size, and eventually joined the ranks of truly big business. Along with improved economic performance, social evaluation of small business underwent a slow, but clear process of upward amendment. The old notion of SMCs as being of a lower social rank gradually faded, and was replaced by the view that they formed a vital majority. The enactment in 1963 of the Basic Law of Small- and Medium-scale Firms (*Chusho Kigyo Kihon Ho*) symbolized the beginning of the change.

This subtle change notwithstanding, many puzzles still linger concerning the economics of small business, including managerial and institutional factors essential for the growth of SMCs (see, e.g. Patrick and Rohlen 1987). For instance, how and where have the managers and owners of small businesses received necessary training as business leaders, prior to the foundation of their businesses? How were their start-ups financed?

Ever since the Meiji period, workers aspired to become independent managers or owners of their own business, however small. Although the gate became narrower and narrower as time went on, the 'Japanese dream' could still be realized as late as in the high-speed growth era. A study revealed that, at the end of the high-speed growth era, as many as a half of the employees working for a very small firm (with 1 to 29 workers) eventually started their own businesses. Naturally the ratio went down as the size increased: 20–30 per cent in the class of firms with 30–99 workers, and 20 per cent in enterprises with 100–299 workers (Koike 1981: 88–9). Such a high incidence of newly formed small businesses has no doubt added dynamism essential for economic growth. But it has never been easy to initiate, maintain and expand one's own business; as an old Japanese saying puts it, 'a small business, just like a tumour, bursts when it grows'. The death rates of small businesses have also been quite high.

Industrial policies of various kinds came forward to assist in the growth of small business. In addition to financial aid in the form of outright subsidies, grants-in-aid, low-interest government loans, etc. the working of public institutions such as experimental stations and vocational training schools warrant due attention.

Local governments were also engaged in active support of SMCs. Highly successful applications of local industrial policy can in fact be identified, which in some cases stimulated competitive spirit among the local governments, encouraging them to engineer better policy devices to help develop local SMCs.

Regional comparative advantage is a matter of great importance that serves as a corner-stone for the development of SMCs. Many small firms have been set up to exploit the resource endowments specific to regional communities, which in turn receive economic benefits by the presence of SMCs.

It will be particularly worthwhile to place the experience of Japanese small business in an international perspective, as the country was one of the first industrialized nations outside the Western hemisphere. International comparisons may help clarify Japan's unique position in the history of world-wide industrialization, and also provide a valuable basis for formulating public policies for development in follower countries.

The Aims and Composition of the Present Volume

Given the foregoing conceptual framework, this volume seeks to identify salient characteristics of SMC development in Western Europe, North America, and Japan. Each chapter has borne in mind questions such as: what factors make up the importance of small business or, conversely, how was each national economy affected by the diversity of SMC activities? Have institutional arrangements contributed to the growth or decline of SMCs? What factors account for the success or failure of SMCs? How were the managers, engineers, and workers in SMCs attracted to small business, trained and motivated? What, if any, role have the public authorities played in helping SMCs develop in various national environments? The subsequent chapters will consider these issues in the respective historical contexts.

The book is divided into three parts: Part I is devoted to the experiences of North America (Canada and the USA), Part II to those of Western Europe (France, Germany, Italy, and the UK), and Part III to those of Japan.

Chapter 1 in Part I takes up somewhat theoretical themes, proposing to expand the objects of research concerning small business beyond manufacturing, embracing a wider choice of topics such as entrepreneurs of ethnic immigrant origin, lawyers and physicians as owners of small business, retailing specialists, workers in leisure industries, repair operatives, and so forth. In this manner one may regain freedom to explore 'the meanings, experiences, and practices of "being in business" ', an almost lost topic in previous industry studies which have been almost solely preoccupied with the development of big business.

Chapter 2 examines interactions between public attitudes, policy-making and the development of small business in the USA. First, the development of policies for small business is related to the high social values attached to the maintenance of the spirit of yeomanry, which opposes the increasing concentration of economic power. Second, cases in manufacturing are examined in search of factors supporting the growth of small business. The chapter ends with a note of warning, however, that small manufacturing companies have not been a particularly robust engine of job creation in recent years.

Chapter 3 represents a portion of a larger study examining the 1871 Canadian census of manufactures with the purpose of uncovering the characteristics of the Canadian economy on the eve of industrialization. By careful treatment of descriptive statistics the author looks for systematic patterns among the relevant variables such as industrial products, firm size, power sources, and population density. The study captures the diversity and flexibility of small business at the time, due generally to the use of family labour, being engaged in manufacturing on a by-employment basis.

Part II brings together contrasting experiences of four European countries. First, in Chapter 4, a survey of changing perceptions of small firms in the UK is undertaken, followed by statistical examination of the contributions by small business in five industrial branches: machine tools, woollen and worsted fabrics, scientific instruments, pharmaceuticals, and cardboard containers. Also examined in the chapter are variations in the extent to which small business contributed to the economic revival of the recent decades.

Chapter 5 reviews the German concept of small business, together with the regulative and corporatist environment in which SMCs were fostered. The author adopts a long-run perspective in evaluating the economic conduct of SMCs inclusive of their financing, manufacturing technologies, relationship to big and small firms by way of subcontracting, etc., convincingly suggesting that small business has served as a catalyst of industrial growth in Germany.

By contrast, Chapter 6 explores reasons for the difficulties that French SMCs have faced in the twentieth century. Factors selected by the author in this regard are changing consumer demand, challenges made by big corporations and by state policies, problems regarding the evolution of financial institutions, and the overall decline of local production systems. As candidate policies supportive of small-firm development, the author suggests improvements in SMCs' market performance, production strategies of management, and the use of lateral networks of SMCs.

Chapter 7 illustrates the debate over Italian small-firm systems which concerns the historical conditions for the formation and the development of local production networks: factors which promote the growth of SMCs despite a rapidly changing economic environment. The author deals here with issues such as pluriactivities of peasants, the rise of rural and urban proto-industries, and, more broadly, the role of local governments, institutions, and large firms in incubating entrepreneurial initiatives which are essential for the success of small business.

The four chapters in Part III of the volume look at the historical experiences of Japanese SMCs. Chapter 8 critically reviews the characteristics of small business development, taking a wider Asian perspective and focusing on the initial conditions for industrialization and on the evolutionary process of labour-intensive sectors where SMCs came to dominate. Specific topics include the quality of entrepreneurship, the nature of craft skills conserved and utilized by the SMCs, the work motivation and discipline of the labour force, and technological innovations and their social origins.

Chapter 9 is a detailed, historical review of the putting-out system, which supported the growth of Japanese indigenous industries, concomitant with the rapid growth of big business. The industry chosen for this study is cotton weaving, providing well-documented evidence of dualistic industrial development in modern Japan. The chapter elaborates the entire process of the establishment, development, transformation, and decline of the putting-out system in the Japanese cotton textile industry, as well as various factors influencing the process.

Chapter 10 examines the significance of higher secondary technical education and night school programmes, both of which supplied eligible workers, foreman candidates, and production engineers to the vast number of SMCs in pre-Second World War Japan. The chapter also traces the inter-war activities of the network of Osaka-based public research institutes, which provided technical and managerial information to small businesses, thereby promoting technological upgrading.

Finally, Chapter 11 presents a case-study of a particular industrial policy at the beginning phase of the post-war high-speed growth era, led by the Ministry of International Trade and Industry. It is an evaluation of the working of the Provisional Law to Promote the Machinery Industry. Chosen here as an object of the study is the auto parts industry, which was dominated by relatively small firms at the early phase of its development, in making a sharp contrast to large assemblers (like Toyota and Nissan). The entire process is examined from its inception through its execution and outcomes are examined and evaluated.

The volume ends with a brief note about the future of SMCs in the countries selected for study, as well as an agenda for further research on small business development in the present-day world.

NOTES

1. For instance, Wharton School of Finance and Commerce at the University of Pennsylvania was established in 1881.
2. All official definitions are as of the time of writing (1997). The definition of 'small business' in the USA differs slightly from one industry to another, but its statistical standard in terms of the number of employees is less than 500 in most cases.

3. The figures for Italy and West Germany include 'craft', or 'hand', industries. The 1956 statistics were used for West German craft industries.
4. The 1880 and 1900 figures are averages for factory, hand, and neighbourhood production, whereas the 1920 figure is average for factory outputs only.
5. On the significance of distinction in the formats of production between building and manufacturing, see Brown (1995, 'Introduction').
6. For a detailed account of the problem of small business in Japan, the reader is referred to (for instance) a series of articles by Takizawa (1974–7).
7. If one adds another item to the classification of product and of technology (e.g. 'hybrid') the total of nine combinations would ensue.
8. Shinohara (1968) surveys the literature on dualism through the mid-1960s. It is noteworthy in this connection that Steindl (1945) was one of the frequently cited reference studies in the Japanese literature of dualism.
9. In some countries the dualism exhibited a continuous spectrum in a given industry of very small-, small-, medium-, large-, and giant-scale firms, being arranged in the ascending order of labour productivity and wages. They should be more properly termed, according to Ohkawa (1972, pt. I) as a 'differential structure' rather than simple dualism. But the essence of dualism is no way affected by the apparent continuity of the differentials.

REFERENCES

Bain, Joe S. (1959), *Industrial Organization*. New York: John Wiley.
Berle, A. A., Jr. and Means, G. C. (1932), *Modern Corporation and Private Property*. New York: Macmillan.
[Bolton, J. E.] (1972), *Small Firms: Report of the Committee of Inquiry on Small Firms*, Nov. 1971. London: HMSO.
Broel, W. G., Jr. (1959), *Precision Valley: The Machine Tool Companies of Springfield, Vermont*. Englewood Cliffs, NJ: Prentice-Hall.
Brown, J. K. (1995), *The Baldwin Locomotive Works, 1831–1915*. Baltimore: The Johns Hopkins University Press.
Bruchey, Stuart W. (1980) (ed.), *Small Business in American Life*. New York: Columbia University Press.
Chamberlin, Edward H. (1933), *The Theory of Monopolistic Competition*. Cambridge, Mass.: Harvard University Press.
Chandler, Alfred (1977), *The Visible Hand: The Managerial Revolution in American Business*. Cambridge, Mass.: The Belknap Press of Harvard University Press.
Drucker, Peter (1960), *The Concept of the Corporation*. New York: Beacon Press (orig. pub. 1946 by John Day).
Ford, Henry (1950), 'Mass Production', *Encyclopaedia Britannica*, xv. London: Encyclopaedia Britannica (orig. pub. in 1926 edn.).
Georgescu-Roegen, Nicholas (1966), *Analytical Economics, Issues and Problems*. Cambridge, Mass.: Harvard University Press.

Gordon, D. M., Edwards, R., and Reich, M. (1982), *Segmented Work, Divided Workers: The Historical Transformation of Labour in the United States*. Cambridge: Cambridge University Press.

Hashimoto, Juro (1989), 'Kyodai Sangyou no Koryu' ['The Rise of Big Business'], in Takafusa Nakamura and Konosuke Odaka (eds.), *Niju Kozo* [*Dual Structure*]. Tokyo: Iwanami Shoten, ch. 2.

Hayasaka Tsutomu Zenshu Henshu Iinkai [Editorial Committee for the Complete Works of Tsutomu Hayaska] (1964) (ed.), *Kosaku Kikai to Bunmei: Hayasaka Tsutomu Zenshu* [*Machine Tools and Civilization: The Complete Works of Tsutomu Hayasaka*]. Tokyo: Komine Kogyo Gijutsu.

Hounshell, David A. (1984), *From the American System to Mass Production 1800–1932: The Development of Manufacturing Technology in the United States*. Baltimore and London: The Johns Hopkins University Press.

Imai, Ken'ichi (1984), *Joho Nettowaku Shakai* [*Information Network in the Modern Society*]. Tokyo: Iwanami Shoten.

Ishikawa, Shigeru (1967), *Economic Development in Asian Perspective*. Tokyo: Kinokuniya Bookstore.

Kato, Seiichi (1967), *Chusho Kigyo no Kokusai Hikaku* [*An International Comparison of Small Business*]. Tokyo: Toyo Keizai Shimposha.

Kiyonari, Tadao (1965), 'Nishi Doitsu ni okeru Shukogyo Gainen ni tsuite' ['On the Concept of Craft Industries in West Germany'], *Kokumin Kinyu Koko Chosa Geppo* [*Monthly Survey*], 51 (June 1965).

Koike, Kazuo (1981), *Chusho Kigyo no Jukuren: Jinzai Keisei no Shikumi* [*Formation of Human Capital in Small Business: Its System and Evaluation*]. Tokyo: Dobunkan.

Marshall, Alfred (1919), *Industry and Trade: A Study of Industrial Technique and Business Organization and of Their Influences on the Conditions of Various Classes and Nations*. London: Macmillan.

Mayr, Otto and Post, Robert C. (1981) (eds.), *Yankee Enterprise: The Rise of the American System of Manufactures*. Washington, DC: Smithsonian Institution Press.

Ohkawa, Kazushi (1972), *Differential Structure and Agriculture: Essays on Dualistic Growth*. Tokyo: Kinokuniya Bookstore.

Osaka Shi (Osaka Municipal Government) (1940) (ed.), *Osaka Shi Kogyo Keiei Chosa Sho: Kinzoku Kikai Kogyo Showa 12-nen* [*A Survey on Industrial Management in the City of Osaka: Metal and Machinery in 1937*]. Osaka.

Patrick, Hugh T. and Rohlen, Thomas P. (1987), 'Small-scale Family Enterprises', in Kozo Yamamura and Yasukichi Yasuba (eds.), *The Political Economy of Japan, 1: The Domestic Transformation*. Stanford: Stanford University Press, 330–84.

Piore, Michael J. and Sabel, Charles F. (1984), *The Second Industrial Divide: Possibilities for Prosperity*. New York: Basic Books.

Robinson, E. A. G. (1935), *The Structure of Competitive Industry*, rev. edn. Cambridge: Cambridge University Press.

Robinson, Joan (1933), *The Economics of Imperfect Competition*. London: Macmillan.

Rostow, W. W. (1960), *The Stages of Economic Growth: A Non-Communist Manifesto*. Cambridge: Cambridge University Press.

Rothwell, R. and Zegveld, W. (1982), *Innovation and the Small- and Medium-Sized Firms: Their Role in Employment and in Economic Change*. London: Francis Pinter.

Sato, Yoshio (1996), 'Ima naze "Chusho Kigyo to wa nanika" nanoka' ['Why the Question "What Is Small Business?" Now?'], in Y. Kobayashi and K. Takizawa, (eds.), *Chusho Kigyo to wa nanika* [*What Is Small Business?*]. Tokyo: Yuhikaku.

Schumacher, Ernest F. (1973), *Small Is Beautiful: A Study of Economics as if People Mattered*. London: Blond & Briggs.

Scranton, Philip. (1991), 'Diversity in Diversity', *Business History Review*, 65/10.

Shinohara, Miyohei (1968), 'A Survey of the Japanese Literature on Small Industry', in Bert F. Hoselitz (director), *The Role of Small Industry in the Process of Economic Growth*, vol. vii of International Committee for Social Sciences Documentation, *Confluence: Surveys of Research in the Social Sciences*, The Hague and Paris: Mouton.

Smitka, Michael J. (1991), *Competitive Ties: Subcontracting in the Japanese Automotive Industry*. New York: Columbia University Press.

Steindl, Joseph (1945), *Small and Big Business, Economic Problems of the Size of Firms*. Oxford: Basil Blackwell.

Takizawa, Kikutaro (1974–7), 'A Comparative Study on the Problems of Small Business in the United Kingdom, the United States and Japan (1)–(5)', *Keizai kagaku* [*Economic Science*], 20/4, 21/3, 23/1, 24/1, and 25/1.

Toike, Masaharu (1971), 'Igirisu Chusho Kogyo Kenkyu josetsu' ['An Introduction to the Study of Small Industries in the UK'], *Hitotsubashi Review*, 66/1.

Weber, Max (1922), 'Bürokratie', in *Wirtschaft und Gesellschaft*, ii. ch. 6, pt. 3. Tübingen: Verlag von J. C. B. Mohr (Paul Siebeck) (English trans. in H. H. Gerth and C. Wright Mills (1947) (eds.), *From Max Weber: Essays in Sociology*, London: Kegan Paul, Trench, & Trubner, ch. 8).

Wing, George A. (1964), 'The History of the Cincinnati Machine-Tool Industry', DBA diss., Indiana University, Indianapolis.

PART I
NORTH AMERICA

1

Moving Outside Manufacturing: Research Perspectives on Small Business in Twentieth-Century America

PHILIP SCRANTON

The reigning orthodoxy in business history, sometimes termed the 'organizational synthesis', is articulated around a dichotomy between 'big' and 'small' enterprises, which legitimizes a research concentration on large, 'centre' firms in national and international economies. In this formulation, small business becomes marginalized as the 'periphery', as a residual if sizeable class of firms that failed to thrive (i.e. become big), that occupy 'secondary labour markets' and economic 'niches', and that frequently depend upon leading enterprises for contracted orders. Their misfortune may derive from weak entrepreneurship, sectoral obstacles to scale economies, or other sources; but in essence, they are positioned as a deficient 'other' whose insignificance helps validate the significance of the 'core' and the historical project of delineating its rise to dominance.

In other fields of historical inquiry, similar dualisms long stood unquestioned. Men made history worth recording and interpreting; women tended children and gardens. The actions of white Americans merited analysis; the activities of Black, Latino, or Asian minorities served as curious contrasts or as evidence of deviations from the mainstream story. The public sphere of politics and the economy represented the heartland of history; the more private worlds of social life, family, leisure, sexuality, and religion occupied its extremities. Within the economy, manufacturing symbolized the engine of progress; agriculture, extraction, construction, and the service trades lagged, dragged, or attended upon the core industrial dynamic. Production was basic, whereas consumption, though necessary, was uninteresting. Union struggles and institutions provided the spine for American labour history; unorganized workers appeared weak, passive, unworthy. Last, science exemplified the advance of rigorous knowledge and the control of nature, with technology as the mere application of its principles and methods, or worse, the utilization of customary rules of thumb and unsystematic practices.

Although these dichotomies of centre and periphery, valued and other, are here exaggerated for effect, the hierarchies of historical knowledge and significance they capture dominated American historiography until perhaps a generation ago. Commencing in the 1960s, an array of scholars developed sustained critiques of the 'master narratives' these orthodoxies relied upon. In addition, they unpacked the assumptions that sustained unreflective canons of importance and rosters of core problems worth study. Thereby, new historical fields have been marked out (gender, ethnic, African-American, and technological specialities) and older ones revitalized (social, rural, labour). Though not without fierce controversy, which continues, this process undermined the centrality of politics, production, and white men in historical studies and scrutinized the professional routines and rewards that had anchored 'normal' research and teaching. The result, depending on one's point of view and/or political leanings, has been either an era of creative ferment and innovation or one of fragmentation and drift away from the proper focus.

In American business historiography, the 1960s brought the Chandler revolution. Whereas earlier studies chiefly featured biographies of entrepreneurs and studies of individual firms or sectors, Alfred Chandler drew together four case analyses in his first effort to move to a more sophisticated level of general analysis, then followed in the late 1970s with *The Visible Hand*, a magisterial, integrative work which established that the path to oligopoly depended upon technical and organizational innovation (Chandler 1962, 1977). Over the last decade, other historians have challenged this interpretation, arguing that it is implicitly teleological, flattens diversity among large enterprises, and passes over the vitality of durable, specialized, and flexible industrial firms, chiefly of middling and small scale (Best 1990; Fligstein 1990; Piore and Sabel 1984; Scranton 1991). These studies have added complexity and contingency to our portrait of manufacturing's development, bringing the industrial 'others' into a different relationship with the core, tracing complementary or simply differently configured tracks. However, like many first-cut critiques, much of this work has had what might be termed a 'contributionist' tone. Just as the first cadre of women's history researchers laboured to document the presence and roles of female inventors or physicians, along with their contributions to science or public health, so too has the wave of studies emphasizing small and mid-size enterprises undertaken to establish their non-trivial place in the larger industrialization process. This approach challenges the interpretation, but not the principles and assumptions, of the core narrative, whether it be the progress of the American nation or the articulation of a modern capitalist economic system. Contributionists have argued, in effect, that their subjects 'were here, too, and did some important things'. To this, the advocates of the mainstream tale have responded: 'We had not noticed, and thanks for your reports. But our subjects [political leaders, major firms] did the *really* important things.' Contributionism is self-limiting in so far as it accepts the standards of significance that accompany the dominant framework for interpretation. Moving beyond these confines demands a further step, which this introduction will sketch by analogy to the course of women's studies.

In the late 1970s, perhaps invigorated by Caroll Smith-Rosenberg's and Joan Scott's provocative studies, women's historians turned from documenting female contributions to a male-dominated society toward probing the meanings, experiences, and practices of 'being a woman' (a mother, a worker, a writer, a slaveowner) in differing eras and contexts of the American past (Smith-Rosenberg 1975; Scott 1974). This attention to identity, relationships, and culture raised a meta-theoretical challenge to the existing assumptions about what historical problems were significant, what sources and methods were appropriate, and what concepts and theoretical perspectives both working and apprentice historians should steep themselves in, in order to create coherent research programmes. In tandem with social historians, who were reconstructing the lifeways of the common people through exacting quantitative review of census documents, probated wills, court records, and land transactions, these scholars fashioned alternative ways of 'doing history' that shifted the landscape of inquiry decisively.

In short order, however, women's historians faced a double challenge within their research paradigm. On the one hand, though all women shared a common social experience of subordination to men and most performed mothering, parenting, and household labour, differences among women (class, race, ethnicity) and even power relations between them (consider mistress vs. slave or servant) could not be ignored as sizeable points of division. Some women were 'others', not simply to men, but to other women as well. Moreover, as individuals, women possessed distinct historical identities, circles of contact, opportunities, and challenges. There did not exist an all-inclusive class or category, 'women', whose collective experience and the meanings drawn from it could be documented. Instead, scholars encountered a welter of clusters: Black or Irish immigrant household servants, Yankee, Southern, and Western rural widows, élite female reformers, and so forth. Indeed, those things first thought common—courting, birthing and mothering, marital interactions and sexuality—proved sharply different for women differently located in time, space, and social structures. (Boydston 1990; Fox-Genovese 1988; Lebsock 1984; Marsh 1990; Peiss 1986; Stansell 1987; Tong 1989; Ulrich 1990). Such recognitions precipitated specialization within the field and dissolved the notion that creating a synthetic history of women was a realizable goal. Given that women had diverse experiences, scholars would work to delineate multiple histories. Indeed, no simple hierarchy of significance among issues and areas to be examined could be defended, though the availability of sources made some topics far more difficult.

If this process involved reshaping women's history's internal 'conceptual map', a second, related challenge concerned expanding and redefining the boundaries of the field. In moving the focus from contributions to experiences and meanings, women's relationships with men, and the concept 'man', became essential matters for explication, for men were historically just as differentiated. Elaborating the varied ideologies, actions, and organizations that defined masculinity across time (Bederman 1995; Carnes and Griffen 1990; Leverenz 1989) brought a redefinition of the discipline as 'gender history' (Scott 1988). This in turn triggered a further and productive critique of the normalization of heterosocial and heterosexual relations as objects of study, an issue Smith-Rosenberg had raised years earlier. As scholars came to consider practices once labelled deviant as simply different, the reconstruction of gay and lesbian lifeways gained professional legitimacy (Berube 1990; Chauncey 1994; D'Emilio 1983).

I would argue that this historiographical dynamic provides an object lesson and perhaps something approximating an agenda for business historians, particularly those concerned with small business. Moving beyond the familiar debates of contributionism can be achieved by a double move that first, shifts the terrain of inquiry from the hierarchy of enterprises in a development saga to the meanings, experiences, and practices of 'being in business,' and second, shifts the object of inquiry outside manufacturing to those many trades small business has dominated for generations. To show that Marx or Keynes were right about capitalism's tendencies to commodification and concentration by outlining the recent rise of American (and international) corporations which sweep aside small business' traditional specializations (speciality retailing; restaurants; real estate sales) essentially extends the standard narrative (Dicke 1992), as does the close review of small- and mid-size enterprises (SMEs), which has proliferated. Instead, it may be useful to explore research issues and opportunities in domains rarely visited by business historians where inquiry into meaning, experience, and practice may be well rewarded and where novel perspectives employed by colleagues in other historical fields may be provocatively mobilized. The arenas I think worth attention can be termed: (1) marginality and business; (2) the invisible centre; and (3) social auxiliaries. In each case, the collective institutions actors fashioned also bear analysis.

Marginality and business refers to that cluster of enterprises conducted by the socially-peripheral: in the USA, women, Blacks, ethnic immigrants.[1] During the twentieth century, particularly after the First World War, such operations have been overwhelmingly concentrated in marginal trades— small retailing, food provision, and personal services, for example. As Glenn Porter recently remarked, 'Marginal people have to find niche markets.' Tracing their strategies and patterns of collective institution-building is a key issue, as are the meanings invested in proprietorship. For economy's sake, this paper will focus on immigrant entrepreneurs.

The invisible centre denotes a cluster of enterprises that figure as the cultural inverse of the marginals: self-employed and grouped professionals. Though the law, medicine, and architecture, for example, have received major attention from historians, the practical businesses of lawyering, doctoring, and designing stand in near silence. Whereas sociologists and some anthropologists have become increasingly fascinated with the mediating roles of such professionals, historians have crafted very few studies, chiefly of august legal firms, in which the business aspects of their practices are carefully sidestepped. Their collective institutions, the American Medical Association, American Bar Association, and the American Institute of Architects are organized centres of professional knowledge, power, certification, and political influence, an unsurprising contrast to the organizations of the marginal.

In the present century, the classic autonomous, client-centred professions have been augmented by management and engineering consultants, industrial, commercial, interior, and museum designers, professional lobbyists, survey research firms, and others, many of which have spawned associations of their own. (Indeed, even an association of association directors and managers now exists.) Second, more recently, other professionals have been creating 'practices' in computer consulting, graphics design, investment advising, etc., either to avoid being enmeshed within large corporations or after having been expelled from them. Unlike the vast majority of the marginals, all these business enterprisers were and are highly-skilled, hold baccalaureate or advanced degrees, and utilize specialized and sophisticated knowledge bases. The relevance to business history of examining the economic and institutional courses of self-employed professionals seems obvious. It is also timely, in that recent American political and economic dynamics appear to be transforming the oldest of these professions (law, medicine) into 'occupations,' in which practitioners increasingly work as corporate employees or dependants (law 'factories' vs. health maintenance organizations), subject to close supervision, dismissal, *et al.* (Galanter and Palay 1991; Gray 1991). A final cultural issue concerns Americans' historically delicate unwillingness to consider the classic professionals in law and medicine as 'being in business', and the dynamics through which this representation has altered in the last generation. Here insights from Michel Foucault concerning the production of knowledge and power and their masking through social institutions may be of value. Again for economy, and due to the richness of the literature outside business history, only law and medicine as enterprises will be here reviewed.

'Social auxiliaries' refers to small firms that directly service the needs of everyday life, an area of late penetration by large enterprises, as mentioned above. These enterprises exist in at least three classes: (1) retailing specialists—from appliance dealers to hardware stores; (2) leisure enterprises—restaurants and bars, nightclubs, music recording firms, hotels and vacation sites; (3) repair operations—especially auto repair. These firms overlap somewhat with the marginals (and not at all with the professionals), but here they will be only mentioned in conclusion as sites for future study, given that sustained research on small retailing, leisure, and repair businesses is only in its infancy.

Marginality and Business: Ethnic Immigrant Entrepreneurs

There is a phrase in the American vocabulary of approval that sums up our national ideal of manhood. That phrase is 'a self-made man'. To such we pay the tribute of our highest admiration, justly regarding our self-made men as the noblest product of our democratic institutions. Now let any one compile a biographical dictionary of our self-made men, from the romantic age . . . down to the prosaic year of 1914, and see how the smell of the steerage pervades the volume!   (Antin 1914: 76)

The significance of immigrant entrepreneurs to American economic development has long been appreciated. Not only were some of those who founded firms that became 'peak' corporations not native-born (e.g., Carnegie, duPont), but thousands of enterprisers who built industrial capacity at smaller firms also came from abroad (Scranton 1983). The latter, when possessing competencies in the English language, industrial technology, and a modest capital, soon blended into the world of production and exchange, aided as well by contacts with earlier-migrating kin or old-country local residents, or as with Quakers and German Lutherans arriving in Philadelphia, through integration within established religious congregations (Scranton 1993). Among non-English speakers, particularly Germans, an array of American clones of European institutions (Turnverein, friendly and fraternal societies, native language newspapers) contributed to their transition (Schneider 1994).

For others, however, the path to proprietorship was tortured. Italian and Eastern European immigrants usually lacked capital, the English language, and industrial experience.[2] Slotted into common labour jobs, they worked to survive and bring family members across the waters or to accumulate funds sufficient to return home and buy land (Wyman 1993). The most entrepreneurial among them moved into contracting for construction work, initiated factory-town saloons or small shops making home-country foodstuffs, and/or invested in housing for rent to the next wave of arrivals (Bell 1976; Byington 1974; Ehrlich 1977; LaSorte 1985; Pacyga 1991). Jewish immigrants from Russia and Austria-Hungary encountered harder obstacles, for they entered an aggressively Christian nation without the minimal religious linkages that made Poles and Italians somewhat comprehensible to Catholic co-religionists or, perhaps less so, to Anglo-Saxon Protestants. Concentrating in urban ghettos at New York and Philadelphia, they also endured the disdain that earlier-migrating European Jewish communities evinced for their provincial folkways and troubling poverty. None the less, they moved with speed into small business, both as workers and employers, most notably in the contract shops of the garment trades (LaMar 1940; Levine 1924; Passero 1978; Seidman 1942; Zangwill 1916). Soon, however, the First World War froze European populations in place and post-war changes in American immigration statutes dramatically reduced the influx of immigrants from Europe. Earlier punitive laws had essentially ended flows from the Pacific as well.

In the railroad years after the American Civil War, hundreds of thousands of (chiefly) Chinese immigrants entered the United States as contract labourers for the completion of western routes. White working-class migrants to California soon objected to this competing pool of cheap labour. In the mid-1870s depression and after, political pressure for exclusion of Asian immigrants mounted amid racist campaigns to preserve the nation's economic opportunities for Caucasians. A series of federal acts to bar Asian immigration followed, but once the railroad-building craze ended, thousands of resident Asians, lawfully admitted, sought to construct livelihoods in a hostile environment. Analogous to Jews in New York, many crafted what scholars have called 'enclave economies' in order to supply one another with culturally appropriate goods and services, most notably in San Francisco (Chan 1990; Light and Bonacich 1988; Saxton 1971).

With the radical reduction of immigration openings, *c.*1924–80, ethnic business owners either faded into the general population (e.g. Italian-American construction contractors) or strove to build businesses within and beyond enclave economies. The latter are more intriguing, for they exemplify the linkage between business entrepreneurship and social and cultural identity, an issue begging for business historians' attention, at least in the USA. Here the work of gender historians is directly germane.

A crucial element of the human life cycle, from adolescence through early middle age, is the challenge of constructing a coherent personal identity, a shell for the self that can, without hesitation, present an individual to diverse social relations. This is no small project, for multiple cultural, familial, and social/economic factors have powerful impacts on individuals' effort to fashion an effective identity. If one is among the 'others' (i.e. not evidently a part of the ruling élite, the established working classes, or a prominent cultural group or family), creating an identity is a massive life-cycle task. For immigrants, as for American Blacks (strangers in their own land) and most women (subordinated to patriarchal expectations), who one was and who one appeared to be were profoundly different matters. Ethnic businesses, in this context, serve as a bridge between the past and the future, especially those which either employ co-ethnics in fair numbers to produce goods and services for the wider society or those which through their activities reinforced a sense of self and place among the immigrant populations. The analysis of immigrant entrepreneurship, thus, is bound up with an appreciation of the complexities of individual and social action and identity-formation and maintenance in alien territories, where one is regarded as an interloper.

With a fresh influx of immigrants after 1960, this theme gains greater momentum in American history. Following Fidel Castro's seizure of power in Cuba (1959), a host of business-experienced Cuban citizens fled to Florida, where they created Miami's classic ethnic enclave economy (Portes and Rumbaut 1990). A decade later, at the close of the Vietnam War, thousands of fugitive South Vietnamese once involved in administration, business, and the military, also sought refuge in the United States, undertaking to start small businesses, though far more scattered spatially than the Cubans (Leba 1985). Long-debated changes in immigration quotas that had excluded most Asians from entry (1965) authorized a sizeable Korean and Filipino migration and opened places for dissidents from the Communist bloc in Eastern Europe and Russia, yielding a second, smaller phase of Jewish immigration (Halter 1995).

Last, despite prohibitions that were arguably unenforceable without militarizing America's southern borders, the explosion of economic development in the Southwest combined with instability in Mexico and Central America to generate a flood of 'illegal' immigrants. Unlike the Second World War era, when Latinos were recruited to jobs in a stressed war economy, or later decades, when Latino labourers were sought for agricultural harvesting tasks, these migrants aimed at permanent residence and work in a democratic state whose political leaders neither welcomed them nor saw them as a resource for growth, as had been the case a century earlier (Briggs 1984).

Here, for the United States, and in other nations experiencing sizeable flows of immigrants (France [North Africans], Germany [Turks], the UK [Pakistanis, Caribbean Blacks, Indians], Japan [Koreans]), there is ample space for business historical research that undertakes to link ethnic enterprise with the preservation and reshaping of immigrant identities in foreign terrains (Portes 1995). As most immigrant-owned firms were without question small businesses, this suggestion intersects with the Fuji Conference's theme. Recent research in this vein by sociologists and ethnic studies specialists with backgrounds in anthropology offer provocative perspectives for business historians' consideration.

One inviting example derives from a project concerning entrepreneurship among Cambodian immigrants to the Boston area, where over 12,000 Khmer refugees have settled in the city of Lowell, with another 8,000 clustered at other regional locales. In Cambodia, as in other East Asian societies

(Viet Nam, Indonesia), Chinese migrants constituted the leading segment of the business population. This pattern has been solidly replicated in American settings, where the Sino-Khmer, representing only 6 per cent of all Cambodian immigrants, constitute 85 per cent of those operating businesses. How is this possible? What meaning has it for the construction and preservation of identities within the immigrant community? What historical referents for this continuity can be identified (i.e. in the earlier history of the resident Chinese or, perhaps, in the two transfers of Central and Eastern European Jews to the USA)? Although Chinese and some other Asian groups have a near-legendary status as merchant enterprisers, their role in small manufacturing is also notable. In 1990, among Los Angeles's 5,000 apparel-producing firms, over half had Asian owners, and they hold a comparable significance among New York City's clothing makers (Loucky *et al.* 1994; Waldinger 1986).

Moreover, distinctive business practices seem to be linked with the collective identity of the Sino-Khmer. One researcher provides a telling example, drawn from her extended interviews with entrepreneurs who shared linguistic competence in a Chinese regional dialect (Teochieu). Having opened a restaurant with insufficient capital, a Teochieu-speaking, Sino-Khmer businessman faced ruin unless he could recruit additional funds. He explained:

I went to my friend who is now a high-school teacher. He's a friend from thirty years ago from Chinese school in Cambodia . . . I just called him and said that I needed money for the restaurant. We didn't sign any papers. He didn't have much cash, but he had a credit card and I asked him to get me a loan of $5,000 on his credit card. I paid it off when I could with the interest to the company. My friend didn't ask for anything, no interest or payment for himself. I also borrowed a couple of thousand from a couple of other friends. Those guys didn't want interest either; they just want[ed] to see the business do well. Most of them I helped sometime too. So we trust each other.   (Smith-Hefner 1995: 150)

This tale of reciprocity, informal lending, and identity runs against the grain of modern business start-up experiences. Business plans, notarized contract documents, or audited accounts played no role in this credit/ capital provision; nor did the friend, whose access to funds saved the business, demand an equity share for his services. Business historians might well explore to what degree such arrangements were common historically among immigrant entrepreneurs, and equally important, what varieties of cultural conventions underlay this realm of trust and reciprocity (Granovetter 1995). As studies of corporate culture proliferate, there is plainly another domain of the cultural facilitation of entrepreneurship that begs for our attention.

A related example comes from analysis of Korean entrepreneurship in Los Angeles, to which immigrants transplanted a venerable Korean capital-raising institution, the 'kye' (pronounced 'key'). 'Kyes' are circles of prospective business owners, each of whom every month contributes a fixed sum to a common fund. When the proceeds have reached an agreed level, they are delivered in turn to each member to support business start-ups. Those receiving early capital funds commit themselves to continue contributions until every member has been afforded the opportunity to draw out blocks of capital and commence business. Once this cycle is complete, the 'kye' dissolves. By convention, no member 'owns' any portion of his/her colleagues' businesses at any point. Some proto-entrepreneurs have evidently participated in multiple 'kyes,' in order to raise larger-than-average sums and, like their colleagues, to avoid high-interest commercial lending markets, and to sidestep outsiders' undesirable demands for equity shares or for liability guarantees (collateral), which would be difficult to meet (Light and Bonacich 1988).

Here issues of trust again are crucial, for cultural expectations of right behaviour must be mobilized to block opportunistic manœuvres by those 'cashing out' early in the investment/contribution cycle. It must be possible to sanction dishonourable practices by participants, necessitating that coherent notions of community and the value of reputation must be reproduced in foreign terrain to buttress this capital-raising institution. If the Sino-Khmer funding pattern was essentially informal, the Korean 'kye' represents its complementary opposite—a demanding investment club with traditional rules for contributions, procedures to organize disbursements, and powerful expectations of continued payments. That this has proven workable not only suggests the power of ethnic collectivities in business development, but also raises fresh questions for business historians to engage. In what circumstances did comparable collective institutions develop among immigrants to the USA (or, for that matter, to other nations)? How effective were such arrangements, over what periods of time, in what locales and trades, and, if gradually extinguished, why?

Another set of research projects indicates just that differentiation of ethnic business patterns that historians would expect. Greek immigrants to the USA have shown a remarkable propensity for entrepreneurial efforts, proportionately more than double that of both the native-born and most other in-migrating groups. This phenomenon has deep historical roots. In early twentieth-century Chicago, Greeks operated one third of all restaurants and roughly 1,000 candy stores. A generation later, Greeks owned 60 per cent of New Haven's eating places during the Great Depression. One scholar, observing this history and the present concentration of Greek entrepreneurs in pizza shops, argued that Greek immigrants regarded self-employment 'as a way of retrieving their sense of identity from an impasse' created by relocation to a nation where their language and skill deficiencies could doom them to lifelong common and irregular labour (Lovell-Troy 1990).

However, the spatial and institutional context of Greek enterprise departs radically from that of Sino-Khmer and Korean efforts. Although many of the latter's businesses located in ethnically concentrated zones, Greek pizza 'parlours' scattered across regional landscapes, departing from their early twentieth-century, big-city clustering. Still, Greek immigrants continue to display a stunning predilection for self-employment. In the 1970s, 59 per cent of Greek-born men in Connecticut towns and cities operated independent businesses, seven-eighths of them running restaurants—an element of continuity across six decades. Moreover, contemporary Greek entrepreneurs recognized a business constraint that might be termed the problem of 'speciality consumption sheds'. Concentrating numerous ethnic, and particularly, pizza restaurants in close quarters would quickly yield intense price competition and diminishing returns. Hence, the location of new pizza restaurants was consciously spread across local markets state-wide.

How was this structuring achieved and what were the collective action implications of this strategy? In the 1950s and 1960s, a pioneering Greek pizza entrepreneur served as a mentor and middleman for new enterprisers, aiding co-ethnics in selecting sites, securing new or used equipment, and training for pizza production in already-operating restaurants. As with the Sino-Khmer, he extracted no ownership shares or ancillary revenues from this service to his fellow immigrants. Upon his death, this informal 'system' of shop training, links with equipment providers, *et al.*, devolved into a network of Greek advisers, who channelled new entrepreneurs toward non-competing sites. Though this was effective for assuring start-ups reasonable chances for success, it also entailed few continuing links among the multiple small firms thus established. Financial support for novices was relatively rare; each restaurant, once launched, sailed forward on its own. Indeed, neither the kin nor the friends of firm owners figured significantly in amassing of initial capitals. Most enterprisers used savings from overtime work, often seven days a week, or secured bank loans to open their businesses (Lovell-Troy 1990; Mavratsas 1995). In consequence, the support network for immigrant Greek proto-entrepreneurs has been documented as centring on training through work in others' restaurants, contacts with suppliers, and informal advice, rather than loans or institutionalized capital-raising devices. Here questions comparing distinctive cultural practices and the differential spatial, skill, and capital requirements for various small-business sectors are salient.

This experiential diversity among business-minded immigrant groups in twentieth-century America also invites business historians to develop longer-term analyses of ethnic entrepreneurship than have been attempted by social scientists who have researched current and recent relationships, opportunities, practices, and contexts. Sociologists and ethnologists have created models for inquiry methods, have conceptualized the struggle for a coherent identity among immigrants of various ethnicities, and have examined business practice since roughly the 1970s. The challenge for business historians is to take up these tools and explicate the dynamics of immigrant enterprise in American communities across the preceding century.

The Invisible Centre: Lawyers and Doctors as Firms

'Don't ye iver go into coort,' says I . . . says he, 'No sir, th' law is a diff'rent proposition fr'm what it was whin Dan'l Webster an' Rufus Choate an' thim gas bags used to make a mighty poor livin' by shoutin' at judges that made less. Th' law to-day is not only a profissyon. It's a business. I made a bigger honoraryum last year consolidatin' the glue inthrests . . . thin Dan'l Webster iver thought was in th' goold mines iv th' wurrld.   (Dunne 1963: 35–6)

The somewhat snobbish blindness of the professions to the business aspects of their own occupations is regrettable. Far from obviating the difficulties of business, this ostrich reaction has simply muddled and multiplied them. Whether he likes it or not, every professional man is engaged in a business of selling his professional skill, and satisfying, if not increasing, the number of his customers.   (Wolf 1938, p. vii)

If analysis of ethnic entrepreneurship illuminates the intersection of enterprise and identity, engaging the professions as businesses highlights the relationship between specialized knowledge and economic power. Yet, as with immigration, period and place relate fundamentally to the historical dynamics of professional development and practice. In the nearly twenty years since Larsen's *The Rise of Professionalism* triggered research and debate, efforts to construct a trans-national or 'essentialist' definition of the 'professional' have not borne fruit. The histories of the classic professions, law and medicine, are sharply different in the USA, UK, Continental European states, and presumably in Asia as well. Two basic contrasts will here suffice, one between private and public ordering and another concerning national culture. In Britain and America, both law and medicine developed as self-managed private sectors to which the state long paid little attention. In France, Germany, and Scandinavia, however, the state more often initiated and regulated professional training and practice, making irrelevant the Anglo-American notions of autonomy and proprietorship. Moreover, the United States has a global reputation as a profoundly litigious society and since the 1940s, as a nation nearly obsessed with health issues. In consequence, the USA supports more lawyers than any other country, nearly a million in the 1990s (a dramatic contrast with Japan, where court challenges appear to be a last, rather than a first, resort), and expends above 12 per cent of gross national product on medical services, again a global peak (Gerson 1984; Larsen 1977; Segrist 1990).

Hence, this section will make no larger claims than to review the peculiar American creation of law and medicine as powerful 'anti-businesses', i.e. profoundly institutionalized, profitable economic agents that, as a matter of principle or ideology, have steadfastly differentiated themselves from 'commerce and trade'. That business historians have taken these self-descriptions at face value is at first puzzling.[3] However, this neglect makes a certain sense in an American context where, until recently, this conception was confirmed in both public opinion and government practice. Two examples of the latter are immediately relevant. In the 1930s, the federal Census Bureau determined that, in the Depression crisis, it was essential to develop a fuller portrait of American economic activity than could be drawn from censuses of agriculture and manufacturing. Thus were launched a series of Censuses of Business, which took account of distribution and services, including in 1935, 'professional service businesses'. However, a note to the tabulated findings (9,000 firms, 50,000 employees, $84 million in payrolls) explained the figures covered 'Accountants, architects, commercial artists, engineers, etc., but not . . . professional businesses such as lawyers, physicians, dentists, etc.' (Census 1937: 5). Thus, though described as 'professional businesses', law and medicine were also not businesses for the Census Bureau's purposes. In situations like this, Foucault's understanding that power is often quietly coded into categories and classifications is relevant to appreciating the significance of lawyers' and physicians' invisibility as businesses and the cultural force of their self-definitions.

Second, in legal terms, both law and medicine were long regarded by courts as immune to investigation and prosecution for restraint of trade, price-fixing, and other violations of anti-trust statutes. Their ideologies of disinterested public service, with one exception in the 1940s,[4] remained a legal bulwark until the mid-1970s. As one commentator noted: 'Although the courts had never squarely so held, it was thought that physicians, lawyers, and perhaps some other professionals were not engaged in "trade and commerce" and that [their collective] professional activities . . . were fundamentally different from similar concerted activities carried out by industrial groups' (Gray 1991: 180). Only after a series of assertive Supreme Court decisions, c.1975–82, was the self-regulation of the 'learned professions' deemed comparable to business collusions that constrained competition. That organized medicine failed to secure specific Congressional exemptions from such scrutiny (and prosecutions) in the 1980s indicates a recent sea change in public and political views.[5]

What characteristics make the anti-businesses of law and medicine germane to American business history? Six features of their common practice beckon: monopoly returns to economic activity, control of entry, a 'fiduciary ethic', a long tradition of small proprietorships and partnerships, the self-regulation and certification of practitioners, and the construction of national trade associations with considerable political leverage. Let us review these in sequence.

'Everyone knows' that American lawyers and doctors earn vast incomes. Of course, what 'everyone knows' is rarely accurate when both history and the distribution of economic opportunities are fully taken into account. From the mid-ninteenth century through the Great Depression, the earnings of most attorneys and physicians stood modestly above those of skilled workers, retail proprietors, and college professors, and well below those of mid-size industrial entrepreneurs. Yet since the Second World War, their professional incomes have escalated sharply, being by the 1980s three to four times the level that production workers could achieve (Gray 1991: 178).[6] Why this should be the case is a substantial problem for business historians to engage.

Further, in a 1968 study of service sectors for the National Bureau of Economic Research, Victor Fuchs examined statistically a wide range of 'industries' to determine differentials between expected earnings, given demographic characteristics of those economically active (age, sex, race, years of schooling), and their actual earnings in 1959. Regressions on these factors 'explained' 70 per cent of 'interindustry differences', a robust finding regarding the relation between individual characteristics and earnings. However, in three professions, Fuchs discovered that 'actual earnings far exceed[ed] expected' returns, suggesting extra-demographic factors were crucial to these extraordinary incomes. Unsurprisingly, these 'upper end' performers were 'security and commodity brokers, medical except hospital [private physicians], and legal' professionals (Fuchs 1968: 135–40). When years of schooling, age, etc. were all factored out, these groups enjoyed incomes inexplicably higher than those having comparable demographic characteristics in other professions. Howso?

The spectre of monopoly cannot but be drawn on-stage here. American attorneys and physicians plied their trades in a post-war environment wonderfully favourable to profiting from their skills. Self-trained rivals or those expounding alternative models for treatment (homeopathy) had been driven out. The complexities of law and healing had overmatched individuals' capacities to represent their own interests at court or communities' capabilities for self-medication and informal care.[7] It is hard not to view the exceptional earnings of lawyers and physicians as the fruits of a complex process of monopolization, to whose elements we now turn.

Actors in all business sectors wish for means to control the entry of rival firms. The construction of oligopolistic barriers was, of course, the classic mode in American economic development, at least among Chandlerist sectors like auto, steel, and meatpacking for most of the century after 1880.[8] Superior skill and creative design requirements or the narrowness of markets also may restrict entry, as in machine tools or shipbuilding. But for services, this challenge is usually overwhelming. Retailers, restaurants, and repair shops can do little individually or collectively to prevent others from initiating competition. Enterprisers in law and medicine had greater capabilities in this regard, and as Fuchs discovered, greater success than other professionals.

After the 1850s, controlling entry had two dimensions. These professionals had both to exclude 'inferior' rivals active in the nineteenth century and to manage the flow of aspiring competitors willing to endure the rigours of professional training as defined by 1900. Conceptualized as 'market closure', this effort to employ claims to expert knowledge and demand extensive training as a means to social power has been carefully documented by sociologists researching the professions (Collins 1990). Focusing on 'resources available for controlling or evading the control of others in organizations and social networks', they have argued that those trades most successful in managing borders and labour supplies become 'professions'. Other trades in which this capability fails represent mere 'occupations' (Collins 1990).

For American lawyers and physicians in the nineteenth century, the first phase of entry control was truly daunting. Prospective attorneys could train with any practising lawyer and set up shop whenever they judged they had absorbed enough practical knowledge (Abel 1989; Galanter and Palay 1991). Candidate doctors could choose among a range of therapeutic systems, learn the basics, and project themselves to clients (never customers, given the prevailing ideology) as experts in healing, without prior examination or regulation (Haber 1991). In a sense, this was a pure market environment for the businesses of law and medicine, for wretched practitioners would be forced out of the trade, at least locally, and sent off to find another set of victims in other territories. Of course the purity of these exchange relations was undercut by the differential positions of consumers and providers. The former rarely had comparative criteria through which to gauge in advance the capabilities of their service professionals. Yet, although the professionals controlled the essential knowledge that gave them status, the local circulation of information about outcomes and reputations served as a market feedback device that could eliminate the weakest firms.

Organization at the national level was crucial to building the capacity to drive out rival vendors in law and medicine. The American Medical Association (founded 1847) battled late in the century to discredit all physicians who followed theoretical models that did not accord with their 'allopathic,' or science-based, format. The American Bar Association (1878) sought the authority to rule on the qualifications of attorneys, and thus 'naturally' decided that women, African-American, and immigrant lawyers, however properly schooled, were beneath their standards (Haber 1991). Surely as important, both organizations converged successfully on defining a single pathway to entry: advanced education in university settings. Only the worthy were admitted; only the most competent among that élite achieved degrees in law and medicine. Once this scheme generalized, market control was solidified, but only so long as the number of training institutions was controlled as well.

Here the twin towers of state licensure and certification of legal and medical educational institutions served to lower the proportion of physicians per 100,000 population from 157 in 1900 to 132 in 1957, while that of lawyers rose modestly from 120 to 150 across the same period (Abel 1989; Harris 1964). Both national and state-level trade associations pressed effectively for legislation regarding licensing of professionals and were instrumental in fashioning umbrella organizations for assessing and accrediting training institutions (increasingly graduate schools), while demanding higher entry qualifications of prospective students. Plainly, physicians were more adept at controlling supply than lawyers, but both professions enjoyed rising demand for their expertise as the twentieth century proceeded.

The differential between clients' knowledge and that of lawyers and doctors, combined with both trades' bans on advertising and the critical nature of clients' problems, created a power differential that could hardly be ignored. To mediate this unequal relationship, lawyers and doctors fashioned a cultural convention, the 'fiduciary ethic', which became the keystone of their 'anti-business' stances. Because clients 'must depend on doctors, doctors must act under legal and ethical constraints that do not apply to businessmen', as must lawyers (Gray 1991: 172). No client can know beforehand how serious his/her difficulties are, how much professional attention they need, or what the cost is likely to be. Hence, it is necessary for the power-holding professional to exercise prudence, to stand as arbiter of the client's interests, and to submit to the judgement of colleagues concerning the probity of the decisions taken. As medical historian Paul Starr notes:

Medicine and other professions have historically distinguished themselves from business and trade by claiming to be above the market and pure commercialism. In justifying the public's trust, professionals have set higher standards for themselves than the minimal rules governing the marketplace and maintained that they can be judged under those standards by each other, not by laymen. . . . This shift from clients to colleagues in the orientation of work . . . represents a clear departure from the normal role of the market.   (Starr 1982: 23)

Lawyers occupy a comparable position, for they long rejected competition to secure clients and regarded one another as the best evaluators of their acuity and effectiveness (Abel 1989).

Business historians interested in the uses of language should find reconstructing the development of the fiduciary ethic a fascinating challenge. To what degree is it analogous to trustees' obligations of 'prudence', for example? Or, from a more critical perspective, is it analogous to industrial ideologies of efficiency employed to transfer shop-floor authority from skilled workers to engineers and managers through claims to specialized knowledge, externally validated (by the market) and opaque to employees? Moreover, an early twentieth-century debate about the business dimensions of both professions developed alongside real engagement with notions of efficiency and system derived from scientific management. Both merit exploration (Cohen 1916; Galanter and Palay 1991; Wiprud 1938; Wolf 1938).

Though the private practice of law and medicine has altered dramatically in recent decades, for the century before the 1960s, the vast majority of professionals in both areas worked as proprietors or partners in small practices. In 1930, for example, 87 per cent of lawyers served in private practices, the balance salaried by either government or businesses. Forty years later, nearly three-quarters of the legal profession remained in private firms, though the advance of partnerships with apprenticed 'associates' had transformed some lawyers into salaried employees (Abel 1989). Another survey revealed that, in 1951, 84 per cent of lawyers operated independent enterprises, two-thirds of these being sole practices. By 1970, solo lawyers represented just over half of the 77 per cent still working outside industry and government (Spangler and Lehman 1982). The development of 'huge' law firms, those with over 100 lawyers, has been quite recent and perhaps overemphasized. In the mid-1970s, about fifty such enterprises employed 6,500 attorneys, whereas a 1993 report located 67,000 lawyers at 250 firms. This tenfold increase, however impressive, showed less than 8 per cent of American attorneys employed by the 'law factories' (Linowitz 1994).

Virtually all physicians worked in solitary practices in 1900, with a tiny minority salaried by the military, public health agencies, or as medical school and hospital personnel. In 'horse-and-buggy' days, town and village doctors enjoyed a spatial monopoly of area clients, for as little as five miles travel made it unlikely that individuals would seek an other-than-local physician. The technological and social changes which the advent of the automobile brought also produced the stirrings of competition among non-urban doctors. MDs with Model Ts could range more widely and more rapidly to reach clients, and more affluent farmers with cars could bypass the nearby physician to seek an alternative in market towns or county seats. In consequence village doctors relocated to larger places; a third of the towns with under 1,000 residents which had had physicians in 1914 had none in 1927 (Berger 1979).

Notwithstanding these centralization dynamics, as late as 1963, 55 per cent of physicians still reported themselves as 'self-employed' and 14 per cent as salaried in office-based practices, with the remaining 30 per cent evenly divided between hospital teaching and administrative staff, and training posts as interns and residents. The pace of recent change is evident in data gathered a decade later, for by 1973 the self-employed share had dropped to 42 per cent as hospital, bureaucratic and training positions neared 40 per cent (McKinlay 1982; Roback 1973). These trends herald a major shift in contemporary entrepreneurial status and prospects in law and medicine, about which much concern has been expressed. The historical autonomy and claims to non-market behaviour that underwrote lawyers' and physicians' special status in American society have been eroded by factors other than court decisions.

Next, both professions fought long and hard to establish their rights to self-regulation and to certify the qualifications of new entrants. The growing scientific base of medicine and its extended training sequences made it relatively easier for physicians to argue convincingly that only those already knowledgeable could evaluate the performance and skills of colleagues and apprentices. By 1900–10, physicians staffed the proliferating state boards of medical examiners which tested incomers and novices. In addition, local medical societies supported members' court defences against malpractice claims (with considerable success), and the AMA 'began grading medical schools according to the record of their graduates on state licensing examinations' (Starr 1982: 104–18). Though the ABA was slow to draw wide membership (being initially an organization of wealthy urban lawyers who met annually at Saratoga Springs, NY, a famous resort), state and local associations readily assumed the responsibility for certifying new lawyers through oral interviews. State-level, formal examinations spread nationally after 1900, and clearly were used to restrict entry in periods of perceived labour oversupply and potential competition, notably in the Great Depression. Though the ABA developed ethical standards for lawyers, a recent analyst argued that attorneys have been far from effective in self-governance and control of malpractice, a failure that has undermined their claims to professional autonomy, as well as their social status (Abel 1989).[9]

Last, both law and medicine are unified professionally through national trade associations that have become politically and culturally far more powerful than those of other small businessmen, professionals, and manufacturers. Perhaps this achievement derives in part from a conflation of public service and personal interest which may be peculiar to these two vocations. Whatever its source, their authority has been considerable throughout the present century (Garceau 1961). Whereas the ABA and its state federations regularly 'certify' judicial prospects as 'qualified' (or not) in electoral and appointment processes, the AMA successfully blocked efforts to develop a national medical care system for half a century after the Second World War. At local levels, both are deeply involved in disciplinary proceedings to disbar attorneys or cancel physicians' licences, often defending those charged with misdeeds. Each association has a research arm that tracks the profession's economic course and generates policy papers for legislators' consideration; and each has collaborative relations with a sizeable set of specialized collective institutions that represent the interests of sub-groups within the profession (trial lawyers, surgeons). For business historians, comparisons of such associations with those in manufacturing and distribution is an obvious opportunity, especially with regard to associations of small business enterprises, such as Chambers of Commerce and Boards of Trade.

Given the distinctive small-business character of American lawyers and doctors, at least until the 1980s, their dramatic transformations in the last fifteen years, and their construction of both authoritative cultural statuses and powerful collective institutions, these two professions should be inviting targets for small-business historians. Their successes should provoke us to ask a range of questions, particularly if we are sensitive to Foucault's arguments about the intersection of knowledge and power and its institutionalization (Foucault 1977, 1980). How was it possible for these knowledge specialists to achieve such economic returns and income stability/growth while retaining a small business format? How were these solitary or small partnership enterprises managed, and with what resonances and contrasts to analogous firms in service sectors or professional activity? When and why were issues of efficiency, scale, or throughput introduced into their discourses and practices? How was entry control legitimized in these trades, while being assaulted and defeated in virtually all other small-business sectors? Why has American society, unlike others, created or tolerated a special 'anti-business' niche for these economic actors, but not for most other professionals? Why the long lag in the consolidation of medical and legal services, much like real estate or banking, as opposed to insurance? What technological and legal shifts transformed the business of medicine and law over the last century and what nexuses of power have threatened their small-business format in recent years?

Surely other questions will arise, but this cluster suggests the open spaces for thoughtful research into the professions when they are considered as small enterprises that have been largely invisible to business historians. The inverse of the marginal, law firms and medical practices are equally deserving of our sustained attention.

Social Auxiliaries

As business historians' interests in recent years have broadened to include enterprises outside manufacturing, studies that address the management of information in insurance, the development of franchising, and the fashioning of a national communications network have enriched our knowledge (Dicke 1992; Lipartito 1989; Yates 1989; Zunz 1990). Yet business historians still lag their colleagues in related fields who are taking account of consumption as a key theme for historical research (Brewer and Porter 1993; Olney 1991; Tomlinson 1990). Other than an enterprise's own use of material and other inputs, consumption is located outside the firm, is the result of marketing and demand, and thus has seemed external to the discipline's concern. In doing so, we overlook the hundreds of thousands of small businesses directly mediating the history of consumption in America. Only advertising and the department store have drawn sustained attention, but rarely by business historians (Leach 1993; Lief 1968; Marchand 1986; Miller 1981; Schudson 1984; Twichell 1996).

Space limitations and the thinness of historical research force brevity, but a sketch of the terrain and its potentials is possible. If it is arguable that advanced industrial capitalist societies have increasingly defined themselves by reference to the consumption goods and practices of individuals, those institutions which facilitate consumption hold special interest for business historians. These auxiliaries include non-financial firms that offer goods and services to individuals, chiefly retailers, leisure operations, and repair specialists, but not banks, loan companies, insurers, wholesale firms, or business service organizations (i.e. advertising agencies). As the vast majority of these enterprises have always been small firms, their significance to this conference's theme is evident. Here, only two tasks will be attempted: a depiction of the extent of social auxiliaries in the USA, drawn from Censuses of Business before and after the Second World War, and presentation of a cluster of possible research questions.

First, some fairly raw data will help focus attention. The American retailing sector in 1929 included 1.5 million enterprises handling $49 billion in sales, only a quarter of which were recorded by stores grossing $300,000 or more. Four years later, in the depression's worst year, 1.5 million shops continued in operation; and while sales had fallen by half, small-firms' shares in the constricted market had little changed (Census 1935a: 34).[10] In miserable 1933, retailing was the locus of 5 million jobs, including proprietors, with 700,000 in auto-related sectors (dealers, gas stations, repair shops), more than were then occupied in manufacturing vehicles (Census 1935a: A-8).[11] Overall, independent retailers accounted for 88 per cent of enterprises and 71 per cent of sales (only a tenth of which flowed through department stores), with chains (25 per cent) and mail-order operations (1 per cent) handling most of the balance. Full-time workers' earnings in all classes clustered around $1,000 per year, or $20 per week (Census 1935a: A-18). Three years after the end of the Second World War, 1.8 million retailers reported $130 billion in sales, a 70 per cent rise in real terms over their 1929 performance. Independent operators represented 90 per cent of all stores, holding a 70 per cent share in sales, while chains accounted for most of the residual. Employment (including proprietors and family workers) had doubled to 10 million, with 1.1 million involved in automobile services. Yet in 1948, paid workers' average earnings reached only $2,000, a figure that, given inflation, yielded purchasing power hardly much improved from that during the Depression (Census 1952a: 9, 17, 22).

American personal service, repair, and amusement enterprises in 1933 summed to 460,000 firms, 1.2 million owners and employees, and $2.1 billion in receipts. Ranging from barber and beauty shops through typewriter repairs to dance halls and hotels, these sectors' total revenues were far smaller than retailers' because their inventory purchases were miniscule. However, in both fields, the mean firm size was three, representing a proprietor and two workers. Here, full-time employees on average took home over $900 in annual pay in 1933, with legitimate theatre performers topping the lists at nearly $3,000 and 'auto launderers' (car washers) trailing everyone else at $600 (Census 1935*b*, table 1.1). With economic recovery by 1939, these three auxiliaries reported 620,000 enterprises, 1.6 million proprietors and workers, and revenues of $2.9 billion, roughly proportional increases that suggest continuity rather than structural change (Census 1941: 4–5).

Initially, the war years were harsh for small business, as population and supply dislocations advantaged the largest industrial corporations. A postwar analysis indicated that 'the total number of enterprises—including retail and service lines—was reduced by one-sixth between Pearl Harbor and the end of 1943', a decline overwhelmingly suffered by small firms. Yet by 1946, the number of American enterprises swelled to 25 per cent above the mid-war low, 'reaching the unprecedented total of 3.5 million' (Kaplan 1948: 2). Personal services, repairs, and amusements did not share in this burst of company start-ups; but they did expand dramatically in other ways. The 1948 reports showed a firm total (633,000) virtually the same as in 1939. However, although the number of proprietors was stable, their work-forces nearly doubled to just under 2 million. More dramatically, receipts tripled to $11.7 billion, well outpacing inflation, which doubled prices, 1939–48. Average worker earnings rose only one-third, sharply lagging inflation and creating opportunities for substantially enhanced profitability. The increase for legitimate theatre personnel (to $4,000) closely tracked this average, whereas car-washers' wages doubled (to $1,200), perhaps in response to minimum wage statutes (Census, 1952*b*: 1.02–3). Of course, interpreting these shifts more precisely will demand further research.

For retailing, it is generally understood that the long-term impact of chain stores on independent businesses has been dramatic and troublesome. Complaints of predatory competition by chains and of overpricing (once locally-owned firms failed) yielded both a Federal Trade Commission investigation late in the Depression, fair trade legislation, and a landmark study of distribution dynamics (FTC 1935; Palamountain 1955; Twentieth Century Fund 1939). Yet as one scholar commented: 'Independents' political attacks on mass distribution and large-scale organization, full of sound and fury, accomplished little.' The chains' advantages have been so heralded that the slow pace of their long advance has been less appreciated. For example, in groceries, chains accounted for 38 per cent of national sales in both 1929 and 1948, as they proved unable to hold a mid-Depression gain to 45 per cent. In restaurants and drinking places, chains held 15 per cent of a $1.3 billion market in 1933, and, forty years later, 21 per cent of a $70 billion market in the mid-1970s (Emerson 1979; Palamountain 1955 (quote,

256); Census 1935*a*: A-18). Business historians might well explore what accounted both for this slow progress and for the evident resilience of small firms in grocery retailing and restaurants through mid-century and well beyond it.

More broadly, how might we assess the larger significance of these 'non-producer' firms within the national economic context? Of course, many service and social auxiliary sectors can be fitted into a narrative that represents their incorporation, belatedly, into secular processes of centralization and consolidation, one that features appropriate attention to obstacles preventing the marginalization of small enterprises until, for example, brand-naming and mass advertising ably promoted consumer interest in chain fast-food outlets or national retailing discounters (Walmart). This, however, would be a traditional exercise. More intriguing would be a set of business historical studies that explored the logics of small entrepreneurship in social auxiliaries. To what extent are such enterprises designed to stake out market niches distinct from the mass delivery systems for goods and services? How did entrepreneurs define their areas of competence and market them? What have been the locational patterns of speciality retail and service firms, and to what degree are these conditioned on the co-location of definable user populations (ethnics, high-income families)? How have such firms responded to the cumulative brand promotions by chain rivals? What organizational efforts have they undertaken to set politically the boundaries of competition, and with what results?[12] How has the state, which in the 1930s showed deep concern for the fate of small service specialists, altered its stance and why (both in terms of legislation and court precedents)?

It is evident that the service segment of the American economy has long been a rich terrain for small enterprise and that its long resistance to amalgamation and concentration has been undercut in recent decades, both in professional businesses like those outlined earlier, and in the consumption-oriented commercial trades. Our collective understanding of these enterprises remains primitive. It is indeed time for that near-silence to be broken.

Conclusion

This chapter represents an exercise in imagining distinctive and provocative futures for the history of small business. Such novel efforts would move beyond contributionist motifs to fresh and perhaps controversial engagements with the subjective significance of 'being in business', the implicit cultural structures that long defined economically important professions as 'anti-businesses', and the centrality to a consumer society of those many small enterprises that serve as social auxiliaries to everyday life. The challenge ahead is twofold: (1) to refine concepts and methods appropriate to researching these territories and histories; and (2) to prosecute sustained inquiries into these little-known worlds of business history. I do hope that the preceding commentaries and arguments will serve to stimulate just such efforts.

NOTES

1. Ethnic immigrants here refers to non-native English speakers, to distinguish them from English, Welsh, Scots, and Irish immigrants whose language capacities rapidly reduced their peripheral status as 'foreigners'. Though the Irish had the greatest difficulty in this regard, particularly in the two decades after the famine, by the 1880s, they had become 'solid citizens' in dozens of urban areas, politically active and economically buoyant. Women entrepreneurs were plainly marginal figures well into the post-Second World War decades, but this has changed substantially in the last generation. In 1987, women owned 30 per cent of all US firms; by 1996, this proportion rose to 36 per cent, representing 8 million enterprises with 18.5 million employees, roughly a quarter of the present private sector work-force (*Philadelphia Inquirer*, 30 Apr. 1996, C1, C8). Black-owned enterprises have made no comparable advance.
2. There were exceptions, of course. Northern Italian immigrants from manufacturing districts moved readily into positions in Paterson, New Jersey's silk trades, for silk production dated to the early modern period in their regions of origin.
3. Specialists in legal and medical history abound in the USA, but rarely focus on the business aspects of practice. Instead, they have crafted fine studies treating the history of legal thought, court precedents, the transformation of training, *et al.*, and for medicine, analogous themes, plus the emergence of the hospital, mental and public health provision, and crucially, the impact of science and technology on medical treatment.
4. In 1943, the Supreme Court upheld a lower court conviction of the American Medical Association for transgressing the Sherman Antitrust Act in its concerted effort to undermine a group pre-paid medical practice in Washington, DC. This precedent lay dormant for 30 years.
5. Ironically, American professional baseball has enjoyed effective legal exemption from antitrust suits since 1922, when Justice Oliver Wendell Holmes ruled that baseball 'was sport, not trade.' See Andrew Zimbalist (1992), *Baseball and Billions*. New York, 8–10.
6. Average incomes for self-employed doctors in 1987 stood at $132,000, whereas few manufacturing workers could expect to earn more than $40,000 per year, and most received less.
7. Physicians fought a continuing and successful battle to prevent pharmacists from prescribing medications, while, as a trade-off, restricting themselves from

selling same. The marginalization of midwives represents another vector in this drive for control.

8. That this was not a timelessly effective strategy should be evident, however. Import barriers and consumer preferences were insufficient to prevent the advance of non-US car and heavy-vehicle makers in the 1970s, generating a major crisis among America's leading firms. In steel, both global technological updating and the creation of domestic non-union, specialized 'mini-mills' undercut U.S. Steel's and Bethlehem's dominance. In meatpacking, the diffusion of slaughtering to secondary cities and the innovation of 'boxed beef' deranged the major packers' positions in the same era. See Brock Yates (1983), *The Decline and Fall of the American Automobile Industry*. New York; Paul Tiffany (1988), *The Decline of American Steel*. New York; John Strohmeyer (1987), *Crisis at Bethlehem*. New York; and Roger Horowitz (1997), *Organizing the Makers of Meat: Shop Floor Bargaining and Industrial Unionism in Meatpacking*, 1930–1990. Urbana, Il. ch. 10.

9. In 1890, there were only 4 state-wide examinations, but by 1917, 37 existed among the 48 states and the District of Columbia.

10. In 1933, firms with $200,000 and above in sales held 22 per cent of retail trade; if half the $100,000–200,000 group were added, to estimate a reduced $150,000 dividing line, the largest enterprises would carry 27 per cent of sales.

11. In 1929, the Detroit area's auto industry, the national hub, alone employed 475,000 workers. By 1931, only 250,000 still had jobs and more were laid off in the next two years (Rothschild 1973: 36).

12. Lizabeth Cohen, in a 1994 presentation at a Hagley conference, indicated that successful activism for 'blue laws' in New Jersey in the 1950s, banning Sunday openings of retail stores, derived largely from independents operating in town centres who faced seven-day competition from chain stores located in the new 'shopping centres' in the state's northern counties.

REFERENCES

Abel, Richard (1989), *American Lawyers*. Oxford University Press: New York.

Antin, Mary (1914), *They Who Knock at Our Doors*. Houghton Mifflin: Boston.

Bederman, Gail (1995), *Manliness and Civilization*. University of Chicago Press: Chicago.

Bell, Thomas (1976), *Out of the Furnace*. University of Pittsburgh Press: Pittsburgh.

Berube, Alan (1990), *Coming Out Under Fire*. Free Press: New York.

Berger, Michael (1979), *The Devil Wagon in God's Country*. Archon Books: Hamden, Conn.

Best, Michael (1990), *The New Competition*. Harvard University Press: Cambridge, Mass.

Boydston, Jeanne (1990), *Home and Work*. Oxford University Press: New York.

Brewer, John and Porter, Roy (1993), (eds.) *Consumption and the World of Goods*. Routledge: London.

Briggs, Vernon (1984), *Immigration Policy and the American Labor Force*. The Johns Hopkins University Press: Baltimore.

Burrage, Michael and Torstendahl, Rolf (1990) (eds.), *Professions in Theory and History*. Sage: London.

Byington, Martha (1974), *Homestead: The Households of a Mill Town*. University of Pittsburgh Press: Pittsburgh.

Carnes, Mark and Griffen, Clyde (1990) (eds.), *Meanings for Manhood*. University of Chicago Press: Chicago.

Census (1935a), US Department of Commerce, Bureau of the Census, *Census of American Business, i: Retail Distribution*. GPO: Washington, DC.

—— (1935b), US Department of Commerce, Bureau of the Census, *Census of American Business, i: Services, Amusements, and Hotels*. GPO: Washington, DC.

—— (1937), US Department of Commerce, Bureau of the Census, *Census of Business, 1935: Non-Profit Organizations, Office Buildings, Miscellaneous*. GPO: Washington, DC.

—— (1941), US Department of Commerce, Bureau of the Census, *Sixteenth Census of the United States: 1940, Census of Business: Service Establishments, 1939*. GPO: Washington, DC.

—— (1952a), US Department of Commerce, Bureau of the Census, *Census of Business, 1948, i: Retail Trade—General Statistics*. GPO: Washington, DC.

—— (1952b), US Department of Commerce, Bureau of the Census, *Census of Business, 1948, vi: Service Trade—General Statistics*. GPO: Washington, DC.

Chan, Suchen (1990), 'European and Asian Immigration into the United States in Comparative Perspective', in Virginia Yans-McLaughlin (ed.), *Immigration Reconsidered*, 37–75. Oxford University Press: New York.

Chandler, Alfred (1962), *Strategy and Structure*. Harvard University Press: Cambridge, Mass.

—— (1977), *The Visible Hand*. Harvard University Press: Cambridge, Mass.

Chauncey, George (1994), *Gay New York*. Basic Books: New York.

Cohen, Julius (1916), *The Law: Business or Profession?* n.p.: New York.

Collins, Randall (1990), 'Market Closure and the Conflict Theory of the Professions', in Burrage and Torstendahl (eds.), *Professions*, 24–43.

D'Emilio, John (1983), *Sexual Politics, Sexual Communities*. University of Chicago Press: Chicago.

Derber, Charles (1982), (ed.) *Professionals as Workers*. G. K. Hall: Boston.

Dicke, Thomas (1992), *Franchising in America*. University of North Carolina Press: Chapel Hill, NC.

Dunne, Finley Peter (1963), *Mr. Dooley on the Choice of Law*. University Press of Virginia: Charlotesville, Va. (repr. of 1905 edn.).

Ehrlich, Richard (1977), (ed.) *Immigrants in Industrial America*. University Press of Virginia: Charlottesville, Va.

Emerson, Robert (1979), *Fast Food: The Endless Shakeout*. Lebhar-Friedman Books: New York.

Federal Trade Commission (FTC) (1935), *Final Report on the Chain Store Investigation*, 74th Congress, First Session, Senate Document No. 4. GPO: Washington, DC.

Fligstein, Neil (1990), *The Transformation of Corporate Control*. Harvard University Press: Cambridge, Mass.

Foucault, Michel (1977), *Discipline and Punish*. Vintage Books: New York

Foucault, Michel (1980), *Power/Knowledge*. Pantheon: New York.

Fox-Genovese, Elizabeth (1988), *Within the Plantation Household*. University of North Carolina Press: Chapel Hill, NC.

Fuchs, Victor (1968), *The Service Economy*. Columbia University Press: New York.

Galanter, Mark, and Palay, Thomas (1991), *Tournament of Lawyers*. University of Chicago Press: Chicago.

Garceau, Oliver (1961), *The Political Life of the American Medical Association*. Archon Books, Hamden, Conn.

Gerson, Gerald (1984), (ed.), *Professions and the French State*. University of Pennsylvania Press: Philadelphia.

Granovetter, Mark (1995), 'The Economic Sociology of Firms and Entrepreneurs', in Portes (ed.), *Economic Sociology of Immigration*, 128–65.

Gray, Bradford (1991), *The Profit Motive and Patient Care*. Harvard University Press: Cambridge, Mass.

Haber, Samuel (1991), *The Quest for Authority and Honor in the American Professions, 1750–1900*. University of Chicago Press: Chicago.

Halter, Maryln (1995), (ed.) *New Migrants in the Marketplace*. University of Massachusetts Press: Amherst, Mass., 43–58.

Harris, Seymour (1964), *The Economics of American Medicine*. Macmillan: New York.

Kaplan, A. D. H. (1948), *Small Business: Its Place and Problems*. McGraw-Hill: New York.

LaMar, Elden (1940), *The Philadelphia Clothing Workers*. Amalgamated Clothing Workers: Philadelphia.

Larsen, Magali (1977), *The Rise of Professionalism*. University of California Press: Berkeley.

LaSorte, Michael (1985), *La Merica: Images of Italian Greenhorn Experience*. Temple University Press: Philadelphia.

Leach, William (1993), *Land of Desire*. Vintage Books: New York.

Leba, John (1985), *The Vietnamese Entrepreneur in the United States*. Zieliks: Houston, Tex.

Lebsock, Susanne (1984), *The Free Women of Petersburg*. Norton: New York.

Leverenz, David (1989), *Manhood and the American Renaissance*. Cornell University Press: Ithaca, NY.

Levine, Louis (1924), *Family Business: A Century in the Life and Times of Strawbridge and Clothier*. McGraw-Hill: New York.

Light, Ivan and Bonacich, Edna (1988), *Immigrant Entrepreneurs: Koreans in Los Angeles*. University of California Press: Berkeley.

Linowitz, Sol. (1994), *The Betrayed Profession: Lawyering at the End of the Twentieth Century*. Maxwell Macmillan: New York.

Lipartito, Kenneth (1989), *The Bell System and Regional Business*. The Johns Hopkins University Press: Baltimore.

Loucky, James, Soldatenko, Maria, Scott, Gregory, and Bonacich, Edna (1994), 'Immigrant Enterprise and Labor in the Los Angeles Garment Industry', in Edna Bonacich (ed.), *Global Production: The Apparel Industry in the Pacific Rim*. Temple University Press: Philadelphia, 346–50.

Lovell-Troy, Lawrence (1990), *The Social Basis of Ethnic Enterprise: Greeks in the Pizza Business*. Garland Press: New York.

Marchand, Roland (1986), *Advertising the American Dream*. University of California Press: Berkeley.

Marsh, Margaret (1990), *Suburban Lives*. Rutgers University Press: New Brunswick, NJ.

Mavratsas, Caesar (1995), 'Greek-American Economic Culture', in Halter (ed.), *New Migrants*, 97–119.

McKinlay, John (1982), 'Toward the Proletarianization of Physicians', in Derber (ed.), *Professionals*.

Miller, Michael (1981), *The Bon Marché*. Princeton University Press: Princeton.

Olney, Martha (1991), *Buy Now, Pay Later*. University of North Carolina Press: Chapel Hill, NC.

Pacyga, Dominic (1991), *Polish Immigrants and Industrial Chicago*. Ohio State University Press: Columbus, Oh.

Palamountain, Joseph (1955), *The Politics of Distribution*. Harvard University Press: Cambridge, Mass.

Passero, Rosa (1978), *Ethnicity in the Men's Ready-Made Clothing Industry, 1880–1950*, unpub. University of Pennsylvania diss.

Peiss, Kathy (1986), *Cheap Amusements*. Temple University Press: Philadelphia.

Piore, Michael and Sabel, Charles (1984), *The Second Industrial Divide*. Basic Books: New York.

Portes, Alejandro (1995) (ed.), *The Economic Sociology of Immigration*. Russell Sage: New York.

—— and Rumbaut, Ruben (1990), *Immigrant America*. University of California Press: Berkeley.

Roback, G. A. (1973), *The Distribution of Physicians in the U.S.* AMA: Chicago.

Rothschild, Emma (1973), *Paradise Lost: The Decline of the Auto-Industrial Age*. Vintage Books: New York.

Saxton, Alexander (1971), *The Indispensable Enemy*. University of California Press: Berkeley.

Schneider, Dorothee (1994), *Trade Unions and Community: The German Working Class in New York City*. University of Illinois Press: Urbana, Il.

Schudson, Michael (1984), *Advertising: The Uneasy Persuasion*. Basic Books: New York.

Scott, Joan (1974), *The Glassworkers of Carmaux*. Harvard University Press: Cambridge, Mass.

—— (1988), 'Gender: A Useful Category of Historical Analysis', in ead, *Gender and the Politics of History*. Columbia University Press: New York, 28–52.

Scranton, Philip (1983), *Proprietary Capitalism*. Cambridge University Press: New York.

—— (1991), 'Diversity in Diversity', *Business History Review*, 65: 27–90.

—— (1993), 'Build a Firm, Start Another', *Business History*, 35: 115–51.

Segrist, Hannes (1990), 'Professionalization as a Process', in Burrage and Torstendahl, (eds.), *Professions*.

Seidman, Joel (1942), *The Needle Trades*. Farrar and Rinehart: New York.

Smith-Hefner, Nancy (1995), 'The Culture of Entrepreneurship Among Khmer Refugees', in Halter (ed.), *New Migrants*, 141–60.

Smith-Rosenberg, Caroll (1975), 'The Female World of Love and Ritual', *Signs*, 1: 1–29.

Spangler, Eve and Lehman, Peter (1982), 'Lawyering as Work', in Derber (ed.), *Professionals*.

Stansell, Christine (1987), *City of Women*. University of Illinois Press: Urbana, Il.

Starr, Paul (1982), *The Social Transformation of American Medicine*. Basic Books: New York.

Tomlinson, Alan (1990), (ed.) *Consumption, Identity and Style*. Routledge: London.

Tong, Rosemary (1989), *Feminist Thought*. Westview Press: Boulder, Colo.

Twentieth Century Fund (1939), *Does Distribution Cost Too Much?* The Fund: New York.

Twichell, James (1996), *Adcult USA*. Columbia University Press: New York.

Ulrich, Laurel (1990), *A Midwife's Tale*. Knopf: New York.

Waldinger, Roger (1986), *Through the Eye of the Needle*. New York University Press: New York.

Wiprud, Theodore (1938), *The Business Side of Medical Practice*. Lea and Febiger: Philadelphia.

Wolf, George (1938), *The Physician's Business*. Lippincott: Philadelphia.

Wyman, Mark (1993), *Round Trip to America: The Immigrants Return to Europe*. Cornell University Press: Ithaca, NY.

Yates, JoAnne (1989), *Control Through Communication*. The Johns Hopkins University Press: Baltimore.

Zangwill, Israel (1916), *Children of the Ghetto*. Jewish Publication Society: Philadelphia.

Zunz, Olivier (1990), *Making America Corporate, 1870–1920*. University of Chicago Press: Chicago.

2

Small Business in America: An Historical Overview

In 1994 a decade-old campaign against Wal-Mart, America's largest retailer, exploded. Protesters chanting 'One, two, three, four—we don't want your Wal-Mart store', opposed the building of new stores in Oceanside, California; Gaithersburg, Maryland; Quincy, Massachusetts; East Lampeter, Pennsylvania; Lake Placid, New York; Gallatin, Tennessee; and other communities. One opponent—a self-employed clothing designer in Fort Collins, Colorado—summarized what was on the minds of many: 'I really hate Wal-Mart. Everything's starting to look the same, everybody buys all the same things—a lot of small-town character is being lost. They disrupt local communities, they hurt small businesses' (*Wall Street Journal*, 11 Oct. 1994). Opposition became so vocal that it attracted the pen of cartoonist Gary Trudeau, who devoted a week of his comic strip 'Doonesbury' to the controversy.

Such opposition illustrates that a concern for small business, and the type of lifestyle that many Americans imagine it engenders, is very much alive in the United States. It mattered little to opponents of Wal-Mart that the stores brought lower prices to consumers or that Wal-Mart's presence generally improved the economies of the communities in which its stores were located (Vance and Scott 1994: ch. 8). What mattered was the firm's imagined harm to small businesses and small towns. However, while the campaign against Wal-Mart caught the attention of Americans, and while many sympathized with small retailers, relatively few took an active part in opposing Wal-Mart. Most Americans liked the company's low prices.

The Wal-Mart controversy laid bare the ambiguous attitudes Americans have long harboured toward small businesses. On the one hand, Americans have held a special place in their hearts for small-business people, their firms, and the individualistic way of life they have been thought to foster. Into the late-twentieth century, some Americans viewed small businesses as bulwarks against too great a concentration of power in the United States.

Yet, on the other hand, Americans have wanted to benefit from the out-pouring of goods from large businesses—companies that they have, until the last decade or so, thought of as being more efficient and productive than small businesses. Most Americans have not tried to use public policies and governmental power in a concerted way to destroy large firms for the bene-fit of smaller ones.

This chapter examines the interactions between public attitudes, policy-making, and the development of small business in America. It begins by looking at public attitudes and federal government policies deriving from those attitudes. The chapter then turns to what actually occurred in terms of the development of small manufacturing firms. Finally, I suggest how historical themes connected to small business are influencing changes in the way big businesses are managed today and looks at the implications of these changes for job creation. No short chapter can encompass all of a field, and mine does not. It says little about small businesses in sales, services, or agriculture. Philip Scranton's chapter in this volume, looks at small busi-ness development in some of these areas.

This chapter looks mainly at manufacturing, because this is the field on which most historical research has focused and because my own work on small business has been mainly in this area. Throughout, I shall be taking an eclectic and functional approach in defining what is meant by 'small'. I shall be defining small businesses less in terms of absolute size and more in terms of their sizes relative to other firms in the same industries and in terms of how they are managed and organized (Blackford 1991: 'Introduction').

Public Attitudes and Federal Government Policies

As the Wal-Mart controversy demonstrated, the attitudes of Americans to-ward small business have been complex. From the 1850s, when large firms began developing, into the 1970s most Americans associated big business with material abundance, efficiency in production methods, and a rising standard of living. None the less, many Americans, especially in the late-nineteenth and early-twentieth centuries, were uneasy with big business, and expressed a sentimental attraction to small business. The development of big business was so sudden and disruptive of traditional ways of work and life that many Americans looked upon it with anxiety. In particular, they feared the concentration of economic power that the rise of big busi-ness seemed to herald.

Government actions to protect small businesses reflected the contradict-ory public discourse. Some protection was afforded from the most blatant abuses of large firms, as the federal courts and Congress sought to prevent vaguely defined forms of 'unfair' competition. For the most part, however, few impediments were placed in the way of the development of big business. As long as large firms developed by reasonable means and submitted to federal and state regulation, they were permitted to grow and prosper. In his *Beyond the Broker State: Federal Policies Toward Small Business, 1936–1961* Jonathan Bean has shown that recent federal government actions with regard to small business progressed through two major stages (Bean 1996). In the first, small business advocates sought to use antitrust legislation, the Robinson-Patman Act of 1936 and the Miller-Tydings Act of 1937, to help small firms. Later, in a more proactive way, they turned to the creation of federal government agencies during the Second World War and the Korean War to spur small business development, culminating in the formation of the Small Business Administration (SBA) in 1953.

A modification of the Clayton Act of 1914, the Robinson-Patman Act ostensibly sought to protect independent retailers from chain store incursions —most importantly by prohibiting growers, manufacturers, and wholesalers from giving chains discounts for large-quantity purchases, even though those savings were often passed on to consumers in the form of lower prices. While originally written by officials of the US Wholesale Grocers' Association, whose members disliked giving discounts to the chains, the bill was, none the less, pictured as an aid to small retailers. In a highly charged debate on the bill, preserving economic opportunity and protecting small-business people were presented as more important than economic efficiency and lower prices for consumers. Proponents of the act hoped to limit concentrations of power, political as well as economic, in America. As Wright Patman, who sponsored the bill in the House, put it: 'There are a great many people who feel that if we are to preserve democracy in government, in America, we have got to preserve a democracy in business operation. We must make some effort to maintain the yeomanry in business' (Palamountain 1955: 211).

The second national measure to win approval was the Miller-Tydings Act, an amendment to the Sherman Act of 1890. Pushed especially hard by independent retail druggists organized in a powerful trade association, the National Association of Retail Druggists, this act sought to standardize prices charged consumers for goods sold at retail. A retail price maintenance measure, the proposal forbade chain stores from selling their goods at prices below those set by manufacturers. Like the Robinson-Patman Act approved the previous year, the Miller-Tydings Act placed the interests of small-business people above those of consumers. For supporters of the Miller-Tydings Act, avoiding too great a concentration of power and preserving a cherished lifestyle were of prime importance. As the secretary of the American Pharmaceutical Association argued:

The small retail distributors are rapidly approaching the time when they will be forced completely out of an independent business existence. . . . These small businesses have been and are the backbone of the communities of this country.... If we ask ourselves honestly, whether we want this country to become a nation of clerks or to remain a nation of opportunity for individual enterprise, there can be only one answer consistent with American ideals.   (Palamountain 1955: 245)

Still, for all the furore surrounding their enactment, the two laws had little impact on America's business structure. Neither had much influence on the chains. The laws contained numerous loopholes that allowed chain stores to continue conducting business with few changes. In the end, the acts were mainly symbolic in significance, allowing Americans to assert symbolic support of small business while continuing to benefit from the work of big business.

The mixed emotions that Americans held toward small and big business continued into the mid-twentieth century. The Great Depression sorely tried the faith of Americans in big businesses, as many blamed them for the coming of hard times. Yet, this break with big business was remarkably brief. By the close of the 1930s, as some prosperity returned, most Americans had affirmed an acceptance of the large corporation. The boom times of the Second World War sealed the pact, and there existed little active opposition to big business in the first quarter century after the war. Still, as in earlier years, Americans had a soft spot in their hearts for small-business people and their firms. Moreover, with the onset of the Cold War, small business came to be seen as distinctly American—as an institution that, by its very nature, could make valuable contributions to the development of America's political and business systems and thereby help defend America against totalitarianism.

Small-business advocates turned to the creation of federal government agencies to protect small firms. In the 1930s and 1940s the Reconstruction Finance Corporation (RFC) had the power to help small firms and occasionally did. Special agencies sought to make sure that some defence dollars went to small companies during the Second World War and the Korean War (with only limited success, especially during the second conflict). During the early 1950s, however, officials in the RFC became involved in a series of well-publicized scandals involving favoritism in granting loans to small businesses.

Coming to power in 1953, President Dwight D. Eisenhower, like many other Republicans, wanted to abolish the RFC, which he viewed as a holdover from the New Deal and as a symbol of political corruption. At the same time, the Republicans realized that they needed to ensure the continuation of aid given by the agency to small business; for, even if the actual amount of aid was not great, its symbolic value was. From these concerns came new legislation ending the RFC and creating the SBA. Small-business people were characteristically divided on the legislation, with some preferring that government leave business affairs altogether. Most politicians, however, agreed with Secretary of Commerce George M. Humphrey who asserted that while he thought that 'in theory there should be no difference between lending money to a large business or lending money to a small business . . . in practice, in just good common sense, I think, there should be some additional body arranged to assist small business' (Parris 1968: 23). As signed into law by Eisenhower, the legislation set up the SBA as a temporary agency in July 1953. At the same time the RFC was abolished. The SBA was made permanent five years later.

Underfunded and lacking consistent leadership, the SBA proved a disappointment to small-business advocates. An administrative assistant to Wright Patman expressed this feeling shortly after the enabling legislation for the SBA had won approval: 'The 1953 act was more to get rid of the RFC than to set up the SBA. It's no more than a sop. The administration wanted only to get rid of the RFC.' For others, disillusionment came later, when it became apparent that the SBA would not fund all desired projects. After studying the record of the SBA, one scholar concluded in 1961 that 'it seems reasonable to suggest that the culmination of eighteen years of activity to establish a separate small business agency actually resulted in a reduction of the government's program for small business' (Zeigler 1961: 111).

The welter of federal government policies designed to protect and promote small business accomplished little. The long-term decline of small business relative to big business continued into the early 1970s. This lack of effective actions on behalf of small business probably accurately reflected public attitudes. Most Americans favoured the growth of big business, which they associated with an outpouring of consumer goods and a rising standard of living. Yet, at the same time most Americans desired that the government take some steps—if only symbolic ones—to preserve small businesses. Politicians took limited steps, passing legislation and setting up federal government agencies designed to help small firms; but, it must be stressed, these were intentionally *limited* actions, mainly *symbolic* in importance.

As the United States national and global business situations changed dramatically from the early 1970s, and especially as Americans came to perceive that large firms might not be the engines of growth they once had been, public discourse on small business changed—particularly with regard to firms in manufacturing. Americans increasingly valued small firms less as defences against the concentration of power, economic or political (although, as the Wal-Mart controversy revealed, this attitude never totally disappeared), and more as imagined sources of growth and efficiency in their nation's economy. This represented a major change in how many Americans viewed small business. They saw small companies as the saviours for their country's faltering business system. Vibrant small firms, especially in manufacturing, would, according to this view, compensate for problems larger companies were having in heightening global competition.

In this new outlook, the role of the federal government was much less significant than economic factors in the recent growth of small business. What were those economic factors, exactly? How did small business develop in the United States? These topics now require examination, with special reference to manufacturing.

Small Business in Manufacturing

With the development of big businesses in industry from the 1880s, small businesses found themselves in an ambiguous position. The proportion of America's industrial output coming from small businesses dropped as large manufacturing ventures rose to prominence. Still, opportunities in the nation's expanding industrial economy beckoned to small-business owners, and small businesses increased in absolute numbers.

Corporations—the legal form assumed by most big businesses, but relatively few small businesses (most small firms remained single-owner proprietorships or partnerships)—accounted for three-quarters of America's industrial production by 1904. By 1914 nearly a third of all industrial workers found employment in plants with 500 or more in their labour forces, and another third in those with 100 to 499. Even so, in 1914 a third of America's industrial work-force found employment in firms with 100 or fewer labourers. If small businesses are defined as those with 250 or fewer workers, 54 percent of those employed by manufacturing concerns worked for small firms. Moreover, some 54,000 little businesses, those with six to twenty workers, were still in operation on the eve of the First World War.

Most small businesses that succeeded in manufacturing did so as flexible firms producing speciality products for niche markets, either on their own or as members of regional business agglomerations. Rather than competing head-to-head with large mass-production industrialists, they coexisted with big businesses by differentiating their products from those of their larger competitors. Doing so often meant producing goods for rapidly changing regional and seasonal markets. Part of the ability to accomplish this task lay in the possession of intelligent, innovative work-forces. Another part lay in the flexible use of the most advanced technologies of the day. This strategy has remained at the core of much small business success in manufacturing to the present day.

There is a growing scholarly literature on small manufacturers in American history, which I have surveyed elsewhere. Rather than repeat myself in detail here, let me touch lightly on several of the most important works and on my own research, and try to draw some conclusions about them.

Philip Scranton's work on the textile industry in Philadelphia has been of great importance for business historians. As the nineteenth century progressed, Scranton argues, America's textile industry divided into two segments (Scranton 1983, 1989). At Waltham and Lowell large factories employed unskilled workers to turn out standardized goods for the mass market. By 1850 12 corporations employed 12,000 textile workers in Lowell. A very different pattern unfolded at Philadelphia. There, in 1850 some 326 firms employed 12,400 textile workers. Two-thirds possessed 25 or fewer workers. Though employing as many workers in the aggregate as their counterparts in Lowell, the Philadelphia firms were capitalized at much less, $4.7 million, about a third of the amount invested in the Lowell companies.

The Philadelphia firms competed successfully throughout the nineteenth century by stressing specialization and flexibility in production and marketing. Few Philadelphia firms tried to master all aspects of textile production. Most specialized in one or two steps which they then did very well indeed, using the most up-to-date machinery and employing skilled workers, often men, at high wages. Productivity levels were high. With skilled work-forces and modern machinery, the Philadelphia mills could rapidly switch to various types of cotton, wool, and other fabrics as needed. Small size and versatility continued to be hallmarks of Philadelphia textile firms into the mid-twentieth century. Only when national economic problems joined particular problems of the Philadelphia mills during the Great Depression of the 1930s did the Philadelphia textile businesses decline.

A similar story developed in America's iron and steel industries. As John Ingham has recently shown, Pittsburgh's iron and steel industries took form as collections of relatively small businesses (Ingham 1991). These smaller firms engaged in only one or two, not all, of the steps involved in turning out iron and steel products and prospered by specializing. Not even the formation of United States Steel in 1901 radically altered the situation. Only a few of the independents became part of United States Steel, and between 1898 and 1901 16 new iron and steel firms were set up in Pittsburgh. In 1901 the 40 independent producers in Pittsburgh had a production capacity of 3.8 million tons of iron and steel, compared to the 2.6 million ton capacity of United States Steel. In 1920 fully 78 per cent of the independents in existence two decades before were still doing business, and even after America's second major merger movement, which occurred in the 1920s, about 50 per cent were active. The Great Depression ended the existence of more, but on the eve of the Second World War 28 per cent of the original independents remained.

The success of small firms in the iron and steel industries was not limited to the Pittsburgh region or to firms that developed as part of regional groupings. The growth of the Buckeye Steel Castings Company of Columbus, Ohio suggests the continuing importance of stand-alone small businesses in manufacturing (Blackford 1982). Formed as a partnership in 1881, Buckeye Steel initially produced a variety of cast-iron goods for the local

market in Central Ohio. Buckeye lacked a speciality product or any other
advantage over its competitors and came very close to failing during the
hard times of the mid-1880s.

However, a new president, Wilbur Goodspeed, changed the direction of
the company. Coming to Columbus from Cleveland in 1886, Goodspeed
had Buckeye Steel develop a speciality product for a niche market, an automatic railroad-car coupler. This technologically sophisticated product gave
Buckeye an edge over its competitors and allowed the company to break
into the national market. In entering this market, Buckeye Steel's executives
relied heavily upon their personal connections with other business people.
While in business in Cleveland, Goodspeed had come to know high-ranking
executives at the Standard Oil Company, which was headquartered in that
city. (Goodspeed and some of the Standard Oil executives set up the
Cleveland Gatling Gun Regiment, a private paramilitary outfit, in the wake
of nation-wide railroad strike in 1877.) Soon after he took over at Buckeye
Steel, Goodspeed negotiated an arrangement favourable to both parties. In
return for receiving a large block of common stock in Buckeye Steel for free,
the Standard Oil executives agreed to use their influence to persuade all of
the railroads that shipped Standard's petroleum products to market (few
long-distance pipelines existed then) to purchase their couplers solely from
Buckeye Steel. Railroad orders soared, and Buckeye Steel emerged as a very
successful business, becoming a medium-size firm by national standards at
the time of the First World War.

Common themes run through the success of those small companies that
proved capable of coexisting with large manufacturing concerns between
about 1880 and 1930. The small manufacturers adopted a growth strategy
that remained one of the keys to success in small business into the late twentieth century: they developed speciality products which they then sold in
niche markets, thereby often avoiding direct competition with their larger
counterparts. To make this strategy work, the firms usually adopted (or developed themselves) the most advanced production technologies available. These small companies were not backward workshops using obsolete
equipment, but were instead among the most advanced industrial establishments of their day. Running the companies were managers deeply committed to their success. Most of the firms continued to be operated as family
enterprises devoid of managerial hierarchies. More than a quest for profits
animated their owner-managers. A sense of personal satisfaction, almost a
sense of craftsmanship, remained an important motivating factor for their
executives and workers.

Factors external to their companies also prepared the way to success. In
some instances government aid helped. Such was the case with Buckeye
Steel. In 1893 Congress passed legislation requiring that all railroad cars be
equipped with automatic couplers within five years. This act was a piece of
safety legislation designed to protect trainsmen who were often injured

while joining cars together with the old-style manual couplers. This law helped create a national market for Buckeye Steel's main product. In other cases, especially where regional groupings developed, favourable local environments proved valuable. In Philadelphia the textile companies benefited from various sorts of local government aid and were also able to join together to support for many years a trade school to insure the availability of a steady supply of skilled workers.

Such strategies continued to bring success after the Second World War. Foreshadowing many of the findings of economists and other scholars a generation later, a perceptive essay in the *Harvard Business Review* in 1957 investigated how some small manufacturers, firms defined as those with no more than 100 employees, succeeded. Some served national markets whose total demand was too small to attract large firms. Others operated in areas that required 'special knowledge and background, special methods and skills in manufacture, and contact with customers by men with particular backgrounds'. Still others manufactured products for regional markets in which service and speed of delivery were of utmost importance. Finally, small businesses succeeded in fields in which flexibility, especially the capability rapidly to turn out small batches of goods in short production runs, was of most significance (Hosmer 1957: 111–22).

A small business I have studied in some detail, Wakefield Seafoods, succeeded as a specialized, vertically integrated food producer. The firm brought Alaskan king crabs to the American table, something no United States company had previously done (Blackford 1979). Lowell Wakefield, who came from a family with experience in Alaska's salmon and herring fisheries, led a group of young men—all of whom knew Lowell and many of whom had been stationed in Alaska with the Navy during the Second World War—in the foundation of Wakefield Seafoods in 1946. Personal ties of acquaintance thus brought together those starting the company. The same ties provided much of the financing for the firm, as Wakefield, together with his family, friends, and business acquaintances, invested their personal savings in the venture. A quest for adventure mingled with a desire for profits in the minds of those starting the company. All had seen their lives disrupted by the Second World War, and at its conclusion were, as one explained, 'casting about for something to do'. They were looking, another later remembered, for 'a lot of glamour and excitement', and were eager to be 'trying something that had never been done'. In addition to private funds, the company depended upon government aid to get started. Two-thirds of the funding came from the RFC.

Despite the federal loan, Wakefield Seafoods began its existence on shaky feet. Like most people starting small businesses, those setting up Wakefield Seafoods were overly optimistic about their company's future, expecting to earn large profits within just two or three years. Such was not to be, for the company encountered unexpected difficulties in every stage of its operations. Within a few years, the problems were solved, but in the meantime they brought Wakefield Seafoods to its knees. By the middle of 1948 the company had accumulated liabilities of $400,000 against assets of only $140,000 (and those consisted mainly of an unsold inventory of crab meat). Wakefield Seafoods was in default of its RFC loan and loans from commercial banks. It could pay neither its fishing crews nor its suppliers of fishing gear. Its officers-investors could take no money out of the company to live on; the company's cash-on-hand had dwindled to a paltry $14!

None the less, Wakefield Seafoods remained in operation and emerged as a very successful company in the 1950s. By 1952 the firm had paid off its most pressing debts, and within just four more years was paying handsome dividends. No single factor contributed to the firm's step back from the brink of bankruptcy. The company's officers eagerly embraced technological advances, many of them spin-offs from the Second World War. Their ship, the *Deep Sea*, was the first to use radar, sonar, and Loran (a navigational device) in fishing, and, similarly, developed new methods to process, cook, and freeze the crabs. Moreover, those starting the company were persistent, willing to endure hard times to get their company moving. When unable to attract fishing and processing crews, the owner-managers manned the nets and processing lines themselves. They operated the company informally, as one later recalled, more as 'a gang of friends' than as a group of managers. Most important, perhaps, were the personal ties that had been so significant in starting Wakefield Seafoods. Personal friendships between the founders of the company and the heads of the Seattle branch of the RFC, Seattle's commercial banks, and the suppliers of fishing gear were especially important in helping secure extensions on the company's loans. Finally, pure, blind luck—an element often underrated by scholars assessing the success and failure of small businesses—saved Wakefield Seafoods. In 1949, for no particular reason, the *Deep Sea*'s officers found twice as many king crabs as in the previous year.

As mentioned earlier, there was something of an increase in the importance of small business in the American economy in the 1970s and 1980s, especially in manufacturing. In fact, firms with fewer than 500 employees increased their share of the nation's total manufacturing output from 33 per cent to 37.4 per cent between 1976 and 1986. As in earlier decades, small firms proved adept at exploiting niche markets with specialized products based upon short production runs. By the 1970s and 1980s, however, perhaps more was involved. Some observers suggested that the ability of small businesses to react quickly to alterations in markets and fluctuating exchange rates in an increasingly unstable economic world helped explain their growing significance. Then, too, the use of computers in computer-aided design, computer-aided engineering, and computer-aided manufacturing allowed small, independent firms to perform tasks that only larger businesses could earlier accomplish, thus allowing more direct competition with their larger counterparts. Some scholars cautioned, however, that by the late 1980s and early 1990s, small businesses were encountering or would soon face limitations in the use of computer technology, because they lacked the capital needed to put entire computer-driven manufacturing systems, automated factories, in place (Acs and Audretsch 1990: ch. 6).

What developed in some fields in the 1970s and 1980s were congeries of small industrial firms, similar perhaps to the textile-makers in Philadelphia studied by Scranton or the independent steel mills in Pittsburgh examined by Ingham. Often located near each other in specific locales, the small firms supported each other and in some fields offered viable alternatives to mass industrial production by big businesses.

High-technology firms in California's Silicon Valley just south of San Francisco provided a case in point. Here few large vertically integrated companies existed. Instead, most of the area's makers of computer hardware and software, producers of communications equipment, and manufacturers of defence products were smaller firms that consciously avoided vertical integration. Instead of trying to internalize all facets of their companies' work in single firms, Silicon Valley entrepreneurs got ahead by forming a large, informal, and very flexible network of linked—but independent—companies. Companies worked very closely with suppliers of components, with venture capitalists, and with specialized legal and marketing consultants. Workers moving from job to job and company to company transferred information across firm boundaries. Located in one area, this agglomeration of many mainly small companies allowed producers to reap economies of scale without forming big businesses.

The system established in the Silicon Valley was a formula for business success. By the close of the 1970s the Silicon Valley possessed nearly 3,000 electronics firms, 70 per cent of which had fewer than 10 employees and 85 per cent of which had fewer than 100. These firms faced a crisis in the mid-1980s, as they lost most of the market for semiconductor memories to Japanese companies. However, as a mark of their flexibility and resilience, most Silicon Valley firms recovered later in the decade as producers of specialized, high-value-added, complex electronics goods. As in the 1970s, most of these companies were smaller firms, which avoided vertical integration (Saxenian 1994).

Should Big Businesses Act Like Small Businesses?

The success of some regional agglomerations such as the group of firms in the Silicon Valley led observers to raise questions about America's business system in the 1970s and 1980s. Many concluded that large industrial businesses should act more like smaller businesses: that they should be more entrepreneurial in their management, that they should be more flexible in their production methods, and that they should stress speciality products for niche markets. Taking these actions, it was argued, would both benefit the individual companies and the American economy as a whole, by making American business more competitive in the global marketplace. Public discourse on small business changed; small business was increasingly valued for its imagined stimulus to the American economy.

Such advice was often wrapped up in a concern about the more general restructuring of American business. As is well known, many large American manufacturers have undergone restructuring in recent years. The unstable global economy marked by energy crises, cycles of boom and bust in consumer demand for durable goods, and rapidly growing foreign competition hurt American firms in a variety of industries. A revival of merger activity, often based on hostile take-overs, placed additional pressures on chief executive officers. Some 143 of the largest 500 industrial firms in the United States were acquired by other companies in the 1980s, and the total value of business assets changing hands in America during the decade came to $1.3 trillion. Restructuring has involved a search for profits, which, in turn, often has led to an increased focus on what business executives consider the core capabilities of their corporations. In fact, about 60 per cent of the unrelated acquisitions made by American manufacturing companies during the 1970s had been divested by 1989.

BFGoodrich was one of America's industrial companies to restructure its operations. Together with my colleague at Ohio State, Professor K. Austin Kerr, I have just finished writing Goodrich's history (Blackford and Kerr, 1996). I would like to look at Goodrich's attempts to restructure its operations and management in the 1980s and 1990s. In doing so, I want to raise the question: can (and should) a big business act like a small one?

Goodrich began as a maker of a wide range of speciality rubber products —everything from fire hose to rubber belting—in Akron in 1870, the first manufacturer to make rubber products west of the Appalachians. The reason Goodrich located in the Midwest and the reason it made speciality products was that it could not compete with better-established eastern firms turning out what was then the commodity rubber product of the day, footwear.

Then occurred the company's first transformation. As Goodrich prospered, it moved into new commodity products, bicycle tyres in the 1880s and automobile tyres from 1896. Goodrich was the first American company to make pneumatic automobile tyres, and by 1912 was America's leading producer of them. Goodrich lost that lead in the 1910s, 1920s, and 1930s. By the early 1930s Goodrich trailed Goodyear, Firestone, and U.S. Rubber as a tyre-maker. Many factors contributed to that decline, but most basically the conservatism of Goodrich's management was responsible. Goodrich's officers proved unwilling to invest in modern tyre plants to as great an extent as their competitors and consequently lost ground to them.

A second transformation at Goodrich began in the 1940s. Led by a new president recruited from outside the firm and spurred by the demands of the Second World War, Goodrich moved in new directions. In tyres, the firm pioneered in the use of synthetic rubber. Equally important, the company developed polyvinyl chloride (PVC) products. A Goodrich scientist had discovered how to plasticize PVC as early as 1926, thus helping start the world's modern plastics industry. During the war, PVC began coming into its own, especially as a replacement for rubber in insulating wires on the Navy's ships (rubber insulation burned too easily). PVC, in turn, led Goodrich to increase its presence in chemicals (the company had worked on rubber chemicals for decades). Many new uses for PVC were discovered in the 1940s and 1950s, as America's and the world's chemical industry was revolutionized; and these developments brought Goodrich growth and prosperity.

By the late 1960s and early 1970s that prosperity was eroding, owing to greatly increased domestic and foreign competition in Goodrich's two major product lines, commodity PVC goods and tyres, setting the stage for a third transformation. Under two chief executive officers since 1971 (O. Pendleton Thomas, 1971–9, and his protégé John Ong, 1979–96), BFGoodrich sold over $2 billion worth of its assets, while making about $1 billion million worth of acquisitions (the difference went mainly to pay off huge debts incurred primarily in the 1980s).

This restructuring of BFGoodrich meant basic changes in the firm's product lines. Goodrich found itself unable to compete in tyres, for its plants were obsolete compared to those of other firms, a legacy going back to the 1920s. Goodrich left the making of original equipment tyres in 1982 and the making of replacement tyres (through a joint-venture with Uniroyal) in 1987. Michelin later bought what was left of this venture. Today all that remains of Goodrich's tyre-making is the Goodrich name. For decades Goodrich's industrial rubber operations, located in an out-of-date hotchpotch of buildings in Akron, had been a major problem, often losing tens of millions of dollars a year. In the mid-1980s Goodrich either sold or closed most of them, including the hose and belt operations with which the company had got its start a century before. BFGoodrich was in the 1970s and early 1980s America's leading producer of PVC, but in the early 1980s the firm ran into major problems in trying to control the raw materials and intermediates that go into the manufacture of PVC. The financial difficulties incurred in trying to integrate backward in PVC almost destroyed the company. Faced with financial problems and growing foreign competition in the making of commodity PVC, Goodrich sold nearly all of its PVC operations in 1993. The firm that had done so much to develop plastics was now out of that industry, except for a few minor operations.

So, what had BFGoodrich become? By the mid-1990s Goodrich consisted of two loosely related divisions, speciality chemicals and aerospace. Both had histories at Goodrich dating back to the 1910s and 1920s, but neither became really important until the 1980s. Since the mid-1980s Goodrich's executives have poured hundreds of millions of dollars into acquisitions to expand aerospace operations. They have tended, by contrast, to develop speciality chemicals more by internal growth. Goodrich has, thus, eschewed the making of commodity products for large homogeneous markets. Instead, the company makes speciality products for niche markets, everything from carbon brakes for America's space shuttle to a wide range of adhesives (and in the case of aerospace Goodrich provides speciality services as well).

BFGoodrich also changed its management. From centralized management it has moved since the Second World War to decentralized management. Corporate executives pushed extensive authority over operations far down the managerial line. By 1996 BFGoodrich consisted of several dozen almost independent business units (or profit centres) set up around products only loosely controlled by the corporate office. Ong explained how management worked. 'No one is in control of you [the manager of a business unit], or can interfere with you. You can do the r&d the way you want, operate your plants the way you want, do marketing the way you want, do your own management hiring and firing, do your own capital spending (within generous limits). You are operating your business almost as if you owned it.' Goodrich's business units operated as relatively small entrepreneurial companies responsible for their own affairs and flexible in responding to alterations in their markets and their technologies. The BFGoodrich of the 1990s was, then, a far cry from the much more centrally controlled company of the 1970s.

How typical is the Goodrich story? There are intriguing suggestions that the recent restructuring of American big businesses—especially in large manufacturing enterprises—is working. Big businesses in manufacturing, by acting as smaller, flexible, entrepreneurial firms—much as Goodrich has done—seem to have been revitalized in recent years. In fact, this revitalization of large industrial companies may be eroding the place of small business in manufacturing.

Two indicators suggest that firms are becoming larger in America. First, America's Gross Domestic Product per company dropped steadily in the 1980s, but has been climbing since 1991—indicating that companies are getting bigger. Second, the share of self-employed workers in America's non-farm work-force reached 8.2 per cent in 1991 (up from less than 7 per cent in the mid-1970s), but has since been falling. In examining these trends in 1995, *The Economist* asked 'What is going on?' And concluded: 'Part of the answer is that small firms are being driven out by large firms which are starting to behave more like their smaller brethren . . . pushing decision-making down through management ranks, restructuring themselves around teams and product-based units, and becoming more entrepreneurial' (*The Economist*, 18 Feb. 1995: 63–4).

The Thorny Issue of Job Creation

Considerations of the relative importance of different company sizes brings my paper to a final issue, the relationship between small business and job creation in America. The question of how important small businesses, especially small manufacturers, have been in creating new jobs has been a very contentious topic, and one rife with significance for government policy decisions.

Much of the controversy has revolved around the very influential work of the consultant David L. Birch. Birch has seen in small business the most vibrant engine of growth in the modern American economy. Using flawed data in his most famous work, *Job Generation in America: How Our Smallest Companies Put the Most People to Work*, published in 1987, Birch characterized big businesses as stagnant firms contributing little to the economic growth of the United States. Birch claimed that 80 per cent of the new jobs created in America between 1969 and 1976 were in companies employing fewer than 20 workers (Birch 1987: 9).

Many have disputed Birch's findings. A study prepared in late 1993 by Steven Davis (of the University of Chicago's Business School), Scott Schuh (of the Federal Reserve Board), and John Haltiwanger (of the Department of Economics at the University of Maryland) is probably the thoroughest analysis of the roles small firms have played in job generation in America in recent years. Its findings do not support the notion that small firms are outstanding as engines of growth. Based on data from the Longitudinal Research Data Database housed at the Center for Economic Studies in the United States Bureau of the Census, their study examines job generation and job destruction in American manufacturing from 1972 to 1988.

The findings are striking. First, the study shows that plants with at least 100 employees accounted for two-thirds of job creation between 1972 and 1988. Moreover, firms with at least 500 employees accounted for nearly two-thirds of the new jobs. It concludes that 'these findings reflect the simple fact that large plants and firms account for the bulk of the manufacturing jobs base'. Second, and most importantly, the report shows convincingly that small manufacturers are no better than their larger counterparts in *net* job creation. Small firms are better at *gross* job creation; but small firms go out of existence more frequently than large companies—thus destroying more jobs: 'Gross job creation rates decline monotonically [unvaryingly] with employer size. The job creation rate averages 16.5 per cent of employment per year for firms with fewer than 20 employees, 9.3 per cent for firms with 500–999 employees, and 6.3 per cent for firms with 50,000 or more employees. . . . Thus, small employers create new jobs at a much higher gross rate than large employers.' But, this is only part of the picture. 'The gross job destruction rate declines sharply by firm size. It averages 18.8 per cent of employment per year for firms with fewer than 20 employees, 9.8 per cent for firms with 500–999 employees, and 8.0 per cent for firms with 50,000 or more employees. . . . How does net job creation vary by employer size? On this score, the empirical evidence produces no strong pattern.' In short, small manufacturing companies have not been robust engines for job creation in the United States (Davis, Haltiwanger, and Schuh 1993: 3, 9, 10).

Conclusions

As they did during industrialization and the growth of national economies in the nineteenth and early twentieth centuries, corporate executives are searching for growth strategies and management structures most appropriate for the global economy of the twenty-first century. That small businesses, despite their problems, will be part of the solution seems assured. Certainly most Americans would favour that; just a year or two ago I saw an automobile bumper sticker in Columbus, Ohio that read: 'There's no business like a small business AND There's no business like your own business.' That historians should continue to be interested in small firms seems evident to me.

Let me close with just a few suggestions for additional research. We need to learn more about the individual small-business firm and its management. As my colleague K. Austin Kerr has pointed out, we need to know more about just how independent small firms really are today (Kerr 1989). Kerr has suggested that their need to prepare business plans when applying for loans and their connections to other companies has made them less independent than in times past. He may have a point. One small business a student of mine has studied, a subcontractor for Honda Motors in central Ohio, is legally independent of Honda; but its assembly line is tied by computer connection directly to Honda's assembly line and is controlled by Honda. How extensive are such controls? Are small businesses autonomous? Along the same lines, it would be interesting to know more about how new technologies, especially computers, are affecting small businesses.

Beyond the individual business firm, a number of topics call for investigation. We need to know much more about the political economy of small business, especially in the years since the Second World War. Jonathan

Bean's work opens new avenues to this topic, but historians have really just begun to scratch the surface on the topic of government–business relations with regard to the development of policies affecting smaller firms. What occurred at the state, as opposed to the federal, level? What has been the thrust of policies since the 1950s? Comparative studies of small firms and government promotion and regulation of them across national boundaries and have begun, but more are needed.

Finally, as we study small business further, we need to bear in mind that the lines between small and large firms can be blurred. There is an indeterminate middle ground. Connections between franchisers and franchisees, links between companies and their subcontractors—as in the case of Honda mentioned above—are some of the areas crying out for historical exploration (Dicke 1992).

REFERENCES

Acs, Zoltan and Audretsch, David (1990), *Innovation and Small Firms*. Cambridge, Mass.: MIT Press.

Bean, Jonathan (1996), *Beyond the Broker State: Federal Policies Toward Small Business, 1936–1961*. Chapel Hill, NC: University of North Carolina Press.

Birch, David L. (1987), *Job Creation in America: How Our Smallest Companies Put the Most People to Work*. New York: Free Press.

Blackford, Mansel (1979), *Pioneering a Modern Small Business: Wakefield Seafoods and the Alaskan Frontier*. Greenwich: JAI Press.

—— (1982), *A Portrait Cast in Steel: Buckeye International and Columbus, Ohio, 1881–1980*. Westport: Greenwood Press.

—— (1991), *A History of Small Business in America*. New York: Twayne Publishers.

—— and Kerr, K. Austin (1996), *BFGoodrich: Tradition and Transformation, 1870–1995*. Columbus, Oh.: Ohio State University Press.

Davis, Steven J., Haltiwanger, John, and Schuh, Scott (1993), 'Small Business and Job Generation: Dissecting the Myth and Reassessing the Facts', Working Paper No. 4492 for the National Bureau of Economic Research, Oct.

Dicke, Thomas (1992), *Franchising in America: The Development of a Business Method*. Chapel Hill, NC: University of North Carolina Press.

The Economist, 18 Feb. 1995.

Hosmer, W. Arnold (1957), 'Small Manufacturing Enterprises', *Business History Review*, 35 (Nov.–Dec.), 111–22.

Ingham, John N. (1991), *Making Iron and Steel: Independent Mills in Pittsburgh, 1820–1920*. Columbus, Oh.: Ohio State University Press.

Kerr, K. Austin (1989), 'Small Business in the United States During the Twentieth Century', unpub. paper presented at a Conference on 'Comparative Management: The Lessons of Business History', Budapest, 13–15 June.

Palamountain, Joseph, Jr. (1955), *Politics of Distribution*. Cambridge, Mass.: Harvard University Press.

Parris, Addison (1968), *The Small Business Administration*. New York: Praeger.

Saxenian, Annalee, (1994), *Regional Advantage: Culture and Competition in Silicon Valley and Route 128*. Cambridge, Mass.: Harvard University Press.

Scranton, Philip (1983), *Proprietary Capitalism: The Textile Manufacture at Philadelphia, 1800–1885*. Cambridge: Cambridge University Press.

—— (1989), *Figured Tapestry: Production, Markets and Power in Philadelphia Textiles, 1885–1941*. Cambridge: Cambridge University Press.

Vance, Sandra and Scott, Roy (1994), *Wall Mart: A History of Sam Walton's Retail Phenomenon*. New York: Twayne Publishers.

Wall Street Journal, 11 Oct. 1994.

Zeigler, Harmon (1961), *The Politics of Small Business*. Washington, DC: Public Affairs Press.

3

The Architecture of an Industrial Sector: Size and Structure in Canadian Manufacturing

KRIS INWOOD

Introduction

A celebrated wave of technological change beginning with the steam engine and improvements in iron manufacture during the eighteenth century created the necessary conditions for mechanizing a wide range of activities in the transportation, mining, and manufacturing sectors (Ashton 1948; Mokyr 1993; Wrigley 1988). A large and still-growing literature investigates the causes and timing of this 'industrial revolution', and its effects on living standards, inequality, working conditions, settlement patterns, and long-distance trade. On one point there is a consensus, that the new technologies improved productivity for large-scale enterprise and thereby contributed to the emergence of big business. And yet small unpowered firms were not eliminated by the multi-faceted influences of industrialization. Observers as diverse as Alfred Marshall (1923) and Ralph Samuel (1977) agree that hand production survived in many places and industries, in some cases because of changes introduced by the incoming technological tide.[1] The importance of small firm survival is reinforced by recent debates about the nature of the industrial revolution (Berg and Hudson 1992; Hoppit 1990).

I am grateful to the Social Sciences and Humanities Research Council of Canada which provided financial support for the research on which this chapter is based. I am grateful as well for helpful critical comments which have been received from Fumikatsu Kubo, Konosuke Odaka, Minoru Sawai, Philip Scranton, and participants in seminar discussion at the Universities of Aberdeen, Alberta, Cambridge, Edinburgh, and Saskatchewan, the London School of Economics, and at the 24th Fuji Business History Conference.

Although small firms remained important, it is difficult to say how much production flowed from small and unpowered establishments at any point after the onset of the industrial era, much less chart their survival over time or explain the patterns. The overall structure and organization, or what we might call the architecture of the manufacturing sector is obscure principally because appropriate sources of information do not exist. Of course, there was much discussion of manufacturing in contemporary trade journals, newspaper and magazine articles, government reports, and the promotional literature designed to attract investors and influence policy-makers. We must rely upon such sources, but most of them reflect the pervasive nineteenth-century fascination with new technology especially as it was embodied in physically imposing structures or machinery. These sources inevitably tell us more about big business than about small-scale enterprise. Small-scale industry attracts attention in many industries most conspicuously when it is in decline, the handloom weavers being the best example (Timmins 1993). Hence the available information is biased to convey the technological marvels of big business and the rather hapless nature of the small.

Careful researchers attempt to overcome this bias, but precise information about the composition of the manufacturing sector remains elusive. In response to this dilemma British historians have turned to census reports of occupational data in order to quantify the overall dimensions of industrial activity. Unfortunately, occupational data are rather imprecise and sometimes treacherous evidence of social structure and/or economic activity. Moreover, knowing that someone was engaged in a trade does not tell us how much was produced or in what circumstances. The reports of the early factory inspectors constitute another importance source. Unfortunately, the Factory Inspector's 1841 survey of Lancashire, which has been called 'the most scrupulous and comprehensive industrial census of the century', covers only the steam and water-powered establishments in one industry and in one county (Gattrell 1977). Even after a substantial broadening of the Factory and Workshop Act during the 1860s it covered only half of the country's installed horsepower and even less of manufacturing workers (Kanefsky 1979). Another census source, the 1851 census of employers, provides the basis for Rodgers' argument for the importance of small industry in urban Scotland. However, this source is incomplete as well. A comparison of national occupation and employer tabulations suggests that the latter describes no more than one-third of all those who report industrial occupations (Rodger 1988).

The incomplete nature of information describing the structure of British industry prompts an interest in sources which might be available in other countries. After all, the technological and organizational changes associated with industrialization left their imprint in a wide range of social and economic environments. Berg and Hudson suggest that we look to North

America whose industrial experience, although different from that of Europe, was deeply intertwined through the migration of raw materials, labour, capital and technological knowledge (Berg and Hudson 1994).

North America businesses eagerly harnessed the new technologies of the industrial revolution as a labour-saving way to expand production for the fast-growing local market. Fortunately, there were few barriers to the trans-Atlantic transfer of technology. Britain and North America in the Victorian era comprised a single intellectual community through which ideas circulated more or less freely. North Americans subscribed to and read the same publications as did British businessmen and artisans. British craftspeople, investment capital, and entrepreneurs migrated across the Atlantic at a rapid rate. Perhaps most important of all, North American managers and investors learned about new technologies directly through their embodiment in imports from Europe (Jeremy 1981).

The ease with which the industrial revolution migrated across the Atlantic is one reason to examine its impact in North America. Another consideration is the richness of available sources. North American governments very early began to collect systematic information about industrial production. These industrial censuses provide a rich description of the structure of business activity in the nineteenth century. The United States attempted its first systematic enumeration in 1820, encountered difficulties and then tried again with more successful results in 1834 and 1850; subsequent enumerations at ten year intervals became progressively more careful and elaborate (Atack 1985*b*; Sokoloff 1984). Industrial census enumeration in Canada began systematically with its 1851–2 census. The data used in this chapter were collected on the industrial schedule of the 1871 census which is arguably the most detailed and complete of all Canadian enumerations.[2]

Canada in 1871

It is useful to begin with an overview of the Canadian context. A merger of the former British colonies of New Brunswick, Nova Scotia, Canada East (Quebec), and Canada West (Ontario) created the federal state of Canada during the summer of 1867. The political landscape was new, but already in 1871 much of the Canadian countryside had been settled by two or three generations of Europeans. Indeed, the lower St. Lawrence Valley and parts of the Atlantic coast has been cultivated by Europeans since the late seventeenth century. Admittedly, some northern regions were still being settled for the first time during the 1860s and 1870s. The transportation system in 1871 was a similar mixture of new and old. Rivers and lakes continued to be important, even though railway lines had been operating for more than a

Kris Inwood

decade and the network of branch lines was being extended rapidly (Drummond 1987; Hamelin and Roby 1971; McCalla 1993; Saunders 1984).

Both rail and water transportation connected the principal cities including Montreal and Quebec City, which had been important centres for 200 years and already equalled the size of many middle-sized European cities. Saint John and Halifax were quintessential port cities. Ottawa, a mill town and staging point for the lumber trade, was fast becoming a government centre after being selected as the national capital. The new and fast-growing cities of Toronto, Hamilton, and London were situated on the northern edge of a rich agricultural hinterland extending continuously into the American Midwest. Although these cities loomed large in the Canadian landscape, we must remember that the largest urban centre, Montreal, had only 120,000 people in 1871. Nowhere in Canada could be found a metropolitan centre comparable to Glasgow, Liverpool, Boston, or Chicago (much less London or New York).

The simplest measure of the degree of urbanization is population density. Such data show that population densities were lower in Canada than in the adjacent American states and much lower than in Britain (Inwood and Sullivan 1993). During 1871 the population density of southern Canada averaged less than that of Scotland outside of Glasgow.[3] The low population density in Canada reflects a lack of large cities *and* the low level of rural population density.

In this rather rural society, as elsewhere in nineteenth-century North America, kinship provided the glue which held together most households. In turn the household provided the principal basis for all social and economic organization (Gaffield 1990). The significance of the household for individual behaviour varied regionally, temporally, and in response to the individual characteristics, but almost everywhere the decisions about fertility, work, production, what and how much to consume, how fast to accumulate, and how to pass assets on to a younger generation were informed by household and often family strategies for survival and betterment. The rural household was especially important because the economy remained predominantly agrarian in character. Roughly half of all commodity income originated in agriculture everywhere in Canada (Inwood and Irwin 1993).

Although agriculture was the principal income in all parts of the country, many and probably most households at some point in their evolution deployed one or more members to non-agricultural pursuits. The patterns of occupational pluralism and intra-household division of labour were diverse, but the need to balance agricultural and non-agricultural demands on the time of family members was ubiquitous (Bouchard 1988; McCann 1988). Non-agricultural activity was most intense for rural families living close to cities or in regions which lacked climate and soil quality permitting a local self-sufficiency in basic foods (such as the north, the western mountains and prairie, and the rocky Atlantic coast). Not surprisingly, non-agricultural wage labour was widespread from an early date (Bitter-mann 1994).

The organizational basis for agricultural production points toward the likely response of rural households to pressures for change. The composition of household labour, for example, was highly heterogenous. People of different ages, gender, and other characteristics allocated labour in a complex range of agricultural and non-agricultural activities, on and off the farm. Adjustment was not costless, indeed it could be very difficult, but the household nevertheless had the flexibility to shift labour from one activity to another if that should prove necessary.

In fact, Canadian rural families during the nineteenth century faced powerful pressures to change. Family expansion and population growth within local communities created inexorable pressures on the limited amount of land that was useful agriculturally. The acreage available for crops and pasture could be increased for a time through the clearing of more forest. However, this strategy was inherently self-limiting. Once the forest was destroyed, this source of growth no longer existed.

Another impetus for change was the competition of grain originating in regions of lower-cost production in the interior of the continent. A reduction of long-distance transport costs during the early part of the century had made it possible for eastern Canadian wheat to enter British markets. Wheat soon became an important source of income and an influence upon the patterns of social relations (McCallum 1980; McInnis 1992). However, continued improvements in transportation gradually made it possible for western wheat to compete with eastern North American producers on increasingly favourable terms (Harley 1980; McInnis 1986). The loss between 1848 and 1866 of preferred access to British and American markets put further downward pressure on the eastern Canadian price of grain. The late 1860s, therefore, was a period of difficult adjustment for rural Canada.

Households responded to these challenges by reducing fertility, modifying inheritance practice, and by migrating to other parts of the continent. From 1851 to 1891, for example, fertility declined by more than one-third in the province of Ontario.[4] Demographic pressures also encouraged farm families to modify their practice for the transmission of savings from one generation to another, in order to preserve farm size and perhaps also to encourage a diversification into non-land assets such as education (Bouchard 1994; Gaffield 1991; Gagan 1981). An especially important adjustment was migration. Many people, indeed entire families left Canada during the later nineteenth century as the country experienced a significant net loss of population through outmigration (Bouchard 1991; Brookes 1976; McInnis 1994).

Those who remained on the land improved agricultural practice through the use of new machinery and science-based innovations of a chemical-biological nature, diversified into new crops and animal products, and turned increasingly to non-agricultural activities (Drummond 1957; Inwood and Wagg 1994; Jones 1946: ch. 16; Marr 1981; McInnis 1982).[5] Forestry work became common among rural men (Kelly 1968: 84–116; Gaffield 1982). Women and girls in the rural household produced butter and cloth, the latter using a blend of local wool and imported cotton yarn (Cohen 1988; Inwood and Wagg 1993). It was common as well for younger women to work as servants within the rural area or in a nearby city. The significance of these adjustments for the manufacturing sector was that rural families were able to deploy considerable labour to industrial pursuits, at a relatively low opportunity cost, especially if the production could be organized on a part-time basis adjacent to the rural household.

The Organization of Manufacturing in Canada

A diverse and lively literature chronicles the evolution of Canadian manufacturing before the First World War. In addition to writing excellent studies of individual companies (Dechêne 1978; McDowall 1984; Noel 1985), historians have compared the pace and structure of manufacturing growth before and after the turn of the century 'wheat boom' (Altman 1987; Bertram 1964; Drummond 1987; Green and Urquhart 1987; Inwood 1991), in different regions (Altman 1986, 1988a; Faucher 1970; Inwood 1987, 1991; McCallum 1980) and internationally (Babcock 1979; Dales 1964, 1966; Inwood and Sullivan 1993; Wood 1989a). Various studies have explored manufacturing in relation to raw material and energy supplies (Altman 1986; Dales 1957; Faucher 1970; Inwood 1985, 1986a, 1992; McNally 1982, 1992; Reid 1983; Walker 1974), and transportation systems (Altman 1988b; Craven and Traves 1979; Cruikshank 1992; Forbes 1977a; Forster 1988; Inwood 1989; Lutz 1988; Tulchinsky 1977). The settlement process (Gilmour 1972; Inwood and Sullivan 1993) has been examined with reference to local rural markets (Courville and Seguin 1991; Grant and Inwood 1990; Inwood and Wagg 1993; McCalla 1985; Noel 1985; Wylie 1990) and urbanization (Acheson 1985; Beeby 1984; Chambers and Bertram 1966; Drummond 1987; Gilmour 1972; McCann 1979, 1981; Middleton and Walker 1980, 1981; Muise 1991a,b; Spelt 1972; Weaver 1981). As in other countries, there is an important literature on the role of national government policy (Acheson 1972a, 1977; Dales 1966, 1979; Dick 1982; Drummond 1987; Forbes 1977b; Forster 1986; Inwood 1989, 1991; Traves 1979) and of financial institutions (Acheson 1979; Evans and Quigley 1990; Frank 1977; Frost 1982; Inwood 1986b: ch. 5–7; Marchildon 1990; McDonald 1975; Naylor 1975; Quigley, Drummond, and Evans 1993). The influence of social history has become important through its consideration of labour (Frank

1976; Delottinville 1980; Heron 1987, 1988; Kealey 1980; Kealey and Palmer 1982; McKay 1978; Reilly 1980; Sandberg 1991), gender (Burgess 1988; Cohen 1988; Cuthbert-Brandt 1981; Inwood and Wagg 1993; McCallum 1989; Muise 1991*b*; Parr 1990; Steedman 1986), and social structure (Acheson 1972*b*, 1973; Craven and Traves 1979; Katz, Doucet, and Stern 1982; Panitch 1981; Sager with Panting, 1990; Wood 1989*a*, 1989*b*; Wylie, 1990). The extent and consequence of Canadian dependence on imported industrial technology also attracts debate (Davis 1986; de Bresson 1982; Naylor 1975; Williams 1983; Wylie 1989). Nevertheless, there has been no comprehensive documentation of the overall structure or composition of manufacturing.

Fortunately, a detailed overview of the architecture of the Canadian manufacturing sector may be developed from an examination of the industrial enumeration of 1871. The Census Branch of the Department of Agriculture structured its instructions to enumerators in a way that reflects the largely rural nature of Canadian society. Enumerators were told to enquire at every residential visit if there was industrial activity on the premises. It was further stated that

an industrial establishment is a place where one or several persons are employed in manufacturing, altering, making up or changing from one shape into another, materials for sale, use or consumption, quite irrespectively of the amount of capital employed or the products turned out. . . . It matters not whether the raw material is in the ownership of the manufacturer or not, whether it is transformed on account of one or another person, whether the working is a profitable or losing business.

. . . in the case of industrial establishments it must be remembered that many farmers or others have attached to their ordinary industries a lime kiln, a saw-mill. . . .   (Canada 1871)

These remarks convey the breadth of coverage intended by census authorities. Industry was defined to encompass a good deal of part-time and small-scale activity that would have been overlooked in other censuses, including the United States census taken ten months earlier. American enumerators in 1870 were instructed to ignore workshops with less than $500 in production and workshops attached to a home or some other building if the artisan 'habitually work[ed] in any other shop which could be separately enumerated'.[6] Indeed, it was thought at the time that the actual enumeration practice frequently overlooked small firms whose production exceeded the threshold level. There is some evidence that enumerators in both countries encountered difficulty fulfilling their instructions with respect to small production units, but certainly the Canadian coverage was intended to be broader than that of many other national censuses (Inwood 1995; Jentz 1982; United States 1872).[7]

Enumeration began in April and was largely complete by the middle of May, although corrections apparently continued for some time afterward. There has been a disappearance of manuscripts in enumeration districts accounting, in total, for slightly less than 2 per cent of Canadian population and presumably a similar proportion of industrial establishments. Only one industry, handweaving, is known to have experienced seriously inconsistent enumeration (Inwood and Wagg 1993). The information collected on the industrial schedule included the name of the proprietor and self-designated type of establishment, number of workers (distinguishing children from adults and males from females), a single figure for wages, an estimate of fixed and floating capital, the type of power used (if any) and the force, months of activity during the year, and the quantities and values of raw materials and products (Canada 1871). Some categories of information are more likely to be missing or misleading, and there is some variation from district to district in the rigour with which enumeration was undertaken.[8] Nevertheless, the source appears to provide a relatively complete profile of manufacturing activity in mid-Victorian Canada.

One way to consider the organizational basis of manufacturing is to examine the proportion of firms which produced more than one product or participated in more than one set of markets. We can identify such firms in three ways. Foundries, smiths and the wood-based hand trades (such as carpentry and turning) whose identity lay precisely in the diversity of their output constitute one set of multi-product firms. Carpenters and blacksmiths typically worked with both wood and iron; they made and repaired a wide range of transportation equipment and its component parts, cultivators and other agricultural machinery, hand tools for various purposes, building materials and pieces, wood machinery and parts, ladders, looms, and so on. The product mix of these firms is so heterogeneous that it seems sensible to designate them, as a group, to be unspecialized.

Even in industries with more specialized firms, it is possible to identify products which, if appearing separately, would merit assignment to distinct industries within the context of an industrial classification system, in this case the system developed for the 1891 Canadian census.[9] A third group of unspecialized firms were those operating two or more industrial processes which were sufficiently distinct that the enumerator returned them as two or more establishments, even though they were directed by the same proprietor, situated beside each other or in the same building and shared power or even labour. In some cases, the enumerator submitted a single return which was divided by the compilers, for ease of tabulation, into industries corresponding to respective industrial processes. I regard these returns as describing separate elements in a complex firm rather than separate establishments.

The importance to some industries of reconstituting the complex firms is illustrated in Table 3.1. Some industries, especially the mill industries and tanneries, are affected a great deal, others not at all. Reconstitution reassigns output among industries so as to increase the average size establishment in most although not all industries.

Table 3.1. *Proportion of establishment records which are linked and output at select points in the size distribution*

	Share of linked	Mean output ($000)	Median output ($000)
Canada	0.05	2,069	440
Ontario	0.04	2,159	560
Quebec	0.07	2,249	333
New Brunswick	0.06	1,761	408
Nova Scotia	0.06	1,363	331
Hand-power	0.01	1,098	391
Steam-power	0.11	11,526	3,211
Water-power	0.19	2,452	469
Carding/fulling	0.54	1,629	590
Flour/grist-mills	0.27	2,403	767
Lathe-mills	0.33	10,510	1,450
Distilleries	0.15	52,530	11,463
Gypsum-mills	0.33	5,838	980
Dyeing/scouring	0.18	1,953	1,255
Match factories	0.07	3,052	886
Saw-mills	0.12	2,462	399
Stave-mills	0.11	2,863	1,149
Flax-mills	0.14	7,219	2,117
Shingle-mills	0.11	902	127
Planing/moulding	0.14	5,235	2,113
Cider-mills	0.13	586	327
Foundry/machine-shops	0.03	12,383	3,745

Notes: A linked firm is operated by a proprietor who operates another adjacent firm in the same enumeration district. Inwood (1995) describes the criteria for establishing a link between two entries and then reconstituting them.

Source: National Archives of Canada, Record Group 31, Ser. 1, 1871, Schedule 6.

Collectively, the three kinds of unspecialized or complex firm accounted for nearly one-half of all industrial establishments active in Canada during the 1871 census. Many unspecialized firms were small but all of them, by virtue of participating in more than one set of markets, faced complex challenges. The proprietors identified in the 1871 manuscripts worked in an environment of constant change. Their survival depended on the ability to compete against goods made elsewhere whose price in the local market fluctuated with the state of the harvest, the technological tide, the local and international business cycle, transportation costs, and other elements beyond the control and largely beyond the knowledge of a local turner or smith. The managers of some firms (foundries are a good example) had the added worry of recruiting specialized labour and keeping up with rapid change in iron-based products. These challenges were no different for the multi-product firm except that there were more of them, by virtue of participation in more than one product market and often more than one set of input markets.

A different kind of complexity was that of a firm operating in more than one location. Historians of business and organizational enterprise have drawn attention to the increasing importance during the late nineteenth century of firms producing at more than one location. Some and perhaps many of these companies were in a position to reduce costs if they were able to undertake the challenge of co-ordinating credit, materials and/or labour. Of course, it is difficult to know how many of the industrial sites enumerated in 1871 represent activity which was part of some larger multi-locational business.

The first step towards resolving the question is a computer search of the industrial records which reveals about 2,300 proprietor names appearing in more than one enumeration division in Canada. Of course, this is only the first step, since there are a great many spurious name matches. The only way to determine whether John Smith, a miller in Wellington County is the same John Smith credited with a blacksmith shop in Quebec City is to identify their residences on the personal schedule 1. If Mr Smith is found living in one location but not the other, then we might suspect that he has two plants. If two Mr Smiths can be identified, we rule out the hypothesis of two plants owned by one man. Unfortunately, it can be very time-consuming to locate a specific person in the personal schedule. Many proprietors lived in the same enumeration division as her or his establishment but some did not. It takes a long time to search an entire county, and a failure to locate John Smith the miller in Wellington County still would not rule out the possibility that he lived somewhere other than Quebec City.[10]

Although it is impractical to mount a comprehensive search through the personal schedules of the census for all proprietors, I have examined a sample of 300 proprietor names recurring at least once in the province of Ontario; each name has an establishment in two or more enumeration divisions. For each name in each of its locations I try to identify an individual with the same name, a consistent occupation and residence close to the establishment. Interestingly, the search is successful in almost all cases. It is possible to locate a nearby residence for all but five or possibly six names. This evidence would suggest that fewer than 5 per cent of the name matches reflect true multi-plant operations. Extrapolation to the 2,300 recurring names suggests that fewer than 100 multi-plant firms existed in 1871. Admittedly, the small sample size and other vagaries of nominal record linkage reduce precision. Nevertheless, these numbers indicate that multi-plant activity spanning more than one enumeration division was relatively rare in 1871 Canada.

Another way to address the same question focuses on the partnerships and companies which probably accounted for a significant share of all multi-plant firms. A search of all proprietor names reveals that the word 'company' or its abbreviation appears in roughly 2 per cent of the records.

Many of these references are contained within a larger set of records which use the word 'and' in patterns such as 'Margaret Jones and Sisters' or 'John Smith and Company'. Roughly 5 per cent of all records fall into this broader class. A manual search of these records reveals only thirty companies and partnerships operating in more than one division. Admittedly, the methodology may fail to capture some multi-plant firms because of variation in the naming of establishments. Even allowing for imprecision in source and method, however, there is no evidence of large numbers of partnerships or companies operating at more than one location.[11]

Almost all of the known multi-plant firms processed local raw materials or assisted in their processing. Flour and/or saw milling companies account for roughly half of all known examples. Other examples include Nova Scotia coal-mines, fish-curing operations in the Bay of Fundy and the Gaspe, Ontario cheese factories, the Canada Peat Fuel Company which operated two plants in rural Quebec, an Oxford County cooper which manufactured its own staves in Perth County, and a Hamilton building company with its own brickyard. A handful of multi-plant companies worked leather and furs in urban areas. The only multi-plant enterprises not directly engaged in resource extraction or processing were the Great Western and Grand Trunk railways which of course earned much of their revenue carrying raw materials.

The Patterns of Establishment Size and Mechanical Power

An examination of the organizational basis for Canadian manufacturing is complemented by an overview of the patterns of establishment size. The firms are divided into industries and the industries into three broad sectors according to their tendency to use mechanical power (steam or water). Industries in the *hand trades* are those in which no more than 5 per cent of the firms used power; the *powered industries* are those in which more than 80 per cent of the firms used steam or water power; the remaining *mixed industries* are characterized by a weaker tendency to use mechanical power.

On these terms more than 27,600 establishments existed in the hand trades, 7,400 in the powered industries and 5,300 in the mixed sector. The average firm in the hand trades had only 3.5 workers in contrast to 8.2 workers in the powered sector, but in the aggregate the hand trades employed slightly more than half of the industrial work-force. The hand trade establishments contributed a smaller but still sizeable share of all industrial product value. Moreover, some 3 per cent of the firms in the powered industries continued to rely exclusively on human or animal labour, as did more than 70 per cent of the mixed industry establishments firms.[12]

Kris Inwood

A typical establishment in the power-using industries tended to be larger than other firms, but a summary description of the eight largest industries in each sector reveals considerable variation within each sector. The data presented in Table 3.2 indicate that two hand trades (clothing and boot/shoes) had a larger average establishment than tanneries and various power-using mills (shingle, stave, carding, and fulling). What accounts for the differences in size of establishment? Clearly part of the explanation lies with

Table 3.2. *Select characteristics of individual industries*

	No. of firms	Mean density	'Urban' share of all firms	Share of firms with power	Mean workers	Mean months
Hand industries	29,338	2,295	0.24	0.02	3.5	9.4
Weaving	3,160	120	0.04	0.06	2.2	5.3
Limekilns	1,006	121	0.04	0.02	2.3	3.5
Blacksmiths	5,677	738	0.11	0.01	1.7	10.6
Coopers	1,606	839	0.15	0.03	2.2	7.1
Carriage-makers	2,601	103	0.19	0.04	3.2	11.2
Harness-makers	1,010	2,028	0.36	0.01	3.6	11.5
Shoe-makers	4,101	2,516	0.24	0.01	4.4	10.9
Carpenters	1,620	2,598	0.24	0.04	3.5	9.7
Clothing	2,442	6,412	0.55	0.00	6.3	11.3
Bakeries	911	6,416	0.59	0.02	3.2	11.6
All other	5,204	3,941	0.37	0.03	5.1	8.4
Mixed industries	5,983	3,097	0.30	0.29	5.8	9.1
Shingle-mills	1,523	49	0.02	0.35	3.6	4.3
Agric. implements	493	661	0.28	0.41	8.2	10.7
Cabinet/furniture	1,062	3,205	0.36	0.18	4.3	10.6
Tanneries	1,027	3,455	0.23	0.25	3.9	11.2
Sashes/doors/blinds	369	3,468	0.30	0.16	3.7	9.0
Breweries	119	4,009	0.71	0.47	6.3	11.1
Printing	358	7,010	0.78	0.16	11.8	11.8
Edge-tools	68	8,056	0.40	0.31	4.6	10.0
All other	964	6,598	0.54	0.36	10.5	9.8
Power industries	7,296	577	0.10	0.98	8.0	6.7
Saw-mills	4,113	94	0.02	0.99	5.9	4.8
Carding/fulling	431	129	0.06	0.98	5.0	6.4
Stave-mills	93	257	0.11	0.98	9.2	6.7
Lathe-mills	137	285	0.07	0.99	23.7	7.7
Flour/grist-mills	1,561	297	0.10	1.00	4.0	9.8
Foundry/ machine-shops	271	4,142	0.56	0.77	18.3	10.8
All other	690	3,067	0.41	0.97	23.9	10.1
ALL FIRMS	42,617	2,113	0.23	0.23	4.6	8.9

Notes: Density is measured in persons per square mile for the census subdistrict in which the firm is located. 'Urban' firms are located in subdistricts with more than 221.3 people per square mile. Powered firms are those using steam or water power. The industries reported separated are the most numerous within each of the three broad groupings. All other industries are reported jointly in the final row of each group.

technological characteristics accompanying individual materials and processes. For example, technology undoubtedly helps to explain why breweries were larger than tanneries, carriage-makers tended to be larger than weavers, and why machinery was more likely to be used in the production of semi-finished wood than final products.

Another influence, however, was the social and economic context in which the processes were situated. One dimension of the socio-economic context is the population density of the firm's immediate environment, which is used in Table 3.2 to order the industries within each sector. Industries with a strong tendency to appear in rural areas appear at the top of each sector; the industries with the greatest urban affinity are at the bottom. This arrangement reveals a pronounced relationship between seasonality and population density in so far as the more urban-centred industries and hand trades tended to work at least eleven months of the year. Rural-dominated mill industries tended to sit idle several months each year presumably because of seasonal fluctuation in the local availability of materials, labour, and water.

The data in this table reveal as well that the more urban industries within each sector tend to have a larger average establishment (workers per establishment). Admittedly the correlation is somewhat imperfect. In order to assess more clearly the correlation of density with other characteristics, the average size of firm in various density classes is shown in Table 3.3. The boundaries among density classes are chosen to allocate equal numbers of firms to the five classes. These data confirm that the average size of firm tended to increase as population density rose above 40 persons per square mile. Density and size correlated even at lower density levels in some industries, but this part of the pattern is much less clear. In almost all industries, however, the average size of establishment rises noticeably as we move from the third density class (R3) to the fourth (R4), and then to the urban group of firms (U).

It seems clear that urban firms tend to be larger especially at densities above 40 people per square mile and in the more urban-centred industries. It is somewhat less clear what to make of this. One could hypothesize a variety of self-reinforcing causal connections which would account for the juxtaposition of urbanity and size of establishment. Resolution of the issue is complicated by a third correlation in so far as the use of mechanical power by itself may have encouraged both bigness and urbanity.

One way to consider the technological possibility is to examine versions of Tables 3.2 and 3.3 for powered establishments and then separately for non-powered establishments. The relevant tables are not shown here, but they demonstrate that the density–size relationship is unaffected. A further examination of power and its correlations is reported in Table 3.4. Within most industries and in the sector as a whole water-powered firms were the most rural and steam firms the most urban.

Table 3.3. *Average number of workers by density class of subdistrict in which the firm is located (average workers/firm)*

	R1	R2	R3	R4	U
Hand industries	2.1	2.1	2.0	2.6	7.6
Weaving	1.2	1.5	1.9	2.9	14.5
Limekilns	3.4	2.1	2.0	2.0	3.8
Blacksmiths	1.8	1.5	1.6	1.6	2.6
Coopers	1.4	1.4	1.8	2.4	5.9
Carriage-makers	2.1	2.2	2.3	3.5	5.7
Harness-makers	5.4	1.9	3.7	2.1	4.8
Shoe-makers	1.7	1.9	1.6	1.7	12.7
Carpenters	1.7	1.8	1.7	1.6	9.2
Clothing	2.4	2.2	2.1	3.5	9.3
Bakeries	3.0	1.7	1.6	3.0	3.7
All other	4.2	4.7	2.8	4.2	7.0
Mixed industries	2.3	2.9	3.2	4.6	12.0
Shingle-mills	2.2	3.3.	4.1	11.2	21.4
Agric. implements	3.4	3.0	3.6	6.4	17.4
Cabinet/furniture	1.7	2.1	1.9	2.0	8.4
Tanneries	2.4	2.7	2.8	2.8	7.9
Sashes/doors/blinds	1.4	1.9	2.1	2.2	7.9
Breweries	4.0*	2.7*	5.7*	5.5*	6.8
Printing	13.7*	3.9	3.3	3.8	14.1
Edge-tools	3.3*	2.8*	1.8*	5.1	5.9
All other	4.3	3.6	4.2	6.4	15.5
Power industries	4.9	5.0	5.5	9.2	27.2
Saw-mills	4.0	4.6	5.6	8.4	40.2
Carding/fulling	4.3	5.1	4.1	5.6	8.3
Stave-mills	7.6	8.7	8.4	7.8*	19.2*
Lathe-mills	19.8	14.3	21.1	27.9	78.8*
Flour/grist-mills	4.1	3.4	3.0	4.3	6.2
Foundry/machine-shops	13.6	4.9	4.4	8.8	26.1
All other	11.5	10.9	10.5	25.5	35.6
All industries	2.9	2.8	2.8	3.8	9.9

* Fewer than 15 observations.

Notes: Density classes are R1 < 25.3 people per square mile (psm), R2 25.3–41.5 psm, R3 41.5–54.7 psm, R4 54.7–221.3 psm, Urban > 221.3 psm.

In almost all industries steam-powered firms were the largest, hand firms were the smallest, with the water-powered firms in the middle. The correlation between size and mechanical power is curiously asymmetric, however, in that almost all large firms used mechanical power but a size-able share of the power-using firms was relatively small (not shown here). The implication appears to be that firms were unlikely to become large without mechanical power, but that steam and water power could be used

Table 3.4. *Size and density by power source*

	No. of firms			Mean density			Workers/firms		
	H	W	S	H	W	S	H	W	S
Hand industries	28,622	329	387	2,288	789	4,104	2.9	16.5	36.5
Weaving	2,979	127	54	94	525	622	1.3	18.6	17.7
Limekilns	985	16	5	121	97	296	2.0	9.2	34.0
Blacksmiths	5,607	40	30	733	46	2,751	1.6	9.2	14.9
Coopers	1,553	21	32	819	1,001	1,736	1.8	14.1	15.2
Carriages	2,502	48	51	1,031	242	2,156	2.8	18.3	8.4
Harness/saddlery	997	2	11	2,047	34	672	2.5	153.0	77.2
Shoe-makers	4,056	10	35	2,428	58	13,428	2.9	8.3	174.0
Carpenters	1,549	21	50	2,529	3,393	4,413	2.8	13.1	21.9
Clothing	2,435	1	6	6,399	60	12,367	6.1	4.5	111.0
Bakeries	889	3	19	6,393	71	8,507	2.7	71.0	15.3
All other	5,070	40	94	3,955	2,115	3,951	4.6	12.0	28.1
Mixed industries	4,273	693	1,017	3,307	414	4,041	2.8	7.4	17.6
Shingle-mills	986	313	224	26	52	151	1.5	6.0	9.9
Agric. implements	291	53	149	258	954	1,343	2.4	14.9	17.2
Cabinet/furniture	867	93	102	3,508	950	2,689	2.3	6.0	19.3
Tanneries	769	61	197	3,837	167	2,984	2.2	5.0	9.9
Sashes/doors/blinds	309	29	31	3,622	1,205	4,043	2.3	8.0	12.9
Breweries	64	4	51	3,063	1,283	5,409	3.4	3.8	10.1
Printing	302	2	54	6,246	362	11,528	6.7	7.5	40.6
Edge-tools	47	16	5	9,671	979	15,528	2.1	10.1	11.0
All other	638	122	204	6,868	537	9,377	4.6	9.7	29.6
Power industries	149	5,600	1,547	1,244	157	1,547	2.9	6.1	20.4
Saw-mills	40	3,455	618	20	63	271	1.8	4.4	14.5
Carding/fulling	8	362	61	34	105	287	1.8	4.5	8.4
Stave-mills	3	54	36	563	23	584	7.3	7.9	11.2
Lathe-mills	1	81	55	120	29	666	3.0	19.1	32.4
Flour/grist-mills	5	1,353	203	33	223	793	2.2	3.6	6.2
Foundry/ machine-shops	63	38	170	1,781	1,894	5,519	3.6	19.9	23.3
All other	29	257	404	2,417	953	4,459	3.8	19.5	28.2
All industries	33,044	6,622	2,951	2,415	215	2,996	2.9	6.1	20.4

H = hand-powered; W = water-powered; S = steam-powered.

efficiently in relatively small production units. It appears that steam was a necessary but not a sufficient condition for a large size.

Conclusion

In 1871 the crucial technological breakthroughs which had launched the industrial revolution were already a century old. Hence the Canadian census data provide a glimpse of manufacturing organization and structure long after the onset of the industrial era. We have seen that in 1871 very few manufacturing enterprises operated at more than one location. Far more numerous and collectively more important were the men and women operating half-specialized workshops and mills closely adjacent to their residences. Many of the firms were small, unpowered and seasonally inactive. Between a third and a half of the establishments were complex in a very local way, producing diverse and sometime unexpected combinations of products. The complexity of these enterprises is more easily explored through an intensive examination of an individual craft or firm, but their importance is revealed clearly by the broad sweep of the census.

What is so interesting about the Canadian evidence is the survival of astonishingly large numbers of unpowered and small businesses. It does not take away from the importance to Canada of the new technologies to recognize that they remained the exception and were not yet the dominant mode of production in most industries, and that the industries in which they had become important comprised only a small portion of the entire manufacturing sector.[13] The limited presence of steam power and large industrial establishments may seem surprising. After all, Canada, like the United States, was a fast-growing market characterized by low-cost transportation and expensive labour (by European standards). These characteristics should have encouraged mechanization and the emergence of big business in Canada, as they did in the United States (Chandler 1977). Of course, small and flexible firms also survived in many regions of the United States (Atack 1985a,b, 1986, 1987; Scranton 1983, 1991). If there is a difference between the two countries, then, it is best seen as one of degree rather than in kind.

In considering which circumstances of Canadian society and economy may have contributed to a distinctive industrial structure, it is useful to remember that the population density of the firm's immediate environment was a significant influence on the nature of manufacturing activity. Some industries were more urban than others, and within most industries the more urban establishments were larger, operated more of the year and (in some industries) were more likely to use steam power.

These observations suggest a model in which economic development is limited by the thinness of local markets. From this perspective, the experience of industrialization in Canada was powerfully conditioned by its low level of population density and by the geographical structure of an economy stretching in a long narrow band from Windsor, Ontario to Sydney, Nova Scotia. Climate and rocky terrain limited the northward extension of settlement. The closest large markets were located south of the border, largely inaccessible to Canadian businesses because of American import tariffs. Although markets were thin and local in character, the cross-sectional correlation between population density and industrial characteristics nevertheless suggests that as the population grew and income increased, the size of Canadian establishments would have expanded. Growth in the scale of production, in turn, would have permitted the use of engines and added machinery, some specialization of both labour and capital, and the intensification of work regimes (Atack 1985*a,b*, 1986, 1987; Chandler 1977; Hunter 1979, 1985; Marglin 1974; Smith 1976: bk. 1; Sokoloff 1984; von Tunzelman 1978).[14]

Direct evidence of these effects is difficult to obtain. Production function and total factor productivity evidence from the American industrial census manuscripts confirms that the factory system improved productivity, with and without mechanized power (Atack 1987; Laurie and Schmitz 1981; Sokoloff 1984; Tchakerian 1994). The Canadian data have not yet been used for a systematic examination of the relationship between size and productivity, but the American studies direct attention at the possibility that a small size of establishment contributed to relatively low levels of productivity in Canada. If that is true, however, then we have to wonder why the Canadian establishments were so hesitant to realize the benefits of a larger size. Many small communities in nineteenth-century Canada hosted more than one cabinet-maker, more than one carriage-maker, more than one cooper and so on. Some and perhaps most of these establishments could have combined in order to capture some of the economies accruing to a larger scale of operation. The reluctance to combine and/or expand requires an explanation.

It is commonly recognized that the advantages for small firms include imperfect competition deriving from both product differentiation and transportation protection, and perhaps also some degree of complementarity between small and large firms (Lyons 1991). A less obvious but perhaps equally important source of support for small Canadian firms may have been their family-based organization of production. The manufacturing sector, as we have seen, was organized on a small-scale and often part-time basis in workshops attached or closely adjacent to the residence of the proprietor. Of course, manufacturing was only one of a range of productive activities organized within the family-based household. Indeed, for many families, manufacturing was a secondary activity undertaken when the demands of the primary activity (often agriculture) were in abeyance.

The use of family labour on a by-employment basis undoubtedly assisted many small firms in their struggle to adapt to a complex and changing environment (Marshall 1923: 236). This strategy, however, implies that the supply of available family labour may have served as a limit to the growth of many firms. Continued expansion beyond a certain point would have required the hiring of additional workers, which in turn would have brought higher wage rates and indirect costs such as financing of the wage bill, the monitoring and supervision of workers, under-utilization of regular employees during downturns in business activity, and so on. The prospect of these added costs undoubtedly offset the attraction of new technologies and deterred the incremental growth of many family-based enterprises.

The particular characteristics and significance of family labour supply invite further investigation. The statistical testing of generalized hypotheses, such as the presumed relationship between scale of operation and productivity, is one line of enquiry. A more demanding method which ultimately may prove to be more fruitful is the examination of individual industries, or individual companies, using a wider range of sources; Scranton (1983) provides an outstanding example. The unique contribution of the census is its broad overview of the structures and patterns of industrial production, which provides a context for the examination of individual companies and industries. The task of developing and confirming analytical hypotheses, however, is best undertaken on a case-study basis. Both approaches are needed to advance the detailed understanding of small enterprise within the Canadian manufacturing sector.

NOTES

1. Phillips (1979) identifies industry-wide external economies as a principal support for small business in Marshall's more theoretical writing.
2. The enumerators' returns survive in National Archives of Canada, Record Group 31, Ser. 31. The Social Sciences and Humanities Research Council of Canada provided funds permitting the creation between 1983 and 1993 of a machine-readable version of the original returns.
3. In order to reinforce the point, the comparison is made after removing from the calculation central and northern areas of Canada which held almost no people and the two Scottish counties in which Glasgow was located. Persons per square mile (psm) 1870–1 as reported by the British and Canadian censuses may be summarized as follows:
   England: 422—287 after excluding the 4 counties in which London, Manchester, Liverpool, and Birmingham are located.
   Wales: 165—126 after excluding Glamorgan in which Swansea and Cardiff are located.
   Scotland: 110—83 after excluding the 2 counties in which Glasgow is located.
   Canada: 11—45 after excluding census subdistricts with less than 10 psm.
4. Fertility declined because of fewer children within marriage and, to a lesser but still important extent, a reduction in the proportion of women who were married (McInnis 1991). Of course, a secular rise in the female share of the population partially offset the decline in the married share of adult women. In older settled areas of eastern North America the fertility decline began much earlier (Berry 1996).
5. In some circumstances, closer integration into international markets may have the effect of 'commercialization' which leads to a specialization of production. However, Canada in this period would seem to resemble parts of the United

States where commercialization brought diversification rather than specialization (Gregson, 1993).

6. United States (1870), *Ninth Census*, iii: *Instructions*, 20. Most farm-based manufacturing was ignored as well; see United States (1900), *Twelfth Census*, vii, p. xxxii. An attempt in 1900 to tabulate some of the activity ignored in earlier years suggests that at least one-fifth, and probably much more, of industrial establishments sold products valued at less than $500 (ibid., p. xxxix).

7. It seems likely that the Canadian enumeration was more sensitive in part because rural small-scale industry was relatively more important in Canada, and especially so in Quebec which provided so many of the senior census staff.

8. Incomplete information for about 10 per cent of the firms makes it necessary to interpolate output using the report of product value, raw materials, or workers. Inwood (1995) describes the procedure.

9. Canada, *Census, 1891*, iii. Each firm in the 1871 database is assigned an industrial class according to the firm's primary product or range of products. The presence of secondary products which, had they been primary, would have led to a different classification signals a lack of specialization.

10. The problem arises because the industrial schedule typically provides no clues as to the residence of the proprietor. Interestingly, all other schedules (agriculture, forestry, fishing, mining, etc.) identify the proprietor and provide a reference to the individual on the personal schedule. Only Schedule 6 (industry) lacks this link.

11. It is worth repeating that by 'more than one location' I mean a proprietor of establishments in more than one enumeration district.

12. The very few industrial establishments which reported the use of animal power are classified here as being unpowered.

13. Even if a new technology was not used in Canada, its influence could have been felt through the price and availability of goods for import into Canada.

14. The reliance of large workplaces on female and child labour reflects organizational modifications as well as an attempt to hire cheaper labour (Berg and Hudson 1992, 1994). Although the data are not reported here, it is worth noting that the female share of the factory work-force in Canada was higher in larger factories and in more urban areas.

REFERENCES

Acheson, T. W. (1972*a*), 'The National Policy and the Industrialization of the Maritimes', *Acadiensis*, 1/2 (Spring), 1–28.

—— (1972*b*), 'The Social Origins of the Canadian Business Elite', in David Macmillan (ed.), *Canadian Business History: Selected Studies, 1497–1971*. Toronto: McClelland and Stewart, 144–75.

—— (1973), 'Changing Social Origins of the Canadian Industrial Elite, 1880–1910', *Business History Review*, 47 (Summer), 189–217.

Acheson, T. W. (1977), 'The Maritimes and Empire Canada', in David Bercuson (ed.), *Canada and the Burden of Unity*. Toronto: Macmillan.

—— (1979), 'The Great Merchant and Economic Development in Saint John', *Acadiensis* (Autumn), 3–24.

—— (1985), *Saint John: The Making of a Colonial Urban Community*. Toronto: University of Toronto Press.

Altman, Morris (1986), 'Resource Endowments and Location Theory in Economic History: A Case-Study of Quebec and Ontario at the Turn of the Century', *Journal of Economic History*, 46/4 (Dec.), 999–1010.

—— (1987), 'A Revision of Canadian Economic Growth: 1870–1910 (A Challenge to the Gradualist Interpretation)', *Canadian Journal of Economics*, 20/1 (Feb.), 86–113.

—— (1988*a*), 'Economic Development with High Wages: An Historical Perspective', *Explorations in Economic History*, 25/2 (April), 198–224.

—— (1988*b*), 'Railways as an Engine of Growth: Who Benefited from the Canadian Railway Boom, 1870–1910', *Histoire Sociale/Social History*, 21/42 (Nov.), 269–82.

Ashton, T. S. (1948), *The Industrial Revolution, 1760–1830*. Oxford: Oxford University Press.

Atack, Jeremy (1985*a*), 'Industrial Structure and the Emergence of the Modern Industrial Corporation', *Explorations in Economic History*, 22/1 (Jan.), 29–52.

—— (1985*b*), *Estimates of Economies of Scale in Nineteenth-Century United States Manufacturing*. New York: Garland.

—— (1986), 'Firm Size and Industrial Structure in the United States during the Nineteenth Century', *Journal of Economic History*, 46/2 (June), 463–76.

—— (1987), 'Economies of Scale and Efficiency Gains in the Rise of the Factory in America, 1820–1900', in Peter Kilby (ed.), *Quantity and Quiddity: Essays in U.S. Economic History*. Middletown, Conn.: Wesleyan University Press, 286–335.

Babcock, Robert H. (1979), 'Economic Development of Portland (Maine) and Saint John (N.B.) during the Age of Iron and Steam, 1850–1914', *American Review of Canadian Studies*, 9 (Spring), 3–37.

Beeby, Dean (1984), 'Industrial Strategy and Manufacturing Growth in Toronto, 1880–1910', *Ontario History*, 76/3 (Sept.), 199–232.

Berg, Maxine and Hudson, Pat (1992), 'Rehabilitating the Industrial Revolution', *Economic History Review*, 45/1 (Feb.), 24–50.

—— —— (1994), 'Growth and Change: A Comment on the Crafts-Harley View of the Industrial Revolution', *Economic History Review*, 47/1 (Feb.), 147–9.

Berry, Brian (1996), 'From Malthusian Frontier to Demographic Steady State in Concord, 1635–1993', *Population and Development Review*, 22/2 (June), 207–30.

Bertram, Gordon (1964), 'Historical Statistics on Growth and Structure in Manufacturing in Canada, 1870–1957', in J. Henripin and A. Asimakopulos (eds.), *Conferences on Statistics, 1962 and 1963*. Toronto: University of Toronto Press, 93–152.

Bittermann, Rusty (1994), 'Farm Households and Wage Labour in the Northeastern Maritimes in the Early Nineteenth Century', in Danny Samson (ed.), *Contested Countryside*. Fredericton: Acadiensis Press, 34–69.

Bouchard, Gérard (1988), 'Co-intégration et reproduction de la société rurale', *Recherches sociographiques*, 29/2–3: 283–312.

—— (1991), 'Mobile Population, Stable Communities: Social and Demographic Processes in the Rural Parishes of the Saguenay, 1840–1911', *Continuity and Change*, 6: 59–86.

—— (1994), 'Family Reproduction in New Rural Areas: Outline of a North American Model', *Canadian Historical Review*, 75/4: 475–510.

Brookes, Alan (1976), 'Outmigration from the Maritime Provinces, 1860–1900', *Acadiensis*, 5/2: 26–56.

Burgess, Joanne (1988), 'The Growth of a Craft Labour Force: Montreal Leather Artisans, 1815–31', *Canadian Historical Association, Historical Papers*, 48–62.

Canada, *Census*, various years.

—— Department of Agriculture (1871), *Manual Containing the Census Act and Instructions to Officers*, Sessional Papers 64.

Chambers, E. J. and Bertram, G. W. (1966), 'Urbanization and Manufacturing in Central Canàda, 1870–1890', in S. Ostry and T. K. Rymes (eds.), *Papers on Regional Historical Statistics*. Toronto: University of Toronto Press.

Chandler, Alfred D., Jr. (1977), *The Visible Hand: the Managerial Revolution in American Business*. Cambridge: Harvard University Press.

Cohen, Marjorie Griffith (1988), *Women's Work: Markets and Economic Development in Nineteenth Century Ontario*. Toronto: University of Toronto Press.

Courville, Serge and Seguin, Normand (1991), 'The Spread of Rural Industry in Lower Canada, 1831–51', *Journal of the Canadian Historical Association*, NS 2: 43–70.

Craven, Paul and Traves, Tom (1979), 'The Class Politics of the National Policy', *Journal of Canadian Studies*, 14: 14–38.

—— (1983), 'Canadian Railways as Manufacturers, 1850–1880', *Canadian Historical Association, Historical Papers*, 254–81.

Cruikshank, Ken (1992), 'The Intercolonial Railway, Freight Rates and the Maritime Economy', *Acadiensis*, 22/1 (Autumn), 87–110.

Cuthbert-Brandt, Gail (1981), 'Weaving It Together: Life Cycle and the Industrial Experience of Female Cotton Workers in Quebec', *Labour/le Travail*, 7 (Spring), 113–26.

Dales, John (1957), *Hydroelectricity and Industrial Development: Quebec, 1898–1940*. Cambridge, Mass.: Harvard University Press.

—— (1964), 'Estimates of Canadian Manufacturing Output by Markets, 1870–1915', in Henripin and Asimakopulos (eds.), *Conferences on Statistics 1962 and 1963*, 61–91.

—— (1966), *The Protective Tariff in Canada's Development*. Toronto: University of Toronto Press.

—— (1979), '"National Policy" Myths, Past and Present', *Journal of Canadian Studies*, 14 (Autumn), 39–50.

Davis, Don (1986), 'Dependent Motorization: Canada and the Automobile to 1930', *Journal of Canadian Studies*, 21/3 (Autumn), 106–32.

de Bresson, Chris (1982), 'Have Canadians Failed to Innovate?', *History of Science and Technology in Canada Bulletin*, 6: 10–23.

Dechêne, Louise (1978), 'Les Enterprises de William Price', *Histoire sociale/Social History*, 1: 16–52.

Delottinville, Peter (1980), 'Trouble in the Hives of Industry: The Cotton Industry Comes to Milltown, N.B., 1879–92', *Canadian Historical Association, Historical Papers*, 100–15.

Dick, Trevor (1982), 'Canadian Newsprint, 1913–30: National Policies and the North American Economy', *Journal of Economic History*, 42/3 (Sept.), 659–87.

Drummond, Ian M. (1987), *Progress without Planning: The Economic History of Ontario from Confederation to the Second World War*. Toronto: University of Toronto Press/ Ontario Historical Society.

—— (1988), 'Ontario's Industrial Revolution', *Canadian Historical Review*, 49/3 (Sept.), 283–99.

Drummond, W. H. (1957), 'Canadian Agricultural Developments, 1850–1900', paper presented to the National Bureau of Economic Research Conference on 'Research in Income and Wealth' (Sept.).

Evans, Lou and Quigley, Neil (1990), 'Discrimination in Bank Lending Practice: A Test Using Data from the Bank of Nova Scotia 1900–1937', *Canadian Journal of Economics*, 23/1 (Feb.).

Faucher, Albert (1970), *Histoire économique et unité canadienne*. Montreal: Fides.

Forbes, Ernest (1977*a*), *The Maritime Eights Movement, 1919–1927*. Kingston and Montreal: McGill-Queen's University Press.

—— (1997*b*), 'Misguided Symmetry: The Destruction of Regional Transportation Policy for the Maritimes', in Bercuson (ed.), *Canada and the Burden of Unity*.

Forster, Ben (1986), *A Conjunction of Interests: Business, Politics and the Tariff, 1825–1879*. Toronto: University of Toronto Press.

—— (1988), 'Finding the Right Size: Markets and Competition in Mid- and Late Nineteenth-Century Ontario', in R. Hall, L. S. McDowell, and W. Westfall (eds.), *Patterns of the Past: Interpreting Ontario's History*. Toronto: Dundurn.

Frank, David (1976), 'Class Conflict in the Coal Industry in Cape Breton 1922', in Greg Kealey and Peter Warrian, (eds.), *Essays in Working Class History*. Toronto: McClelland and Stewart 161–231.

—— (1977), 'The Cape Breton Coal Industry and the Rise and Fall of BESCO', *Acadiensis*, 7/1 (Autumn), 3–34.

Frost, James (1982), 'The Nationalization of The Bank of Nova Scotia', *Acadiensis* 12/1 (Autumn), 3–38.

Gaffield, Chad (1982), 'Boom and Bust: The Demography and Economy of the Lower Ottawa Valley', *Canadian Historical Association, Historical Papers*, 172–95.

—— (1990), 'The Social and Economic Origins of Contemporary Families', in Maureen Baker (ed.), *Families: Changing Trends in Canada*, 2nd edn. Toronto: McGraw-Hill Ryerson.

—— (1991), 'Children, Schooling and Family Reproduction in Nineteenth-Century Ontario', *Canadian Historical Review*, 71/2 (June), 157–91.

Gagan, David (1981), *Hopeful Travellers: Families, Land and Social Change in Mid-Victorian Peel County, Canada West*. Toronto: University of Toronto Press.

Gatrell, V. A. C. (1977), 'Labour, Power and the Size of Firms in Lancashire Cotton in the Second Quarter of the Nineteenth Century', *Economic History Review*, 30/1 (Feb.), 95–139.

Gilmour, James (1972), *The Spatial Evolution of Manufacturing: Southern Ontario 1851–1891*. Toronto: University of Toronto Press.

Grant, Janine and Inwood, Kris (1990), 'Labouring at the Loom: A Case-Study of Rural Manufacturing in Leeds County, 1870', *Canadian Papers in Rural History*, 7: 215–36.

Green, Alan and Urquhart, M. C. (1987), 'New Estimates of Output Growth in Canada: Measurement and Interpretation', in Douglas McCalla (ed.), *Perspectives on Canadian Economic History*. Toronto: Copp, Clark, Pitman, 182–99.

Gregson, Mary (1993), 'Rural Response To Increased Demand: Crop Choice in the Midwest, 1860–1880', *Journal of Economic History*, 53/2 (June), 332–45.

Hamelin, Jean and Roby, Yves, *Histoire économique du Québec, 1851–1896*. Montreal: Fides.

Harley, C. Knick (1980), 'Transportation, the World Wheat Trade and the Kuznets Cycle, 1850–1913', *Explorations in Economic History*, 17: 218–50.

Heron, Craig (1987), 'The Great War and Nova Scotia Steelworkers', *Acadiensis*, 16/2 (Spring), 3–34.

—— (1988), *Working in Steel: The Early Years in Canada, 1883–1935*. Toronto: McClelland and Stewart.

Hoppit, Julian (1990), 'Counting the Industrial Revolution', *Economic History Review*, 43/2 (May), 173–93.

Hunter, Louis C. (1979/85), *A History of Industrial Power in the United States, 1780–1930, vols. i and ii*. Charlottesville: University Press of Virginia.

Inwood, Kris (1983), 'Resource Discovery and Technological Change: The Early Years of Steel Production in Nova Scotia', *Bulletin of the Canadian Institute of Metallurgy*, 59–65.

—— (1985), 'Productivity Change in Obsolescence: Charcoal Iron Revisited', *Journal of Economic History*, 45/2, 293–8.

—— (1986a), 'Local Control, Resources and the Nova Scotia Steel and Coal Company', *Canadian Historical Association, Historical Papers*, 254–82.

—— (1986b) *The Canadian Charcoal Iron Industry, 1870–1914*. New York: Garland.

—— (1987), 'The Iron Industry', in I. M. Drummond (ed.), *Progress Without Planning: The Economic History of Ontario, 1870–1939*. Toronto: University of Toronto Press.

—— (1989), 'Transportation, Tariffs and the Canadian Iron Industry, 1867–1897'. Guelph: University of Guelph Department of Economics, Discussion Paper.

—— (1991), 'Maritime Industrialization from 1870 to 1910: A Review of the Evidence and Its Interpretation', *Acadiensis*, 21/1 (Autumn), 132–55.

—— (1992), 'The Influence of Resource Quality on Technological Persistence: Charcoal Iron in Quebec', *Material History Review*, 36 (Autumn), 36–46.

—— (1995), 'The Representation of Industry in the Canadian Census, 1871–91', *Histoire sociale/Social History*, 28 (Nov.).

—— and Irwin, Jim (1993), 'Canadian Regional Commodity Income Differentials at Confederation', in Kris Inwood (ed.), *Farm, Factory and Fortune: New Essays in the Economic History of the Maritimes*. Fredericton: Acadiensis Press, 93–120.

—— and Stengos, Thanasis (1991), 'Discontinuities in Canadian Economic Growth, 1870–1985', *Explorations in Economic History*, 28: 274–86.

—— and Sullivan, Tim (1993), 'Nineteenth Century Ontario in its Regional Context', *Canadian Papers in Business History*, 2.

—— and Wagg, Phyllis (1993), 'The Survival of Handloom Weaving in Rural Canada circa 1870', *Journal of Economic History*, 54/2 (June).

—— —— (1994), 'Wealth and Prosperity in Nova Scotian Agriculture, 1851–1871', *Canadian Historical Review*, 75/2: 239–64.

Jentz, John B. (1982), 'A Note on Evaluating the Errors in the Gilded Age Manufacturing Census: The Problem of the Hand Trades', *Historical Methods*, 15/2 (Spring), 79–81.

Jeremy, David (1981), *Transatlantic Industrial Diffusion: The Diffusion of Textile*

Technologies between Britain and America, 1790–1830s (North Andover and Cambridge, Mass.: Merrimack Valley Textile Museum/MIT Press).

Jones, Robert L. (1946), *History of Agriculture in Ontario, 1613–1880*. Toronto: University of Toronto Press.

Kanefsky, John (1979), 'Motive Power in British Industry and the Accuracy of the 1870 Factory Return', *Economic History Review*, 3 (August), 360–75.

Katz, M., Doucet, M., and Stern, M. (1982), *The Social Organization of Early Industrial Capitalism*. Cambridge: Cambridge University Press.

Kealey, Greg (1980), *Toronto Workers Respond To Industrial Capitalism 1867–92*. Toronto: University of Toronto Press.

—— and Palmer, Bryan (1982), *Dreaming of What Might Be: The Knights of Labour in Ontario, 1880–1900*. Cambridge: Cambridge University Press.

Kelly, Kenneth (1968), 'The Agricultural Geography of Simcoe County Ontario', University of Toronto Ph.D. diss.

Laurie, Bruce and Schmitz, Mark (1981), 'Manufacturing and Productivity, The Making of an Industrial Base, Philadelphia, 1850–80', in Theodore Hershberg (ed.), *Philadelphia*. Oxford: Oxford University Press, 43–92.

Lutz, John (1988), 'Losing Steam: The Boiler and Engine Industry as an Index of British Columbia's Deindustrialization, 1880–1915', *Canadian Historical Association, Historical Papers*, 168–208.

Lyons, John (1991), 'Competitiveness or Complementarity in the Survival of Proto-industry', unpub. paper.

McCalla, Doug (1985), 'The Internal Economy of Upper Canada', *Agricultural History*, 59/3 (July), 397–416.

—— (1993), *Planting the Province: The Economic History of Upper Canada, 1784–1870*. Toronto: University of Toronto Press.

McCallum, John (1980), *Unequal Beginnings: Agriculture and Economic Development in Quebec and Ontario until 1875*. Toronto: University of Toronto Press.

McCallum, Margaret (1989), 'Separate Spheres: The Organization of Work in a Confectionery Factory, Ganong Bros., Saint Stephen, New Brunswick', *Labour/le Travail*, 24 (August), 69–90.

McCann, Larry D. (1979), 'Staples and the New Industrialism', *Acadiensis*, 8/2 47–79.

—— (1981), 'The Mercantile-Industrial Transition in the Metal Towns of Pictou County, 1857–1931', *Acadiensis*, 10/2 (Spring), 29–64.

—— (1988), ' "Living a Double Life": Town and Country in the Industrialization of the Maritimes', in Douglas Day (ed.), *Geographical Perspectives on the Maritime Provinces*. Halifax: Goresbrook Institute, 93–113.

McCullogh, Alan (1992), *The Primary Textile Industry in Canada: History and Heritage*. Ottawa: Environment Canada.

McDonald, L. R. (1975), 'Merchants Against Industry: An Idea and Its Origins', *Canadian Historical Review*, 56: 263–81.

McDowall, Duncan (1984), *Steel at the Sault*. Toronto: University of Toronto Press.

McInnis, Marvin (1982), 'The Changing Structure of Canadian Agriculture, 1867–1897', *Journal of Economic History*, 41/1 (March), 191–8.

—— (1986), 'The Emergence of a World Economy in the Latter Half of the Nineteenth Century', in Ninth International Economic History Congress, *Debates and Controversies*. Zürich: Verlag der Fachvereine, 83–110.

—— (1991), 'Women, Work and Childbearing: Ontario in the Second Half of the Nineteenth Century', *Histoire sociale/Social History*, 24/48 (Nov.), 237–63.

—— (1992), 'The Early Wheat Staple Reconsidered', *Canadian Papers in Rural History*, 8, 17–48.

—— (1994), 'Immigration and Emigration: Canada in the Late Nineteenth Century', in Tim Hatton and Jeffrey Williamson (eds.), *Migration and the International Labour Market*. London: Routledge.

McKay, Ian (1978), 'Capital and Labour in the Halifax Baking and Confectionary Industry', *Labour/le Travail*, 3: 63–90.

McNally, Larry (1982), *Water Power on the Lachine Canal, 1846–1900*, MS report 56. Ottawa: Parks Canada.

—— (1992), 'Technical Advance and Stagnation: The Case of Nail Production in Nineteenth-Century Montreal', *Material History Review*, 36 (Autumn), 38–45.

Marchildon, Greg (1990), 'Promotion, Finance and Merger in the Canadian Manufacturing Industry, 1885–1918', unpub. doctoral diss., London School of Economics and Political Science.

Marglin, Stephen (1974), 'What Do Bosses Do? The Origins and Functions of Hierarchy in Capitalist Production', *Review of Radical Political Economics*, 6: 33–60.

Marr, Bill (1981), 'The Wheat Economy in Reverse: Ontario's Wheat Production 1887–1917', *Canadian Journal of Economics*, 14/1 (Feb.), 133–45.

Marshall, Alfred (1923), *Industry and Trade*, 4th edn. London: Macmillan.

—— (1924), *Money, Credit and Commerce*. London: Macmillan.

Middleton, Dianne and Walker, David (1980), 'Manufacturers and Industrial Policy in Hamilton, 1880–1910', *Urban History Review*, 8: 20–40.

—— (1981), 'Manufacturers and Industrial Development Policy', *Urban History Review*, 9: 23–46.

Mokyr, Joel (1993) (ed.), *The British Industrial Revolution: An Economic Perspective*. Boulder, Colo.: Westview.

Muise, Del (1991*a*), 'The Great Transformation: Changing the Urban Face of Nova Scotia, 1871–1921', *Nova Scotia Historical Review* (Autumn).

—— (1991*b*), 'The Industrial Context of Inequality: The Female Participation in Nova Scotia's Paid Labour Force, 1871–1921', *Acadiensis*, 20/2 (Spring), 3–31.

Naylor, Tom (1975), *The History of Canadian Business*. Toronto: Lorimer.

Noel, Francoise (1985), 'Chambly Mills, 1784–1815', *Canadian Historical Association, Historical Papers*, 102–16.

Panitch, Leo (1981), 'Dependency and Class in Canadian Political Economy', *Studies in Political Economy*, 6 (Autumn), 7–33.

Parr, Joy (1990), *The Gender of Breadwinners: Women, Men and Change in Two Industrial Towns*. Toronto: University of Toronto Press.

Phillips, Joseph (1979), 'The Theory of Small Enterprise: Smith, Mill, Marshall and Marx', *Explorations in Economic History*, 16/3 (July), 331–40.

Quigley, Neil, Drummond, Ian, and Evans, Lou (1993), 'Regional Transfers of Funds through the Canadian Banking System and Maritime Economic Development, 1895–1935', in Kris Inwood (ed.), *Farm, Factory and Fortune: New Essays in the Economic History of the Maritimes*. Fredericton: Acadiensis Press.

Radforth, Ian (1993), 'Confronting Distance: Managing Jacques and Hay's New Lowell Operations, 1853–73', *Canadian Papers in Business History*, 1: 75–100.

Reid, Richard (1983), 'The Rosamond Woollen Company of Almonte: Industrial Development in a Rural Setting', *Ontario History*, 75.

Reilly, Nolan (1980), 'The General Strike in Amherst, Nova Scotia, 1919', *Acadiensis*, 9/2 (Spring), 56–77.

Rodger, Richard (1988), 'Concentration and Fragmentation: Capital, Labour and the Structure of Mid-Victorian Scottish Industry', *Journal of Urban History*, 14/2 (Feb.), 178–213.

Sager, Eric with Panting, Gerald (1990), *Maritime Capital: The Shipping Industry in Atlantic Canada, 1820–1914*. Montreal and Kingston: McGill-Queen's.

Samuel, Ralph (1977), 'The Workshop of the World', *History Workshop*, 3: 6–72.

Sandberg, Anders (1991), 'Dependent Development, Labour and the Trenton Steel Works, Nova Scotia c.1900–1913', *Labour/le Travail*, 27 (Spring).

Saunders, S. A. (1984), *The Economic History of the Maritime Provinces*, ed. T. W. Acheson. Fredericton: Acadiensis Press.

Scranton, Phillip (1983), *Proprietary Capitalism*. Cambridge: Cambridge University Press.

—— (1991), 'Diversity in Diversity: Flexible Production and American Industrialization, 1880–1930', *Business History Review*, 35: 27–90.

Smith, Adam (1776), *The Wealth of Nations*. London.

Sokoloff, Ken (1984), 'Was the Transition from the Artisanal Shop to the Non-mechanized Factory Associated with Gains in Efficiency?', *Explorations in Economic History*, 21/4 (Oct.), 351–82.

Spelt, Jacob (1972), *Urban Development in South-Central Ontario*. Toronto: McClelland and Stewart.

Steedman, Mercedes (1986), 'Skill and Gender in the Canadian Clothing Industry, 1890–1940', in Craig Heron and Tony Storey (eds.), *On the Job: Confronting the Labour Process in Canada*. Kingston and Montreal: McGill-Queen's), 152–76.

Tchakerian, Viken (1994), 'Productivity, Extent of Markets, and Manufacturing in the Late Antebellum South and Midwest', *Journal of Economic History*, 54/3 (Sept.), 497–525.

Timmins, Geoffrey (1993), *The Last Shift: The Decline of Handloom Weaving in Nineteenth-Century Lancashire*. Manchester: Manchester University Press.

Traves, Tom (1979), *The State and Enterprise: Canadian Manufacturers and the Federal Government, 1917–31*. Toronto: University of Toronto Press.

Tulchinsky, Gerald (1977), *The River Barons: Montreal Businessmen and the Growth of Industry and Transportation, 1837–53*. Toronto: University of Toronto Press.

United States (1870), *Ninth Census*, iii: *Instructions to Assistant Marshals*. Washington, DC: GPO.

—— (1872), *Ninth Census*, iii: *The Statistics of the Wealth and Industry of the United States*. Washington, DC: GPO.

—— (1900), *Twelfth Census*, vii: *Report on Manufactures*, pt I. Washington, DC: GPO.

Urquhart, M. C. (1986), 'New Estimates of Gross National Product, Canada, 1870 to 1926', in S. Engerman and R. Gallman (eds.), *Long-Term Factors in American Economic Growth*. Chicago: University of Chicago Press, 9–88.

—— (1988), 'Canadian Economic Growth 1870–1980', Queen's University, Institute of Economic Research, Discussion Paper no. 734.

von Tunzelman, G. N. (1978), *Steam Power and British Industrialization to 1860*. Oxford: Oxford University Press.

Walker, David (1974), 'Energy and Industrial Location in Southern Ontario, 1871–1921', in D. Walker and J. Bates. (eds.), *Industrial Development in Southern Ontario*. Waterloo: University of Waterloo, 41–68.

Weaver, John (1981), 'The Location of Manufacturing Enterprise: The Case of Hamilton's Attraction of Foundries, 1830–1890', in Richard Jarrell and Arnold Roos (eds.), *Critical Issues in the History of Canadian Science, Technology and Medicine*. Thornhill: HSTC, 197–217.

Williams, Glen (1983), *Not for Export*. Toronto: McClelland and Stewart.

Wood, Phillip (1989*a*), 'Barriers to Capitalist Development in Maritime Canada, 1870–1930: A Comparative Perspective', *Canadian Papers in Business History*, 1: 33–58.

—— (1989*b*), 'Marxism and the Maritimes: On the Determinants of Regional Capitalist Development', *Studies in Political Economy*, 29 (Summer), 123–53.

Wrigley, E. A. (1988), *Continuity, Chance and Change: The Character of the Industrial Revolution in England*. Cambridge: Cambridge University Press.

Wylie, Peter J. (1987), 'When Markets Fail: Electrification and Maritime Industrial Decline', *Acadiensis*, 17/1 (Autumn), 74–96.

—— (1989), 'Technological Adaptation in Canadian Manufacturing, 1900–29', *Journal of Economic History*, 49/3 (Sept.), 569–91.

Wylie, W. T. (1990), *The Blacksmith in Upper Canada, 1784–1850*. Gananoque: Langdale.

PART II
EUROPE

4

Small Firms in the UK

C. F. PRATTEN

Introduction

The changing role of small firms in the *manufacturing* sector of the UK economy is of particular interest because the UK was the first country to industrialize and so changes in industrial structure which occurred in Britain may have been, and may in the future be, followed by other countries. Britain's industrial revolution was a small firms' phenomenon. The focus of this chapter is to trace the contribution of small firms after the industrial revolution and the reasons for the changing role of small firms. By way of introduction, the first three sections of the chapter outline perceptions of the role of small firms in the literature, summarize data quantifying the actual contribution of small firms to the UK economy, and provide a concise comparison of the changing contribution of small firms in the UK with the position in other countries—Japan, Italy, and the USA. The objective of this first part of the chapter is to identify questions about the role of small firms in the UK.

The purpose of the second part of the chapter is to answer the questions identified in the first part. To do this, the contribution of small firms in five industries is examined. The industries are the machine-tool and woollen-textiles industries, industries in which UK firms established an international lead in the nineteenth century, but which have had difficulty meeting international competition during the post-1950 period. Two industries, the instruments and pharmaceutical industries, are included to represent industries where the UK has been relatively more successful during the post-1950 period. Finally, in part two, some interesting developments in a section of the paper-converting industry are described. The third part of the chapter takes a wider perspective. Developments in other sectors of the

I am grateful for the assistance with the preparation of this chapter provided by Nick Collier and James Tatch.

economy and changes in the practice of financial institutions and the government are outlined.

Perceptions of Small Firms

In 1776 Adam Smith used the fragmented pin industry to illustrate his insights to the benefits of specialization and competition (Adam Smith 1937 edn.). This view of manufacturing industry made up of many competing small firms held sway among economists until the beginning of the twentieth century. As late as 1923 Marshall wrote:

Thus so far as the 'productive' side of business is concerned, it may be concluded that though the volume of output required for maximum efficiency . . . is increasing in almost every industry—yet, at any given time and in any given condition of industrial technique, there is likely to be a point, beyond which any further increase in size gives little further increase in economy and efficiency. And this is well; for small businesses are on the whole the best educators of the initiative and versatility, which are the chief sources of industrial progress.   (Marshall 1923)

From the inter-war period there was a shift in economists' perceptions of the contribution of small firms to the economy, led by Schumpeter:

Traditional theory . . . has since the time of Marshall and Edgeworth been discovering an increasing number of exceptions to the old propositions about perfect competition . . . that have shaken that unqualified belief in its virtues cherished by the generation which flourished between Ricardo and Marshall. . . . Especially the propositions that a perfectly competitive system is ideally economical of resources and allocates them in a way that is optimal with respect to a given distribution of income—propositions very relevant to the question of the behaviour of output—cannot now be held with the old confidence.   (Schumpeter 1942)

Steindl writing in 1945 concluded that:

The survival of small firms is thus dependent on a series of factors not very creditable to our economic system: Monopsonistic exploitation of labour, imperfection of markets due to 'irrational' reasons, unemployment, and the 'gambling preference' of small entrepreneurs.   (Steindl 1945)

The views of economists circa 1960 are summarized in the following comments, by Robertson and Dennison,

on the whole there is a tendency for production to be conducted on an ever larger and larger scale—for the large concerns to oust and supplant the small. (Robertson and Dennison 1960)

The emphasis on small firms operating in an environment of 'free competition' and being the engine of economic growth was replaced by a pragmatic approach which argued that imperfect competition would be as capable as perfect competition in reaching economic welfare goals. Prices might then be lower than in conditions with many firms operating at sub-optimal scale. The process of industrial restructuring seemed to be in one direction towards greater concentration and the increasing dominance of large firms. New small firms might set up in new industries, but, for the development of many new products, Schumpeter's assessment was that large firms had advantages. Economists were not hostile to small firms, but the future seemed to lie with the large firms and research concentrated on them.

Simultaneously there were political pressures to extend the public sector and for the use of centralized planning. Harold Macmillan who became the Conservative Prime Minister in 1958 had written 'The Middle Way' in the 1930s advocating rationalization of mature/declining industries and forms of planning. Extending the public sector by nationalization of, for example, electricity generation and supply, resulted in the creation of giant national monopolies and sporadic attempts at planning and government intervention in the 1960s and 1970s focused on the reorganization of, and mergers of, large companies.

The Schumpeterian view represented a new orthodoxy that lasted throughout the 1950s and 1960s. However, in Britain the relative decline of UK industry, encapsulated in a falling share of world exports of manufactures from more than 20 per cent in 1950 to less than 10 per cent in 1972, demonstrated that manufacturing industry lacked competitiveness. Although the UK economy grew during the 1950s and 1960s, growth was slower than in some competitor countries, notably Germany and Japan. During the 1970s and early 1980s growth slowed and unemployment soared. Some giant UK companies, particularly British Leyland, an amalgamation of the indigenous car producers, and the quintessential large-scale manufacturing company, were hit very hard during the recession circa 1980. Some economists were already questioning the emphasis on large firms, for example, Jewkes, Sawers, and Stillerman (1958) had reported that small firms in the UK had played an important role in innovation despite the major advantages for innovations claimed for large firms.

The Bolton Committee

The Bolton Committee was set up under a Labour government in 1969 to enquire into the role of small firms at a point in time which in retrospect can be seen to have been a watershed for small firms. The Bolton Report published in 1971 distinguished the important contributions of small firms to the economy, including the filling of niche markets that would not be worthwhile for a large firm to enter; their role as providers of actual and potential competition; and their innovation in products, techniques, and services, but it claimed that the most significant role of small firms was one in which there was not necessarily any private return to the entrepreneur:

A vigorous and successful small-firm sector, by its very existence, keeps open channels of entry into business and provides a continuing incentive to the ambitious and enterprising to start up in business on their own account ... This 'seedbed' function, therefore, appears to be a vital contribution of the small-firm sector to the long-run health of the economy.

This suggests that when assessing the contribution of small firms special attention should be paid to new small firms which grow.

The Contribution of Small Manufacturing Firms

The share of employment accounted for by small firms is a useful, though qualified, measure of the contribution of small firms to manufacturing industry. The UK Census of Production data for firms (enterprises) which are only available for the period since 1935, indicate that between 1935 and about 1970 the employment share of small firms with less than 200 employees in UK manufacturing industry halved to approximately 20 per cent of total employment.[1] Although reliable estimates for the earlier period are not available, there is little doubt that this fall was a continuation of a long-term historical trend. That was the view of the Bolton Committee: 'the small-firm sector is in a state of long-term decline, both in size and its share of activity' (Committee of Inquiry on Small Firms [*Bolton Report*] 1971). A detailed analysis of the long-run changes in large- and small-firm shares, and in the changes in industry definitions, can be found in Hughes (1993).

During the industrial revolution most industries were organized in clusters of firms. The Lancashire cotton-textile industry, the single most important industry of the period, was made up of a large number of firms.[2] Gatrell (1977) using Horner's Census of Lancashire Textile Firms taken in 1841, towards the end of the industrial revolution, concluded that there was a 'familiar pyramidal hierarchy of firms in which large firms were still few, and small to middling (and single-process) firms were preponderant'. However, in terms of employment there were many firms which would not be classified as small. Only 12 per cent of employees were in factories with less than 100 employees. The important point is that the largest firm employed about 1 per cent of the total labour force in the industry and 64 per cent of employees were employed in factories with less than 500 employees. Compared with contemporary pyramid structures, the structure of the cotton industry in 1841 was relatively flat. In most other industries the proportion of employees in firms with less than 100 employees was probably greater than in the cotton industry. Nevertheless there were medium-size firms in some industries, including potteries and iron manufacture.

Some economic historians have argued that the fragmented vertical and horizontal structure of the textile industry was a handicap as overseas competitors emerged, though this assessment is not universally accepted. A feature of the textile industries and some other leading industries of the industrial revolution—machinery and metal goods—was that, at least with the technology available at the time, they were industries in which the economies of scale were limited, in contrast to the leading, mid-twentieth-century industries such as motor vehicles and aeroplane production. If small firms are defined as employing less than 100 employees it is difficult to assess the proportion of the labour force in small firms in 1850. Clearly the employment share of firms employing more than 1,000 employees was small. Between 1850 and 1970 the share of manufacturing employment in firms with less than 200 employees fell to 20 per cent. It is possible that there were temporary setbacks to the process of concentration, but statistics are not available to test this.[3]

Since 1970 there has been a remarkable reversal of the decline in the relative share of manufacturing attributable to small firms. Between 1970 and 1990 the share of small firms rose to about 30 per cent of total manufacturing employment. Until the 1970s the effectiveness of the structural concentration of many UK industries was not really tested by competition. From 1970 onwards the pressure of competition from overseas, which had hit the cotton-textile trade from the inter-war period, spread to most sectors of manufacturing. The competition forced many firms to shrink in size and the accompanying high unemployment provided an incentive for people to search for opportunities to set up new businesses. The release of employees from firms also provided a source of knowledgeable and experienced employees for existing and new small firms.

Innovation is of critical importance for the competitiveness of manufacturing industries but is difficult to measure. It has been estimated that small- and medium-size firms' share of innovation in UK manufacturing industries has risen steadily since the 1940s and that small firms' share of innovations was only slightly less than their share of employment in the early 1980s (E. Wood 1997).

International Comparisons

Comparisons of the share of employment in manufacturing industry accounted for by firms with less than 100 employees show that the contribution of small US and UK firms to their economies is lower than for Japanese and Italian small firms. Given the much larger total output of many US industries, a smaller percentage contribution of firms with less than 100 employees in the USA compared to small firms in Japan and Italy, is not, perhaps, entirely surprising. The important point here is that in some contexts, a definition based on the *relative* size of firms, which allows for differences in the size of markets, may be more meaningful than a definition based on absolute size. However, differences in the size of domestic markets do not explain the lower contribution of small firms to the UK economy. Another feature of international comparisons is the post-1970 recovery/increase in the share of small firms in the manufacturing sector of the USA and particularly the UK.[4]

The Industries

There was a revival in both the competitiveness of UK manufacturing industry, as measured by its share of world exports of manufactures, and the contribution of small firms to employment in manufacturing industries from the 1970s. In this part of the paper the experience of small firms in five industrial sectors is examined to answer the question: How important was their role in the revival of manufacturing industries?

Each of the five industrial sectors has distinct characteristics. The machine-tool industry, an investment-goods industry which supplies engineering industries is very cyclical and, in order to be competitive, firms have to be highly profitable during periods of boom. Technical progress, including the introduction of electronic controls and innovation—developing improved models of tools—is important. For the woollen industry changes in fashion and the prices of raw materials, as well as cyclical changes, affect the performance of firms. For most firms in both the instruments and pharmaceutical industries innovation is of critical importance. The patent system enables pharmaceutical companies to hold temporary monopolies for many new drugs, and patents can be important for instrument companies. In each of the first four industries there is a high degree of specialization by firms. The part of the paper converting industry concerned with making cardboard boxes is different again. Product development is only important on some fringes of the market, while cost minimization and the quality of service to customers are of key importance.

Plainly the existence of economies of scale is an important determinant of the role of small firms. Scale economies are of least importance for spinning and weaving wool. For the manufacturing operations such as dyeing and finishing for which scale economies are more substantial, production in the UK is concentrated among specialist firms and has been for many years. For cardboard-box manufacture there are economies of long production runs of identical products but there are few economies for manufacturing large numbers of different products in short runs. For this type of production there would have to be duplication of equipment and personnel. There are significant economies related to spreading sunk costs of research and development of new machine tools, instruments, and drugs—the greater the output of products the lower the research and development costs per unit. For some new pharmaceuticals the sunk costs are enormous, while for both machine tools and instruments development costs vary a great deal for different products. The extent of economies of scale for marketing and selling a range of products, particularly in overseas markets, are again substantial for pharmaceuticals and are probably significant for machine tools and instruments.

Table 4.1 summarizes the development of the five industries since the 1920s and Table 4.2 indicates the changing contribution of small companies

Table 4.1. *The development of five UK industries*

Year	Machine tools	Woollen and worsted	Instruments	Pharma-ceuticals	Cardboard boxes
(a) Net output as a percentage of nominal GDP					
1924	0.06	1.36	0.10	0.20	0.10
1930	0.11	0.86	0.13	0.22	0.15
1935	0.18	0.94	0.13	0.28	0.18
1951	0.45	0.85	0.23	0.35	0.27
1970	0.35	0.39	0.47	0.56	0.27
1992	0.11[a]	0.10	0.25[b]	0.93	0.60[c]
(b) Industry employment as a percentage of total manufacturing employment					
1924	0.23	4.93	0.34	0.46	0.43
1930	0.35	3.77	0.49	0.36	0.64
1935	0.48	3.85	0.51	0.41	0.77
1951	1.18	2.57	0.89	0.68	0.69
1970	0.96	1.67	1.53	0.77	0.85
1992	0.63[a]	0.66	1.32[b]	1.81	2.65[c]

[a] In the 1992 Census of Production the industry definition for manufacture of machine tools was widened to include manufacture of engineers' small tools. In Tables 4.1 and 4.2 the figures for the machine-tools industry have been adjusted using a scaling factor calculated as the ratio of the corresponding figures for the old and new industry definitions, as given in the 1970 Census of Production. This assumes (implausibly) that the relative size of firms for the two sub-industries remained the same between 1970 and 1992.

[b] Prior to the 1970 Census the manufacture of scientific instruments was counted together with the manufacture of photographic and document-copying equipment, and of surgical instruments and appliances. In Tables 4.1 and 4.2 the figures for the scientific instruments industry pre-1970 have been calculated as the ratio of the corresponding figures for the post- and pre-1970 industry definitions, as given in the 1970 Census. In the 1992 Census of Production the industry definition was divided into two and widened to include manufacture of photographic and document-copying equipment. In Tables 4.1 and 4.2 the figures for the scientific instruments industry have been calculated as the ratio of the corresponding figures for the old and new industry definitions, as given in the 1970 Census of Production.

[c] In the 1992 Census of Production the industry definition for manufacture of cardboard boxes was widened to include the manufacture of corrugated paper sacks, household and sanitary goods, paper stationery, and wall-coverings. In Tables 4.1 and 4.2 the figures for the cardboard-box industry have been adjusted using a scaling factor calculated as the ratio of the corresponding figures for the old and new industry definitions, as given in the 1970 Census of Production.

Table 4.2. *The share of small firms in the five UK industries*

Year	Machine tools	Woollen and worsted	Instruments	Pharma-ceuticals	Cardboard boxes
(a) Net output of firms with fewer than 100 employees as a percentage of the total in the industry					
1935	19.4	19.4	30.9	23.7	39.7
1951	22.5	25.3	21.9	16.0	25.6
1970	17.8	14.6	14.6	5.2	14.7
1992	42.0[a]	22.4	35.4[b]	2.4	25.9[c]
(b) Employment in firms with fewer than 100 employees as a percentage of the total in the industry					
1935	20.5	17.9	34.8	27.1	44.4
1951	23.6	22.5	19.5	16.2	30.0
1970	17.0	16.2	13.4	6.3	19.2
1992	42.4[a]	22.9	37.8[b]	4.5	32.5[c]

See Table 4.1 for footnotes.

to these industries. The data which are derived from Censuses of Production are subject to three main qualifications. First, changes in definition make time series comparisons difficult: serious breaks in the series are indicated in the tables by underlining of figures. Secondly, the Census provides a series of snapshots, whereas panel data would be helpful to trace and analyse the setting-up of new firms, and the growth and contraction of firms over time. Thirdly, enterprises in one particular trade commonly engage in activities in other trades and separate trades are combined together for census purposes.

(i) Machine tools

The 'census' machine-tools industry includes firms which specialize in making standard and bespoke machine tools *and*, in addition, firms which repair machine tools. For the censuses since 1980 the 'machine-tool' industry also has included manufacturers of engineers' small tools. Ideally, separate figures for manufacturers of standard and bespoke machine tools—the industry *narrowly defined*—would be available, and would include a total of about 100 UK enterprises in 1992.

The figures available for the widely defined industry shown in Table 4.1 indicate a substantial fall in the relative importance of the machine-tools industry since the early post-war period, although this is overstated because 1992 was a trough year in the business cycle. The changing fortunes of the industry are summarized in the following quotation.

The UK is now the seventh largest producer of machine tools in the world. Its relative decline in world terms from its pre-eminence in the last century, can be gauged from the fact that only four UK firms are in the largest 130 in the world as defined by American Machinist. (Senbenelli and Simpson 1993)

Beesley and Troup (1958) reported that large-machine tool plants existed, but that they tended to be agglomerations of different engineering processes, foundries, machining and assembling and making many different specifications of machine tools, thus not taking advantage of scale economies. This applied to Alfred Herbert, the largest firm in the industry, which contracted and finally collapsed in the 1980s. In contrast, the largest firms in the industry now specialize on quite narrow ranges of products such as machining centres. The data in Table 4.2 are compatible with the employment share of small firms having risen between 1970 and 1992, but the figures for the widely defined industry are not necessarily representative for the narrowly defined machine-tools industry.

(ii) Woollen and worsted

Table 4.1 shows the relative decline of the woollen and worsted industry in terms of its contribution to the wider UK economy. While employment in the industry as a whole has been falling, the employment share of small firms has risen since 1970.

(iii) Instruments

The analysis of this sector is hugely complicated by changing definitions in the Census of Production. Again, the data are compatible with an increase in the employment share of small firms between 1970 and 1992. Also, the employment figures for 1992 show that small firms are an important part of this industry. A recent study identified 2,100 UK firms with less than 20 employees which manufactured instrumentation and control equipment in 1994.

(iv) Pharmaceuticals

From Table 4.1 it is clear that pharmaceuticals is a 'growth' industry in the UK; its share in national output rising by 368 % between 1924 and 1992 and the industry has retained a 10 per cent share of world exports. There has been an apparently clear trend *away* from small firms in this industry, as shown in Table 4.2. It is possible that the table is misleading because new small pharmaceutical firms may be classified to other trades e.g. chemicals or in the service sector as research organizations. Also, there have been many new start-ups in the industry recently. It has been estimated that there are now 221 biotechnology companies in the UK with 11,000 employees (*Financial Times*, 25 April 1977).

(v) Paper converting—cardboard boxes

The cardboard-box trade has expanded relative to the rest of the economy (Table 4.1) and small firms have increased their share of the trade since 1970.

The Reasons for Differences in the Performance of the Industries

Before surveying the role of small firms, some developments in the industries are described.

Markets

The UK machine-tools industry was hit hard by the recessions in the early 1980s and early 1990s, that depressed demand from an already relatively weak domestic engineering industry. The scientific-instruments industry, has benefited from the better performance of science-based industries in the UK, such as chemicals and pharmaceuticals, and higher education and utilities which are important customers for its products. The woollen and worsted industry has had to contend with a diminished market for its product owing to the fashion for lighter artificial and natural fabrics besides intensifying international competition. By contrast, the pharmaceuticals industry has not only enjoyed burgeoning demand from the National Health Service in the UK, but more significantly has an excellent export record. The Commission of the European Community (1988) reported that:

the UK-owned pharmaceutical companies hold only a minor part of their home market, but they are both large and have excellent records of research and a markedly international outlook. The appreciable share of sales in the USA and the rest of the EEC held by UK firms is highly significant.

Demand for cardboard boxes has increased and international trade in boxes is limited because of the costs of transport.

Scientific resources

There are differences in the scientific resources available to industries. The absence of graduate engineers in the machine-tool industry during the early post-war period was notorious and managers in the industry consider that UK universities and institutes seem not to be as well organized to provide technical support for firms in the industry as do their counterparts in Germany. The woollen and worsted industry relies more on creative/artistic, rather than scientific, resources, but the instruments and pharmaceuticals industries have benefited from the strong chemical and medical scientific research orientation of UK universities, which has spurred innovation, as well as providing a strong flow of qualified graduate staff into the industries.

Government Support

The degree to which the government has supported the industries varies. For the instruments industry the National Physical Laboratory provides wide-ranging expertise in measurement technology. The long-standing, substantial government-funded scientific underpinning of the industry contrasts with the position of the machine-tool industry, where government funded research is limited and is far less than in Germany. Since the 1970s the woollen and worsted industry has had little assistance not available to other industries. The pharmaceuticals industry has benefited from a stable regulatory regime operating upon an almost entirely voluntary basis. Hancher (1990) observes that: 'British-based industry could bargain and negotiate with a single, unified health department, which was at once its partner, regulator and major customer.'

Inward Investment

Overseas firms have played significant, but differing roles in the industries. In terms of employment, machine-tool businesses which manufacture in the UK and which are owned by overseas-based companies, account for about 40 per cent of the narrowly defined UK industry. The woollen industry has seen little inward investment but, as with machine tools, the instruments industry has been seen as attractive to foreign investors. The sales of the UK operations of companies based overseas account for 30 per cent of the sales of the UK industry when widely defined to include medical and optical instruments. Even so, it is in the pharmaceuticals industry where inward investment is probably most important. Most of the leading drug companies in the world set up facilities in the UK owing to the conducive environment and market. Companies based in Scandinavia have interests in the UK paper-converting industry including cardboard box manufacture.

International Comparisons

(i) Machine tools

Japan and Germany are the leading machine-tool manufacturing nations and in the 1993 list of the leading world machine-tool manufacturers, fourteen Japanese and five German companies were in the top twenty-five (*American Machinist*, August 1993). It is noteworthy that Japan and Germany are the two advanced industrial countries with the most successful and innovative mechanical engineering and motor vehicle industries—the main users of machine tools. Several UK machine-tool companies make machines for the aerospace industry, an engineering industry in which the UK has been relatively successful.

The trend in the German machine-tools industry has been away from small firms and towards large enterprises (Table 4.3). Audretsch *et al.* (1993)

Table 4.3. *Small firms in West German machine-tools industry (Percentage of employees in small enterprises with less than 100 employees)*

Year	%
1951	23.0
1960	10.3
1970	8.1
1980	8.9
1990	6.4

Source: Audretsch *et al.* (1993).

argue that increased globalization, especially in terms of competition from Japan, may have exerted 'competitive pressures on the smallest sub-optimal scale plants, resulting in both employment loss and ultimately exit from the industry'.

(ii) Woollen and worsted

Italian firms are the principal competitors for UK firms in the woollen and worsted industry. According to Owen (1993): 'Italy's success has been mainly in the wool, worsted and knitwear sectors. It is based on a combination of design flair and flexible production arrangements; the dense network of companies, mostly very small, in the principal centres of Prato, Biella and Como has been widely praised as a new form of capitalism which other industrial countries have been unable to match.' After a crisis *c.*1951 during which some large integrated firms switched to buying out operations from sub-contractors, many of which were new firms set up by ex-employees using machinery acquired from their former employers, the Italian industry expanded rapidly. In 1961 there were 7,000 textile firms in the Prato region with 41,000 employees and by 1981 there were more than 14,000 firms with 61,000 employees, a striking contrast to the contraction of the UK industry portrayed in Table 4.1. Many of the firms are small-scale weavers who work as subcontractors for larger firms. Advantages of this structure include low and flexible labour costs for family workers and low overheads, especially where businesses are located in the homes or extensions to the homes of the owners. Replacing employees with small firms acting as subcontractors effectively creates wage flexibility—during recessions the income of subcontractors falls.

One feature of the Prato industry is the existence of an active trade association which among other tasks, monitors technical and fashion changes relevant to the industry. Striking the most effective balance between competition and co-operation within a district is difficult. One alternative to an industry structure with many small firms allied to co-operative arrangements to take advantage of economies of scale for activities where they apply, as in Prato, is consolidation through mergers such as those which have taken place in Yorkshire in the UK.

(iii) Instruments

The USA, Japan, Germany, and the UK are the leading international instrument-manufacturing nations. The USA has a strong advantage because of its huge domestic market which has enabled firms there to spend more on

R&D and to spread the costs of developing instruments over a larger output than their competitors; as a consequence US firms have developed some products with superior performance. (The large US market does not alone explain the success of the American firms, as American car and TV set manufacturers had similar advantages.) An important feature of the industry is the international spread of the operations of many companies (including some UK-based companies). Typically, international companies do not duplicate the production of the same instruments in different countries; instead they manufacture different products in different countries and distribute the products internationally. Reasons for this international specialization are to avoid the costs of duplicating technical expertise and to make use of specialized knowledge which has been built-up by businesses which have often been acquired by their present owners to obtain access to this expertise.

(iv) Pharmaceuticals

The major world players in the pharmaceuticals industry are based in the USA and Europe. The US drugs industry has over one-third of world sales outside the command economies, and dominates its own large and highly competitive domestic market. It is the major source of new products. American dominance in the early post-war period is described by Thomas (writing in 1958). He argued that the substantial domestic market 'encourages large-scale production and specialization'. Despite the advantages of giant companies in the pharmaceuticals industry, many new companies have been set up, particularly in the USA, to develop drugs and delivery systems for drugs.

A Survey of Small Firms

The purpose of the survey of small firms reported in this section was to identify reasons for the increasing relative importance of small firms since 1970.

(i) Machine tools

The UK machine-tool industry (narrowly defined) has made an astonishing recovery from the recession of the early 1990s. Many companies in the industry were forced to make fundamental changes—replacing managers, rationalizing and/or redesigning product ranges and production facilities, and increasing reliance on bought-in components, and—aided by a competitive exchange rate and a recovery in demand—profitability was restored. At present it is difficult to assess whether there has been a fundamental improvement in the international competitiveness of the UK industry—the author's assessment is that the improvement *is* more than a cyclical recovery.

The recovery has been led by the largest companies in the industry. Eight of the ten largest producers in the UK are owned by companies based overseas. None of these ten companies is a new firm or existing small firm which has grown very rapidly. Small companies have played a part, but the recovery has certainly not been limited to small firms: overall their contribution has probably been modest.

How do small firms compete in the machine-tool industry? To answer this question a cluster of small machine-tool firms in and around Halifax, a town in Yorkshire which has had a machine-tool industry since the industrial revolution, was surveyed. Some of the firms manufacture lathes— superficially an unpromising product, as lathes are manufactured in large volumes by Japanese and other companies, including the largest UK-based machine-tool manufacturer, the 600 Group. How could these small firms compete?

One company, Crawford Swift had 75 employees in 1996 and is an example of a large machine-tool company which has shrunk. It had been part of a subsidiary of Staveley Industries, Craven Bros, which in the 1970s had 1,500 employees making machine tools. Crawfords now specializes in rebuilding and supplying electronic controls for machine tools designed to machine large components. Crawfords is an example of small firms emerging from the ruins of much larger companies. Advantages of such companies include the goodwill and brand names of the larger companies which gives them advantages for winning contracts to repair tools and supplying parts for existing machines. Brand names also seem surprisingly important for an industry which sells to other manufacturers rather than the public. Other relatively small firms have taken over the machine-tool businesses formerly run by BSA, TI, and Wickmans.

Asquith Butler, another Halifax manufacturer, also manufactures machine tools for machining large components. Since 1992 it has been part of a group with more than 100 employees, so it does not qualify as a small firm. Prior to 1992, Asquith and Butler were parts of much larger groups. The history of takeovers of the family-controlled machine-tool manufacturers around Halifax including Crawfords and Asquith Butler, suggests that take-overs are not a recipe for creating international competitiveness if the acquired firms lack it.

A third company in Halifax, Benford, operates at the other end of the size range—it makes small lathes which it sells primarily to educational establishments, though it also sells lathes to industrial users. Another small company in Halifax, Beaver, had been a machine-tool repairer. It acquired the rights to manufacture Beaver lathes from a company of that name to which receivers were appointed in 1992.

A few small firms have entered the machine-tool manufacturing industry in recent years. One, Douglas Curtis, manufactures grinding machines to very close tolerances. This company was set up in the early 1970s. It developed machine-tool repair and rebuilding and machining divisions. It started to build new bespoke machine tools in the early 1990s and has exported some machines. It acquired expertise in designing machine tools from experience of repairing and rebuilding machine tools.

No account of the UK machine-tool industry and small firms would be complete without mention of Renishaw, a new firm which was founded in 1976. It pioneered the development of measuring electronic probes for use in machine tools. Renishaw's initial success was built on patent protection for its high quality innovative products, allowing it to maintain high profit margins, and on the use of advanced, flexible manufacturing systems. It has grown into an international company with a stock market capitalization of £320m.

(ii) Woollen and worsted

The recession of the early 1980s hit the woollen industry very hard, but the recession of the early 1990s was much less traumatic—very few woollen firms were forced to close. This suggests that the industry had by 1990 achieved an internationally competitive structure.

The statistics quoted earlier report the shrinkage of large firms in the industry. This involved a process of shrinking output and closure by large firms which had concentrated on the manufacture of standard-commodity products. The increasing relative importance of small firms does not reflect a process of splitting up of large firms and subcontracting as in Prato or the setting up of new small firms. Rather the small firms were concentrated in the sectors making specialized products such as cashmere scarves, and high-quality fabrics for sports jackets and suits, and their markets have not been as adversely affected by increased international competition. The surviving firms tend to produce products for the top end of the market where price competition is less important, while many overseas manufacturers choose to attack products with mass-market appeal. Greater flexibility for producing short runs of products efficiently and not being vertically integrated which facilitates switching to different fabrics may have contributed to the relative success of small firms. Nor is there much evidence of small firms growing very rapidly. Interestingly, the example of a company which had grown rapidly, but not to a very large size, was a firm which marketed upholstery fabrics for office furniture. It had moved into manufacturing after it had established a business selling products made for it by other firms. Entry to the industry requires knowledge of processes and markets, but a small number of Asian immigrants have set up weaving businesses since the mid-1970s.

(iii) Instruments

Of the five industries included, new small firms have had greatest impact in the instrument industry. Renishaw, whose growth was described in the section on machine tools, is an instrument company and it is not alone in developing new products and achieving rapid growth. Another instrument company which has achieved explosive growth is Siebe, much of it by takeovers. In terms of growth these are stars, but many new small firms have been established in this industry during the post-war period. Often these firms were set up to manufacture new instruments designed for use in research laboratories or new versions of existing instruments by, for example, replacing mechanical parts with electronics and software. Other examples of new instruments are data loggers to measure chemical composition for pollution and environmental control, and instruments to detect explosives. An influence reducing the size of some instrument companies measured in terms of employment has been a reduction in vertical integration. Many instrument companies have spun off or closed their machine shops and similar facilities. This has two effects on the size distribution of firms: the instrument firms shrink in size in terms of employment and other small firms can supply the components.

(iv) Pharmaceuticals

The statistical analysis indicated that small firms are less important for the pharmaceutical industry. However, as in the instrument industry, new firms have been set up to make pharmaceuticals and, at least in terms of stock market capitalization, a few of them have recently achieved spectacular growth. Revolutionary changes in biotechnology have opened up new opportunities for developing drugs; the costs of development have been reduced by, in some circumstances, the increased scope for predicting the effects of compounds by computer modelling and other techniques, and by speeding up the preparation of, and screening (testing) of, compounds, but there are enormous costs of developing drugs for the market. A small firm attempting to develop and market a major drug on its own has to grow very rapidly indeed. It can to some extent avoid this by concentrating on drugs for use by terminally ill patients for which controls are less onerous, or delivery systems for drugs. Another more widespread solution is to enter joint ventures with large companies to test and market new formulations. A snapshot of the number of small firms in this industry is likely to provide an inadequate indication of the contribution of small firms because successful new firms will grow rapidly and/or be taken over; they nevertheless speed the development of new drugs.

(v) Paper converting—cardboard boxes

In the 1970s the cardboard-box trade was dominated by large firms. In common with many sectors of industry there was considerable slack in their operations with chronic labour-relations problems at some factories. A number of new small firms entered the trade and were able to compete successfully with the industry leaders. The small firms had advantages for supplying local users of boxes and for manufacturing short runs. Also, the quality of the service provided for customers is important. A progressive change in organization to just-in-time stock-holding by customers aided the small firms because it resulted in shorter runs and a need for flexibility. One of the new firms grew very rapidly by take-overs including the acquisition of the box- and paper-making facilities of some former competitors. Some of the small firms were able to manage their labour force more efficiently; they organized long, twelve-hour shifts with employees working five and sometimes six shifts a week, albeit for high wages. Some employees were engaged on a temporary basis providing flexibility to deal with peaks and troughs of demand which occur through the year. A less attractive source of lower costs for one small firm was that it did not have a pension scheme. The small-firms sector now has a share of nearly 30 per cent of the trade while the large firms have reduced slack and closed factories.

The cardboard-box industry provides an example of small firms creating changes in industries and illustrates the speed of structural change. Managers with experience of the industry were able to set up new small firms and put pressure on the leading firms in the industry which were not under much pressure from international competition. New management teams were formed which in time took over some of the assets previously managed by large companies.

A Wider Perspective

So far the focus has been on UK manufacturing. A recent government report estimated that firms with less than 100 employees now account for about 50 per cent of employment in the private sector. This includes self-employment which is particularly common in the construction industry. In some circumstances self-employment is tax efficient. The process of concentration has proceeded in other sectors, most obviously in parts of the retail trade, but more than 50 per cent of employment in the retailing, wholesaling, and repairs sector is still with firms with less than 100 employees.

An interesting example of a trade where the tide of concentration and domination by national chains was reversed is estate agencies—agents who sell residential property. During the 1980s, financial organizations such as banks, building societies, and insurance companies bought up great numbers of independent local estate agencies. For some of these organizations the expansion which was intended to provide synergies with other financial services, such as selling insurance and banking services, proved disastrous. Many small estate-agency businesses have been set up and some of the financial organizations have withdrawn. Unlike retailing, there are no economies for buying in bulk for estate agents. Knowledge of local housing markets and the ability to help and inspire confidence in home owners and those seeking to buy homes and to deal with transactions of which customers have little experience is of great importance.

The fastest growth of small firms in the UK has been in the service sector. Between 1985 and 1990 the total stock of service-sector firms grew by 184,000, 22 per cent, compared with only 14,000 or 9.3 per cent for manufacturing. The growth of service-sector firms has been led by professionally based, information-intensive activities such as management consultancy and computer services (Keeble, Bryson, and Wood 1993). Many of these service-sector firms sell services to manufacturers. Also, a surprisingly high proportion of them export (Cosh and Hughes, 1996).

In the USA and the UK, capital markets and institutions have an important role in promoting changes to the structure of industries. Two noteworthy changes of approach have emerged since the 1980s. The City of London is now disenchanted with conglomerate companies, companies with interests in a diverse range of industries, which were very fashionable in the 1970s and 1980s. The share prices of the leading conglomerate companies have fallen. Financial institutions have encouraged companies to sell off or demerge their non-core activities. If existing companies are to stick to their core businesses this leaves more gaps for small and new firms. The financing of new ventures—venture capital—by City of London institutions and other investors may still be inadequate, but provision of venture capital has been substantially increased, in part stimulated by tax concessions for this type of investment.

No account of the changing role of small firms in the UK would be complete without reference to the revolution in the government's support for small firms. Whether the extraordinarily wide range of initiatives, including advice and training schemes the government has put in place to aid and encourage small firms actually enables many new and existing small firms to survive and grow is difficult to assess, but there has certainly been a change of emphasis. Under the Conservative governments since 1979 a major and, perhaps, main focus of government support for industry has been on small firms. With historically high levels of unemployment, the role of small firms and self-employment to create jobs has been an important reason for this focus. The increased government support for small firms has been matched by much greater media attention to small businesses. Also, there may have been important changes in aspirations; setting up and running a business in Britain may have higher status in 1997 than it had in 1970, but such changes which may be important cannot be measured. Since 1979 the number of small businesses has increased by 50 per cent.

Conclusions

The UK was the first country to industrialize. In the middle of the nineteenth century clusters of small businesses were the predominant form of industrial structure. In manufacturing concentration increased and the dominance of small firms was progressively reduced. In the 1970s the UK faced an industrial crisis—its protected colonial and domestic markets had been opened to fierce international competition which tested the industrial structure that had evolved and which exposed a widespread lack of international competitiveness. It is outside the scope of this chapter to describe and assess all the ingredients for the remarkable recovery that has since occurred: we have focused on the role of small firms.

Plainly, small firms have played an important part in the revival. Nevertheless, in two of the five industries surveyed, machine tools (narrowly defined) and pharmaceuticals, the recovery has been led by large UK- and overseas-based companies. Some small machine-tool firms have emerged from the ruins of large firms and new small pharmaceutical—biotechnology —firms have been set up. In woollen textiles and instruments industries the role of small firms has been more important. Existing small firms have had more success in maintaining employment than large firms in the woollen industry, many new firms have been set up in the instrument industry and some of these have achieved spectacular growth, and small firms account for a substantial share of the output of the industry. In the cardboard-box trade, a trade not directly exposed to much international competition, small firms have played an important part in increasing efficiency and improving the service provided for customers.

The government has made small firms a major focus of its industrial policy and since 1979 there has been spectacular growth of the number of small firms. It is too early to fully assess the long-term impact of the revival of small businesses in the UK, but there can be little doubt that the creation of new businesses has increased employment[5] and though some of the experiments with small firms, like some of the earlier experiments with large companies, will fail, there have been, and will continue to be, many successes.

NOTES

1. The Censuses of Production prior to 1935 did not collect information for enterprises.
2. Between 1835 and 1840 exports of cotton goods accounted for nearly *half* of total British exports and in 1913 cotton goods still represented nearly a quarter of Britain's export trade (G. C. Allen 1951).
3. It has been shown that the share of the largest 100 firms in manufacturing net output in the UK *fell* between 1930 and 1950, but there is good reason to believe that the share of small firms continued to fall, with the firms between the small firms and the largest 100 companies gaining share (Hannah and Kay 1977).
4. For a detailed comparison of small firms' employment shares, see Driver and Dunne 1992.
5. Attempts to quantify the increase in employment are fraught with difficulties. The problems in accurately assessing the employment impact of small firms are discussed in OECD Employment Outlook (July 1994).

REFERENCES

Allen, G. C. (1951), *British Industries and Their Organization*. London.

Audretsch, D., Carree, M., Fleischer, M., Monsted, N., Price, Y., and Yamawaki, H. (1993), *Shifts in the Firm-Size Distribution and Underlying Causes: A Case Study of the Machine Tool Industry*, in Z. J. Acs and D. Audretsch (eds.), *Small Firms and Entrepreneurship: An East–West Perspective*. Cambridge.

Beesley, M. and Troup, G. (1958), 'The Machine-Tool Industry' in D. Burn (ed.), *The Structure of British Industry*, 2 vols. Cambridge.

Central Statistical Office, *Business Monitor, Report on the Census of Production, PA1002*, various issues. London.

Commission of the European Communities (1988), *Research on the 'Cost of non-Europe'—Basic findings: The Cost of non-Europe in the Pharmaceutical Industry.* (Luxembourg).

Committee of Inquiry on Small Firms (1971), *Report of the Committee of Inquiry on Small Firms [Bolton Report]*, Cmnd. 4811. London.

Cosh, A. and Hughes, A. (1996), *The Changing State of British Enterprise*. ESRC Centre for Business Research, Cambridge.

Department of Trade and Industry (1996), *Small Firms in Britain*. London.

Driver, C. and Dunne, P. (1992), *Structural Change in the UK Economy*. Cambridge.

Gatrell, V. A. C. (1977), 'Labour Power and the Size of Firms in Lancashire Fallen in the Second Quarter of the Nineteenth Century', *Economic History Review*.

Hancher, L. (1990), *Regulating for Competition: Government, Law and the Pharmaceutical Industry in the United Kingdom and France*. Oxford.

Hannah, L. and Kay, J. A. (1977), *Concentration in Modern Industry*. London.

Harrop, J. (1985), 'Crisis in the Machine Tool Industry: A Policy Dilemma for the European Industry', *Journal of Common Market Studies*, 24/1: 61–75.

Hughes, A. (1993), 'Industrial Concentration and Small Firms in the United Kingdom: The 1980s in Historical Perspective' in Acs and Audretsch (eds.), *Small Firms and Entrepreneurship: An East–West Perspective*. Cambridge.

Jewkes, J., Sawers, D., and Stillerman, R. (1970), *Sources of Invention*, 2nd edn. London.

Keeble, D., Bryson, J., and Wood, P. (1993), *Management Consultancy Small Firms: Creation, Growth and Dynamics in the UK*. Cambridge.

Macmillan, H. (1938), *The Middle Way*. London.

Marshall, A. (1923), *The Modernisation of Old Industries: The Case of Textiles and Clothing in Britain*, Centre for Economic Performance, Working Paper no. 403.

Robertson, D. and Dennison, S. (1960), *The Control of Industry*. Cambridge.

Schumpeter, J. A. (1950), *Capitalism, Socialism and Democracy*, 3rd edn. New York.

Senbenelli, A., and Simpson, P. (1993), *The UK Machine Tool Industry*, Ceris-CNR Working Paper no. 3/1993. Turin.

Smith, A. (1937), *An Inquiry into the Nature and Causes of the Wealth of Nations*, ed. E. Cannan. New York.

Steindl, J. (1945), *Small and Big Business*. Oxford.

Thomas, C. (1958), 'The Pharmaceutical Industry', in Burn (ed.), *The Structure of British Industry*.

Wood, E. (1997), *Small and Large Firms in the Innovation Process*, mimeo. Cambridge.

5

Small-Scale Business in Germany: The Flexible Element of Economic Growth

ULRICH WENGENROTH

Small-scale business was a flexible element of economic growth in Germany,[1] and it was flexible in two ways: First, it transformed itself from a pre-modern and anti-industrial stronghold of corporatism to a competitive partner in a rapidly changing industrial society. Secondly, in providing technology-intensive services and tailor-made applications, it paved the way for the advance of mass-produced industrial goods into domestic markets. Earlier than industry, small-scale business blurred the distinction between manufacturing and services, thereby reconciling economies of scale in industrial production with growing diversity on the side of consumption. Rather than direct competition and marginalization, co-evolution of small and big business has been characteristic of the last century of German economic history. To be sure, the position of small business during this period was always challenged, and survival was never guaranteed. Only by flexibly adapting to new functional requirements in an economy that was ever more dominated by large enterprise, did small-scale business continue to flourish. Small-scale business did not control the many vicissitudes to which it was exposed. It is no surprise, therefore, that small businessmen mostly tried to resist the transformation of the German economy, which at the same time they were so successfully helping to bring about. And, when it came to institutions, small business never lost its historical backward orientation, inventing traditions of a golden past that never was. Thus, despite well-proven adaptability, the mentality of its entrepreneurs, as well as a large portion of the institutional arrangements and legislation for small firms, can only be understood if viewed against the backgound of retrospective ideals.

'Mittelstand'—the German Idea of Small Business

Small-scale business in manufacturing and distribution in Germany grew out of two pre-industrial traditions: the guild crafts and trades in the towns, and the rural putting-out system. After the introduction of 'Gewerbefreiheit' (freedom of trade) and the creation of a national customs union in the first half of the nineteenth century, these two traditions began to merge into the single socio-economic unit of small business. Gradually over the twentieth century, and especially after the Second World War, the formerly distinct and often mutually hostile groups of artisans, petty industrialists, and merchants found their common identity in the 'mittelständische Unternehmen' (middle-class enterprises). On the local and regional level they are organized and represented by semi-public Craft Chambers and Chambers of Commerce and Industry.[2]

The term 'Mittelstand', literally 'middle-estate', has strong corporatist overtones. It creates a collective unity of small business as a pre-modern 'estate' and betrays continuing mental reservations against *laissez-faire* capitalism. Its ideological roots are to be found in the pre-industrial possessive individualism which distinguished it from the 'new' middle class of white-collar workers and professionals.[3] Until well after the Second World War the term 'Mittelstand' invoked anti-modern feelings in setting a small family-centred and self-reliant economic unit against the antagonistic classes of industrial society. Not surprisingly the 'Mittelstand' was successfully wooed by the Nazis during the years of rapid modernization and economic upheaval in the late 1920s.[4]

'Mittelstand' has always been a defensive concept, very unlike the recent optimism for highly innovative small business. The latter is typically presented as 'young' or 'specialized' enterprise, not mentioning family ties but stressing anonymous entrepreneurial qualities. A great variety of legal forms notwithstanding, most small firms are still family-owned, even if ever more management is being recruited from outside. The gradual transition from stressing family embeddedness to stressing market embeddedness has been long and often imperfect, and the effort to bridge the tension between 'Mittelstand' and 'Unternehmertum' (enterpreneurship) in creating the category of 'mittelständische Unternehmen' for small-scale business was never fully successful. Small-scale business in Germany has been Janus-faced throughout the twentieth century.

The size of what has been understood to be small-scale business has changed notably over the last hundred years. In the early years of Imperial Germany, companies with more than 50 employees were already considered to be large firms, and those with 6–50 were described as middle-sized; this categorization held well into the inter-war years (Gantzel 1962: 108). To some of today's sources, companies with up to 49 employees are small firms, while those with 50–500 employees fall into the category of medium-sized business, although others would include these larger firms in small-scale business as well (Institut für Mittelstandsforschung 1976: 1–30; Boswell 1972: 15–16).[5] The latter group would have been in the top category before the First World War.[6] Other parameters, like output, can lead to almost absurd juxtapositions. A modern mini-mill in the steel industry, employing not more than 400 workers, can turn out as much steel annually (1 million tons) as the complete German steel industry did in 1870, then employing more than 56,000 workers.[7] Growing capital intensiveness made companies 'small' although their output grew immensely. The latter is especially true for some formerly labour-intensive industries like textiles, where investment costs in spinning are up to $1 million per job created and new companies have very little employment.[8] The 'smallness' of small-scale business is not unambiguous.

For most of the post-war years small business has been looked down upon as business that failed to grow. In the inter-war years, however, it was seen as a pillar of social stability, and in recent years the big business strategy of 'downsizing' has had a dramatic effect on the ruling paradigms of industrial efficiency. No longer are 'mittelständische Unternehmen' and their continuous demands for protection and tax preferences a source of embarrassment to conservative and liberal politicians. Today, all hopes for industrial revival and job creation are pinned upon them, while their much-praised flexibility all too often turns out to include a more or less voluntary withdrawal from the market. Their greater capacity to suffer, as much as their greater ability to redirect their resources, always made them popular in times of economic crisis and upheaval. The recent paradigm shift from 'big' to 'lean' is a shake-up of the industrial and social structure where flexible elements are needed, and small business immediately comes to mind.

In German history the issue of small business has always been prominent in times of continuing economic stress. The first major inquiry into the situation of the crafts in competition with big industry dates from the end of the Great Depression of the late nineteenth century,[9] and the next inquiry into 'Handwerk' (craft) was published in 1930 (Ausschuß zur Untersuchung der Erzeugungs- und Absatzbedingungen der deutschen Wirtschaft 1930). At the time of the latter inquiry, a research team of economists was also formed to investigate in the possibility of transferring the then crisis-proof small-business culture of Württemberg to the problem-stricken province of Ostpreußen. This was the first time in Germany that small business was explicitly presented as a panacea to severe structural problems in times of economic crisis and decline (Preiser 1937). The increasing number of small craftshops after the Second World War, when returning soldiers and refugees from the Eastern provinces could not find employment in industry, corroborated this view (Puderbach 1967: 135–6). Today's discussion takes place in view of persistently high unemployment and de-industrialization since the mid-1970s, when the first wave of literature on 'small is beautiful' made its appearance.[10] If historians of small business are to welcome this revived interest in their subject, the vicissitudes of related public debate must also form part of the analysis.

Regulation and Corporatism: 'Handwerk' and Shopkeepers

A peculiarity of the German discussion of small-scale business is the prominent role played by 'Handwerk' (craft). Most research and investigations concerning small business focused on this large subgroup, which had grown out of the guild crafts of pre-industrial times. The two inquiries of 1895–7 and 1930 concentrated on 'Handwerk', and much of the 'Mittelstandsforschung' (Mittelstand-research) of the Federal Republic was in fact research into the conditions of 'Handwerk'. To German politics, 'Handwerk' as a social entity has been more important than small-scale business. And, since 'Handwerk' is often small scale, it has been taken to represent small business in international comparisons as well as in the national accounts of 'Kleingewerbe', which translates into 'small business'. Because of this tradition in history, economics, and social science, much research on German small business continues to suffer from this bias in the literature and in statistical data. Since a 'Handwerk' business could have over 1,000 employees in the fairly recent past (Fischer 1972*a*: 350), the elaborate 'Handwerk' statistics are of limited use only if bona fide small business is at issue. With an average work-force of close to 9 employees per 'Handwerk' business in the 1980s, 'Handwerk' is very close to the average of 10.4 for all business in Germany (Statistisches Bundesamt 1995: 128–31; Lenger 1988: 210–11). When it comes to mentality and the public image, however, 'Handwerk' continues to be almost a separate institution. Until today 'Handwerk' other than small-scale industry has connotations of quality, high skills, local embeddedness, and tradition, all of which are anchored to formal apprenticeship and corporate quality control. Both were strengthened at the time of the first 'Handwerk' inquiry.

In 1897 the Imperial Parliament passed legislation that allowed for the setting up of official guilds and established 'Handwerkskammern' (Craft Chambers) as semi-public bodies. Guilds, which had been reintroduced in 1881 as voluntary organizations, could again be made compulsory at the request of the local craftsmen. They regulated submissions, vocational training, and watched over quality standards. Finally, in 1908, formal control over apprenticeship was re-enforced. Much of the earlier freedom of trade legislation was revoked in favour of corporate regulations (Wernet 1952:

156).[11] In 1934 the new Nazi government made all guilds compulsory and for the first time gave them control over new business by insisting on a master's diploma issued by a craft chamber (Kaufhold 1979: 131).[12]

This neo-corporate legislation was reaffirmed after the Second World War when the Allies eventually lost control over trade regulation in Western Germany. The American military government had abolished all the institutional pillars of corporatism, including compulsory guilds, the master's diploma requirement, price regulations, and submission cartels, and had reintroduced freedom-of-trades legislation as in the nineteenth century. But with new legislation on 'Handwerk' in 1953, regulatory politics became reminiscent of the Nazi years, and it was again prohibited to open a business in one of the local crafts without a formal 'großer Befähigungsnachweis' (major certificate of qualification) by the crafts chambers.[13] Crafts chamber membership was not dependent on the size of business, whether in terms of employment or financial turnover. Therefore, many substantial manufacturing businesses with up to several hundred employees would benefit from the same corporate networks, and participate in the same submissions regulations. Small-scale business was regulated and constrained in its competitive freedom whenever it fell into one of the categories of 'Handwerk', and, while entrepreneurial activity was not stifled, it was shaped in a strongly corporatist fashion. The anti-*laissez-faire* ideology of the 'Mittelstand' had its stronghold in the corporatist world of 'Handwerk', which continuously spilled over into other small-scale business.

In the Empire, 'Handwerk' had been part of the self-styled 'Schaffende Stände' (productive estates) as opposed to merchants, bankers, pedlars, etc., who were 'mere' capitalists or 'usurers'. The pride of 'Handwerk' went beyond entrepreneurial values and constituted moral claims on protection from market forces. A fair clientele for every master according to the premodern 'Nahrungsprinzip' (principle of sustenance) was the linchpin of political claims. One of the craft journals argued that 'a strong broad middle stratum is indispensable for the social structure' (Blackbourn 1984: 50), and craftsmen felt that competition from putting-out labour was as much or even more of a nuisance than mass-produced industrial commodities. Pedlars and consumer co-operatives, both offering cheap products from outside the region, were the targets of incessant complaints; self-exploitation of the craftsmen and their families became the rule.[14]

In a revolution of rising expectations, 'Handwerk' had grown spectacularly in numbers after the freedom-of-trades legislation in the first half of the nineteenth century. When this expansion subsided towards the end of the century, and many groups of 'Handwerk' fell visibly behind general economic growth,[15] craftsmen turned against the liberal institutions of industrial Germany and enforced the reintroduction of corporate organizations. Alongside coal-mining, the iron and steel industry, estate owners, and peasants, 'Handwerk' was one of the noisiest if not one of the best organized interest groups before the First World War (Blackbourn 1984: 35)—much more audible than shopkeepers.

Retailers, it is true, did on average benefit more from urbanization and industrialization, since chain stores and department stores were slow to develop in Germany. From 1895 to 1907 the number of retail outlets with less than five employees rose from 560,000 to 800,000 (Gellately 1974: 13). The somewhat differently composed census of 1925 shows 1.1 million businesses in the category 'commerce and traffic' with a labour force of more than five million, two million of whom worked in places with not more than three employees (Preller 1949: 109–15). If there were some protective measures in individual states against competition from consumer co-operatives, however, the greatest grievance of enterprising small retailers was dearth of capital, not least to cover the extended credits they gave to their customers.[16]

While the Nazi government did not live up to its earlier proclamations to expropriate the big department stores, it did place a temporary ban on further retail outlets in May 1933, and controlled concessions for retailing afterwards (Gesetz zum Schutz . . . 1933). With an average work-force of 2.6 per shop in 1933, trading was dominated by very small business. Antisemitic propaganda had focused on the 'middleman in the background', the wholesale merchant, and eventually left retailing alone (Tiburtius 1935). More important in limiting competition and the effects of economies of scale on the structure of retailing was enforceable resale price maintenance. Until January 1974 branded articles had fixed prices and left handsome profit margins. Nevertheless, this did not prevent supermarkets from offering non-branded food at bargain prices, thereby causing a massive decline in small grocers' shops ('Ladensterben') from the 1960s onward. This was counterbalanced, however, by the creation of more specialized shops. Mass retailing took off with the wide diffusion of private automobiles, and there were still some efforts in the 1970s to ban additional 'large surface' shopping centres (Winkel 1990: 200). The trend since the 'supermarket revolution' has been ambiguous. While the number of retail outlets fell in the 1960s and early 1970s, it grew again in the 1980s as a result of increasing differentiation and specialization, sometimes quite spectacular in prosperous cities. In Munich, for example, the total number of retail outlets grew from 26,150 in 1980 to 39,503 in 1988 (Winkel 1990: 201). In the long run, the number of businesses in retailing was remarkably stable, with about 460,000 from 1950 to 1970 and a subsequent decline to 400,000 in 1987 (Winkel 1974: 150; Statistisches Bundesamt 1995: 131).

As mass-consumption gathered momentum, many self-employed craftsmen turned to selling industrial products, which they would then service. Reliable data on the importance of retailing among 'Handwerker' do not exist for the early period, but in 1935 about 10 per cent of all returns of 'Handwerk' came from retailing. Thereafter its share grew continuously to surpass 25 per cent around 1960. Differences between trades were significant.

In 1955 clockmakers and radio and television electricians had the highest share at 80 per cent, while house-painters had a mere 4 per cent (Beckermann 1959: 101–2; 1966: 84). Without the protection of enforceable resale price maintenance, however, 'Handwerk' came under pressure from department stores and specialized chain stores for durable consumer products.

Small retailing business was usually well embedded in its social environment. Although informal consumer credits lost importance when banks and credit card organizations offered ever more financial services to ordinary people, personal acquaintance with customers continued to be the rule. A field inquiry in the early 1960s showed that 70 per cent of all retailers, including 'Handwerk', did most of their business with regular customers (Institut für Mittelstandsforschung 1962: 161–5). In this context it has been argued by experts of Chambers of Commerce and Industry that small businesses were virtual monopolists in their neighbourhood markets ('Zum Begriff des Mittelstandes', 1959: 163). With an average labour force of 6.3 per firm compared with an average of 10.4 in the whole economy, retailing is still dominated by small business. Half of all sales staff in 1987 were in the category of business with fewer than 20 employees (Statistisches Bundesamt 1995: 131).

Financial Services for Small-Scale Business

Since the great banks would not lend to small business in the nineteenth century, enterprises in this category had to resort to municipal savings-banks and co-operative credit-unions (Kreditgenossenschaften). Funding by these unions virtually exploded in the half-century before the First World War from around 8 million marks in 1860 to close to 4 billion marks in the first decade of the twentieth century. Their share of all banking investment went from 2.9 per cent (early 1860s) to 7 per cent (1910s) (Fischer 1972*a*: 347). At the same time, city councils helped with the creation of a growing number of local savings banks backed up by municipal guarantees. Their numbers grew continually through the nineteenth century, reaching 3,133 by 1913, with total deposits of nearly 20 billion marks. This compares with 21 billion marks for all private German credit banks combined (Tilly 1976: 591). These savings banks were introduced to encourage saving among the petty bourgeoisie, artisans, and workers. They had no own capital, sufficing with a back-up guarantee from the municipality, and they did not pay trade tax. Beginning in the 1880s the savings banks increasingly transformed themselves into a German-type universal bank for small business. Legally this process was settled in 1908 when they were authorized to issue cheques and to conduct transfer business (Born 1977:

204–8). It has been estimated that the total deposits of small-scale business in savings banks amounted to 6 billion marks in 1913, which would have made them the most important financial institution for craftsmen, shop-keepers, and petty industrialists (Fischer 1972*a*: 346).

Today co-operative banks and savings banks provide a complete range of financial services to their small-scale business clients. They have close contacts to the Chambers of Commerce and Industry and offer specialized information services on local and regional levels, where they often perform better than the great credit banks. After the Second World War, Chambers of Commerce and Industry together with local savings banks, co-operative banks, and government, created credit guarantee institutions to finance small-scale business (Sauer 1984: 85–6). An important boost was given to small business in the 1950s by low-interest loans, as the federal government provided easy access to capital by making large loans from the European Recovery Program available for small business (Winkel 1974: 166–7). Even thirty years after the war, these funds, which were repaid and re-lent on an ongoing basis, continued to be an important capital source for small busi-ness. During the economic crisis of the 1970s the federal government in-creased the total loans to small business, rising to almost 2 billion DM by 1981. Interest rates for these loans were typically 2–2.5 per cent lower than the market rate (Sauer 1984: 85–6).

Small-Scale Manufacturing and Technology

With the advent of machine tools and electric motors,[17] it becomes very difficult to distinguish between crafts and small-scale industry on the basis of capital goods or products. Sociologically, however, it was of great differ-ence whether small companies settled complacently within the corporate framework or broke out of the strait-jacket of compulsory guilds and sub-missions regulations. Small firms outside the protective order of 'Handwerk' often had their roots in the rural putting-out system and the proto-industrial setting of early modern 'Gewerbelandschaften' (trade and manufacturing regions) with their highly decentralized, light manufacturing industries.[18]

The critical moment in their development came with mechanization and technological economies of scale, as power requirements for production machinery had created an industrial divide. Unless small-scale water power was still available or had been in the possession of a small concern from pre-industrial times, the investment costs of and regulations for steam engines often proved to be an unsurmountable barrier of entry. The vast literature on small motors (water-power, kerosene, gas, petroleum, hot air, steam, electricity) gives evidence of this technological trap for small business. The human motor was often not powerful enough to operate the new machine tools. Scaled-down versions of models from industry were just sufficient for the odd repair job (Benad-Wagenhoff 1989: 151–75).

Many observers in the second half of the nineteenth century believed that small, easy-to-handle motors would be a panacea for all the problems of cottage industries and craft-shops. Most designers of small motors had small business in mind. Nikolaus Otto, inventor of the four-stroke gas motor, had learned about the misery of putting-out labour when he was assistant to a textile merchant in the Rhineland. Siemens, Pirelli, Diesel, and others all had hoped to bring industry back to the fold of the family with the help of small motors (Wengenroth 1989a: 177–89). A working solution for the majority of trades was eventually brought about by robust electric motors after the turn of the century.[19] The rapid expansion of decentralized 'model regions' of small manufacturing business, such as Württemberg, only began when regional electrification gathered momentum in the early twentieth century and the inter-war years.[20] Before this, small manufacturing enterprise could only thrive when it had little or no competition from industrial producers of the same commodities. This explains the expansion of small-scale builders' companies or, in the absence of mass retailing before the 1960s, the flourishing of local bakers and butchers.

Case-studies

The great variety of small-scale business and the absence of useful aggregate data make it very difficult to properly assess specific alternatives and entrepreneurial strategies during the last century. Between the Scylla of meaningless homogenization and the Charybdis of chaotic detail, the following case-studies seek to illuminate some ideal types within small-scale business history.

Innovations for Manual Production

A good example for the impact of 'appropriate' technologies on small business was cigar-making (Kölling 1997). Cigars were very popular before the First World War, and cigar-making was a rapidly expanding business. The number of German tobacco factories soared from 3,322 in 1861 to 19,357 in 1907. Total employment then stood at 200,000 and was equal to employment in the steel industry (Jersch-Wenzel and Krengel 1984: 409; Kölling 1997).[21] This means that the average-size 'tobacco factory' had 10 employees; since the average number of employees had been near 20 in 1861, the tobacco industry did in fact decentralize while growing. This expansion was largely based on demand for cigars using 65 per cent of all tobacco in 1912 against 43 per cent in 1877. Total production went from 5 billion to more than 8 billion cigars annually.

Rolling and wrapping cigars had been an exclusively manual process until the 1850s when the first cigar-forms were introduced. With these forms the bodies of twenty cigars could be made simultaneously and only the wrapper had to be applied manually. From the 1860s cheap cigars for mass consumption were all made with these forms. Production per team of one 'roller' and one 'wrapper' increased from 1,500 to 2,500 cigars per week, allowing for lower-priced, mass-consumption cigars. The forms reduced the skills necessary to roll cigars, although wrapping continued to be a very delicate job, and cigar-makers now began to employ mostly female helpers. In the 1880s the share of female labour in the tobacco industry exceeded 50 per cent with women eventually working as 'wrappers' as well. Centres of small-scale cigar manufacture were rural regions in Saxony and Baden, where cigar-making often replaced jobs in declining textile trades like home-weaving, thus becoming a stabilizing element in rural labour markets.

All efforts to mechanize cigar-making failed. This was not the case with cigarettes, however. At the eve of the war 103 cigarette machines in Berlin alone turned out more than 8 million cigarettes annually. When male cigar-makers were recruited to the army, and as cigarette machines continued to operate, consumer preference eventually shifted to cigarettes and the cigar industry went into decline.

The fate of the cigar industry demonstrates that small-scale business did benefit from technical innovation—the forms—as long as it was not capital-intensive. Such an innovation could even reverse the trend towards con-centration for several decades and still create a large industry in terms of total employment. A second important observation is that small-scale cigar manufacturing was not replaced by large-scale cigar manufacturing, but by a similar product that could be mass produced employing automatic power-driven production machinery. This shift in consumer preferences, however, resulted in large measure from the impact of the First World War on cigar supplies. Although cigarettes had been around for decades, they had failed to win a large market share until the war.

From Manufacturing to Servicing

Cigar-making was atypical of expanding small-scale manufacturing, in so far as it could be done without motors. That the introduction of motorized machine tools had ambiguous effects on the prospects of small business has been shown in a comparative study of wheelwrights and blacksmiths who co-operated in providing the means for rural transport (Mende 1989: 93–129). At first sight wheelwrights could benefit more from electric motors since these motors could drive a great number of machine tools from jig-saws to band-saws, drilling machines, planers, wood-chipping machines, etc. Blacksmiths would not be able to use many motorized tools for horse-shoes, ploughshares, scythes, and axles.

Growing demand for agricultural vehicles was the backbone of business for both, and led to close co-operation. Nevertheless, wheelwrights were soon to suffer from side-effects of new technology since rubber tyres were substituted for iron hoops and required wheels and axles of steel. This ef-fect alone reduced the wheelwright's share of the sales price of a hay-cart from 35 per cent to less than 10 per cent, while the blacksmith could at least sell and service the new wheels. As bad, however, was that electric motors, specifically electric circular-saws and electric hand tools, were also avail-able to farmers. The wooden construction that was left of rubber tyre hay-carts could now be repaired on the farm. Wheelwrights, fully equipped with electric machine tools, gave up.

Meanwhile, the skills of blacksmiths in working with the more difficult materials of iron and steel could be transferred from horseshoes and ploughshares to tractors and reapers, and thence to automobiles. The trans-ition from timber to steel in rural transport and agricultural machinery opened more than just a survival strategy for blacksmiths, who became ser-vice agents for industrial products. In only seven years, from 1949 to 1956, the number of 'blacksmiths concentrating on agricultural vehicles', i.e. tractors and reapers, grew by 385 per cent (Beckermann 1959: 39).

The same was true for many plumbers and mechanics who turned from manufacturing simple tools and utensils to selling and servicing more soph-isticated industrial products. They benefited from a growing diversity of industrial products which found their way into private households and eventually required more labour for servicing during their lifetime than for manufacturing in the first place. In these instances small-scale business was the precondition for mass consumption, and therefore mass production of industrial products. Instead of devastating competition from industry, as was feared in the above-cited inquiries into the state of 'Handwerk', there often arose mutual dependency and symbiosis in making complex indus-trial products available for consumption, with the classic example being the private motor car.

The Locality of Resources

Business history has many examples of industrial enterprise going from one product to another while preserving its productive resources. A German example would be Opel, going from sewing machines to bicycles and eventually to automobiles. A farrier's shop turned into a sales and service point for cars follows the same pattern. In both cases accumulated skills are better reference points for entrepreneurial continuity than inventory and locality. Given the strong local embeddedness of small-scale business and its premises, however, there is a second path to continuity that can be observed. The case-study of a paper-mill in Southern Germany, which has been a local resource for small business for more than two hundred years, exemplifies this (Schmidt 1989).

The mill was started in order to make paper using local water power. When it turned out that competition by major paper-makers could not be successfully met, the owners converted it to make cardboard. Because of the regional practice of partible inheritance, the mill changed owners and partners repeatedly and was continuously adapted, extended, and rebuilt for new products. In the nineteenth century the water power was used to add a sawmill, an oil-mill, a hemp-brake, and a tanning-mill. In 1890, when the water supply finally proved insufficient for the plethora of different activities in 1890, a gasoline motor was added. Thirty years later it was replaced by a more powerful Diesel engine. Outside electrical supply came in 1941, and the first turbine in 1951. Today the paper-mill is a restaurant and a local attraction. There was nothing stagnant about what was a focus of local entrepreneurial activity through two centuries. The place never lay idle.

A history of the many 'firms' operating on the premises of the paper-mill in the past would be a history of many short-lived business careers and would smack of failure. A business history concentrating on the institution of the legal firm would never discover two centuries of uninterrupted entrepreneurial activities. Small-scale business has often been ridiculed as 'easy in, easy out', assuming that the longevity of a firm was the litmus test of success. The flexibility of small-scale business, however, seems to positively incorporate a strategy of 'easy in, easy out', thereby making small firms transitory events for transitory needs and opportunities. The paper-mill in our case-study did not perish for two centuries, instead it provided the basis for a number of transitory opportunities which were taken advantage of by alternating entrepreneurs. It had more in common with a shopping-mall housing a number of boutiques run by regularly changing managers than with an industrial enterprise.

Since these shopkeepers usually don't go bankrupt when they wind up one business to start the next, the longevity of a particular small-business environment seems a more appropriate yardstick for the success of this form of business than the lifetime of the 'firm'. The long-lasting economic stability of traditional European centres of crafts, trades, and services also points in the same direction, directly contrasting with the desperate problems of 'new' (i.e. nineteenth century) industrial conurbations. Very often the conditions of successful performance of a service to the economy—

local, regional, or national—reside in smallness. In this sense, as in many other respects, the question of large versus small business, which had dominated the major inquiries into the state of 'Handwerk', is beside the point.

Decentralized Industry

Mass production in Germany, like anywhere else, has fostered large industrial enterprises which came to dominate the public image of industry. It has often been overlooked, however, that even mass production of a very limited range of standardized goods is based on a great variety of inputs, and that the production of these inputs does not necessarily require or benefit from large organizations. Satisfactory statistics concerning small-scale industry are often lacking, and here again we have no aggregate data to quantitatively assess the importance of subcontracting. We must therefore resort to available examples. A well-documented case of the post-war situation is the car manufacturer Daimler-Benz, where subcontractors supplying material and services for less than 20,000 DM (about $4,750) annually have been recorded (Herrigel 1996: 155–6). In 1950, 90 per cent of the company's 12,643 suppliers fell into this category. Eight years later the small suppliers composed 82 per cent of the total of 15,388. These suppliers were not necessarily all small-scale businesses, but they show the extent to which a large manufacturer needed small specialized inputs, thus creating a vast scope of business opportunities in the vicinity. In the late 1950s almost two-thirds of the costs of production at Daimler-Benz resulted from supplier sales to the company. Gary Herrigel called this a 'new hybrid mass-production strategy', where suppliers were used 'as external sources of manufacturing capacity' (Herrigel 1996: 155).

The 1960s were a high-water mark of the literature on the transformation of small manufacturing business into subcontractors and suppliers to big industry. It was the time when small firms became conspicuously more capital-intensive, as has also been noted in the studies on the transformation of 'Handwerk'. Capital-intensity in this category increased fourfold from the mid-1950s to the early 1970s with technology-intensive services like automobile and television repair being the leading growth sectors (Beckerman 1974: 110–14; Fischer 1972*a*: 355–6). Small-scale manufacturers, however, caught the most attention in the 1980s, albeit without unanimity over their success.[22] The problem often remains as one of interpreting survival as a sign of profitability and therefore economic success, when the borderline between company funds and private means of the owners is in fact opaque. It cannot be outruled that the survival of small companies is to a large extent an expression of their greater endurance under unfavourable conditions, as has been cynically praised by buffer theorists of small-scale business in the past (Wengenroth 1996).

Another problem is where to draw the dividing line between small- and medium-scale business, as has been discussed in the introduction. If one restricts small business to the two lower categories of the Federal statistics, i.e. 1–19 employees, the most recent history as well as the outlook for small manufacturing business appears rather sombre. But the picture changes if one includes the category of 20–499. The individual success stories in most cases are medium-scale, with a labour force between 200 and 1,500. Gary Herrigel's admirable account of 'decentralized industrial order since 1945' (Herrigel 1996: 143–204) is full of examples from this category, which lies across those of the official statistics. The same is true for the 'hidden champions', small- and medium-sized manufacturing firms which have dominating positions in the world market. They tend to have about 1,000 employees, with few exceptions below 200.[23]

Small Scale for the World Market

Small-scale business is mostly associated with local or at best regional demand, while geographically extensive markets are seen to be the privilege of big firms. The orthodox view maintains that world-wide trading overtaxes the management resources of small firms. However, this does not always seem to be case. To cite an admittedly extreme example, consider the case of *Carl Jäger*, a firm with 10 employees and a share of the world market in its product range (incense cones and sticks) of 70 per cent. Another example is *Söring*, with a labour force of 20 and a 36 per cent share of the world market for ultrasonic cut-off devices (Ultraschall-Trenngeräte). Other German small-scale manufacturers selling worldwide are *Baader*, with 90 per cent in fish-filleting machinery, or *Pustefix*, a maker of liquid for blow-bubbles with an unknown, since unrecorded, market share, but which exports to more than 50 countries (Simon 1996: 12, 26, 55, 77). It is difficult to see how these extremely successful activities could benefit from bigger company structures. What the products of these 'hidden champions' lack in public attention, they make up for in diversity and number. As long as there are children who love blow-bubbles, and Catholics and orthodox Christians who attend mass, small-scale business like the examples above will be the most appropriate form to serve these needs. In arriving at a monopolistic position in the world market, they have achieved everything a manufacturing enterprise can hope for. If they are not typical of small-scale business, this is no different from large-scale business, which also does not typically maintain monopolistic positions.

Conclusion

Small-scale business in Germany has been a flexible element of economic growth in many respects. It translated mass production of consumer durables into mass consumption. It was a source of skills for industry in particular and society in general. It was the external skeleton of industrial production. It provided the decentralized and highly flexible provision networks for growing conurbations. It was a buffer for the labour market. And it was an optimum efficient scale of production for a huge variety of commodities.

Small business was the catalyst of industrial growth in providing the background of skills and services which alone made possible the mass consumption of industrial product. Jean Baudrillard has observed that in economic growth the corollary of productivity is consumptivity, being the ability of industrial society to increasingly absorb its own products (Baudrillard 1972: 87–9).[24] Growing consumptivity is as much a cultural achievement as growing productivity; the two are mirror-imaged twins. Had small business not been able to make industrial products intelligible, usable, and durable through servicing, repair, installation, and advice, consumer skills for the plethora of often complicated modern artefacts would never have developed to the extent that they did (Wengenroth 1997). In giving up production of artefacts and turning to their selling and servicing, many small businesses opened the outlets for economies of scale in production and made economic growth happen.

Small business in Germany was probably more skill-conscious than small business in many other countries. The corporate strategy of 'Handwerk' to defend social status through skill control helped to provide a large pool of highly qualified labour which could cope with both production and servicing of technology-intensive novelties, although this does not necessarily mean that German small business was technologically superior to its foreign counterparts. On one hand, formal skill control guarantees a high level of minimum competence among the work-force; on the other, it introduces rigidities in skill formation and is notoriously slow in embracing new and changing technologies. In the very recent past, i.e. the late 1980s and the 1990s, there have been indications that some of the rigid effects of formal skill control and its legal skeleton were detrimental to the adaptibility of decentralized small-scale manufacturing,[25] but empirical proof is still hard to find.

The secondary effects of strictly regulated apprenticeship seem to have been as valuable for the formation of a skilled work-force as was formal education in the dual system of schools and workshops. In promoting a professional ethos and self-esteem among journeymen and many blue-collar workers, small business significantly contributed to the formation of a corps of highly motivated and 'responsible' manual workers and technicians with basic technological competence. To a large extent, this contribution manifested itself as much in the creation of attitudes toward technology as in the intellectual and physical command of it. These 'social' skills of engineering were certainly as important for the diffusion of technology-intensive consumer goods and services as was the more formal knowledge of the underlying technologies.

Since these 'social' skills of engineering among small-scale business were an unintended side-effect of formal apprenticeship, one would expect them to arise under different conditions and in other countries as well and constitute a more general and essential characteristic of small-scale business in industrial societies. Strict formal skill control was a particularly German way to achieve this end. Whether it was a particularly economical way, let alone the only way, is open to debate and probably very difficult to test. Corporate skill control was certainly expensive, since it limited access to and competition in a large sector of small-business activities with more than 100 different trades. The balance of the trade-off between high skill levels and regulated markets is unknown. One should not overestimate the importance of formal skills, therefore, but rather include the 'professional' attitude into the skill pattern of German small business.

High and highly differentiated skills of this dual nature made small-scale business a perfect external skeleton to industry. It was a resource that massproducers could rely upon to provide the many variable inputs that were necessary and concentrate on economies of scale. The inevitable narrowmindedness of bulk-processing and homogenization of product was preserved by outsourcing long before 'outsourcing' became a catchword.

The qualities to provide the external skeleton of industry were very similar to those demanded by growing conurbations and increasing differentiation of lifestyles. Continuously shifting demand patterns on the micro level necessitated a continuous reappraisal of activities with local endowments and environments rather than production lines constituting continuity. Being part of the permanent flux of local opportunities and demand, not an outside source to provide for them, small-scale business anticipated the last cry of the boundary-less firm. Many small businesses were centred on neighbourhoods, local opportunities, and personal relationships, rather than on a legal existence as a particular 'firm'. Small-scale business was often more a strategy than an institution for tackling small-scale economic missions.[26]

These missions did not always have to be transitory nor did they have to grow. In this instance small scale was the optimum efficient scale of operations. With labour productivity incessantly increasing, one should expect ever more specific needs to fall into the category of small-scale production. What is incense and blow-bubbles today might be cold-rolled strip steel tomorrow, none of which are distinctly German. In this respect, the recent history and near future of small-scale business in Germany is quite unlikely to differ noticeably from that of other countries.

With hindsight, the whole controversy over whether small-scale business was a winner or a loser of industrialization was beside the point. Small-scale business was not a miniature version of big industry which failed to grow, nor was it industry without the rigidities of 'bigness'. It was neither 'superior' nor 'inferior' to large enterprise, but has been the appropriate organizational form for a great variety of economic activities in the past. If some activities crossed the borderline between 'big' and 'small', this is no reason to disqualify either of these categories.

NOTES

1. The former German Democratic Republic is not included in this survey. Temporary state socialism in this part of Germany created strikingly different conditions for small-scale business which were no continuation of a German tradition and which are very unlikely to become part of future traditions in the making. It was a history in its own right which cannot be done justice to in a short synthesis on 'Germany'.
2. Craft Chambers (Handwerkskammern) and Chambers of Commerce and Industry (Industrie- und Handelskammern) were not always separated. The crafts left the common chambers in the early 1900s, were incorporated again in 1934/1942, and left them again in the early 1950s. There was often a feeling among self-employed craftsmen that the Chambers of Commerce and Industry were dominated by 'big' companies. For an example of these discussions see Winkel (1990: 24–6, 150–2). The German term 'Handwerk' does not translate easily into English. It goes beyond 'craft' and is narrower than 'trade'. 'Handwerk' includes about 125 different occupations requiring a high level of non-academic skills and formal apprenticeship. Butchers, bakers, carpenters, engineers, tailors, hairdressers, plumbers, car mechanics, opticians, TV and computer servicepersons, etc. all fall in the category of 'Handwerk' and get their certificate of qualification (journeyman and master) from the local or regional Craft Chamber.
3. A high-water mark of the literature on the 'estate' nature of 'Mittelstand' is Marbach (1942). Twenty years later the 'Institut für Mittelstandsforschung' (literally: Institute for Middle-estate Research) still published books on the 'essence' of the 'middle-estate enterprise' (Gantzel 1962). The author presents 102 definitions of 'Mittelstand' from earlier publications and comes to the conclusion that in spite of all fundamental criticism 'Mittelstand' still was a qualitatively separate form of personal enterprise with a distinct 'Gesinnung' (mental attitude) of the entrepreneur (ibid. 279–86). He explicitly repudiates the

'pragmatic' American notion of 'small business' as being merely quantative (ibid. 114–21).

4. On the 'Nazification' of 'Mittelstand' see Leppert-Fögen (1974: ch. 4) and Winkler (1976: 1–18). In the German version of this article 'small business' is 'Mittelstand' (middle-estate) (Winkler 1978).

5. The census of the Federal Statistical Office on company size has four categories: 1–9, 10–19, 20–499, and 500+. The average size of all German business in the last census of 1987 was 10.4. While the two lower categories are clearly small business, the trouble begins with the category of 20–499 unless one includes all of them in small business. Average employment in this category was close to 64 in 1987, which would suggest that the majority of firms in this category were small firms with certainly less than 50 employees. In a balanced three-category scheme small business with up to 19 employees and big business with more than 500 both had 7.5 million employees in 1987. The intermediate category with a total of 6.9 million employees had little less (Statistisches Bundesamt 1995: 128–31).

6. The categories of the Imperial Statistics were: 1–5, 6–50, and 50+. Since the statistical office based its investigation on shops and workshops and not on companies, the data overemphasize the share of small business to an unknown extent (Kaiserliches Statistisches Amt 1914: 59; Hoffmann/Grumbach/Hesse 1965: 212).

7. The figures for 1870 include all wrought iron which was the equivalent of today's steel (Jersch-Wenzel and Krengel 1984: 409).

8. Figures for new spinning plant in Saxony in 1995. Personal communication, company, and location kept anonymous upon request.

9. *Untersuchungen über die Lage des Handwerks in Deutschland mit besonderer Rücksicht auf seine Konkurrenzfähigkeit gegenüber der Großindustrie* (Schriften des Vereins für Socialpolitik, vols. 62–70. Leipzig 1895–7). The 'Verein für Socialpolitik' was an association of liberal economists and social scientists. Between the census of 1882 and 1895 both the number of small businesses (up to 5 employees) and the total number of employment in this category had hardly declined (small business from 2,173,083 to 1,987,733; employment from 3,264,322 to 3,187,296) while industry was rapidly expanding. The share of small business (up to 5 employees) of the total labour force sank from almost 60 per cent in 1882 to 43 per cent in 1895 and eventually to less than 32 per cent in 1907. The same was true for small business' share of total manufacturing product (Kaufhold 1979: 109–12, 121). Small business was visibly suffering from relative decline.

10. On the importance of the 'traditional sector' (small business) for full employment and the inability of industry to redress the problem see Lutz 1984.

11. There is some debate over the effectivness of this legislation, however. For a sceptic view see Blackbourn 1977: 418–19.

12. See also the speech of the 'Reichshandwerkführer' (Führer of the Reich's crafts) of 17 May 1934, reprinted in Haupt 1985: 273–7.

13. Handwerksordnung, Para. 7 (1953). To the 'Handwerk' historian Friedrich Lenger this was an act of blunt restoration (Lenger 1988: 210).

14. On the trade-offs between growing market opportunities and intensifying competition before the First World War see Blackbourn 1989.

15. Between 1875 and 1907 the share of labour employed in companies with less than six workers had fallen from two-thirds to one third (Fischer 1972a: 343;

Kaiserliches Statistisches Amt 1914: 59). There were, however, many trades which benefited very much from urbanization. Among the success stories were builders, bakers and butchers, while most tailors and shoemakers could only survive with repair shops. Between 1849 and 1895 the number of self-employed masons almost doubled while the total number of masons more than tripled. There was concentration, however, with the ratio of self-employed : employed going from 1 : 5.5 to 1 : 10. The growth of butchers' shops was similar (Thissen 1901: 32).

16. The government of Hessen taxed consumer co-operatives because of 'the present difficult situation of small shopkeepers and the interest of the state in preserving the greatest possible number of independent "Mittelstand" existences' (34th Hessian Parliament 1908–11 (Blackbourn 1984: 51)). On capital shortage see ibid. 42. Blackbourn argues that generous consumer credits made small shops very attractive *vis-à-vis* less flexible department stores and anonymous retailing firms. The price premium was effectively an interest payment on advance delivery.

17. On the impact of electric motors in small-scale industry and the part played by small workshops in the electrification of German cities see Wengenroth 1989*a*: 177–205.

18. Gary Herrigel gives a very stimulating and often unorthodox account of these decentralized light industries (Herrigel 1996: chs. 2 and 5).

19. It was one of the main findings of the Parliamentary Inquiry in the late 1920s that very much to the surprise of most experts small manufacturing business had not declined in numbers since the turn of the century, and that electric-driven machine tools had to be credited for much of this effect (Ausschuß zur Untersuchung der Erzeugungs- und Absatzbedingungen der deutschen Wirtschaft 1930: 188–91).

20. On the electrification of Württemberg and the promotion of electric motors for small-scale business (Leiner 1985: i. 192, 200–1, 222; ii. 30–1). On the late but eventually very successful expansion of the decentralized manufacturing sector in Württemberg see Megerle 1982: 180–2.

21. All figures for cigar-making from Kölling. Since most of the literature on small-scale business in the Empire concentrated on 'Handwerk' and the question whether it did decline or not, only few authors noticed the simultaneous emergence of many small- and medium-scale industries like cigar-making.

22. For an enthusiastic view see Stephanie Weimer 1990. A more qualified assessment is given in Bade 1986.

23. Prominent examples of successful 'mittelständische Betriebe' quoted by Simon are: *Matthias Hohner*, accordions and mouth-organs, 85 per cent of world market, 1,050 employees; *Arnold & Richter*, 35 mm-film cameras, 70 per cent of world market, 700 employees; *Märklin*, toy railways, 55 per cent of world market, 1,700 employees; *Hensoldt & Söhne*, telescopic sights, 50 per cent of world market, 960 employees (Simon 1996: 26).

24. Baudrillard was of course not the first to make observations of this kind. An earlier, less well-remembered discussion of this problem is given in Knight 1951 [1935]: 22–3.

25. Herrigel is among the sceptics and provides interesting, though not fully conclusive evidence. It still seems to be too early to fully appreciate the current

problems of small German business in the manufacturing sector (Herrigel 1996: 198–204).
26. I owe the idea of 'business as a strategy' to Günter Bechtle (Bechtle 1980).

REFERENCES

Ausschuß zur Untersuchung der Erzeugungs- und Absatzbedingungen der deutschen Wirtschaft (1930), *Das deutsche Handwerk (Generalbericht). Verhandlungen und Berichte des Unterausschusses für Gewerbe: Industrie, Handel und Handwerk (III. Unterausschuß), 8. Arbeitsgruppe (Handwerk)* [*German Crafts (General Report). Proceedings and Reports of the Sub-committee on Trades: Industry, Commerce, and Crafts*]. Berlin: E. S. Mittler.

Bade, Franz-Josef (1986), 'The Economic Importance of Small and Medium-Sized Firms in the Federal Republic of Germany', in David Keeble and Egbert Wever (eds.), *New Firms and Regional Development in Europe*. London: Croom Helm.

Baudrillard, Jean (1972), *Pour une critique de l'économie politique du signe* [*For a Critique of the Political Economy of the Sign*]. Paris: Gallimard.

Bechtle, Günter (1980), *Betrieb als Strategie. Theoretische Vorarbeiten zu einem industriesoziologischen Konzept* [*Business as strategy: Theoretical preparations for a concept of industrial sociology*]. Frankfurt am Main: Campus.

Beckermann, Theo (1959), *Das Handwerk—Gestern und Heute* [*The Crafts—Yesterday and Tomorrow*]. Essen: Rheinisch-Westfälisches Institut für Wirtschaftsforschung.

—— (1966), 'Konjunktur und Konjunkturbeobachtung' ['Business Cycle and Business-Cycle Observation'], in W. Abel (ed.), *Das Handwerk in der modernen Wirtschaft und Gesellschaft* [*Crafts in Modern Economy and Society*]. Bad Wörrishofen: Holzmann.

—— (1974), *Das Handwerk im Wachstum der Wirtschaft* [*Crafts in a Growing Economy*]. Berlin: Duncker & Humblot.

Benad-Wagenhoff, Volker (1989), 'Spanabhebende Werkzeugmaschinen im metallverarbeitenden Betrieb' ['Metal-cutting Machines in Engineering Workshops'], in (Wengenroth, *Prekäre Selbstständigkeit*.)

Blackbourn, David (1977), 'The Mittelstand in German Society and Politics, 1871–1914', *Social History*, 4.

—— (1984), 'Between Resignation and Volatility: The German Petty Bourgeoisie in the Nineteenth Century', in Geoffrey Crossick and Heinz-Gerhard Haupt (eds.), *Shopkeepers and Master Artisans in Nineteenth-Century Europe*. London: Methuen.

—— (1989), 'Handwerker im Kaiserreich: Gewinner oder Verlierer?' ['Craftsmen in the Empire: Winners or Losers?'], in Wengenroth, *Prekäre Selbstständigkeit*.

Born, Karl Erich (1977), *Geld und Banken im 19. und 20. Jahrhundert* [*Money and Banks in the 19th and 20th Centuries*]. Stuttgart: Kröner.

Boswell, Jonathan (1972), *The Rise and Decline of Small Firms*. London: Allen & Unwin.

Fischer, Wolfram (1972a), 'Das deutsche Handwerk im Strukturwandel des 20. Jahrhunderts' ['German Crafts Under Structural Change During the 20th

Century'], in Wolfram Fischer, *Wirtschaft und Gesellschaft* [*Economy and Society*]. Göttingen: Vandenhoeck & Ruprecht.

—— (1972*b*), 'Die Rolle des Kleingewerbes im wirtschaftlichen Wachstumsprozeß in Deutschland 1850–1914' [The Role of Small-scale Business During Economic Growth in Germany, 1850–1914], in Fischer, *Wirtschaft und Gesellschaft*.

Gantzel, Klaus-Jürgen (1962), *Wesen und Begriff der mittelständischen Unternehmung* [*The Essence and Notion of the 'Middle-estate' Enterprise*]. Cologne: Westdeutscher Verlag.

Gellately, Robert (1974), *The Politics of Economic Despair: Shopkeepers and German Politics 1890–1914*. London: Sage.

Gesetz zum Schutz des Einzelhandels vom 12. Mai 1933. *Reichsgesetzblatt*, no. 50, 13 May 1933, pt. 1, p. 262.

Haupt, Heinz-Gerhard (1985) (ed.), *Die radikale Mitte. Lebensweise und Politik von Handwerkern und Kleinhändlern in Deutschland seit 1848* [*The Radical Centre: Way of Life and Politics of Craftsmen and Petty Retailers in Germany Since 1848*]. Munich: DTV.

Herrigel, Gary (1996), *Industrial Constructions: The Sources of German Industrial Power*. Cambridge: Cambridge University Press.

Hoffmann, W. G., Grumbach, F., and Hesse, H. (1965), *Das Wachstum der deutschen Wirtschaft seit der Mitte des 19. Jahrhunderts* [*Growth of the German Economy Since the Mid-19th Century*]. Berlin: Duncker & Humblot.

Institut für Mittelstandsforschung—Betriebswirtschaftliche Abteilung (1962), *Die Konkurrenzsituation mittelständischer Unternehmungen* [*The Competitive Situation of 'Middle-estate' Enterprise*]. Cologne: Westdeutscher Verlag.

—— (1976), *Zur Problemsituation mittelständischer Betriebe* [*On the Problems and Situation of 'Middle-estate' Firms*]. Göttingen: Vandenhoeck & Ruprecht.

Jersch-Wenzel, Stefi and Krengel, Jochen (1984), *Die Produktion der deutschen Hüttenindustrie 1850–1914. Ein historisch-statistisches Quellenwerk* [*The Production of the German Iron and Steel Industry: Historical-Statistical Sources*]. Berlin: Colloquium.

Kaiserliches Statistisches Amt (1914), *Statistisches Jahrbuch 1914* [*Statistical Yearbook 1914*]. Berlin: Schmidt-Verlag.

Kaufhold, Karl Heinrich (1979), 'Das Handwerk zwischen Anpassung und Verdrängung' ['Crafts Between Adaptation and Marginalization'], in Hans Pohl (ed.), *Sozialgeschichtliche Probleme in der Zeit der Hochindustrialisierung 1870–1914* [*Social-historical Problems in the Period of 'High Industrialization' 1870–1914*]. Paderborn: Schöningh.

Knight, Frank H. (1951 [1935]), *The Ethics of Consumption*. London: Allen & Unwin.

Kölling, Bernd (1997), 'Das zweite Brot. Technische Innovation und Arbeitsleben in der deutschen Zigarrenindustrie' ['The Second Bread: Technological Innovation and Working Life in the German Cigar Industry'], *Technikgeschichte*, 64.

Leiner, Wolfgang (1985), *Geschichte der Elektrizitätswirtschaft in Württemberg* [*History of the electric-power industry in Württemberg*], 2 vols. Stuttgart: Energieversorung Schwaben AG.

Lenger, Friedrich (1988), *Sozialgeschichte der deutschen Handwerker seit 1800* [*A Social History of German Craftsmen After 1800*]. Frankfurt am Main: Suhrkamp.

Leppert-Fögen, Anette (1974), *Die deklassierte Klasse. Studien zur Geschichte und Ideologie des Kleinbürgertums* [*The Downtrodden Class: Studies in the History and Ideology of the Petty Bourgeoisie*]. Frankfurt am Main: Fischer.

Lutz, Burkart (1984), *Der kurze Traum immerwährender Prosperität. Eine Neuinterpretation der industriell-kapitalistischen Entwicklung im Europa des 20. Jahrhunderts* [*The short dream of Everlasting Prosperity: A New Interpretation of Industrial-Capitalistic Development in 20th-Century Europe*]. Frankfurt am Main: Campus.

Marbach, Fritz (1942), *Theorie des Mittelstandes* [*Theory of the 'Middle-estate'*]. Berne: A. Francke.

Megerle, Klaus (1982), *Württemberg im Industrialisierungsprozeß Deutschlands. Ein Beitrag zur regionalen Differenzierung der Industrialisierung* [*Württemberg in the Process of German Industrialization: A Contribution to Regional Differentiation of Industrialization*]. Stuttgart: Klett.

Mende, Michael (1989), 'Verschwundene Stellmacher, gewandelte Schmiede. Die Handwerker des ländlichen Fahrzeugbaus zwischen expandierender Landwirtschaft und Motorisierung 1850–1960' ['Vanished Wheelwrights, Transformed Blacksmiths: The Craftsmen of Rural Vehicle-Manufacturing Between Expanding Agriculture and Motorization 1850–1960'], in Wengenroth, *Prekäre Selbstständigkeit*.

Preiser, Erich (1937), *Die württembergische Wirtschaft als Vorbild. Die Untersuchungen der Arbeitsgruppe Ostpreußen-Württemberg* [*The Wurttemberg Economy as a Model: Investigations of the Working Group East Prussia/Württemberg*]. Stuttgart: Kohlhammer.

Preller, Ludwig (1949), *Sozialpolitik in der Weimarer Republik* [*Social Policy in the Weimar Republic*]. Stuttgart: Franz Mittelbach.

Puderbach, Klaus (1967), 'Die Entwicklung des selbständigen Mittelstandes seit Beginn der Industrialisierung in Deutschland' ['The Development of self-employed 'Middle-estate' Since Early Industrialization in Germany'], Diss. University of Bonn.

Sauer, Willibrord (1984), 'Small Firms and the German Economic Miracle', in Cyril Levicki (ed.), *Small Business. Theory and Policy*. London: Croom Helm.

Schmidt, Frieder (1989), 'Pappenfabrikation als Marktnische' ['Cardboard Manufacturing as a Market Niche'], in Wengenroth, *Prekäre Selbstständigkeit*.

Simon, Hermann (1996), *Die heimlichen Gewinner. Die Erfolgsstrategien unbekannter Weltmarktführer* [*The Hidden Winners: Success Strategies of Unknown World-Market Leaders*]. Frankfurt am Main: Campus.

Statistisches Bundesamt (1995), *Statistisches Jahrbuch 1995 für die Bundesrepublik Deutschland* [*Statistical Yearbook of the Federal Republic of Germany, 1995*]. Stuttgart: Metzler-Poeschel.

Thissen, O. (1901), *Beiträge zur Geschichte des Handwerks in Preußen* [*Contributions to the History of the Crafts in Prussia*]. Tübingen: Laup.

Tiburtius, Joachim (1935), 'Der deutsche Einzelhandel im Wirtschaftsverlauf und in der Wirtschaftspolitik von 1925 bis 1935' ['German Retailing During the Fluctuations and the Economic Policy from 1925 to 1935'], *Jahrbuch für Nationalökonomie und Statistik, 1935*.

Tilly, Richard (1976), 'Verkehrs- und Nachrichtenwesen, Handel, Geld-, Kredit- und Versicherungswesen 1850–1914' ['Transport and Information, Commerce, Money, Credit and Insurance 1850–1914'], in Hermann Aubin and Wolfgang Zorn (eds.), *Handbuch der deutschen Wirtschafts- und Sozialgeschichte* [*Handbook of German Economic and Social History*], ii. Stuttgart: Union.

Untersuchungen über die Lage des Handwerks in Deutschland mit besonderer Rücksicht auf seine Konkurrenzfähigkeit gegenüber der Großindustrie (1895–7) [*Investigations in the Situation of the Crafts in Germany with Special Consideration to its Competitiveness vis-à-vis Big Industry*] (Schriften des Vereins für Socialpolitik, vols. 62–70). Leipzig: Duncker & Humblot.

Weimer, Stephanie (1990), 'The Federal Republic of Germany', in Werner Sengenberger, Gary Loveman, Michael Piore (eds.), *The Re-emergence of Small Enterprises: Industrial Restructuring in Industrialized Countries*. Geneva: International Institute for Labour Studies.

Wengenroth, Ulrich (1989a) (ed.), *Prekäre Selbstständigkeit. Zur Standortbestimmung von Handwerk, Hausindustrie und Kleingewerbe im Industrialisierungsprozeß* [*Vulnerable Independence: An Assessment of Crafts, Cottage Industry and Petty Industry During Industrialization*]. Stuttgart: Steiner.

—— (1989b), 'Motoren für den Kleinbetrieb: Soziale Utopien, technische Entwicklung und Absatzstrategien bei der Motorisierung des Kleingewerbes in Deutschland' ['Motors for Small Enterprise: Social Utopias, Technological Development and Sales Strategies During the Motorization of Small-scale Business in Germany'], in Wengenroth, *Prekäre Selbstständigkeit*.

—— (1996), 'Mittelständische Unternehmen—der flexible Kern des industriellen Systems' ['Middle-estate' Firms: 'The Flexible Centre of the Industrial System'], *Stahl und Eisen*, 10.

—— (1997), 'Technischer Fortschritt, Deindustrialisierung und Konsum. Eine Herausforderung für die Technikgeschichte' [Technological Progress, Deindustrialization and Consumption: A Challenge for the History of Technology], *Technikgeschichte*, 64.

Wernet, Wilhelm (1952), *Handwerkspolitik* [Crafts Policies]. Göttingen: Vandenhoeck & Ruprecht.

Winkel, Harald (1974), *Die Wirtschaft im geteilten Deutschland 1945–1970* [*The Economy in Divided Germany 1945–1970*]. Stuttgart: Steiner.

—— (1990), *Wirtschaft im Aufbruch. Der Wirtschaftsraum München-Oberbayern und seine Industrie- und Handelskammer im Wandel der Zeiten* [*Economy on the March: The Economic Region of Munich and Upper Bavaria and its Chamber of Commerce and Industry in Changing Times*]. Munich: C. H. Beck.

Winkler, Heinrich August (1976), 'From Social Protection to National Socialism: The German Small Business Movement in Comparative Perspective', *Journal of Modern History*, 48.

—— (1978), 'Vom Sozialprotektionismus zum Nationalsozialismus: Die deutsche Mittelstandsbewegung in vergleichender Sicht' [From Social Protection to National Socialism: The German 'Middle-estate' Movement in Comparative Perspective], in Heinz-Gerhard Haupt (ed.), *'Bourgeois und Volk zugleich?' Zur Geschichte des Kleinbürgertums im 19. und 20. Jahrhundert* [*'Bourgeois and People at the Same Time?' On the History of the Petty Bourgeoisie During the 19th and 20th Centuries*]. Frankfurt am Main: Campus.

'Zum Begriff des Mittelstandes' (1959) ['On the Notion of Middle-estate'], *Mitteilungen der Industrie- und Handelskammer zu Köln*, 14/8: 163.

6

Small- and Medium-Size Industrial Enterprises in France 1900–1975

MICHEL LESCURE

Introduction

The purpose of this chapter is to explore the ways used by French small- and medium-size manufacturing enterprises (SMEs) to adapt themselves to the new economic context of the twentieth century. It must be recalled that at the beginning of the twentieth century most French industrial sectors were composed mainly of small- and medium-size enterprises. In 1906, France had 58 per cent of its factory labour in very small plants (employing fewer than 10 wage-earners). No more than 12 per cent of the labour force was employed in plants with more than 500 wage-earners.

The weight of SMEs was in part the consequence of the first stage of industrialization. The resource endowment of the country, shortly stated as a well-trained and abundant work-force coupled with the high cost of coal, had led French industry to specialize in the output of quality individualized products manufactured in small rural workshops using labour-intensive and capital-saving technologies. But the second stage of industrialization that the French economy experienced from 1895 onwards was to give a new impetus to the multiplication of small firms. Among other reasons, there was the fact that a large part of several new industries (for instance automobiles and primary steel transformation) were launched not by old, established large enterprises but by new and innovative small firms.

However, throughout the twentieth century, the general context has tended to become less and less favourable to SMEs. The ensuing section will examine the new context in which SMEs have had to operate. The third section will survey the extent to which SMEs have been able to survive while the following sections will focus on the ways chosen by SMEs to adapt themselves.

New Conditions for SMEs

During the twentieth century five kinds of factors have combined to reduce the place left to small- and medium-scale operators.

New Characteristics of the Consumer Markets

The first came from shifts in the consumer markets. During a major part of the nineteenth century, SMEs had benefited from the geographical and social compartmentalization of the domestic market. High costs of transportation coupled with a low level of urbanization and industrialization meant that demand for manufactured goods remained very differentiated in nature. By 1900, 59 per cent of the total population was still living in small villages, while self-employed workers and small employers accounted for nearly 50 per cent of the working population. Tastes differed from region to region and from one social group to another. In part, the role played by SMEs reflected adaptation to a narrow, rural, and dispersed home market.

During the three opening decades of the twentieth century and again during the so-called 'Thirty Glorious Years' of 1945–75, two periods during which French economy experienced fast growth, the market for manufactured goods expanded quickly while the process of urbanization and industrialization tended to make the structure of demand more homogeneous. In 1968 the urban population comprised 66.2 per cent of the total population (compared with 41 per cent at the beginning of the century) and the proportion of wage-earners exceeded 77 per cent of the working population.

The growth of urban markets and the change this implied in the pattern of demand made possible the development of the corporate sector. From 1920 onwards, large corporations came into being in the sectors that supplied markets with mass-produced goods (automobiles, paper, food, beverages, textiles) (Lévy-Leboyer 1980).

The Strategy of the Large Corporations

Of course the growth of the corporate sector did not necessarily imply the decline of SMEs, but the strategy followed by large firms was to make the position occupied by small firms more difficult. Actually, not only were SMEs losing the markets which were integrated into mass production, but during a large part of the period under review they were also likely to lose those coming from their collaboration with large organizations.

During the period running from 1930 to the early 1950s, the role of SMEs as suppliers or subcontractors declined. Except in civil engineering, the subcontracting system did not play more than a modest part in French industry by 1950. At that time, subcontractors were considered as 'simple drudges', unable to be involved in the large plans of production, and they were thus restricted to small and low-ranked markets.

In addition to the traditional distrust of public authorities towards a practice which was thought to generate multiple levels of profit, this situation can be ascribed to the tendency for large firms to internalize activity that they had formerly subcontracted to SMEs. This tendency was apparent in some firms such as Renault as early as the 1920s, but it expanded to a new dimension in the following two decades under the impact of the new conditions brought about by depression and autarky. In the post-war years, the poor constitution of the majority of SMEs was a further reason not to resort to subcontracting. Suppliers were considered to be too small, not specialized enough, and suffering from a lack of flexibility to adapt themselves. These limitations on the supply side resulted in the first experiences of near-integration pioneered by industries such as metals and engineering (Ministère de l'Industrie 1978; Houssiaux 1957).

State Policy

The policy followed by the State caused further difficulties for SMEs, although this policy had long been favourable to SMEs, especially the smallest ones. The social ideal of the Radicals, the predominant party at the beginning of the century, was a society of small independent property-holders. The Radicals' aversion to giant companies was shared by a large fraction of the peasants who feared that their fertilizer supply would fall under the domination of large monopolistic chemical firms, as well as by certain military circles who raised the division of the markets to the status of a doctrine, especially in the industrial sectors where they had lost control of the innovation process (Chadeau 1987; Daviet 1983). Even though the experience of the First World War had stimulated a fruitless but intense discussion on the renovation of French economy, this policy was to receive a new impetus during the depression of the 1930s. The falling of prices and profits led firms to resume entente building in order to limit overproduction and excessive competition among firms. External and internal protectionism was reinforced. The State, for instance, encouraged the formation of cartels, and in some sectors (for instance retail trade and the shoe industry) it intervened directly to prevent the creation of new chain stores and plants.

Following the Second World War, this policy was to be severely criti-cized. Not only was protectionism said to be responsible for the economic backwardness of the country, but SMEs, which were supposed to have bene-fited most from these measures, were viewed as anachronistic relics that would disappear when the protectionist arsenal was dismantled. Men who managed the French economy in the post-war period were 'impressed by the ethics of the large production units' (Bloch-Lainé quoted by Guillaume in 1987). They thought that the time had come for the substitution of large-scale enterprises for small ones, and that it was the role of the State to pro-mote industrial concentration. The Monnet Plan (1947–52) provides a good illustration of this frame of mind since the entire amount of this investment programme was oriented towards large-scale (most of them newly nation-alized) enterprises operating in basic sectors (e.g. coal, electricity, steel, transport, cement, and farm machinery).

The policy followed by the State from 1950 to 1970 to improve the pro-ductivity of the economy was a continuation of the same logic. On the one hand, the State strove to restore a climate of competition among firms. If it did not succeed in solving the problem of internal rigidities, a problem inherited from the previous period, it did succeed in opening the French economy to external competition. The opposition of the General Confedera-tion of SMEs to the creation of the Common Market shows clearly that many SMEs were very much threatened by the removal of protectionism (Szokoloczy-Syllaba 1965). On the other hand, the State promoted indus-trial concentration in several sectors such as steel, textiles, petroleum, and machine tools. During the Fifth Plan (1965–70) the State sponsored a vast campaign of mergers in order to endow each industrial sector with large competitive national groups.

The Evolution of Financial Institutions

The evolution of financial institutions was a fourth factor of difficulty for SMEs. As technological changes generated a wide range of indivisible investments (in textiles for instance), it became more difficult for local SMEs to raise funds. This was the result of the process of concentration of finan-cial institutions. With regard to financial markets, a high level of concentra-tion was observable very early in France, since the stock exchange of Paris recorded more than 90 per cent of the transactions made in France at the be-ginning of this century. However, the process of concentration carried on and accelerated in the 1960s (Mayoux 1978). Furthermore, the process was spreading to the banking system that had remained very decentralized at the beginning of the century. The decline of the regional banks (in the 1960s the 132 local and regional banks accounted for only 7.6 per cent of total banks deposits) and the emergence of balanced branch banking systems, strongly dominated up to the early 1970s by metropolitan higher management, resulted in a highly centralized banking system. This in turn reduced the direct involvement of the banks in regional/local economies. At the end of the 1970s nearly 70 per cent of the value of the demands for credits addressed to bank branches were submitted to the Parisian management for approval.

The process of concentration coupled with the centralized structure of the large commercial banks helps to explain why short-financing channels (those characterized by the proximity between saver and borrower) were in decline throughout the twentieth century. The specialization of financial institutions and the regulations governing banking activities since 1945 led to the same results. Given the rules they had to follow, decentralized banking institutions such as local and regional banks, and popular banks, tended by the end of the 1960s to become mere purveyors of resources for long-financing channels (through, for instance, the monetary and the mortgage markets). In addition, it must be recalled that in France the non-banking decentralized institutions such as saving and mutualistic banks did not take part in the financing of local SMEs in the same proportion as they did in many Western industrial countries. Thus, it was the whole decentralized financial system that was led away from significant industrial commitments.

The Decline of the Local Productive Systems

In addition to their direct and negative effects on SMEs, the foregoing factors had serious consequences for the survival of the local industrial systems in which many SMEs operated at the beginning of this century.

According to the classical views of Piore, Sabel, and Zeitlin (1984 and 1985), the characteristics of the French local systems broadly corresponded to the Marshallian pattern of industrial districts: production of a wide range of closely specified products to suit the needs of highly differentiated markets and constant alteration of the assortments of goods in response to changing tastes; flexible use of productive and widely applicable technologies; skill-intensiveness and a high degree of specialization of SMEs involved in batch production; as well as the active role of local institutions, including municipal authorities, to balance co-operation and competition among firms, to promote innovation, and to guarantee the mobility of resources (through the creation of vocational schools and insurance and credit systems).

Although in some cases flexible production continued to innovate, many local industrial systems declined or were drawn into mass production during the twentieth century. Some of them went into retreat as early as the

1920s, as was the case of the ribbon industry of Saint Étienne. Changes in clothing habits brought about a gradual decline in the demand for ribbons, while local producers were faced with growing competition from Germany. Fragmented industrial structures were not adapted to the new standardized production and conflicts of interest retarded innovative adaptation (Reynaud 1989). Several other local industrial systems followed this pattern during the period from 1930 to 1950. The Thiers cutlery industry, for instance, collapsed because of the excessive individualism of its craftsmen, their outdated equipment and methods, and the replacement of their traditional small customers by powerful representatives of large chain stores. But the ultimate assaults on local industrial systems were launched in the 1960s when the State sponsored a campaign of mergers. In Lyon, this policy furthered the intrusion into the local economy of large French and foreign multinationals pursuing mass-production strategies. The loose federations of specialists which had previously ensured the success of traditional Lyonnais products were now broken up (Sabel and Zeitlin 1985; Laferrère 1960).

The result was that only a few local systems survived by 1970. They were located in the eastern and western parts of the country (Jura, Savoie, Anjou, Choletais, Vendée) and they belonged mainly to textile industries.

The Performances of SMEs

These unfavourable circumstances appear to have had little influence on the position occupied by SMEs in industrial structures. Of course, excepting the 1930s, the process of technical concentration (i.e. the concentration observed at the level of the plant, the local unit of production—not at the level of the firm, which is the legal and economic unit) continued but, as can be seen from Table 6.1, this process was fed mainly by the decline of self-employed persons and craft workshops (units with less than 5 workers) and it benefited small- and medium-size plants as much as it did large ones.

The evolution of economic concentration (i.e. the concentration observed at the level of the firm) cannot be followed with the same accuracy but the evidence is that its progress was slow and limited to very short periods, such as the late 1920s and the period running from 1965 to 1974, when large firms were encouraged by the State to initiate a wave of mergers. Otherwise, during a large part of the 'Thirty Glorious Years', for instance from 1955 to 1963, the share of the largest firms in manufacturing output did not increase. Rather it was decreasing in those sectors which experienced the fastest growth (e.g. electrical and mechanical engineering and pharmaceutical industries). Given the falling number of small businesses (80,000 firms

Michel Lescure

Table 6.1. *Distribution of the work-force according to industrial plant size (percentages)*

No. of wage-earners	1906	1926	1931	1936	1954	1962	1966
0–4	53	35	28	33	19	16	14
5–10	5	6	6	6	6	5	6
11–20	5	5.9	6.6	6.1	6	6.3	6.4
21–100	11.8	15.9	17.8	16.5	21	22.1	23.2
101–500	13	17.7	19.8	18.3	23.3	25.3	26.4
500 +	12.2	19.5	21.8	20.1	24.7	25.3	24
TOTAL	100	100	100	100	100	100	100

Source: Didier and Malinvaud (1969).

less between 1951 and 1963) this was an unexpected but easily explainable issue since the importance of medium-size firms had been enlarged.

The result was that, far from being marginalized, SMEs remained prominent figures at the end of the period under review, and that French industry maintained its originality. In 1962, France had 61.4 per cent of its labour force in small- and medium-size manufacturing enterprises (employing less than 500 wage-earners), whereas in Germany the figure was 54 per cent, and in the United Kingdom 33.2 per cent.

Not surprisingly, the hierarchy of the industries according to their degree of concentration did not differ from that observed in other countries (with SMEs accounting for a larger share in employment and output in the consumer goods industries than in other industries; see Table 6.2). However it was the degree of concentration inside each industry which was lower in France than in other countries. This was true both in the traditional industries where the level of concentration remained very low (textiles, metals, and food) and in the more recent ones which featured a higher degree of concentration (engineering and vehicles) (Lévy-Leboyer 1974).

These developments concerning the evolution of concentration in industry are broadly in line with what is known of firms' performance. Even though they are thought to be less capital-intensive and less productive than other firms (which is true for industry as a whole—see Table 6.3, cols. 2 and 3—although not in several sectors), SMEs performed better than large firms in terms of growth and profitability (Table 6.3, cols. 8–12) during the largest part of the two phases of fast expansion that French industry experienced.

For growth the best sizes seem to have been the medium ones (roughly, from 20 to 100/500 employees); the smallest firms were characterized by a wide dispersion of their results which negatively affected overall performance of the group. With regard to profitability, the best size (small or medium size) varied according to the ratio used to measure it and according to the

Table 6.2. *SMEs in French industry in 1973 (percentages)*

	No. of enterprises			No. of employees			Value of turnover		
	A	B	C	A	B	C	A	B	C
Gas, water electricity	76	21	3	0	5	95	4	7	89
Food, drink	96	4	0	23	38	39	19	41	40
Intermediate goods	86	13	1	7	37	56	9	32	59
Consumer goods	89	11	0	12	56	32	17	52	31
Capital goods									
Professional	79	20	1	5	35	60	7	32	61
Domestic	70	27	3	3	29	68	4	28	68
Vehicles	79	18	3	2	17	81	2	9	89
Building, civil engineering	95	5	0	30	45	25	32	41	27

A = firms with less than 20 wage-earners.
B = firms employing from 20 to 499 wage-earners.
C = firms with more than 499 wage-earners.

Source: Brocard and Gandois (1978).

Table 6.3. *Characteristics of French industrial firms according to size by the mid-1960s*

(a) Economic and financial characteristics (1962)

No. of wage-earners	Investment per employee	Value added per employee	Fixed assets/ turnover	Own capital/ total liabilities (%)	LT debt/ ST debt
6–9	1.46	12.6	0.27	46	0.20
10–19	1.82	17.3	0.28	42	0.23
20–49	2.10	17.6	0.31	38	0.27
50–99	2.23	17.8	0.33	38	0.19
100–199	2.40	18.4	0.40	40	0.20
200–499	2.80	19.9	0.53	44	0.28
500–999	3.35	20.8	0.68	50	0.25
1000 +	5.43	28.6	1.10	42	0.92

(b) Economic and financial performance (1965–1966)

Value of turnover (million F)	Growth of turnover (1965–6) (%)	Growth of profits (1965–6) (%)
0–10	7.4	5.6
10–50	8.4	4.8
50–100	9.9	6.7
100–500	7.9	6.1
500 +	6.8	10.8
TOTAL	8.0	7.7

(c) Economic and financial performance (1964)

Value of turnover (million F)	Rate of profitability in 1964[a]	Firms recording no profits in 1964 (%)
0–5	7.7	21.4
5–15	13.1	14.2
15–40	17.6	10.8
40–75	18.8	9.7
75–200	16.5	6.1
200–400	15.2	5.4
400–750	13.0	6.1
750 +	10.4	2.1

[a] Profit + provision for depreciation as % of permanent capital.

Sources: Industrial Census of 1962; Babeau (1971); Didier (1969); Morvan (1967).

sector or the time frame. If the medium sizes were frequently associated with the best profitability, the small ones were not systematically excluded since in some cases the high productivity of their capital (Table 6.3, col. 4) enabled small firms to compensate for the small portion of their value added devoted to profits (Brocard and Gandois 1978; Vasille 1982; Morvan 1967; Evraert 1978).

Two nuances should be noted here with regard to this general pattern. First, during the peak years of each phase of expansion the growth of large firms tended to surpass that of SMEs. The strategy of external growth followed at that time by large firms is not enough to explain the shift. Further reasons are to be found in the special circumstances of these years, namely the shortage of labour in the late 1920s and the strength of inflation in the early 1970s, two factors which appeared to be more prejudicial to SMEs than to large firms (Lescure 1996; Evraert 1978). Second, it is likely that during the slump of the 1930s the profitability of SMEs fell behind that of larger firms (Villa 1992). This can be partly explained by the differences existing in the rate of concentration and consequently of deflation between upstream sectors (electricity, transport, and capital-goods industries), as most of them were sheltered from sharp competition by cartels or the monopolistic structure of their markets, and downstream sectors where the majority of SMEs was located. Further difficulties came in 1936 when the Popular Front gave priority to satisfying working-class grievances. Given the share of their value added devoted to wages and their relatively low wage levels, the purchasing-power policy implemented through wage increases and the 40-hour week was more detrimental to small firms than to large ones.

These developments remained marginal, however, and one must wonder why SMEs continued to perform so well even though conditions had become less favourable. Of course one reason may be that large firms did not strive to exploit fully the advantage they drew from their scale. In the 1960s, many of them were organized as loose-knit groups; 'for managerial purposes, they did not offer an efficiency comparable to that of the multidivisional organization' (Lévy-Leboyer 1980). Nevertheless the main reasons had to do with the SMEs. The following sections will survey the extent to which markets remained opened to small producers, the industrial and organizational strategies followed by SMEs to adapt themselves to the new circumstances, and the benefit drawn by these firms from the industrial policy of the State.

SMEs' Markets

The ability to carve out market niches for their products remained a leading reason for the persistence of successful SMEs, but the various ways used to develop these niches illustrates the wide variety of economic roles played by these firms in the French economy.

The Exploitation of Technological Specialization

The first of these ways was specialization in sophisticated production processes or the use of specific technologies. By developing products or processes of their own, SMEs acquired distinctive competence that gave them significant competitive advantages. Of course access to this kind of market was closely dependent on innovative capacity. Even though SMEs were perceived to suffer serious handicaps stemming from their relative inability to promote R.&D. and to access available technological information, there is nothing to indicate that French SMEs were less innovative than large firms. In the 1920s, for instance, the proportion of firms which had innovated in the previous three years was 8.6 per cent for firms with less than 100 employees against 9.6 per cent for those with more than 100. According to a public enquiry, 56 per cent of the most important innovations that took place in France were ascribable to SMEs (Lescure 1996; Barnier 1981).

During the 'Thirty Glorious Years', for instance, it was this innovative capacity that enabled SMEs to occupy leading positions in new and large consumer-goods markets (for example Camping-Gaz, Bic, Poclain, and Rossignol), and an avant-garde position in smaller professional markets, as intermediate-goods markets were opened by the creation of a new linked-product market (Clapets T. J. at Châlon-sur-Saône or Fonderies Gailly at

Meung-sur-Loire) and capital-goods markets were opened by the special equipment requirements of a number of industries (firms such as Secmer S.A. or S.O.A.F.) (Barreyre 1975).

Batch Production

A second way to develop market niches was to specialize in batch production designed to supply those segments of the markets that mass-producers could not meet. This type of market segmentation was not unusual in capital-goods industries (especially in tools and machinery) but it was in the consumer-goods industries that it was the most frequent. Its import-ance was closely dependent on the evolution of market structures.

Obviously, if the progress of large firms using continuous-process mass-production methods paralleled that of mass consumption, it must be emphasized that numerous opportunities remained to other formats of production, especially those grounded in flexibility and custom products. First, a wide disparity continued to characterize the distribution of the country's wealth, which favoured the maintenance of a highly differenti-ated product demand. In 1929, at the bottom of the social ladder, 25 per cent of households received 10 per cent of total incomes while at the top 25 per cent controlled 56 per cent. Furthermore, it must be added that the rising standards of living that occurred during the 'Thirty Glorious Years' brought with them a new enlargement of the disparities, especially from the mid-1950s to the mid-1960s: the ninth and the first deciles in the wage ladder were in a ratio of 3.8 in 1972 compared with 3.4 in 1954 (Parodi 1981). It is also possible that the consequences of the low densities observed at the centre of the salary scale have been accentuated by the cultural-value en-dowment of the country, since the growth in real incomes was likely to pro-long the slow diffusion of differentiated aristocratic tastes to the popular classes. In any event, the 1970s witnessed an increasing propensity to make the means of social differentiation more sophisticated, which tended to strengthen the position of batch-producers (Goblot 1925; Kurgan-Van Hentenryk and Chadeau 1990; Zeldin 1973; Weisz 1987).

Second, the extension and acceleration of fashion generated a growing number of short-lived products, the output of which could be easily left to flexible batch-producers. The dressmaking industry provides a good illus-tration of this process. In the 1920s, the simplification of female clothing and the constant change of fashion went hand in hand. The result was that manufacturers no longer produced large batches of the same style but small batches of changing styles (Omnès 1993). New changes occurred in the 1960s and in the 1970s when rising standards of living coupled with popu-lation increase led to another extension of fashion. A new generation of clothes designers pioneered the creation of 'stylish' ready-made dresses. Their models were supposed to appeal to new kinds of customers (young people and new socio-professional categories) eager to escape from conventionality and ready to accept that fashion had to change constantly. The growth of 'stylish' ready-made dresses implied the relative decline of standard products (classical clothes and traditional fashion dresses) whose rhythm of renewal was slow and regulated by commercial conventions (biannual collections) and their substitution for very unstable products. This evolution (speeded up by economic crisis) favoured flexible small operators to the detriment of large integrated firms (Battiau 1976; Delattre and Eymard-Duverney 1984).

Subcontracting Markets

For SMEs that developed neither a technological speciality nor a market niche, subcontracting systems provided further opportunities not only to stay afloat but sometimes to achieve good results.

Subcontracting systems had expanded rapidly during the three opening decades of the century. The financial and organizational risk borne by over-integrated large firms, the fear held by the first large distribution bodies of falling under the domination of a few too-powerful suppliers, and the public encouragement given to subcontracting systems in aeronautical industries were factors that furthered the collaboration between large firms and SMEs. The further upsurge of the subcontracting system during the 'Thirty Glorious Years' involved similar reasons. Special attention should be paid to the successive difficulties felt at that time by many large firms, such as difficulties in anticipating and adapting themselves to the growth and the shifts in demand in the 1950s, as well as difficulties in overcoming the falling tendency in capital productivity from 1965 onwards. The opportunity for large firms to resort to smaller operators was increased by the fact that, at that time, the share of production capacities remaining unused was chronically larger in the latter than in the former (Houssiaux 1957; Saglio and Tabuteau 1971; Delattre 1982).

The slump and the disorganization of the subcontracting markets that occurred between 1930 and 1950 now required a special drive to stimulate and to improve their smooth functioning. The first initiatives came from the national professional unions. In 1948, for instance, the National Union of General Engineering created the 'Bureau Technique d'Orientation des Offres de Travaux' (BTO). Its aim was to provide big enterprises with information concerning the equipment and the work schedules of the subcontractors that were members of the union (800 small firms with 150,000 employees), and also to make contact easier between large firms and subcontractors. The creation of regional bodies (subcontracting Exchanges, entrepreneurs' associations, and subcontracting departments of Chambers of Commerce or regional unions) had similar goals, but the people who initiated these creations thought it was more effective to organize subcontracting markets on a regional and multi-sectorial basis, and about fifteen regional bodies came into being between 1959 and 1965. The State also pushed a bit because it considered that this would help to reach full employment of production capacity. While the national professional unions strove to improve the subcontracting system in matters of specialization, regional institutions focused on the so-called subcontracting of capacity.

The efficiency of these different kinds of institutions should not be overestimated. Given the crucial lack of suppliers in the years following the end of the war, the BTO, as an example, was approached by many firms up to the late 1950s, but the downward trend that appeared at that time stimulated the propensity of big enterprises to internalize a larger part of their processes of production, and the activity of the BTO declined. Regional bodies were not more successful. Because of their tendency to stimulate regional industrial development, they were blamed for encouraging local autarky. Above all, they did not play the role that they were expected to. In 1972, only two subcontracting Exchanges were still operational (those at Nancy and Tours). Most of them had collapsed because they suffered a lack of financial means and placed too large an emphasis on purely commercial transactions for which they were in competition with private businesses. As a general rule, the constituents of these organizations remained limited. In the early 1970s, no more than 27.5 per cent of principal firms were reported to have dealt with such bodies. On the side of the subcontractors, less than 20 per cent turned to them in order to find new customers, and, with the exception of the Nancy Exchanges, the geographical scope of these institutions never exceeded 50 kms (Ministère de l'Industrie 1974, 1978; Champeux 1976; Lanoizelée 1975).

Despite these disappointing circumstances, the subcontracting system expanded rapidly from 1950 to 1970 under the pressure of demand. In 1975, work subcontracted to other firms accounted for 5 per cent of the total output of manufacturing firms (Table 6.4). But its markets remained opaque and compartmentalized. This factor, coupled with the weakness of the commercial organization of subcontractors (in the 1970s only 8.8 per cent of small subcontractors had a commercial section), made these firms very dependent on a few big customers. In the early 1970s, 68.5 per cent of the small subcontractors (here those with less than 200 wage-earners) had no more than ten customers (Ministère de l'Industrie 1974).

Further difficulties for SMEs derived from the reasons for which large firms subcontracted to them. Unlike American, German, or Swedish large corporations, French big firms have been very slow to experiment with a strategy of structural subcontracting, that is to say, a strategy characterized

Table 6.4. *Work subcontracted to other firms with more than 20 wage-earners as a proportion of total output in various industrial sectors, 1975*

Industry	%
Aeronautical	31.0
Shipbuilding	17.4
Civil engineering	11.3
Textiles	8.2
Metals	8.1
Paper	7.6
Mechanical engineering	7.5
Electrical	5.8
Vehicles	5.5

Source: Ministère de l'Industrie (1978).

by some degree of planning in the orders and of stability in the relations between principal firms and subcontractors. At the beginning of the 1970s, 57.5 per cent of the principal firms used subcontractors as a safety valve in times of business fluctuations. Even in those sectors such as metal-cutting and stamping where long-standing relationships existed between principal firms and subcontractors, the main interest found by the former in subcontracting was to transfer to the latter the risk coming from short-term economic fluctuations. The shape given to agreements between firms reflected the same preoccupations; 60 per cent of these agreements were simple orders including only conditions of quantity, price, and delivery time. Open orders, including both firm orders and forward-looking ones, did not account for more than 32 per cent, and, in two cases out of three, the forecast did not exceed one year. Contract orders, which are firm and long-term, represented only 8.5 per cent of the total agreements, and in three cases out of four the principal firm was not French.

Thus, even though some improvements could be recorded during the period, the position of being a subcontractor was seen as a constraint by most of the SMEs. Except in some sectors of mechanical engineering, characterized by a low degree of competition among firms and a rather high degree of near-integration between parent firms and subcontractors, most SMEs strove to escape from subcontracting (Ministère de l'Industrie 1974; Champeux 1976).

The Productive Strategies of SMEs

Whatever the market, SME performance remained closely dependent upon two very different kinds of conditions: the upholding of a high degree of industrial specialization, and the adoption of management methods liable to reconcile the growth of the firm with the concerns of proprietary capitalism. Specialization remained the best instrument in the success of fast-growth small firms. Several studies have emphasized the relationship existing between the degree of specialization of the SMEs and their innovative capacity or the size of their markets. In the 1920s, for instance, the market size was national and international for the 34 per cent of the SMEs whose production was the most specialized, against 14 per cent for those which were the most diversified (Lescure 1996).

The problem is that the degree of specialization, which is usually much higher in small firms than in large ones, fell sharply in the 1930s and the 1940s. Diversification expanded so much that it seemed logical in the 1950s to ascribe it to the character of French managers (Landes 1951). More simply, this situation was the result of the contraction of markets and the increasing influence of protectionism that came about during this period. Firms (whether small or large) have found in polyvalency a compensation for too narrow outlets.

In the ensuing period, excessive diversification remained characteristic of many firms in several sectors. According to the members of the Mechanical Engineering Committee of the Sixth Plan, SMEs 'are too polyvalent to reach the degree of competitiveness required for each kind of production'. This negative appraisal, however, should not lead to an underestimate of the efforts made by many firms to increase their specialization. Growing competition operated as a driving force, while the State pressed firms to quicken the pace of change. From the Second Plan onwards, better specialization had become a key objective for industrial policy. In order to increase their specialization, firms could resort to agreements with other firms, as these agreements allowed them to divide up orders and to externalize some part of the process of production. Specialization accordingly gained ground during these years. In aeronautical industries, for instance, the decline of polyvalent enterprises dating back to the previous period reflected the advantage now given by the new State policy to subcontractors involved in a monospeciality under the dependence of aeroplane manufacturers (Allinne 1993). In the motor car industry, similar choices were made by medium-size subcontractors who provided car manufacturers with mass-produced elements (Vennin 1975). The same tendency, here oriented toward a technical specialization, was found in batch production. In mechanical engineering, for instance, a sector in which 53 per cent of SMEs are batch producers, no more than 21 per cent of small firms were highly specialized in the early 1970s, but 50 per cent of them strove to increase the specialization of their activities. In addition, SMEs did their best to diversify their markets because growth in the number of their customers was expected to reduce the risk accompanying close specialization (Lanoizelée 1975; Champeux 1976).

Except for firms which were condemned by the unoriginality of their products to stay barely afloat by multiplying the number of those products they offered to local customers, diversification tended to amount to the development of related technologies (Lanoizelée 1975; Barreyre 1975; Hirigoyen 1984).

Management of SMEs

Ways to satisfy the second requirement for success (the adaptation of management methods) were much more difficult. The main problem encountered by SMEs was how to overcome the tendency of many owner-managers to put a brake on their growth because of their desire to keep close control of both the everyday management of the firm and of its long-term future.

Many studies confirm that for a majority of SMEs growth was not the most important objective. On the contrary, it was seen rather as something to avoid. In the sector of mechanical engineering, for instance, at the beginning of the 1970s, the main objective for 58 per cent of medium-size enterprises was to experience no growth (Lanoizelée 1975). According to another statistical survey of that time, no more than 30 per cent of French SMEs strove to grow (Herblay 1973). Of course there were many reasons to explain this attitude, such as the wish to protect the financial autonomy of the firm or the organizational flexibility of small business, but the main reason was the will of the entrepreneur to keep absolute control of the decision-making process. If only one-fifth of the businessmen who launched their firms between 1950 and 1970 are said to have accepted growth without any restriction, it is because a majority of new businessmen refused to delegate any part of their authority (Laufer 1975). According to another survey, one-third of French employers were ready to delegate and to adopt management 'by objective' (Gervais 1978).

For a majority of SME managers, the goal of enterprise remained the highest possible profit. Given the close dependence of SME investments on the level of past profits, this goal allowed harmonization of the growth of the firm with its independence. Above all, this goal was compatible with the aspiration for security and for stability of managerial structure (Hirigoyen 1984; Lanoizelée 1975; Horowitz and Demillère 1978; Besse 1983).

One mark of these preoccupations can be seen in the very centralized structure of a majority of SMEs. In 1975, the organization 'en rateau', in which the manager supervises everything, was found in 52.3 per cent of the medium-size family concerns located in Aquitaine. The first steps towards a functional organization were found in 38.6 per cent of the same firms, but only 9 per cent of them fully adopted this type of organization and experimented with some degree of operational delegation (Hirigoyen 1984; Zouggari 1985). Of course the information system on which depended a great part of the firms' efficiency was also based on the same centralized pattern.

Consequently, methods of controlled forward-looking management expanded little. Yet one of the main interests of these methods was to allow managers of medium-size enterprises to delegate some part of their authority while keeping overall control on management. In 1977, 38 per cent of medium-size industrial enterprises (compared with 85 per cent of large firms) had adopted a system of long-term planning through which different kinds of plans and budgets could be connected. In a majority of cases planning was operational in nature, not strategic, and it was no more than an extrapolation of budgetary management (Hirigoyen 1984).

In addition to the risk of having growth curbed by the reluctance of managers to delegate some part of their authority, SMEs also incurred risk linked to the desire of a majority of owner-managers to make their firms family concerns handed down from generation to generation. This type of firm tends to generate conservative strategies (in relation to the will of the family group to protect its independence and to ensure its security) and to experience decreasing efficiency in management (because of the lack of institutional procedures to govern the turnover of their equipment, structures, and managers).

These kinds of risks must not be overestimated. First, the proportion of SMEs concerned was not as significant as it might appear. Even though SMEs were 96 per cent (in the 1920s) or 80 per cent (in the 1980s) proprietary or family-owned firms, the proportion of those which successfully remained under family control for several generations was much lower (Table 6.5).

During each period, the proportion of managers belonging to the second generation or beyond never exceeded 35 per cent. The inheritance of ownership in small industry remained something rarely found in France. This was due both to the difficulties experienced by SMEs in ensuring their transmission within the family group and to the permanent turnover of the SMEs (with nearly 50 per cent of their managers having founded the firm).

Table 6.5. *Origin of the position occupied by SME managers (%)*

	1920s	1973	1987(a)	1987(b)
Foundation	46.7	42	58	58
Inheritance	26.9	35	7	14
Others	26.4	23	35	28

Notes: 1. Data for the 1920s and 1987(b) refer to industrial SMEs, those for 1973 and 1987(a) refer to all SMEs. 2. Data are not rigorously comparable from one column to another.

Sources: Lescure (1996); Herblay (1973); Crédit d'Equipement des PME (1987).

Second, as shown by the great number of large family businesses in France, the family character of the firm was not always an obstacle to its development. With regard to financial problems, for instance, several devices were available that enabled SMEs to reconcile the satisfaction of their financial requirements with the preservation of their independence and family control. On the assumption that savers were more interested in high rates of return than in power, many large and medium-size family firms issued preference shares in the 1920s and this opportunity recurred from 1978 onwards. The creation of a holding company was another device to slow down the erosion of family control while allowing external capital to take part in the financing of the subsidiaries. Similarly, many SMEs strove to overcome the tendency for family firms to decline under the pressure of decreasing quality in management. Following the example given by long-standing large family firms located in the east of the country (especially in Alsace), many firms have adopted careful rules regulating the right of each branch of the family to introduce a member into the organization and setting up strict criteria for the selection of the managers. Some of them went so far as to establish a charter designed to protect the firm both from interference by family shareholders and from mismanagement by family directors (Gelinier and Gaultier 1972).

But it was only a minority of large family SMEs which resorted to such devices, and their results remained questionable. The consequence of this can be seen in the influence of age on SME performance. In the 1920s, just as in the 1950s and the 1960s, ageing brought about a decline in SME performance while it had no influence on growth of large firms (Alla 1974; Fizaine 1968; Lescure 1996).

SME Networks

For SMEs, as well as for some large firms, one solution to these problems of control, autonomy, and flexibility has been found in the constitution of family networks.

During each phase of fast growth that the French economy experienced, a significant proportion of SMEs has chosen to expand through the creation of subsidiaries rather than through linear growth. As illustrated by the examples of SMEs like TRECA, SICLI, or Vibrachoc, three firms which occupied a leading position in their specialities in the 1960s, the constitution of a group of sub-enterprises provided for both fast growth together with the preservation of organizational flexibility and overall control of the decision-making process.

This could also mean compatibility of the development of the firm and the preservation of family control. With this aim in view, SMEs could either create a central family holding designed to maintain the unity of the group, or constitute a divisible family system with several firms independent from each other but related to the same family group.

In addition to the organizational advantages it provided to the family group, the constitution of such networks gave significant competitive advantages to the several companies involved. Networking enabled the firms to enjoy a higher degree of specialization as well as a better access to market information, and there was a pooling of technical and management skills (Barreyre 1975; Gelinier and Gaultier 1972; Lescure 1996).

As a matter of fact, these groups were not new in France. It must be recalled than in many regions (in the North or in Alsace for instance) the typical nineteenth-century firm operated as part of a network of firms. These networks resulted from the tradition followed by family firms to see the entry of a son, son-in-law, or nephew into their management as an opportunity to promote a new activity by providing the new member with a business project to establish. The 'système Motte', for instance, was 'to pair each family member . . . with an experienced craftsman . . . , provide them with start-up capital . . . and have them together establish a new company specializing in one of the requisite phases of production' (Sabel and Zeitlin 1985). The upholding of this kind of strategy coupled with the management problems of fast-growth small firms explains why family networks, far from declining during the twentieth century, remained a central feature of French industrial structures. If we take into account personal 'participations' held by owner-managers in other firms, a widespread practice among firms under control of several unrelated owner-managers and designed to secure stability of income for each entrepreneur, 32 per cent of SMEs in the 1920s (as well as in the 1980s) were part of a network of SMEs. Among them 58 per cent were centralized family networks (Lescure 1996, Huppert 1981).

State Policy

Networks of firms were endogenous factors of adaptation for SMEs. Exogenous factors coming from the new orientations of State policy provided further stimulus.

As already mentioned, in the immediate post-Second World War period the priority of the State was given to the improvement of industrial productivity by promoting the growth of the corporate sector. This policy was to be continued all through the 'Thirty Glorious Years' but it became clear very quickly that another way to increase the productivity of French industry was to help SMEs to modernize their management and their equipment. The policy of national and regional development launched in the 1950s pushed in the same direction. By 1955, the Fund for Economic and Social Development, a public fund designed to finance the equipment programme of the Plan, had been allowed to grant loans to firms (small or large) involved in operations of conversion or decentralization. Further financial assistance programmes followed.

Two leading themes can be drawn from the wide range of public aid and encouragement initiated during these years. They concerned markets (especially foreign markets) and financing.

SMEs' Markets

During the 1920s, French SMEs had been very active in foreign markets, particularly those which operated in traditional sectors (Table 6.6). But fifteen years of economic difficulties had led to a vast retreat to the domestic market. The overvaluation of the franc coupled with the permanent excess of internal demand over supply was to prolong this tendency up to the late 1950s.

Table 6.6. *Proportion of exporting firms according to size (%)*

No. of employees	1926–9	1976
1–20	21.6	
21–100	41.9	60.8
101–199		79.3
101–500	50.9	
200–499		89.9
500 +	60.0	96.5

Sources: Lescure (1993); Brocard; Lombard; Varieras (1982).

For SMEs, the reopening of foreign markets did not imply only a problem of cost of production or of choice of product. It also implied a problem of information and commercial organization. Not only was the marketing staff of most of the SMEs minimal, but very few firms resorted to companies specialized in international trade. The latter themselves were generally small firms which had to visit industrial firms (and were not visited by them as in other countries) to offer them their services (Vidal 1980).

To solve this problem, groups of exporters have been constituted from the mid-1950s, and were sometimes initiated by SMEs themselves. In several industrial districts local authorities strove to sponsor the creation of a local association designed to group together exporting enterprises but, as illustrated by the example of Thiers, failure was a frequent outcome. It became the responsibility of the State to promote new structures. Two kinds of institutions with important fiscal advantages came into being: the State-agreed companies ('sociétés conventionnées'), and the groups of economic interest (GEIs). The former, created in 1959, were designed as joint ventures whose general purpose was to help their parent firms to prepare themselves for the Common Market. They were intended to prospect new markets inside the EEC but also to further a better specialization of the SMEs and a reduction of their costs. The latter, instituted in 1967, were more flexible and less-specialized organizations since the goal of the group could be exportation as well as research, purchase, stocking, management, etc.

The success of these organizations was not uniform. Even though many small firms in sectors such as electrical engineering and metallurgy did not hesitate to create 'sociétés conventionnées', these companies did not expand. GEIs were more successful, as 1,200 of them were recorded in 1972, but their number stopped increasing and only some of them had a commercial purpose. This is not to deny any utility to these institutions; they have lent useful but incomplete support to the reintroduction of SMEs to foreign markets (Crédit Hôtelier 1972; Chaibddera 1976).

SMEs' Financing

The lack of financial facilities for SMEs was the second motive for State intervention. As shown through the large share of their balance sheet occupied by short-term debts (most of them credits granted by suppliers), SMEs have been short of permanent capital throughout the period under review. This was the consequence of the shifts in financial structures previously analysed.

As an attempt to remedy a situation that made small firms very fragile bodies, the State had created semi-public institutions in the inter-war period. The goal of the 'Crédit National' and the 'Crédit Hôtelier' was to improve the provision of SMEs with medium-term credits. This policy was carried on during the 'Thirty Glorious Years', but it was slightly altered to take into account the new financial requirements of the firms. During the rapid growth of the 1960s, the lack of own-capital became a crucial issue. On the firms' side, this lack could be related to the limited volume of family resources and to the fear of owner-managers of losing the control of their firms if new shareholders joined the company. From 1963 to 1973, only 52 per cent of SMEs increased their capital; among them 85 per cent have contented themselves with calling on capital from relatives or friends (Herblay 1973). On the savers' side, the reluctance to hold shares of SMEs stemmed from the low liquidity and the high risk inherent in this kind of investment. Furthermore, the profitability of such investments was rather low since only a minority of SMEs distributed dividends (the proportion was 14 per cent in the sample studied by Hirigoyen in the mid-1970s) and the return was 25 per cent lower than in large firms (Mayoux 1978).

For the solution to this problem, the State relied on Companies for Regional Development. These institutions, which have been created from 1955 onwards to stimulate national and regional development, were private companies (with 45 per cent of their capital held by banks) but they enjoyed important financial and fiscal advantages. At the national level, their action was complemented by that of the Institute for Industrial Development created in 1970. One of the roles of the Companies was to acquire a minority interest in regional SMEs and to grant long-term loans. In matters of fund-raising, this second part of their activity was as innovative as the first since a special pattern of the loans was formed by the flotation of joint debenture bonds that enabled SMEs to access financial markets. In 1978, the shareholdings of the fifteen metropolitan companies amounted to 2.5 billion francs and their loans (with a part of their rate of interest borne by the State) rose to 10 billion francs. Thus new regional State-sponsored organizations (subcontracting Exchanges, Companies for Regional Development) tended to replace declining spontaneous organization (local banks, regional stock-exchanges, and industrial districts).

However, this new type of organization did not meet SMEs' expectations. The direct involvement of the Companies for Regional Development in local economies remained modest. Their operations expanded slowly and they were rather unprofitable. Above all, the firms to which they were committed were the larger SMEs not the smaller ones. It was not until crisis speeded up the contraction of SMEs' own capital (this falling from 47.1 per cent to 33.7 per cent of their resources between 1967 and 1976) that new public and private initiatives were taken.

One reason why the State was slow or unsuccessful in satisfying firms' financial requirements is found in the role played by commercial banks in the management of institutions (Crédit National, Companies for Regional Development) which were supposed to support SMEs. As banks were inclined to consider these institutions as potential competitors, they tended to limit their growth and to strictly select their clientèle from firms that they could not afford to satisfy directly.

These difficulties are a striking illustration of the limits of State policy in favour of SMEs. None of the great problems that SMEs faced found a solution before the beginning of the crisis. With regard to subcontracting problems for instance, the reflection dated back to 1969, but the first measures were decided only in 1973 and 1975, and they concerned only public markets. All through the 'Thirty Glorious Years', the main problems associated with the subcontracting system (instability of relations between subcontractor and principal firm, lack of training and information for the subcontractor, and poor quality control by the subcontractor) remained unsolved

(Ministère de l'Industrie 1978). Obviously the State delayed finding alternatives to the insufficient development of near-integration by large firms.

It also delayed finding solutions to the difficulties encountered by SMEs in acquiring direct access to sources of information, financing, and development of innovation and it was only in the early 1970s that the first measures were decided upon (Barreyre 1975; Barnier 1981).

Conclusion

The consequences of these delays have to be appreciated in relation with those factors that acted upon SME efficiency. As already mentioned, age is one of these factors since SMEs do not benefit by those institutional procedures that enable large organizations to govern efficiently the turnover of their equipment, structures, and managers. Given the close and negative relationship existing between the age of SMEs and their performance, their contribution to economic growth can be expected to depend less directly on the turnover of their constitutive elements than on the permanent turnover of the firms themselves.

Yet it was only in the early 1970s that the formation of new businesses became a political issue, and the conclusions of the first official reports on this question were rather pessimistic. Not only was France supposed to suffer a crucial lack of entrepreneurship, this in relation with the special cultural and social values of the country, but the new entrepreneurs were described as being badly trained and poorly provided with information, financing, and staff. Furthermore, no public institution on the model of the American SBA could compensate for such deficiencies (Mialaret 1973).

Evidence of the influence of this negative factor on the rejuvenation of SMEs and the renewal of the industrial fabric is inconclusive. However, it is possible to put forward some hypotheses. Under the assumption that the creation of new companies reflected the formation of new businesses as a whole (in the 1980s companies accounted for only 31 per cent of the total number of SMEs) it is difficult to instance lack of entrepreneurship as a permanent characteristic of French society: 15,700 new (industrial and commercial) companies were launched annually in the 1920s and in the years 1945–65; this was twice the figure reached on the eve of the First World War. Among them 85 per cent were general or limited partnerships or SARL, a new category of company created in 1925 and specially designed to provide small entrepreneurs with limited liability. The burgeoning of new and very small enterprises in the recession years of the 1930s was not as significant since it was generated by unemployment and, in all likelihood, frequently led to a misallocation of resources.

Most important was the decline in the supply of new entrepreneurs from 1966 onwards since public authorities determined in 1973 that 'the number of firms created each year is insufficient' (Mialaret 1973). Furthermore, if the formation of new businesses can be seen as a good indicator of the entrepreneurship that drives the economy, it is not enough to guarantee a suitable renewal of SMEs. In the inter-war period the rejuvenation of the industrial fabric met serious difficulties resulting from the over-mortality of young firms in the 1920s and from the under-mortality of old firms in the 1930s. Over-mortality resulted from the imbalanced financial organization of new firms; the continuous problem of the lack of financial facilities for these firms to raise long-term capital was worsened by the financial troubles of the inflationary years 1920–6 (Lescure 1994). Under-mortality in the recession years of the 1930s came from the growing leniency of the political authorities towards firms in difficulties; devices to keep unprofitable enterprises alive introduced barriers to entry and made competition no longer a driving force. Given their need for turnover, small firms were the most affected by these circumstances (Detoeuf 1943). Thus, in contrast with countries where the State tended to sponsor small businesses to protect competition among firms, in France the State shelved competition to protect SMEs, in fact penalizing them.

Given the prominent position of SMEs in French industrial structures, it is legitimate to assume that these developments were not completely unrelated to the poor performance recorded by the French economy during the first half of the twentieth century. Although these difficulties did not stop suddenly after the Second World War, the evidence is that their influence was declining throughout the 'Thirty Glorious Years' and that the process of renewal of the industrial fabric and SME rejuvenation was greatly improved. Therefore, it is also legitimate to assume that these new conditions were important contributions to the French economic recovery of these years.

REFERENCES

Alla, J. (1974), 'Age et évolution de l'entreprise' ['Age and Evolution of the Firm'], *Revue Economique*, 25/6.

Allinne, J. P. (1993), 'De l'externalité à la flexibilité: l'exemple de la sous-traitance aéronautique dans le sud-ouest de 1917 à nos jours' ['From Externality to Flexibility: The Example of the Subcontracting System in the Aeronautical Industry in the South-West of France from 1917 to Today'] in *Histoire, Gestion et Management*. Toulouse: ESUG.

Babeau, A. (1971), 'La croissance et le financement des petites entreprises industrielles' ['The Growth and the Financing of Small Industrial Enterprises'], in *La capacité de concurrence de l'industrie française*. Paris: Bordas.

Barnier, M. (1981), *L'innovation technologique et les PME, rapport au Premier Ministre* [*Technological Innovation and SMEs, Report to the Prime Minister*]. Paris: La Documentation Française.

Baroin, D. and Fracheboud, P. (1983), 'Les PME en Europe et leur contribution à l'emploi' ['SMEs in Europe and their Role in Employment'], *Notes et Etudes Documentaires*, 4715–16.

Barreyre, P. Y. (1975), *Stratégies d'innovation dans les MPI* [*Innovation Strategies in Medium and Small-Size Industries*]. Suresnes: Hommes et Techniques.

Battiau, M. (1976), 'Les industries textiles de la région Nord-Pas-de-Calais: Etude d'une concentration géographique d'entreprises et de sa remise en cause' ['Textile Industries in the Region Nord-Pas-de-Calais: Case-Study of a Geographical Concentration of Firms and its Crisis'], Ph.D. diss., Lille University.

Besse, J. (1983), 'PMI et politique industrielle' ['SMEs and Industrial Policy'], *Revue d'Economie Industrielle*, 23.

Brocard, R. and Gandois, J. M. (1978), 'Grandes entreprises et PME' ['Large firms and SMEs'], *Economie et Statistique*, 96.

—— Lombard, N., and Varieras, D. (1982), 'Forces et contraintes des PME' ['Strengths and Constraints of the SMEs'], *Cahiers Economiques et Monétaires*, Entreprises, 16.

Chadeau, E. (1987), *L'industrie aéronautique en France 1900–1950* [*Aeronautical Industry in France 1900–1950*]. Paris: Fayard.

Chaibddera, M. (1976), 'Les explications de la survie des petites entreprises industrielles: Analyse de l'économie française' ['The Reasons for the Survival of the Small Industrial Enterprises: Study of the French Economy'], Ph.D. diss., Rennes University.

Champeux, A. (1976), 'Le développement des entreprises de sous-traitance métallurgiques du secteur découpage-emboutissage' ['The Growth of the Sub-contractors in the Cutting-out and Stamping Industries'], Ph.D. diss., Paris University.

Crédit d'Equipement des PME (1987), *Les PME et leurs dirigeants* [*SMEs and their Managers*]. Paris: CEPME.

—— (1991), *La transmission des PME* [*The Making Over of SMEs*]. Paris: CEPME.

Crédit Hôtelier, Commercial et Industriel (1972), *Les moyennes et petites industries: Expériences et solutions* [*Medium and Small-Size Industries: Experiences and Solutions*]. Paris: EME.

Daviet, J. P. (1983), 'La Compagnie de Saint-Gobain de 1830 à 1939' ['The Company of Saint-Gobain from 1830 to 1939'], thesis diss., Paris University.

Delattre, M. (1982), 'Les PME face aux grandes entreprises' ['SMEs Facing the Large Enterprises'], *Economie et Statistique*, 148.

—— and Eymard-Duverney, Fr. (1984), 'Le progrès des PME dans la crise: signe d'un relâchement du tissu industriel' ['The Progress of the SMEs During the Crisis'], *Critiques de l'Economie Politique*, 119–32.

Detoeuf, A. (1943), 'L'avenir en France des petites et moyennes entreprises' ['The Future of SMEs in France'], in *12e Cycle d'Etudes de la CEGOS*. Paris: CEGOS.

Didier, M. (1969), 'Croissance et dimension des entreprises' ['Growth and Size of Firms'], *Collections de l'INSEE*, E.I.

—— and Malinvaud, E. (1969), 'La concentration de l'industrie s'est-elle accentuée depuis le début du siècle?' ['Has Concentration in Industry Increased since the Beginning of the Century?'], *Economie et Statistique*, 2.

Evraert, S. (1978), 'Croissance, efficacité et rentabilité des petites et moyennes entre-prises' ['Growth, Efficiency and Profitability of SMEs'], Ph.D. diss., Toulouse University.

Fizaine, F. (1968), 'Analyse statistique de la croissance des entreprises selon l'âge et la taille' ['Statistical Analysis of the Growth of Firms according to Age and Size'], *Revue d'Economie Politique*, 78/4.

François, J. P. (1976), *Les moyennes entreprises dans l'économie industrielle [Medium-Size Enterprises in the Industrial Economy]*. Paris: Ministère de l'Industrie et de la Recherche.

Gelinier, O. and Gaultier, A. (1972), *L'avenir des entreprises personnelles et familiales [The Future of Individual and Family Firms]*. Paris: Hommes et Techniques.

Gervais, M. (1978), 'Pour une théorie de l'organisation PME', ['For a Theory of the Organization of SMEs'], *Revue Française de Gestion*, 11.

Goblot, E. (1925), *La barrière et le niveau* [The Gate and the Level]. Paris: P.U.F..

Guillaume, S. (1987), *Confédération Générale des Petites et Moyennes Entreprises* [General Union of Small and Medium-Size Enterprises]. Bordeaux: P.U.B.

Herblay, M. (1973), 'La vérité sur les PME' ['The Truth on SMEs'], *L'Expansion* (Oct.).

Hirigoyen, G., (1984), 'Contribution à la connaissance des comportements fin-anciers des moyennes entreprises industrielles familiales' ['Contribution to the Knowledge of the Financial Strategies of Medium-size Industrial Family Firms'], Ph.D. diss., Bordeaux University.

Horowitz, J. and, Demillère, M. C. (1978), 'La vraie nature de la PME française' ['The True Nature of the French SME'], *Revue Française de Gestion*, 11.

Houssiaux, J. (1957), 'Le concept de quasi-intégration et le rôle des sous-traitants dans l'industrie' ['The Concept of Near-integration and the Role of the Sub-contractors in Industry'], *Revue Economique*, 2.

Huppert, R. (1981), 'Stratégies de développement des PMI françaises' ['Strategies of Development of the French Industrial SMEs'], *Revue d'Economie Industrielle*, 17.

INSEE (1974), 'Fresque historique du système productif' ['Historical Fresco of the Productive System']. *Les Collections de L'INSEE*, E 27.

Jenny, F. and Weber, A. P. (1974), *Concentration et politique des structures industrielles [Concentration and Industrial Structures Policy]*. Paris: La Documentation Française.

Kurgan-Van Hentenryk, G. and Chadeau, E. (1990), 'Structure et stratégie de la pe-tite et moyenne entreprise depuis la révolution industrielle: rapport général' ['Structure and Strategy of the SME since the Industrial Revolution'], in H. Van der Wee and E. Aerts, (eds.), *Debates and Controversies in Economic History, A-sessions, Proceedings Tenth International Economic History Congress*. Louvain: Louvain University Press.

Laferrère, M. (1960), *Lyon ville industrielle [Lyons Industrial City]*. Paris: P.U.F.

Landes, D. (1951), 'French Business and the Businessman: a Social and Cultural Analysis', in M. Earle (ed.), *Modern France: Problems of the Third and Fourth Republic*. Princeton: Princeton University Press.

Lanoizelée, F. (1975), 'La stratégie des moyennes entreprises de mécanique' ['The Strategy of Medium-Size Mechanical Enterprises'], Ph.D. diss., Paris University.

Laufer, J. (1975), 'Comment on devient entrepreneur' ['How One Becomes an Entrepreneur'], *Revue Française de Gestion*, 2.

Lescure, M. (1993), 'Les petites et moyennes entreprises et l'exportation en France au XXe siècle' ['SMEs and Export in Twentieth-Century France'], in *Le commerce extérieur français de Méline à nos jours*. Paris: Comité pour l'Histoire Economique et Financière de la France.

—— (1994), 'Small and Medium-sized Industrial Enterprises Through the Inflation of the 1920s in France', in Muller (ed.), *Structure and Strategy of Small and Medium-Size Enterprises*.

—— (1996), *PME et croissance Economique: L'expérience française des années 1920* [*SMEs and Economic Growth: The French Experience in the 1920s*]. Paris: Economica.

Lévy-Leboyer, M. (1968), 'Les processus d'industrialisation: le cas de l'Angleterre et de la France' ['The Processes of Industrialization: The Cases of England and France'], *Revue Historique*, 2.

—— (1974), 'Le patronat français a-t-il été malthusien?' ['Were French Entrepreneurs Malthusian?'], *Le Mouvement Social*, 88.

—— (1980), 'The Large Corporation in Modern France' in A. D. Chandler, Jr., and H. Daems (eds.), *Managerial Hierarchies, Comparative Perspectives on the Rise of the Modern Industrial Enterprise*. Cambridge, Mass. and London: Harvard University Press.

—— (1984), 'The Large Family Firm in the French Manufacturing Industry', in A. Okochi and S. Yasuoka (eds.), *Family Business in the Era of Industrial Growth, Its Ownership and Management*. Tokyo: University of Tokyo Press.

Martin, C. (1981), 'Forces et faiblesses des PME en France' ['Strengths and Weaknesses of French SMEs'], *Profils Economiques*, 5.

Mayoux, J. (1978), *Le développement des initiatives financières locales et régionales* [*The Development of Local and Regional Financial Initiatives*]. Paris: La Documentation Française.

Mialaret, M. (1973), *Pour entreprendre* [*To Undertake*]. Paris: La Documentation Française.

Ministère de l'Industrie (1974), 'L'organisation des marchés de sous-traitance' ['The Organization of the Subcontracting Markets'], *Etudes de Politique Industrielle*, 8.

—— (1978), 'Commission Technique de la Sous-Traitance, premières réflexions' ['Technical Committee for Subcontracting System: First Thoughts'], *Etudes de Politique Industrielle*, 20.

Morvan, Y. (1967), 'Influence de la dimension sur la rentabilité des firmes' ['Influence of Size on Firms Profitability'], Ph.D. diss., Rennes University.

Muller, M. (1994) (ed.), *Structure and Strategy of Small and Medium-Size Enterprises since the Industrial Revolution*. Stuttgart: Franz Steiner Verlag.

Omnès, C. (1993), 'Marchés du travail et trajectoires professionnelles: Les ouvrières parisiennes de l'entre-deux-guerres' ['Labour Markets and Professionnal Trajectories: The Parisian Female Workers of the Inter-War Period'], Ph.D. diss., Paris University.

Parodi, M. (1981), *L'économie et la société Française depuis 1945* [*Economy and Society in France since 1945*]. Paris: Armand Colin.

Piore, M. J. and Sabel, C. F. (1984), *The Second Industrial Divide: Possibilities for Prosperity*. New York: Basic Books.

Reynaud, B. (1989), 'L'industrie rubannière dans la région stéphanoise, 1898–1975' ['The Ribbon Industry in the Region of Saint-Étienne, 1898–1975'], Ph.D. diss., Saint-Étienne University.

Sabel, Ch. and Zeitlin, J. (1985), 'Historical Alternatives to Mass Production: Politics, Markets and Technology in Nineteenth-Century Industrialization', *Past and Present*, 108.

Saglio, A. and Tabuteau, B. (1971), 'L'utilisation des capacités de production dans l'industrie' ['The Utilization of Production Capacity in Industry'], *Economie et Statistique*, 21.

Schnetzler, J. (1973), 'Les industries et les hommes dans la région de Saint-Étienne' ['Industries and People in the Region of Saint-Étienne'], Ph.D. diss., Lyons University.

Straus, A. (1985), 'Les marchés régionaux de valeurs mobilières: une approche comparative' ['Regional Stock Exchange Markets: A Comparative Study'] in *Banque et investissements en Méditerranée à l'époque contemporaine*. Marseille: C.C.I.

Szokoloczy-Syllaba, J. (1965), *Les organisations professionnelles françaises et le Marché commun* [*The French Professional Unions and the Common Market*]. Paris: F.N.S.P. .

Vasille, L. (1982), 'Les PME: fragilité financière, forte rentabilité' ['SMEs: Financial Fragility, High Profitability'], *Economie et Statistique*, 148.

Vennin, B. (1975), 'Pratiques et signification de la sous-traitance dans l'industrie automobile en France' ['Practices and Significance of the Subcontracting System in the French Car Industry'], *Revue Economique*, 26/2.

Vidal, M. Cl. (1980), 'Le rôle des PME dans le redéploiement industriel' ['The Role of the SMEs in Industrial Redeployment'], Ph.D. diss., Paris University.

Villa, P. (1992), *Productivité et accumulation du capital en France depuis 1896* [*Productivity and Capital Accumulation in France since 1896*]. Paris: INSEE.

Weisz, R. (1987), 'L'intégration de la production et de la distribution: rationalisation ou renversement de la logique industrielle?' ['The Integration of Production and Distribution: Rationalization or New Industrial Logic?'], *Entreprises et Produits*, 30.

Zeldin, Th. (1973), *France 1848–1945*. Oxford: Oxford University Press.

Zouggari, M. (1985), 'Organisation et croissance de la PME' ['Organization and Growth of the SME'], Ph.D. diss., Paris University.

7

Small Manufacturing Firms and Local Productive Systems in Modern Italy

AURELIO ALAIMO

Introduction

Historical research on industrial development in Italy has been marked by some contradictions. International historiography has given scarce attention to the Italian phenomenon. The latter has often been considered just one of the many cases of latecomer countries, for which the task was simply to identify the substitutive factors of industrialization. Moreover, Italian historians themselves have shown little interest in the economic development of the last two centuries. Modern historians have dwelt on the classic themes of political and institutional history, while economic historians have shown a clear preference for the study of pre-industrial economy and of its extraordinary evolution, from great prosperity to its rapid decline.

The situation has been undergoing change for some time. In Italy a new generation of economic historians, in particular business historians, has begun to investigate the great unexplored issues of modern industrialization: the structure and strategy of the larger industrial enterprises, the organization of credit, and patterns of public intervention. Sociologists and economists have greatly stimulated historical research on Italian industrialization. These scholars, having examined the most recent successes of Italian industry, have hypothesized that such successes were favoured by the historical traditions already existing in some regions. At the same time, we have witnessed a partial revision of the dominating approach in the economic history of industrialization. Newer studies offer more attention to

I wish to thank the editors of the book, the discussants, and the participants to the 24th Fuji Conference, for their helpful comments during and after the conference. I am also grateful to Robert Gwizdala for his co-operation in the English translation of the paper.

the elements of continuity and gradualness of industrial development. This then has led to a view of development which pays close attention to the role played by local traditions and by pre-industrial experiences.

The meeting of these different tendencies has favoured a renewed interest in modern Italian industrial development. Thanks to business historians, we are more familiar today with the major protagonists of economic growth. Some studies closely examine the classic issues of an industrial development process. Others favour the 'revisionist' arguments proposed by some economic historians. Still others have concentrated their analysis on firms and sectors previously considered of lesser importance, but recognized today for their strategic importance. In any case, both fieldwork and the comparison of different schools of thought help to refine the techniques and methods employed in the study of these issues. The early result produced by this work suggested the following conclusion: the analysis of the Italian case, so strongly characterized by the persistence of structures and traditions from a distant past, may lead to an important contribution regarding the shape taken by European industrialization. Far from being considered a minor episode, the study of these phenomena in Italy may open new perspectives for international comparison.

Within this context, the research on small-firm systems has aroused growing interest. These very recent studies constitute a new current in research. They examine those forms of regional industrial development that have drawn a part of their resources from the local communities and from the choices of a plurality of subjects. As a consequence, a new interpretation of the Italian industrialization process has been advanced. In this perspective, local economic traditions and social relationships preceding real industrial development have taken on a particular relevance.

This chapter offers a synthesis of the historical studies on small-firm systems, and discusses their implication for a more general reconsideration of Italian industrial development. The first aim of the chapter is to show the important role played by small-firm systems in the Italian industrialization. However, this analysis also has a more ambitious goal. The study of local productive systems can allow understanding of some mechanisms which have fostered the whole industrialization process, including large-firm based development.

The chapter is divided into three parts. The first section illustrates the terms essential to the discussion of the small-firm systems in Italy, as the social sciences have defined them in the last few years. The second section presents the main results obtained by the historical analysis of these issues, dwelling on the great variety of development paths in various regional areas. The third section provides an overall view of these paths, identifying the central common characteristics and indicating some possible hypotheses for further investigation. The conclusion offers a short synthesis and mentions some still unresolved questions, in particular on the subject of the economic regulation of productive systems. This chapter is, for the most part, based on existing studies, many of which are still works in progress. Also, a large portion refers to research conducted by myself, in particular on industry in the region of Emilia Romagna. Such research has provided the impetus to discuss hypotheses and theoretical notions used in empirical studies.

The Debate on the Italian Small-firm Systems

Scholarly research on the Italian small-firm based industrial development—the so-called *industrializzazione diffusa* ('widespread industrialization')—has constantly grown in the last two decades. The initial appeal came from the excellent performance of these firms during the 1960s and 1970s. Several empirical investigations have since indicated that many of these small firms displayed innovative capacities as well as considerable organizational and productive flexibility. Such characteristics helped them reach a position from which to compete successfully within the most fluctuating international markets. It has also been observed that small innovative firms have clustered in the central and north-eastern regions of Italy. Their competitive advantage clearly came out in the business-cycle slump stages, when the rigidity of large firms hindered organizational changes and innovations.[1]

The 'discovery' of widespread industrialization has profoundly transformed the current vision of the Italian economy. First, it has pointed out the existence of a particular form of industrial development, conceptually in need of clearer formulation, yet certainly distinct from the best-known growth processes—that is those based instead on the large enterprise with standardized production and a rigidly hierarchical organization. Furthermore, the study of the territorial clustering of these firms has forced scholars to review the traditional dualistic interpretation of Italian economic development.

In a schematic way, one can state that the dualistic interpretation was based on a dichotomy. The large-firm based industrialization of the North, in particular the three north-western regions of the so-called 'industrial triangle', was opposed to the backwardness of southern Italy (see Map 7.1). The latter seemed to be destined to remain dominantly agricultural: its main contribution to the Italian industrialization was limited basically to the work-force migrating from the South towards northern industrial areas (Lutz 1962). But this idea of a territorial dualism did not allow one to grasp the peculiarities of the areas covered by the widespread industrialization phenomenon. Taken together, these areas represented a sort of 'third Italy' (Bagnasco 1977; Fuà and Zacchia 1983). Unlike the industrial triangle, they did not experience a large-firm based industrialization. However, they

Map 7.1. *Map of Italy, showing the borders of the twenty Italian regions, the main Italian cities, and the names of some regions and cities mentioned in the chapter. The regions of the so-called 'Third Italy' are represented by the shaded areas (from south to north: Marche, Toscana, Emilia Romagna, Veneto, Friuli Venezia Giulia; however, some scholars include other areas). The regions of the 'industrial triangle' are: Lombardia, Piemonte, Liguria. Several local productive systems can be found in many other areas, even in Southern Italy. The map has been drawn by Giuliana Chiodini.*

were by no means comparable to the backward South, as far as the dynamic and innovative small-firms activity was concerned. And moreover, third Italy regions presented a certain homogeneity, even from the point of view of political and social systems, being characterized by the presence of strong political subcultures (communist or catholic local subcultures; see Trigilia 1986, 1989*b*).

A closer examination of this line of research has allowed avoidance of making generic reference only to the size of the firm. At once, the research turned its attention to the existing connections between the different units involved in the same productive sector and located in a circumscribed area (small-firm clusters). In this direction, an important contribution has come from the analysis of a group of scholars headed by the economist Giacomo Becattini. This analysis made use of some of the indications present in Alfred Marshall's work, upon which Becattini made new elaborations and applied the notion of 'industrial district' (Becattini 1987).[2]

In general terms, the notion of district may point to a population of firms, mainly small ones, specialized in the same industrial sector (or in a *filière*, that is a vertically integrated sector) and located in a circumscribed territory (generally around a small town). From this territory, the firms derive resources necessary for their activity and their success. Thus, the essential characteristic of the district is the existence of economies external to the single enterprises, yet internal to the district. Examples are the diffusion of particular professional skills, a continuous information exchange about the market and technology, an inter-firm division of labour, and the possibility to count on a network of qualified suppliers. This group of elements—the 'industrial atmosphere' evoked by Marshall—allows for a limitation (though not the exclusion) of competition among the firms, while instead favouring co-operation. One may thus contend that both the functioning and success of an industrial district largely depend on the unity of its community relations, and on its capacity to organize, at times informally, the economic activity of a vast number of enterprises.

The notion of district, here briefly explained, has not only revealed itself to be of great utility in the empirical investigation, but has also met with great success.[3] The idea of a district even appears in the contributions of other scholars, who perhaps arrived at this notion while having undertaken independent and at times divergent paths (Brusco 1986, 1989; Gobbo 1989). The discussion on Italian districts has also involved European and American scholars and may constitute a point of departure for comparative investigations (Goodman 1989; Pyke, Becattini, and Sengenberger 1990; Zeitlin 1990). By now, commentators have begun speaking of districts in news and television inquiries, a true testimonial to the rapid progress made by this idea (Moussanet and Paolazzi 1992; Prodi 1992, ch. 3).

As often happens in these cases, the proliferation of research has modified the original proposals; and if perhaps some theoretical rigour has been lost, it is certainly true that what gains have been made concern the empirical knowledge of the phenomena studied. Emerging from the various inquiries, we have a differentiated picture of small-firm systems. Many of them are even located outside the third Italy, notably in some areas of the industrial triangle, and also in other central and southern regions. Then some scholars have tried to group these systems into a broad variety of models and interpretative proposals: not only true industrial districts, but also flexible specialization systems, industrial sub-systems, co-operative districts ... (Piore and Sabel 1984; Seravalli 1988; Capecchi 1990*a*; Alaimo 1994). Though present in different forms, and not always well specified, these productive systems share a common element. Their identity is characterized by the strong grounding in the areas where they are settled, and by their ability to exploit the resources offered by local communities.

In this way, a further difference from the typical development of many large firms has been clarified. Not merely in terms of size and economies of scale, it is more important to note that in the large-firm areas economic growth has been fostered above all (though not exclusively) by exogenous forces. Within a latecomer economy like the Italian, these forces may have assumed particular importance. Some examples are: State intervention, bank credit, foreign capital, and international trade tendencies. Conversely, the development resulting from the small innovative firms represents to a great extent the outcome of an endogenous path. This path, still in need of retracing, may have been favoured by the opportunities present in a given period and by a plurality of subjective choices made within the same community. It means that in order to understand the reasons behind the success of the widespread industrialization, it is not sufficient to study firms and entrepreneurs, but is necessary to examine *local productive systems*, considered as a whole (Garofoli and Mazzoni 1994). To be sure, such a vast reference to local productive systems runs the risk of being generic. But it reminds us that understanding of these productive systems requires the use of interdisciplinary methodologies able to go beyond (and to 'complicate') the economic analysis.

From what has been said it appears evident that historical research can play an essential role in the comprehension of these phenomena. It is worth observing that on various occasions sociologists and economists were responsible for advancing hypotheses on the evolution of local systems. Such hypotheses proposed to identify a possible tie between the historical inheritances—family structures, agrarian contracts, political subcultures—and their recent economic successes (Paci 1982; Becattini 1986; Trigilia 1986). Despite the considerable interest in these and other ideas, Italian economic historiography has been slow in undertaking empirical research in this field. The existing research today, while still taking shape, may be characterized as fragmentary and heterogeneous. This research may nevertheless furnish us with some important indications. First of all, it reveals which conditions

favoured the initial development of widespread industrialization and how
this evolution occurred in these areas. Furthermore, historical research in-
forms us of how widespread industrialization contributed to the overall
development of Italian industry.

The following paragraphs examine such questions. Yet we should bear in
mind that literature on this subject is scarce. Various research projects are
underway, with others limiting themselves to the exposition of proposals
and hypotheses in need of verification. While the results may require a
necessary degree of caution, it is perhaps more important to draw attention
to both the questions and the problems raised by recent studies.

Development Paths of Local Productive Systems

Pluriactivity and Protoindustry

One of the most interesting indications of the formation of local productive
systems concerns the role played by the widespread *pluriattività* in the
Italian countryside. In brief, rural pluriactivity can indicate the carrying out
of two different types of work by the same individual. In these cases, a chief
agricultural occupation was backed up by a second activity, generally (but
not always) in the manufacturing sector. Pluriactivity can even refer to the
simultaneous presence of incomes of different origin within the same family (or household) (Villani 1989). This experience is tied to the most varying
forms of family management of agriculture, such as sharecropping and
small ownership. Yet it probably expanded more among day-labourer families attempting to augment incomes derived from this most precarious activity (Biagioli 1989; Pescarolo 1989).

The Italian economy of the nineteenth century, and even late into the
twentieth, presents numerous examples of pluriactivity, many of which are
important in understanding the industrialization process. Actually, this experience is not necessarily associated with the widespread industrialization phenomenon. An interesting case is the silk industry. Up to the First
World War this industry constituted the most important manufacturing
sector in terms of employees, capital, and exports, and was characterized
by the presence of steam-powered medium-sized units (Federico 1988).
Other studies have demonstrated the presence of peasant/worker families
in the cotton industry located in the area north of Milan (the *Alto Milanese*).
This is a sector and an area beyond the borders of the third Italy, considered
as a paradigmatic example of 'classic' industrialization, founded on the
productive concentration and favouring the growth of large industry and

the urban expansion (Romano 1990; a partially different view in Cento Bull 1989; Corner 1993).

Nevertheless, the successive evolution of an intensely industrialized portion of the Alto Milanese tells a different story, one in which the old tradition of pluriactivity seems, in recent years, to have favoured the formation of small-firm systems. Mauro Magatti (1991), a sociologist mindful of historical transformations, has shown that this area experienced a surprising process of restructuring and productive disintegration (between the 1950s and the 1970s). The previous dualistic structure, characterized by the dominating presence of large-scale, vertically integrated factories, transformed itself into a 'scattered factory': that is into a system of small and subdivided firms. Magatti maintains that this transformation was made possible by the habit, still in use even after the Second World War, of families integrating agricultural and industrial incomes. It would have been precisely this form of income integration that created the favourable conditions for the diffusion of autonomous and entrepreneurial initiatives. The willingness to run the risk of new initiatives drew upon the protection offered by family incomes as well as by community relations (Magatti 1991: 134–42).

These hypotheses should be verified with greater attention, in so far as the area under examination is the site of a long and complex industrial history. However, in areas of recent industrialization and more clearly characterized by the presence of small firms, the connection between pluriactivity and local productive systems appears more evident and better established. A model case is the slow industrialization of the Marche, a region of central Italy which represents an essential reference point for any study of the local productive systems.

The history of the Marche is one of a predominantly agricultural region which, from national unification in 1861 to the Second World War, was distinguished by its rural and sluggish economic structures (Sabbatucci Severini 1987). Yet, despite this apparent immobility, beginning in the 1950s numerous small-firm productive systems developed. These systems spread out rapidly into all of the territory, thanks to the accomplishments of the production and export of mass-market products (Sori 1991).

This surprising evolution may be better understood by referring to the long pluriactivity of sharecroppers and, in general, of farmers in some areas of the Marche (Moroni 1989*b*; Sabbatucci Severini 1996, ch. 5). In this case, however, pluriactivity often asserted itself through the presence of truly protoindustrial productions spread out among the countryside and even in small rural towns (D'Attorre 1991).[4] According to Ercole Sori (1987), the 'pillar' of the protoindustry of the Marche was silk manufacturing, which for some decades symbolized the 'classic intermediary between the city and the country' (p. 334). This activity was, however, smaller and more backward compared to its counterpart in northern Italy. Other textile activities, namely hemp and flax, were of minor importance. Around the end of the century they were scattered among the firms/families in the country-side and, though secondary, were deeply rooted in the territory. Actually both the silk manufacturing and the other textile productions, some earlier than others, met with an irreversible decline. It is probable however, that this diversified protoindustrial experience in some way constituted a 'pre-condition' (Sori 1987: 333), whether indirectly or not, of the subsequent industrial development. This represented an activity forming a predomin-antly female, multipurpose labour force, within an agricultural economy and rural territory. At the same time, it laid the foundations for the growth of entrepreneurship, which later in the century, successfully met the chal-lenges of international markets (Amatori 1987).

While in the textile industry we find only a few indirect preconditions of successive widespread industrialization, in other cases the connection be-tween protoindustrial traditions and recent tendencies appears more dis-tinct. I am referring to those old productive activities, still existing in the twentieth century, in which a remarkable new development occurred be-ginning in the 1950s. In these cases, the skills acquired during the previous decades made it possible to seize the opportunities presented by the new international trade openness and by the expansion of markets.

As an illustration, let us examine the history of the footwear district, per-haps the best-known of the many districts of the Marche. Today, shoe fact-ories are present in many areas of the region. In the town of Montegranaro (south of Ancona), which constitutes the historic nucleus of this district, the protoindustrial tradition goes back to the beginning of the last century. The research of Moroni (1989*a*) illustrates how protoindustrial productive organ-ization foretold the implementation of work-at-home and seasonal work (see also Sabbatucci Severini 1996, ch. 8). In this way the protoindustry al-lowed connections with agricultural activities and integration of different incomes; and this still in the early decades of the twentieth century. This, however, differed from other protoindustrial experiences—those in which manufacturing production was located in the countryside and was often conditioned by the rhythms of the agricultural cycle. In the case of Monte-granaro, we encounter a protoindustry that grew within a town, albeit a small one. This activity, moreover, developed due to the initiative of a class of rising entrepreneurs, such as merchants and artisans, who were able to sell their products (slippers and eventually inexpensive shoes) in even distant markets. Besides the work conducted at home, these entrepreneurs man-aged to organize the working of the raw materials inside centralized work-shops. This experience reinforced the nascent district in its attempt to meet the challenges of mechanization and to create the first technically organ-ized shoe factories. The most remarkable development occurred after the Second World War, concurrent with the expansive phase of the business cycle.

The case of the footwear industry of the Marche is not an isolated one. Research on the historic origins of widespread industrialization has shed light on the existence of urban, protoindustrial (or, more generically, manufacturing) traditions, even in other sectors and in various areas of the third Italy. An example is the hide and musical instruments workshops in the Marche (Sori 1991), or the working of leather and furniture in Tuscany (Becattini 1986). A slightly different though particularly interesting case concerns the area in and around the town of Carpi, in Emilia Romagna (north of Bologna). An important knitwear district developed there in the 1950s and today is in a leadership position on the international markets (Solinas 1982).

Even in the history of the Carpi district one finds earlier protoindustrial experience—the production of wood shavings (Cigognetti and Pezzini 1992). This activity consisted of the production of semifinished goods— straw plaits made from vegetable fibres—which could be sold directly or used in the production of hats. The production of wood shavings dates back to the sixteenth century and had developed with alternating fortunes in the successive centuries, predominantly with day-labourer and sharecropper families. In the twentieth century, it experienced a strong relaunching, demonstrated both by the creation of genuine industrial plants and by a joint-stock company. However, during the 1930s, and even more so after the Second World War, the old activity had an irreversible crisis. Eventually it was replaced by the vast growth in knitwear manufacturing in and around Carpi. This successful productive reconversion was made possible by the experience derived from the manufacturing traditions of the past, such as the ability to organize the work at home spread out into many areas, the international commercial skills of agents and middlemen, and the entrepreneurial skills of producers and traders. The fluctuating market tendencies required a change in production, with a flexibility which is the distinctive trait of the district. Nevertheless, the commercial and organizational forms remained those already used by the labourers and by the firms committed to the production of wood shavings.

Let us then attempt to synthesize an illustrative outline. The various experiences, such as pluriactivity of peasants, rural and urban protoindustry, and the manufacturing traditions, all contributed in creating favourable conditions for the formation of local productive systems. Naturally, it is a rather simple matter to note that these developments were possible in the sphere of light industry and in particular, in the production of those mass-market products that required neither heavy investments nor particularly complicated technology. One may also object that in many other contexts, protoindustrial experience did not produce similar positive results. Our aim however, is not to propose coherent and unassailable models, but rather it is to identify some possible lines of evolution.

Then we can state that the cases examined describe a path of development strictly bound to the country and to agriculture, or to small towns surrounded by a vast rural territory. The entrepreneurial initiative, to be sure, seems to come particularly from merchants and artisans. But the labour force, usually residing in rural towns and in the countryside, often remained attached to this world, even if in many different ways. Therefore in the origins of widespread industrialization we discern a 'minor' Italy with firmly established traditions, characterized by a dense network of relationships between the city and the country. In this path of development, the gradualness and the persistence of centuries-old structures, not fully 'modernized', seem to prevail over the drastic breakups common in many other industrialization processes.

Towns, Institutions, Firms

Besides the rural and protoindustrial routes, there are some cases in which the formation of productive systems followed divergent paths. Political and economic systems in small- to medium-sized towns sometimes played the role of 'incubator' for entrepreneurial initiatives. In many cases the same role was played by thriving firms. Although here we appear to be far from the gradual development of rural pluriactivity, this different route also led to one of the many variations of widespread industrialization.

The most important examples of an urban development path are detectable in Emilia Romagna, another region of the third Italy which has been for some time an object of analysis at home and abroad (Brusco, 1982; Capecchi, 1990a).[5] This region possessed ample protoindustrial precedents, such as that already mentioned in regards to Carpi, tied to relatively prosperous and well organized agricultural activities (D'Attorre 1991; D'Attorre and Zamagni 1992). In Emilia Romagna, however, perhaps more than elsewhere, the formation of local productive systems was fostered by opportunities and resources available in the larger towns.

Bologna, the most important Emilian city, and one of the main Italian cities, is an exemplary case. During the last few decades, the territory of Bologna with its immediately surrounding municipalities, has undergone intense industrialization through the support of a complex system of small- to medium-sized firms. However, unlike other areas of the third Italy, Bologna does not meet the commonly accepted standards of a district. Though engineering industries prevail, no specific sector is dominant. Instead, we find a series of industrial subsystems formed by thousands of small firms in continuous evolution (Capecchi 1990b). Moreover, Bologna with its commercial service, large and prestigious university, and its wealth of cultural activities, possesses a social and economic system which cannot be associated in any single way with its industrial production, as frequently occurred in the small integrated towns of authentic districts.[6] Nevertheless, the resources promoting the formation of this productive system derive precisely from the city itself. This is most evident in the development of the engineering industry which is the driving sector of the system.

In Bologna, the earliest engineering firms were already active at the end of the nineteenth century, producing agricultural and other simple machines (such as motors, pumps, and boilers). The following decades saw this initial nucleus develop into a cluster of firms dedicated to specialized and small series production, predominantly of industrial components and intermediate goods, but also of durable consumption good (such as motor cycles). A strong impetus for these productive activities came from the war commissions of the 1930s (D'Attorre 1980). Finally, in the 1950s and 1960s, the engineering industry established itself as far and away the most important local industry (Zamagni 1986; Capecchi 1990*b*).

Among the factors that most favoured this long growth process, we must emphasize the role played by the municipal technical institute, Aldini Valeriani. During its long history, this school, founded in the first half of the nineteenth century and still active, produced multifaceted personnel able to read a technical design, to work on universal machine tools, and already prepared for the needs of the many craftsmen's workshops present in the city. To these workshops, the school furnished specialized workers and technicians skilled in moving from one productive process to another. This contributed to the creation of a remarkable degree of diversified production and promoted flexibility in responding to the changing demands of a still restricted and unstable market (Comune di Bologna 1980; Capecchi 1990*b*).

In the inter-war years, public technical schools with multiskilled graduates were situated in other Emilian towns near Bologna, such as Modena and Imola (Berselli and Telmon 1983). Moreover in recent years, regional and municipal governments have furnished services and infrastructures, for example on data about market tendencies, that may have contributed to the process of widespread industrialization (Nanetti 1988, ch. 6; Brusco and Righi 1989). These forms of indirect public intervention should be better examined. They introduce a new subject to our investigations, namely that of the local public institutions. It is a subject which, in the growth processes most closely tied to the country, had never emerged before (at least not so visibly). Of course, we are not speaking of actual development strategies, nor of 'visible hands' intent on programming industrial routes. We are dealing, however, with subjective choices that back up and orient the autonomous formation process of the local productive system.

The role of subjective choices becomes clear even when considering the activity of some larger firms, particularly in the engineering industry. Though larger than others, by comparison with the national average, some of these firms can be considered medium or even small- to medium-sized (see note 1). Yet in many areas, they had created a point of reference for the formation and spread of skills to be used later within the system. At times this happened in a direct fashion. In the 1930s, for example, some of the larger firms in the area created internal courses for apprentices working with machine tools. It was the case of Ducati in Bologna, Reggiane in Reggio Emilia, and Bubba in Piacenza (the last two towns are located to the north-west of Bologna). The most significant contributions appeared during the period of intense development, though in a more indirect way. In the 1950s and 1960s many firms offered formative opportunities to technicians and skilled workers who, only a few years later, were to quit their work to start up new businesses as craftsmen and entrepreneurs. At first, the original firms benefited from this tendency. They found it was convenient to de-centralize a part of their production, as well as guaranteeing orders to their suppliers (when necessary even giving some form of assistance). However, these craftsmen quickly became autonomous and began to find specific niches in the market for their own products, leading at times, to direct com-petition with the parent company.

Once more, the area in and around Bologna offers the most striking ex-ample of this form of spin-off development. Examples are the engineering and electrotechnical sectors (Capecchi 1990*b*: 172–3; D'Attorre and Zamagni 1992: 14), as well as the production of packaging machinery, which is the most important local industry. Even in other provinces, we have evidence of analogous processes, sometimes by firms started with public funds or with capital coming from banks or other larger groups, such as Reggiane in Reggio Emilia (Basini 1995), or OCI in Modena. The decisive role played by a large firm is recorded in that area of Carpi previously described as a knitwear district. A stimulating study by the economist Solinas (1993) shows how those actors, such as technical schools, large firms, and crafts-men workshops, who helped in the formation of mechanical skills, were ab-sent in Carpi, until at least the middle of the century. The situation changed during the Second World War when, in order to escape bombing, the Marelli plant (car components) was transferred from Lombardia to Carpi. The presence of this plant encouraged the creation of skills formerly absent in this area, through training courses, worker/manager administrative councils, and in particular, organizational innovations introduced in the factory. Later, the sackings of the 1950s drove many employees to set up new businesses in the production of engineering components: woodwork-ing machines, biomedical products, and automatic machines. All this rep-resents the outcome of a process more casual than intentional. Unlike in Bologna or Reggio Emilia, the 'large' firm in Carpi arose as an imported exogenous operation. Yet, it managed to stimulate local energies in the for-mation of a productive system (even though the knitwear industry pre-vailed in Carpi).

From the examination of industrialization in Emilia Romagna, we find a development path centred on the experience obtained in the towns, and above all on the diffusion of specific technical and economic skills. These skills spread out through various channels: a public school or a company training course, the experience gathered in a large firm either in expansion or in crisis, as well as the opportunities offered by war or by productive reorganization. In some cases, more informal mechanisms have been documented, such as information exchange between friends and relatives. Nevertheless, the essential vigour was always provided by industry, whether of old local tradition or from recent development. This is particularly true in the case of the electrotechnical and engineering industries. It is not surprising then to discover that in the latter case many entrepreneurs possessed experience from urban and industrial contexts (Barbagli, Capecchi, and Cobalti 1988: 176–89).

The role of local institutions and larger firms in the formation of local productive systems is distinguishable in other areas of the third Italy or in sectors other than engineering. In some cases, larger firms enacted conscious decisions in favour of decentralization and of smaller firms. This was particularly true in the Veneto region (the third most important industrial region in Italy), where the great textile producers and the local authorities often preferred the decentralization of production and the scattering of factories. This choice was dictated not only by economic reasons, but also by the intention to safeguard the unity of their communities and their bonds with the surrounding country (Roverato 1984). More recently, a similar tendency has occurred in for example, the entrepreneurial choices made in the 1970s by the Merloni family in the Marche, who divided their production of home appliances into eight factories located within a circumscribed area (Amatori 1987: 623–6). In other cases, the widespread industry was the outcome of a gradual disintegration of the productive cycle set up in old industrialized areas. So it was in the already mentioned cotton factories of the Alto Milanese (Magatti 1991), as well as in the wool industry in Prato, in Tuscany (near Firenze (Florence)), which after the Second World War met the overproduction crisis of its plants by turning to the small family firms as a solution (Nigro 1986; Trigilia 1989*a*). In the 1960s, the vertical disintegration was also the choice of the ceramic tile district, around the town of Sassuolo in Emilia Romagna (north-west of Bologna), another classic example of widespread industrialization. In this case, however, productive disintegration has been backed up by the tendency to managerial and proprietorial integration, characterized by the presence of entrepreneurial families linked in different ways with each other (Russo 1985; Sorrentino 1991). There are, as always, many variations. However, the common trait remains the decisive presence of a local industry, even of limited size, but able to stimulate a development sequence that led to the formation of a productive system.

In conclusion, it is clear that some aspects of this specific process are similar to the path of development strictly bound to the country and to small rural centres. Even the industrialization of the urban areas occurred gradually, though transformations were more decisive than in rural regions. Local initiative also prevailed in this process, while exogenous intervention did not seem decisive (an important exception may be made for orders tied to the war effort). The local channels were particularly instrumental in ensuring the diffusion of skills necessary for the formation of productive systems. The differences reside, if anywhere, in the different quality of these skills. Generic commercial or entreprenurial backgrounds were not sufficient for starting up engineering or electrotechnical firms. Instead, specific technical knowledge was necessary. This knowledge was directly picked up in the workplace (learning by doing), or more formally in public (state and municipal) schools and on company training courses.

An Overall Evaluation

The succession and overlapping of many industrial events in different areas and sectors can create a confusing impression, that of a fragmented story, in which the conditions which made it possible escape our attention. The risk is perhaps inevitable; particularly in this phase of the research, when the available evidence does not lead to a satisfying synthesis. Moreover, we must bear in mind that this account is largely incomplete. This is true not only because we are considering only a portion of the existing studies, but more importantly because we are focusing our attention on territorial and entrepreneurial events, while neglecting other essential elements of the industrialization process. One model example is the conditions describing access to credit.

To further complicate the picture, we could mix those development paths already outlined. Some interesting examples of this mixture are the productive systems of the Veneto, the region with probably the most complex situation in our history. Since the 1920s this region has hosted simultaneously, basic industry, large textile firms, and a vast system of predominantly small textile and engineering firms. A study of the province of Vicenza (west of Venezia (Venice)), one of the most industrialized in Italy, has examined precisely the collaborative relationships between large firms and specialized districts (Fontana 1994). This sort of alliance would have motivated the formation of a widespread industrial culture, on which the great expansion of the last decades was based. The development of small-firm clusters was therefore complementary to the permanence and growth of innovative large firms.

Then one can state that any attempt to arrive at clear classifications and development sequences would be in vain. We are far from the initial opposition between large and small firms or between productive integration and decentralization. History has, instead, revealed the presence of hybrid forms of industrial development which avoid rigid modelling. This idea is confirmed by the fact that in recent years many large firms have adopted organizational models partially drawn by the district experience in order to define a new internal structure and their relations with suppliers (Regini and Sabel 1989). Of course, this does not mean that we should abandon efforts to identify some unifying elements. This will be my aim, while pausing at those points which seem of most interest.

The first way to understanding this process can be offered precisely by its fragmentation. In the case-histories examined, we have observed that the formation of local productive systems is not arranged according to any sequence of linear development, nor does it constitute the outcome of a well-established strategy. Yet some strategic choices on the part of public institutions, of entrepreneurs, and workers, were made. At times, these choices favoured processes already under way, as in the example of the public technical schools. In other situations, they brought about unintended results, while at other times, they had unforeseen consequences. The transfer of a plant from Lombardia to Emilia Romagna, for example, was not designed to stimulate the development of local industry. Large firms who encouraged their own employees to start up independent businesses did not imagine that they were 'breeding' some of their future competitors. On the whole, it seems therefore that the most twisting and not always predictable paths prevailed: a combination of subjective choices and unexpected opportunities, at times casual and definitely not intentional.

When the timing of the entire process is considered, the fragmentation of such varied paths appears in part to recompose itself. Actually, even in this case the first impression is one of remarkable differences. We have seen that some manufacturing and protoindustrial traditions were already active during the twentieth century, while others even had roots in pre-industrial times. Some areas registered forms of widespread industrialization in the first half of the twentieth century. Others 'exploded' only after the war and in the 1960s. In recent times, new districts arose in unexpected ways in some regions of southern Italy. For all these differences however, two indications emerge from the existing research. The history of local productive systems must necessarily consider a long-term perspective, in searching for skills and traditions slowly established in limited areas. Yet, the peculiarities of this form of industrial development clearly come out only in that specific growth period, between post-war reconstruction and the early 1960s, that culminated in the so-called 'economic miracle'. The presence of many local productive systems consolidated itself in the late 1960s and in the subsequent years, concurrent with the crises and difficulties met by the large public and private enterprises.

The current state of research is unable to go beyond these simple indications. Economic historiography on the Italian 'miracle' is only beginning (Zamagni 1992). This research is still scarce and heterogeneous. Of course, we must not forget that the economic development of these years, and hence even the impulse to form local productive systems, depended to a large degree on international conditions: for example the opening of markets, the growth in consumption, and the long expansive cycle of the European economies. In other cases, the formation of local productive systems seemed mostly bound to the specificity of the Italian situation (and that is mainly true for the most recent developments). For example, in the 1970s the organizational difficulties and the social conflicts which occurred in the large centralized structures fostered the productive decentralization tendency. In all of these situations however, forces external to the local communities played the crucial role in the development of widespread industrialization.

Thus the establishment of local productive systems would never have taken place in the absence of these and other conditions of development. But all this is not sufficient as an explanation of why these productive activities clustered in precisely some areas, and why they took on the characteristics already described. Instead, the historical study of some specific cases allows us to grasp the local dimension of these systems and, in so doing, to understand their peculiarity.

Finally the reference to the periodization permits us to put forward another simple consideration. Inasmuch as this development process has occurred in less than linear fashion, in recent decades it has given birth to dynamic and innovative productive systems.

Such a statement calls for several clarifications. First of all, the positive outcome of this story does not exclude the fact that in many cases there may have been some failures (but research says little on this point). Moreover, we should avoid making unilateral appraisals of the characteristics of local productive systems (Amin and Robbins 1990). It is true, for example, that co-operative relationships within both districts and firms were often accompanied by forms of exploitation of the labour force, such as low salaries and oppressive piece-work wages. Nor should we forget that productive and organizational flexibility may have created particularly harsh and uncertain working conditions, especially in artisan and home workshops. In different spheres, other limits may have been provoked by the insufficient capitalization of the small firms, or by the difficulties in competing with multinationals in the basic high-technology industry, a place reserved (inevitably?) for large-scale enterprises. We have to bear in mind, therefore, that elements of structural weakness were not absent in these forms of development.

Notwithstanding these clarifications, it is certain that widespread industrialization made a contribution of great importance to the Italian 'economic miracle'. It remains difficult to quantify the extent of this contribution. The absence of quantitative reconstructions is one of the greatest limits of the studies under scrutiny. Historical statistics are very scanty. Even economic studies referring to the last years often give only some data on specific areas or sectors.

Nevertheless, it is easy to understand that local productive systems were responsible for the creation of new jobs. Some general data on small firms can give a rough idea of this contribution. In 1961, for instance, 46.8 per cent of employees in manufacturing industry worked in small and very small firms. After twenty years this share was 51.7 per cent while total employment in manufacturing remarkably increased (+ 35.6 per cent, equal in all to 6.1 million employees, of which medium-size firms accounted for 29.7 per cent).[7] Moreover, small-firm systems have favoured the increasing flow of exports, mostly to industrialized nations. An overall survey of 65 industrial districts, only a part of the more general phenomenon of local productive systems, shows an average of 41.8 per cent of total sales were destined for export (Moussanet and Paolazzi 1992, app.). And in some cases, a significant example being that of automatic machines in Bologna, the development of a local system allowed Italy to conquer the international leadership of a sector already dominated by other countries (Alaimo 1992).

Beyond any quantitative estimation however, there is room to suppose that the main contribution of widespread industrialization to the Italian 'great transformation' resides in a more evasive and yet more important circumstance. This hypothesis may be tentatively formulated as follows: the formation of local productive systems may have fostered the creation of economic cultures and organizational models, able to overcome hostilities and mistrust towards industrial development and towards the exigencies of a market economy.

This hypothesis can be tested in those areas in which there is a deep-rooted opposition political subculture, such as Bologna and more generally Emilia Romagna. It is probable that in these areas the socialist and later communist (reform-oriented) tradition drove many specialized workers to refuse the rigid and hierarchical structures of large integrated enterprises. This attitude may have instead favoured the independent entrepreneurial activities, in which former employees could experiment with more flexible organizational forms. The creation of systems of co-operative enterprises shows a more explicit rejection of the large-firm rationality. These systems are particular cases of 'co-operative districts' bound to the socialist and communist movements, and in general headed by a sectorial organization (for example a consortium). The leaders of these organizations have tried to pursue a democratic and collective management system of economic activity. The results have been contradictory. Yet in following this path, they have pushed their members (in perhaps unintentional ways) to meet the challenges of the market economy and of the industrial enterprise organizational constraints (Alaimo 1994; Fabbri 1994). Similar results have been obtained by following very different paths, as in many areas of the extremely catholic Veneto. We have witnessed in these cases, how the entrepreneurs and parish priests, fearful of the social and political consequences of urbanization and of the proletariat diffusion, favoured the tendency to create a 'factory for every parish' (Roverato 1984: 213).

Examples of mistrust of large industry are plentiful. Within recent Italian history, it is not difficult to find a hostile attitude towards large industry, though often with very different motivations. Yet neither can one regard this attitude as an exclusively Italian characteristic. This is precisely the reason for which the experience of local productive systems is particularly interesting. They are a form of industrial development which, because of its widespread characteristics, lent itself to being accepted by a dynamic local community, even when the latter was contrary to uncontrolled industrial and urban growth.

Once again some clarification is necessary. The fear of the worst consequences of industrialization does not mean that this development process held an essentially 'defensive' meaning. This idea of the 'defence from the market', that is many local communities refusing the effects of market penetration, comes out in some sociological studies of these issues (the best example being Trigilia 1986). Moreover, such an idea has the merit of illustrious origins, which go back to Polanyi's (1944) classic indications.

Historical studies reveal instead a different side. The history of local productive systems shows that the refusal of the more devastating aspects of industrialization slowly translated itself into the invention of a different form of development, able to compete successfully on international markets and gain economic efficiency. Such a process was possible precisely because the experience of market was by no means unknown to those local communities we have been observing. The various experiences prior to the real development of local productive systems—such as pluriactivity, protoindustry, and firms in leadership positions—already provided the possibility to confront the market with its constraints, and allowed for the timely exploitation of the opportunities offered by economic expansion. Our history thus demonstrates that industrialization cannot be conceived of as an entirely external process, superimposed on the local situations. Nor as an impersonal force animated by inevitable stimuli with respect to which there remained nothing but the possibility of defence or of supine resignation. From the evolution of local productive systems, we find evidence of the active role played by subjective choices, institutions, and community resources in fostering the forms of development (and not only in self-defence).

Conclusions

At the beginning of this chapter it was stated that local productive systems were the outcome of a largely endogenous development process. My impression, notwithstanding many clarifications and complications, is that the studies examined confirm this idea. In summary, one may claim that the development of local productive systems in Italy has followed a path which is at least in part spontaneous (and only partially induced). This path has been made possible by the local diffusion of specific skills. The origin and evolution of these productive systems appear in very different forms. Nevertheless, we can identify some common elements: the non-deterministic nature of different development paths; a relatively homogeneous periodization; an important contribution—on an economic and cultural level—given to Italian industrial development.

Once again, it is important to remember the temporary nature of these indications. In this field, historical research is in constant motion as so many subjects need exploring. On the other hand, economic and theoretical analysis is undergoing changes in the light of new investigations, those particularly conducted in southern Italy. The historical studies already in progress are entrusted with the task of enriching the modest framework of our knowledge of these subjects, to verify some of the hypotheses discussed, and to propose new research objectives.

It is only right to mention some of the questions still remaining unanswered about which it is still not possible to provide well-defined information. Such questions may be formulated in two different ways. Which mechanisms made the functioning and success of local productive systems possible? To what degree did these mechanisms intervene even in the functioning of systems characterized by the prevalence of large firms? These questions clearly refer us back to a recurring theme in economic analysis, the understanding of what are the governing and regulating forms of a productive system.

Some partial responses have already been provided by the studies examined. These investigations have shown, first of all, how important the regulation entrusted to the free market has been. One may think, for example, of the entrepreneurial activities started up by former employees of the large enterprises. In other situations, the intervention of mechanisms of reciprocity has been identified, for example in those cases in which family and community relations favoured the appearance of new firms. On the other hand, mechanisms of political exchange and hierarchical organization have appeared less important (except perhaps in co-operative districts).[8] These few generic arguments certainly do not exhaust the subject of the regulation of local productive systems. The main problem is to understand how it was possible to ensure the co-ordination of very articulated systems lacking a centralized guide, yet able to compete successfully in international markets. To summarize by quoting a persuasive remark by a journalist: 'But how is it possible for a headless organism to live and grow and remain competitive?' (Carini 1996).

The search for the answers to these questions involves confronting the more general theme of industrial development in Italy. The difficulty of identifying a regulatory mechanism is evident even in the studies of large public and private enterprises. It was clear that Italian industry, for a long time protected in different ways by public policies, did not place much trust in the free market. Nor can we suppose that the 'visible hand' of hierarchic organization prevailed in large industry. On the contrary, the history of many of the larger firms, if anything, reveals how difficult it was to provide themselves with an efficient and durable structure. Therefore these difficulties show that in understanding Italian industrialization, we should refer to intermediate forms of economic regulation, other than market and hierarchies. In this perspective, notions such as 'network' and 'business groups'— proposed in the last years by economists and sociologists—can be very helpful in shedding some light on regulatory mechanisms both of small-firm systems and of large enterprises.

In conclusion, studies of local productive systems can play a twofold role. First of all, these studies simply present a more complete picture of Italian economic development, which includes areas and sectors until recently neglected by economic historiography. Moreover, it is possible that the categories emerging from these investigations demonstrate their utility even for the analysis of more classic forms of industrialization. One could find, for example, forms of reciprocity in the internal relationships of a large hierarchically organized enterprise, or understand the cautious strategies of medium-sized, family-owned firms by referring to the weight of family relationships in a particular community.

These are, of course, only some brief suggestions which would benefit from more careful theoretical analysis. Yet these observations convey an essential idea. The study of the evolution of local productive systems must not involve the substitution of the old theoretical structure with a new one, such as gradualism in place of breakups, small instead of large, flexible rather than rigid. The most useful results will only be achieved when the indications obtained from these studies are incorporated within a wider conception of industrial development in Italy. The final objective will be to provide a useful contribution to the comparative study of the various national cases.

NOTES

1. The definition of small enterprise in manufacturing is not a simple one. Roughly speaking, today we could consider as a small enterprise that with less than 50 employees, while the middle-size could include the group of between 50 and 499 employees (size classification changes slightly in different censuses). These simple definitions can work just as a point of reference. But actually each definition must be a pragmatic one: perception of what is small, medium, or large can

change remarkably in different periods and places. In this chapter, moreover, I will consider only those small- and (to a lesser extent) medium-size enterprises which are flexible and innovative units of a productive system (the latter will be better identified later on). Thus I am not interested in the small firm in itself, and I do not consider those backward units destined to disappear or to have an arduous survival.

2. It should be borne in mind that many books mentioned in this paragraph actually contain essays already published in previous years. It is the case with Becattini (1987), whose first essay was published in 1979.

3. Literature on industrial districts is now very vast, but sometimes repetitive. Among the most recent works of synthesis see Bellandi and Russo (1994), as well as Nuti (1994); both books contain useful bibliographical references. Useful essays in Barca (1997) were published too late for consideration in this chapter.

4. In these pages terms such as 'pluriactivity' and 'protoindustry' are used in their general and descriptive meaning, without being concerned with all the aspects of the historiographical discussion about them.

5. Remarks on Emilian productive systems largely draw both on my own research (Alaimo 1990, 1991, and 1994; Alaimo and Capecchi 1992), and on a work in progress on the case of Bologna. References to other studies will be mentioned below.

6. During the 1950s the population in Bologna was about 400,000, while the *comprensorio* (Bologna and surrounding municipalities) was more than 500,000 and the province more than 800,000. The city was among the ten largest Italian cities. In early modern centuries Bologna was one of the medium-sized cities in Europe.

7. These and many other data can be found in Bellandi (1989), who has processed the surveys of the Trade and Industry Censuses. However, as the author himself points out, these data are not always reliable. Other interesting tables are given in Sforzi (1990). (See also n. 1 for some general remarks on statistics.)

8. This outline of possible regulation mechanisms in the small-firm systems has been drawn by Bagnasco (1988, ch. 2); a partially different view by Magatti (1991, ch. 1).

REFERENCES

Alaimo, A. (1990), *L'organizzazione della città. Amministrazione comunale e politica urbana a Bologna dopo l'Unità* [*The Organization of the City: Municipal Administration and Urban Policy in Bologna After the Unification*]. Bologna.

—— (1991), 'La ricerca della specializzazione: l'industria meccanica in Emilia (1850–1950)' ['The Research of Specialization: Engineering Industry in Emilia (1850–1950)'], in Pedrocco and D'Attorre (eds.), *Archeologia industriale in Emilia Romagna Marche*, 133–52.

—— (1992), 'Una storia paradossale? L'industria internazionale delle macchine automatiche in un prospettiva storica (1870–1990)' ['A Paradoxical History? International Automatic Machines Industry in the Historical Perspective (1870–1990)'], *Scuola officina*, 2: 37–40.

Alaimo, A. (1994), 'Governare un distretto: la Federcoop di Ravenna dalla rico-struzione al boom (1945–1962)' ['Managing a District: Ravenna Federcoop From the Reconstruction to the Economic Boom (1945–1962)', in P. P. D'Attorre (ed.), *Il 'miracolo economico' a Ravenna* [The 'Economic Miracle' at Ravenna]. Ravenna, 225–55.

—— and Capecchi V. (1992), 'L'industria delle macchine automatiche a Bologna: un caso di specializzazione flessibile (1920–1990)' ['Automatic Machines Industry in Bologna: A Case of Flexible Specialization (1920–1990)'], in D'Attorre and Zamagni (eds.), *'Distretti, imprese, classe operaia'*, 191–238.

Amatori, F. (1987), 'Per un dizionario biografico degli imprenditori marchigiani' ['Toward a Biographical Dictionary of Marche Entrepreneurs'], in Anselmi (ed.) *Le Marche*, 592–627.

Amin, A. and Robins, K. (1990), 'Industrial Districts and Regional Development: Limits and Possibilities', in Pyke, Beccatini, and Sengenberger (eds.), *Industrial Districts and Inter-firm Co-operation in Italy*, 185–219.

Anselmi S. (1987) (ed.), *Le Marche* [Marches]. Turin.

Bagnasco, A. (1977), *Tre Italie* [Three Italys]. Bologna.

—— (1988), *La costruzione sociale del mercato* [The Social Construction of the Market]. Bologna.

Barbagli, M., Capecchi, V., and Cobalti, A. (1988), *La mobilità sociale in Emilia Romagna* [Social Mobility in Emilia Romagna]. Bologna.

Barca, F. (1997) (ed.), *Storia del capitalismo italiano dal dopoguerra a oggi* [History of Italian Capitalism Since the Second World War]. Rome.

Basini G. L. (1995), *L'industrializzazione di una provincia contadina. Reggio Emilia (1861–1940)* [The Industrialization of a Peasant Province: Reggio Emilia (1861–1940)]. Rome and Bari.

Becattini, G. (1986), 'Riflessioni sullo sviluppo socio-economico della Toscana in questo dopoguerra' ['Reflections on Socio-economic Development in Tuscany after the Second World War'], in Mori (ed.), *La Toscana*, 899–924.

—— (1987) (ed.), *Mercato e forze locali: il distretto industriale* [Market and Local Forces: The Industrial District]. Bologna.

Bellandi, M. (1989), 'The Role of Small Firms in the Development of Italian Manufacturing Industry', in Goodman, Bamford, and Saynor (eds.), *Small Firms and Industrial Districts in Italy*, 31–68.

—— and Russo, M. (1994) (eds.), *Distretti industriali e cambiamento economico locale* [Industrial Districts and Local Economic Change]. Turin.

Berselli, A. and Telmon, V. (1983) (eds.), 'Scuola e educazione in Emilia Romagna fra le due guerre' ['Schools and Education in Emilia Romagna in the Inter-war Years'], special issue (3) of *Annale Istituto per la storia della Resistenza dell'Emilia Romagna*. Milan.

Biagioli, G. (1989), 'Dall'Italia della mezzadria all'Italia dell'industria diffusa: per-corsi economici e demografici di un mutamento' ['From Italy of Sharecropping to the Italy of Widespread Industry: Economic and Demographic Journeys of Change'], in Villani (ed.), 'La pluriattività negli spazi rurali', 113–22.

Brusco, S. (1982), 'The Emilian Model: Productive Decentralization and Social Integration', *Cambridge Journal of Economics*, 2: 167–84.

—— (1986), 'Small Firms and Industrial Districts: The Experience of Italy', in D. Keeble and E. Wever (eds.), *New Firms and Regional Development in Europe*. London, 184–202.

—— (1989), *Piccole imprese e distretti industriali* [*Small Firms and Industrial Districts*]. Turin.

—— and Righi, E. (1989), 'Local Government, Industrial Policy and Social Consensus in Modena', *Economy and Society*, 18/4: 405–24.

Capecchi, V. (1990a), 'A History of Flexible Specialisation and Industrial Districts in Emilia-Romagna', in Pyke, Becattini, and Sengenberger (eds.), *Industrial Districts and Inter-Firm Co-operation in Italy*, 20–36.

—— (1990b), 'L'industrializzazione a Bologna nel Novecento' ['Industrialization in Bologna in the Nineteenth Century'], in W. Tega (ed.), *Storia illustrata di Bologna* [*An Illustrated History of Bologna*]. Bologna, iv. 341–60, and v. 161–80.

Carini, A. (1996), 'Dal Nord-est al Sud i segreti d'un sistema che continua a crescere' ('From the Northeast to the South, the Secrets of a Still Growing System'], *La Repubblica: Affari e Finanza*, 16 Sept., p. 3.

Cento Bull, A. (1989), 'Proto-industrialization, Small-scale Capital Accumulation and Diffused Entrepreneurship: The Case of the Brianza in Lombardy (1860–1950)', *Social History*, 2: 177–200.

Cigognetti, L. and Pezzini, M. (1992), 'Dalle paglie alle maglie. Carpi: la nascita di un sistema produttivo' ['From Straw to Knitwear, Carpi: The Birth of a Productive System'], in D'Attorre and Zamagni (eds.).

Comune di Bologna (1980), *Macchine, scuola, industria: dal mestiere alla professionalità operaia* [Machines, Schools, Industries: From Craftsmen to Professional Workers]. Bologna.

Corner, P. R. (1993), *Contadini e industrializzazione. Società rurale e impresa in Italia dal 1840 al 1940* [*Peasants and Industrialization. Rural Society and Enterprise in Italy from 1840 to 1940*]. Rome and Bari.

D'Attorre, P. P. (1980), 'Piccola industria e classe operaia' ['Small Industry and the Working Class'], in A. Berselli (ed.), *Storia della Emilia Romagna* [*History of Emilia Romagna*]. Bologna, iii. 771–817.

—— (1991), 'Emilia Romagna Marche: problemi di storia industriale' ['Emilia Romagna Marche: Problems of Industrial History'], in Pedrocco and D'Attorre (eds.), *Archeologia industriale in Emilia Romagna Marche*, 25–38.

—— and Zamagni, V. (1992) (eds.), 'Distretti, imprese, classe operaia. L'industrializzazione dell'Emilia Romagna' ['Districts, Firms, and workers: The industrialization of Emilia Romagna'], special issue (7–8) of *Annale. Istituto per la storia della Resistenza dell'Emilia Romagna*, Milan.

Fabbri, F. (1994), *Da birocciai a imprenditori una strada lunga 80 anni. Storia del Consorzio Cooperative Costruzioni 1912–1992* [*From Carters to Entrepreneurs, a Journey of 80 Years: History of the Consortium of Building Co-operatives*, 1912–1992]. Milan.

Federico, G. (1988), 'Per una storia dell'industria serica italiana' [Toward a History of the Silk Industry in Italy], *Annali di storia dell'impresa* 4: 112–30.

Fontana, G. (1994), paper presented to the Assi seminar on 'Piccola e media impresa: esperienze a confronto in una prospettiva storica' ['Small and Medium-size Enterprises: Comparing Historical Experiences'], Luic, Castellanza, 9 May.

Fuà G. and Zacchia, C. (1983) (eds.), *Industrializzazione senza fratture* [*Industrialization Without Breaks*]. Bologna.

Garofoli, G. and Mazzoni, R. (1994) (eds.), *Sistemi produttivi locali: struttura e trasformazione* [*Local Productive Systems: Structure and Transformation*]. Milan.

Gobbo, F. (1989) (ed.), *Distretti e sistemi produttivi alla soglia degli anni '90* [*Districts and Productive Systems at the Beginning of the Nineties*]. Milan.

Goodman, E. and Bamford, J., with Saynor, P. (1989) (eds.), *Small Firms and Industrial Districts in Italy*. London.

Lutz, V. (1962), *Italy: A study in Economic Development*. London.

Magatti, M. (1991), *Mercato e forze sociali. Due distretti tessili: Lancashire e Ticino Olona 1950–1980* [*Market and Local Forces. Two Textile Districts: Lancashire and Ticino Olona 1950–1980*]. Bologna.

Mori, G. (1986) (ed.), *La Toscana* [*Tuscany*]. Turin.

Moroni, M. (1989*a*), 'Nel cuore del futuro distretto industriale. Montegranaro: economia e società dal primo Ottocento al 1920' [In the Heart of the Future Industrial District. Montegranaro: Economy and Society from the Early Nineteenth Century to 1920], in S. Anselmi (ed.), *L'industria calzaturiera marchigiana* [*The Marche Shoe Industry*]. Fermo, 123–65.

—— (1989*b*), 'La pluriattività in un'area mezzadrile: la tessitura nelle campagne fidardensi dell'Ottocento' ['Pluriactivity in a Sharecropping Area: Weaving in the Castelfidardo Countryside in the Nineteenth Century'], in Villani (ed.), 'La pluriattività negli spazi rurali', 197–204.

Moussanet, M. and Paolazzi, L. (1992) (eds.), *Gioielli, bambole, coltelli* [*Jewels, Dolls, Knives*]. Milan.

Nanetti, R. Y. (1988), *Growth and Territorial Policies: The Italian Model of Social Capitalism*. London and New York.

Nigro G. (1986), 'Il "caso" Prato' ['The "case" of Prato'], in Mori (ed.), *La Toscana*. 821–65.

Nuti, F. (1994) (ed.), *I distretti dell'industria manifatturiera in Italia* [*Districts of Manufacturing Industry in Italy*]. Milan.

Paci, M. (1982), *La struttura sociale italiana* [*The Italian Social Structure*]. Bologna.

Pedrocco, G. and D'Attorre, P. P. (1991) (eds.), *Archeologia industriale in Emilia Romagna Marche* [*Industrial Archeology in Emilia Romagna Marches*]. Milan.

Pescarolo, A. (1989), 'Le trecciaiole della campagna fiorentina tra Ottocento e Novecento: una protoindustria marginale che prepara l'industrializzazione diffusa' ['The plait-maker women of the Florence Countryside Between the Nineteenth and Twentieth Centuries: A Marginal Protoindustry Which Prepared the Way for Widespread Industrialization'], in Villani (ed.), 'La pluriattività negli spazi rurali', 179–86.

Piore, M. J. and Sabel, C. F. (1984), *The Second Industrial Divide*. New York.

Polanyi, K. (1944), *The Great Transformation*. New York.

Prodi, R. (1992), *Il tempo delle scelte. Lezioni di economia* [*The Time of Choices: Lessons of Economics*]. Roma.

Pyke, F., Becattini G., and Sengenberger, W. (1990) (eds.), *Industrial Districts and Inter-firm Co-operation in Italy*. Geneva.

Regini, M. and Sabel, C. F. (1989) (eds.), *Strategie di riaggiustamento industriale in Italia* [*Strategies of Industrial Restructuring in Italy*]. Bologna.

Romano, R. (1990), *La modernizzazione periferica. L'Alto Milanese e la formazione di una società industriale 1750–1914* [Peripheral Modernization: The Alto Milanese and the Formation of an Industrial Society, 1750–1914]. Milan.

Roverato, G. (1984), 'La terza regione industriale' ['The Third Industrial Region'], in S. Lanaro (ed.), *Il Veneto*. Turin, 165–230.

Russo, M. (1985), 'Technical Change and the Industrial District: The Role of Interfirm Relations in the Growth and Transformation of Ceramic Tile Production in Italy', *Research Policy*, 6: 329–43.

Sabbatucci Severini, P. (1996), *Continuità e mutamento. Studi sull'economia marchigiana tra Ottocento e Novecento* [*Continuity and Change: Studies of the Marche Economy Between the Nineteenth and Twentieth Centuries*]. Ancona.

Seravalli, G. (1988), 'Le cooperative e i distretti industriali' ['Co-operatives and Industrial Districts'], *Il Ponte*, 6: 23–39.

Sforzi, F. (1990), 'The Quantitative Importance of Marshallian Industrial Districts in the Italian economy', in Pyke, Becattini, and Sengenberger (eds.), *Industrial Districts and Inter-Firm Co-operation in Italy*, 75–107.

Solinas, G. (1982), 'Labour Market Segmentation and Workers' Careers: The Case of the Italian Knitwear Industry', *Cambridge Journal of Economics*, 4: 331–52.

—— (1993), 'Competenze, grandi imprese e distretti industriali. Il caso Magneti Marelli' ['Competences, large firms, and industrial districts: The Magneti Marelli Case'], *Rivista di storia economica* 10: 79–111.

Sori, E. (1987), 'Dalla manifattura all'industria (1861–1940)' [From Manufacture to Industry (1861–1940), in Anselmi (ed.), *Le Marche*, 301–92.

—— (1991), 'I nuovi distretti industriali nelle Marche' ['New Industrial Districts in Marches'], in Pedrocco and D'Attorre (eds.), *Archeologia industriale in Emilia Romagna Marche*, 209–33.

Sorrentino, T. (1991), 'Appunti per una storia del distretto ceramico di Sassuolo' ['Notes for the History of the Ceramic Tile District in Sassuolo'], *Annali di storia dell'impresa*, 7: 273–317.

Trigilia, C. (1986), *Grandi partiti e piccole imprese* ['Large Political Parties and Small Firms']. Bologna.

—— (1989a), 'Il distretto industriale di Prato' ['The Prato Industrial District'], in Regini and Sabel (eds.), *Strategie di riaggiustamento industriale in Italia*, 283–333.

—— (1989b), 'Small-Firm Development and Political Subcultures in Italy', in Goodman, Bamford, and Saynor (eds.), *Small Firms and Industrial Districts in Italy*, 174–97.

Villani, P. (1989) (ed.), 'La pluriattività negli spazi rurali: ricerche a confronto' ['Pluriactivity in Rural Areas: A Comparison'], special issue of *Annali, Istituto Alcide Cervi*, 11. Bologna.

Zamagni, V. (1986), 'L'economia' ['The Economy'], in R. Zangheri (ed.), *Bologna*. Rome and Bari, 247–314.

—— (1992), 'The Italian "Economic Miracle" Revisited: New Markets and American Technology', in E. Di Nolfo (ed.), *Power in Europe?*. Berlin and New York, 197–226.

Zeitlin, J. (1990), 'Industrial Districts and Local Economic Regeneration: Models, Institution and Policies', paper presented to the International Conference on 'Industrial Districts and Local Economic Regeneration', International Institute for Labour Studies, Geneva.

PART III

JAPAN

8

Historical Features of Japanese Small and Medium Enterprises: A Comparative Economic Approach

JOHZEN TAKEUCHI

Through the 1960s small and medium enterprises (SMEs) were commonly associated with symbols of Japanese social backwardness representing cheap labour, low productivity, and other negative factors. In fact, there was indeed a serious wage and productivity gap known as 'the dual structure', which was considered by many academicians to be a unique feature of Japanese capitalism. However, the economic conditions of SMEs were improved significantly in the 1970s and social critics became less interested in the matter.

At the same time, some professors maintained that the development of SMEs had become a mainstay of Japanese economic growth, and gave high marks to certain SMEs, known as 'chuken-kigyo' or 'middle and leading enterprises' (Kiyonari 1972; Nakamura, H. 1976). The development of these firms was increasingly examined in the 1980s but supporting historical research did not attract corresponding interest.

Before the Second World War, not a few Japanese academicians and bureaucrats regarded the development of SMEs as an important field of research for the identification of various characteristics of Japanese society. By the 1970s, however, this approach had largely been abandoned. Furthermore, intellectuals had became neither interested in the long-term perspective nor focused on the historical experience of industrialization and the unique functions of SMEs therein.

Despite this shift, Takafusa Nakamura's historically oriented analyses was quite influential, providing academic stimulus to a younger generation of economic historians (Nakamura, T. 1976). He successfully utilized macro-economic data to verify that traditional economic surveys had underestimated the scale of the social significance of Japanese SMEs. He also stressed that many industries had been transferred from abroad and re-organized into a system which was similar to much of Japanese traditional manufacturing. His approach was strongly sympathetic with that of those social scientists who had been keenly interested in the large and complex stratum of SMEs in the dark days of the 1930s (Takahashi 1936; Arisawa 1940).[1] They concentrated mostly on their own fact-finding and success-fully avoided the pitfall of merely plugging the Japanese experience into Western models. Here, it is possible to perceive one of the most impressive but small academic streams of Japanese social sciences.

Inspired by the analysis of T. Nakamura, a few young academicians began serious study of SMEs in the 1980s. Some of them adopted modern macro-economic and econometric analyses in their regional or sectorial investigations, while others concentrated on developing a methodological and theoretical framework to accommodate Professor Nakamura's findings. These analytical activities formed two basic streams of research regarding Japanese SMEs, which can be introduced via a brief look at historical treat-ment of the textile industry.

The tradition of historical analysis of the textile industry was well estab-lished even before the Second World War, although SMEs were not scrutin-ized *per se*. Given this background, a new approach was successfully adopted by O. Saitoh (1985) and T. Abe (1989) who clarified the regional features of the development and mechanization of the cotton-spinning and weaving sectors. They integrated traditional methods of regional study and sectorial analysis with an econometric approach, and a similar method was adopted by Y. Kiyokawa in his study of the silk-reeling industry (Kiyokawa 1995). In addition, other scholars applied the case-method to analysis of textile-related enterprises (Tanimoto 1987, 1992; Kagotani 1989; Matsumura 1992).

Meanwhile, perhaps because the textile industry was the leading indus-try in Japan at least through the 1950s, insufficient attention has been paid to surveys of SMEs in the machine-tool and other industries. Some scholars have investigated the expanding socio-historical role of engineers, but not with particular regard to the development of SMEs (Morikawa 1981; Sawai 1990*a,b*). A survey of the subcontracting system of the machine-tool sector during the Second World War has also been carried out by H. Ueda (1989), and his study provides a number of key factors for consideration of the present Japanese machine-tool industry. In addition, J. Suzuki (1996) suc-ceeded in obtaining an abundance of useful data that convincingly reverses the commonly held perception that the sector had not significantly de-veloped during the Meiji era (1868–1911), and K. Hang (1992) has success-fully documented the developmental process of the textile-machine industry in urban areas.

Recently, not only in these major industrial sectors, but also in less promin-ent sectors such as food-processing, several historical analyses have been undertaken (Kagotani 1990; Takeuchi, J. 1991; Tanimoto 1996). Many sectors remain to be further investigated, but it is noteworthy that we now have a rudimentary foundation on which to conduct a reconsideration of the basic historical features of Japanese industrialization.

However, the complexity and variety of development and reorganization processes, not only among sectors but also within small subsectors, should not be overlooked. In fact, this complexity is a key factor driving Japanese industrialization under the threat of colonization during the latter half of the nineteenth century. There was already a wealth of traditional business practice upon which to draw in the integration of new concept and technologies introduced from outside, or, stated differently, the existence of long-established traditional ways of doing things meant that new systems could not simply be transplanted in unmodified form. Thus, there were numerous opportunities for SMEs to develop by seeking out unique ways of applying new methods and technologies to both existing and emerging social and economic needs. It is against this complicated background of rapid socio-economic change that the development of late-starting countries (not necessary limited to Japan) must be considered.

This chapter will concentrate on this background, seeking to identify some of the basic features of Japanese industrialization and business activities through the analysis of a variety of factors including business type, market conditions, skill formation, and technological innovation. However, the scope of presentation does not permit the introduction of many important aspects and functions of agricultural production, which strongly impacted on Japan's labour market and industrialization processes.[2]

Types of Capital and SMEs

Merchants and Manufacturers

There has long been heated debate among Japanese scholars as to whether fundamental leadership of Japanese industrialization was taken by the merchant class or by artisans and manufacturers. More detailed historical analysis of SMEs could well resolve this dispute, but the result of empirical surveys have not been widely introduced into the discussion. Admittedly, the use of empirical data vastly complicates the debate, but lack of historical consideration of SMEs has turned the argument into something of a circular academic exercise.

In the history of SMEs, there can be found many cases in which traditional merchants changed into modern manufacturers, as well as numerous examples where small manufacturers developed into larger-scale business owners. Nevertheless, the business systems of SMEs, such as transaction networks, employment systems, and skill formation, are extremely complicated in actual practice. Still, it is possible to see that certain fluctuating factors (e.g. market conditions and technological adaptation) tended to define the leadership for the modernization of each manufacturing sector.

International interactions are becoming increasingly intensive and complicated, suggesting that a better understanding of differences in social conditions and historical backgrounds is necessary. In some newly industrializing economies (NIEs), the reorganization of industrial sectors and social structure is surprisingly clear-cut, especially compared with the historical experiences of industrialized countries. This simplicity is an important factor allowing rapid development, but the resulting foundational structure is too primitive to cope with modern industrial sophistication. One reason for this facile approach is the tendency for over-application of simplified models of economic development by Western economists,[3] while another is that they have not always been sufficiently aware of the historical complexity of their own countries and the consequent implications for industrial and entrepreneurial development.

It would be misleading to explain Japanese industrial experience without sufficient comments on its wider historical origins. For example, M. Tanimoto (1990, 1996) has suggested that, in addition to traditional regional merchants (TRMs) and small-scale manufacturers (SSMs), traditional regional landowners (TRLs) were a third prototype for modern entrepreneurs. Tanimoto found that landowners often came to engage in manufacturing businesses such as rice wine and soy-processing, and that their conservative and parochial attitudes have contributed to the behavioural patterns of modern business people in Japan.

T. Abe (1989, 1996), a leading analyst of the history of the Japanese textile industry, has cited many cases of TRMs metamorphosing into modern manufacturers. He has paid extensive attention to differences in market conditions and technological achievements, and stresses that these were the decisive factors causing many TRMs to change their managerial systems over the long run. He has also classified the types of businesses pertaining to inter- and intra-regional competition, and has shown that, under certain limited conditions, only TRMs could evolve into the modern entrepreneurs as in the cases of cotton-weavers in Sen'nan (southern Osaka) and carpet-weavers in Sakai City. In these regional industries, technological conditions were stable, the cost of machinery was high, and the market for final products was expanding rapidly. Because TRMs were typically much better capitalized than SSMs, and could therefore afford to purchase modern machinery, this combination of business conditions was to their advantage. Moreover, since the SSMs suffered from a lack of market information, the latter were unable to appropriately adjust their strategies over time. Especially in carpet-weaving, where there was no domestic market and all production was exported, trading merchants were the sole channel for market information. New industrialists emerged from among these merchants, and they became the first organizers of the Export Goods Dealers and Manufacturers Association (*Juyo Yushutsuhin Dogyo Kumiai*) in and around Osaka City (OMO 1933).

The textile industry was by far the leading industry in pre-war Japan and there were numerous regions where TRMs and SSMs were competing against each other for further development. However, there were many different industries concentrated in particular regions, and a number of new surveys have appeared since the 1980s (Takechi 1990; Yamada, K. 1995; Sawai 1996; Omori 1997). Their analytical frameworks differ, but utilizing these studies, it is possible to get sufficient information to classify various market and production conditions. In spite of the decisive gap in initial conditions, it should be noted that numerous SMEs emerged and expanded around developing industries and/or businesses in many industrial regions throughout the country, excluding Northern Japan.[4] Considering the industrialization of NIEs where large enterprises have developed quickly but have not been paralleled by the development of SMEs, this historical experience is worthy of greater attention.

Socio-Economic Background of Type-Classification

In introducing type-classification analysis, it should be noted that the implication of the concept varies according to the historical background and initial conditions of the countries in question. Karl Marx and Max Weber explained merchant capital (*Handels Kapital*) as a kind of universal concept, and it is possible in many cities of Asia to observe this type of capital. However, the situation was utterly different in Japan, where merchants were strictly prohibited from going abroad, and did not even enjoy freedom of movement domestically, until the latter half of the nineteenth century. This experience had a significant impact on Japanese merchants, and they were unable to cultivate the cosmopolitan activity and dynamism which characterized the major merchant houses of the world.

Lacking such dynamism, they formed several introverted types (Fig. 8.1). Following the lifting of the former restrictions, some of them preferred to stay in urban areas and maintain a contact with political powers (A), while others opted for the countryside (B). Many adopted traditional production systems without showing any interest in new technology and/or materials (1), but some were keenly interested in new developments (2). The A-1 type is the classical 'merchant capital', and the B-2 shows innovative community merchants (ICMs) who intended to take a radical role for reorganizing regional transaction systems in certain advanced regions near

	(A) URBAN TYPE	(B) RURAL TYPE
(1) TRADITIONAL TYPE	Marx–Webber Model	Tanimoto Model
(2) INNOVATIVE TYPE	Omori–Yamada Model	ICMs

Fig. 8.1. *Types of Japanese merchants.*

Osaka in the middle of the eighteenth century and failed.[5] It should be noted that M. Tanimoto (1992, 1996) originally identifies the B-1 type, while K. Yamada (1995) and K. Ohmori (1997) introduced the A-2 type.

Although the geographical extent of their business was ordinarily small, they did not tend to depend upon ties of kinship and birthplace as did many Asian merchants and merchant tribes. On the other hand, they were not innovative in arranging new transaction systems like the urban commission systems and the craft/guild relations which were virtually universal in European society. Instead of these traditional customs and feudal systems, they preferred to maintain complex webs of business relations among themselves and/or with small manufacturers and artisans, and these resulted in the appearance of numerous types of middlemen. Notwithstanding, their intimate system became a critical factor providing traditional merchants and middlemen with sufficient ability to evaluate the quality of products and semi-finished goods, as well as the efficiency of the tools and/ or systems used by artisans and SSMs.

The historical experience of Japanese traditional merchants suggests that there might be numerous sub-types of merchant capital in response to differing conditions and varied business networks. Fig. 8.2 shows representative patterns of these confusingly varied networks among TRMs and SSMs, and in the textile industry the network shifted from stage 1 to stage 2, 2 to 3, and so on to the modern factory system, although the Japanese historical process took time to shift to it, and the middle-stage types tended to expand and sometimes became quite complicated as in stage 4. However, there were also various cases in which the local network stabilized at a particular stage, as well as TRMs which directly started up modern factory systems (Yamada 1995; Takeuchi, J., Abe, and Sawai 1996; Ohmori 1997). Nevertheless, there was an overwhelming tendency to remain in a particular stage from 1 to 4. Fig. 8.3 shows the case of shell-button manufacturing in pre-war Japan (i.e. stage 4), which eventually disappeared without ever evolving into a modern factory system (Takeuchi, J. 1991).

At stages 3 and 4, there was a peculiar social division of labour among SSMs, and organizing agents (OAs) served as intermediaries between SSMs and merchants, and these agents generally came up from among the ranks of SSMs.

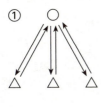

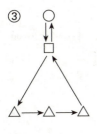

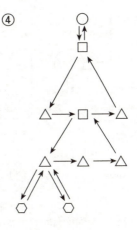

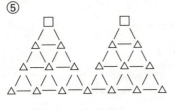

1, 2	traditional putting-out system	○ wholesale merchant
		□ organizing agent
3, 4	integration organized by organizing agents	△ small producer
5	linkage among industrial sectors	⬡ domestic system

Fig. 8.2. *Reorganization of the Japanese putting-out system.*
Source: Johzen Takeuchi (1988).

In many sectors of machine- and metal-manufacturing, various parts and/or manufacturing processes were necessitated, and numerous kinds of SSMs developed independently. Some of them took advantage of the chance to supply their parts or processing services to multiple manufacturers, thus enabling them to improve their technological backgrounds, and not a few of them were able to greatly expand their businesses over the long run (Takeuchi, J. 1991). In such sectors, the SSMs needed to have sufficient modern technology and/or skill and they or their sons usually had some educational background obtained at vocational schools or technical colleges.

Although social scientists generally attempt to set up 'universal' concepts (mostly extracted from the European experience), the point here is to

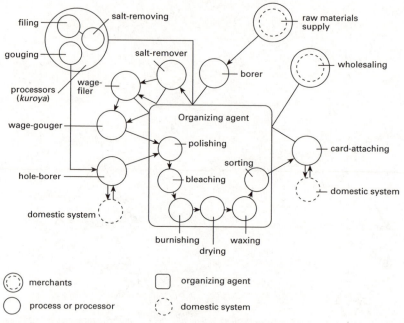

Fig. 8.3. *Organization chart of shell-button manufacturing.*

Source: Osaka Municipal Office (1930), *Osaka no Botan Kogyo [Button Industry in Osaka]*. Osaka: OMO, 25–30.

decompose such a concept into small 'sub-concepts'; this complexity is a historical factor explaining the development of various kinds of TRMs and SMEs during the course of Japanese industrialization. It also demonstrates that, while the European development process lends itself to analysis broadly defined, it is not necessarily 'universal'.

Local Autonomy and Entrepreneurs

In Japan, there is a small academic school of economic historians who stress the comparative immaturity of modern Japanese local autonomy and its impact on society and manufacturing systems. They interpret this immaturity, as well as the overwhelming presence of 'traditional' SMEs, as the historical result of Japanese social backwardness. However, different historical experiences can only be fairly compared when their initial conditions are similar.

In the early stage of European industrialization, technological development was limited and traditional regulations on the social life of the people were restrictive, but they already had a sense of human rights and a rich tradition of local autonomy, in addition to the early appearance of materialistic tendencies. Under these conditions, Europeans experienced distinct social stratification and lively social struggle over the course of the industrial revolution.

On the contrary, traditional social restrictions were weakened in Japan in the latter half of the nineteenth century, but the tradition of their local autonomy had been strangled since the latter half of the sixteenth century (albeit in an orderly way), and materialistic desire was minimized even as the traditional and tiny tea rooms of Japanese gardens. Furthermore, Japan was on the brink of being colonized. These factors tended to prioritize industrialization over democratization until well after the Second World War (Lockwood 1955). Japan thus became the first state to promote industrialization policy without democracy, and this authoritarian strategy became popular among Asian countries after the war.

The East Asian experience after the war was strangely unique, as these countries set about promoting industrialization policy without any SSMs or even TRMs. Instead, a few urban merchants took exclusive leadership in transferring foreign technology, capital, managerial systems, etc. Many of them were immigrants and they usually resided in certain large cities where it was easy for them to maintain a favourable and informal contact with native political leaders. From the 1960s, they were able to freely utilize foreign funds, and it became easy for them to introduce new production systems which substituted technology for traditional skill accumulation, thereby depriving potential SSMs of their chance to develop. Here, it is obvious that the initial conditions for industrialization had changed completely. However, it is doubtful whether such an authoritative society could develop independent-minded (i.e. innovative) SSMs in the near future.

Market Structure and Human Factors of SMEs

Stratified Structure of Production and Market

Investigating Japanese SMEs and the features of their markets, some scholars examining the marketing strategy of SMEs by means of case-studies noticed a qualitative difference between domestic and foreign markets. They also stressed that market scale had a decisive impact on decisions as to whether or not to adopt new technology (Sawai 1987; Abe 1989). Before the Second World War, traders and SMEs had to cope with serious fluctuations in world markets, including the cases of their own colonies. As a late-starting imperialist country, Japan could not afford to establish indirect-rule systems, thus resulting in resistance from native peoples, and intensified market fluctuations. Unstable market conditions also induced speculative activities and fraud, which further accelerated the fluctuations.

Even in a small industrial sector like shell-button manufacturing, market conditions precluded innovation in the manufacturing system. The market was highly unstable, except for a few special products such as decorative buttons made of Mexican abalone. Manufacturers were obliged to maintain an amazingly complicated social division of labour among themselves as in Fig. 8.3. TRMs and OAs were able to utilize SSMs as a social buffer in case of business decline. Under the circumstances, not a single TRM was reported to have become a modern factory owner (Takeuchi, J. 1991).

Compared with exports, the domestic market was far more stable, but the scale was almost negligible as traditional Japanese kimonos do not need buttons, and TRMs had to depend on SSMs for production. In other industrial sectors where TRMs were able to gradually expand in stable growing markets, modern factories could be started up. However, such TRMs still did not abandon the subcontracting system, and modern factories co-existed with different kinds of subcontracting systems ranging from stages 1 to 4 (Fig. 8.2). Similar situations could be found in some luxury sectors of the textile industry, and TRMs tried to maintain their traditional networks for the supply of limited regional specialities (Abe 1989; Matsumura 1992).

Provided the export market featured sufficient scale and stability, TRMs were encouraged to introduce new technology and systems for expanded production. Accordingly, they downgraded their relations with SSMs, as can be observed in sectors like cotton-weaving in southern Osaka, silk weaving in the Hokuriku region, and hosiery knitting near Osaka (Abe 1989; Takeuchi, J. 1991).

However, market scale and stability were not the only factors which induced TRMs to establish modern factories. In metal-button manufacturing, although the market was indeed favourable because of substantial and constant demand for the uniforms of soldiers and students, a new and compact press technology eliminated the need for the traditional skills of the SSMs. Meanwhile, it was difficult for SSMs to establish modern factories; they only maintained traditional workshops capable of certain limited processes, they were unable to obtain enough information about modern markets and new technology, and they lacked the capital resources to expand (Takeuchi, J. 1991).

In some traditional sectors like lacquer-ware (known as 'japan' in contrast to 'china'), the situation between TRMs and SSMs was rather different. In the Aizu and Yamanaka regions, where TRMs had long ago taken leadership in seeking new markets and introducing the latest designs, they completely integrated SSMs into their business networks. However, in Kagawa, where TRMs depended more upon the skills of SSMs, the latter were able to keep their independence. The better-known artisans could freely select merchants, as long as they did not require advance payments. Further, in

Wajima, the major of artisans were able to form their own market, and some of them actually became nation-wide distributors for their own products and for those of other artisans. This region was (and is) famous for supplying supremely high quality goods.

It should be noted that the range of market stratification of the industrialized countries, especially that of the USA, was so wide that Japanese SMEs could supply cheap goods which would not have had any marketability at all in Japan. It was easy for late-starting countries to supply goods for low-end export markets. Subsequently, they began climbing up the socio-economic ladder of the stratified market, assuming they had sufficient industrial potential to supply better-quality goods. Japanese SMEs gradually were able to shift towards higher markets.

Asian countries adopted similar strategies from the 1960s, although differences in ladder-climbing potential are now becoming more obvious.

Interaction between Traditional Skills and Modern Technology

It was one of the features of Japanese industrialization that traditional manufacturers had a variety of responses to modern technology transferred from abroad. The term 'technology transfer' is generally used to mean a direct introduction of modern technology to newly industrializing countries. However, the 'adaptation' of modern technology was far more popular in Japan.

Modern technology was separated into its component functions by Japanese craftsmen, and corresponding series of compact instruments and machines were arranged. They thereby succeeded in achieving the same results as the latest technology, but by using traditional skills and systems together with abundantly available labour. One of the earliest cases of this kind of adaptation is the silk-reeling industry, where locally available materials were substituted for the brass, steel, and glass used in the original European equipment (Wada 1969). Similarly, localized equipment became popular in various industrial sectors in which SMEs or SSMs undertook the major part of production. Such adaptations were usually implemented in place of parts that were likely to require replacement, and instruments, and maintenance costs consequently became surprisingly cheap. However, the resulting production systems had to be supplemented by the accumulation of various skills and often by long working hours.

As traditional craftsmen showed their flexible ability to substitute for modern technology, they began to try to catch up to the level of industrialized countries, and some of them actually succeeded. Toyota and Suzuki, for example, started by adapting power looms, and later developed as manufacturers of world-wide competitiveness. It is noteworthy that their attitude of adaptation was one of the human factors which accelerated their much deeper technology transfer. Other examples include traditional wooden-ship builders who later became famous engineers of modern ship-building (Takeuchi, J. 1992b; Odaka 1993).

Adaptation became one of the determinants of Japanese competitiveness in labour-intensive products for international markets, but it should be pointed out that cheap labour and long working hours were not always the key factors for further adaptation. SSMs accumulated skills and concentrated on their work, despite the fact that they did not receive immediate financial reward for doing so.

When traditional production networks and new adaptations were combined with such commitment on the part of SSMs, SMEs could compete with modern enterprises using the latest equipment. Furthermore, there were a number of industrial sectors from which modern large-scale factories were obliged to retreat due to their high cost structure, leaving only SMEs to continue with production. This is the very reason why numerous industrial sectors were referred to as 'small and medium-scale industries' (SMIs) in Japan. SMIs began increasing at the turn of the century and expanded rapidly from around the First World War.

Additional factors were intensified in accordance with the development of SMIs including: (1) the daily mobilization of family work forces including children; (2) the reinforcement of the authoritative atmosphere within nuclear families; and (3) the utilization of cheap labour from colonized areas. Some of these factors were regarded as having been 'traditional' or 'feudal' factors, but they actually emerged in conjuncture with the acceleration of Japanese industrialization. As these factors were diffused among the transferred industries, they also began penetrating other sectors, both traditional and modern.

Superficially, they appeared to be 'feudal', but they did not feature either mutual assistance or solidarity, both of which were compensating factors in the older system. As some humanistic reportages revealed vividly, people were often obliged to live under the norms of both ruthless modern efficiency and traditional restrictive introversion (Yokoyama 1899; Hosoi 1925).

As industrialization continued, the restrictive and stratified labour market expanded to exploit more cruelly the cheap labour from colonies (OMO 1931). Cottage industries were also spread around the outskirts of big cities and in rural districts, taking advantage to the furthest extent of the untapped labour force of women and children (Yamashiro 1956).

Certain observers have regarded this exploitation as a kind of 'job creation', but they fail to take into account the resulting stagnation in technological innovation. The cheap labour system did not have adequate flexibility to cope with new market conditions, and, when new materials and/or commodities were introduced from outside, these cheap labour-oriented industries declined. In particular, whenever large enterprises introduced a far-reaching technology from abroad, numerous industrial subsectors were quickly wiped out (Takeuchi, J. 1991).

On the other hand, when modern factories were unable to achieve sufficient technological progress to cope with cheap labour-oriented production networks, they too were forced to decline. There were also a few sectors which had sufficient accumulations of traditional skills so as not to require new technology introduced from outside. They were able to supply modern products by utilizing traditional skills (Takeuchi, J. 1991). Combining various social factors, Japanese SMEs and SMIs tended to flourish in sectors where there were not any conflicting innovations.

Craftsmanship and Entrepreneurship

While some economists have stressed the 'semi-feudalistic' social restrictions which kept people from free and innovative activities, others have emphasized the favourable 'performance' of the Japanese economy from the 1970s. The former considered the subcontracting system of Japanese SMEs to be typically feudalistic, while the latter held the potential of SMEs in high regard and explained that they were a key factor in Japanese economic dynamism. However, there was also another small academic group which evaluated the Japanese native system in a completely different way. This group organized a kind of social movement for maintaining traditional skill formation and regional culture, known as the *Mingei-undo* (fork craft movement). They neither regarded Japanese labour intensity as a positive element of quantitative efficiency, nor as negatively interpreted labour exploitation. Instead, they placed great emphasis on the aspect of self-training and self-assessment of highly skilled Japanese workers and craftsmen (Yanagi 1958).

Whatever industrialization policies are implemented, the issue of craftsmanship must be carefully considered. The type of craftsmanship referred to here can be defined as possessing the following characteristics:

(1) It is composed of groups of skilled artisans and workers who are comparatively free from restraints imposed by traditional practices or political authority,

(2) it is centred on small-scale family business,

(3) it possesses its own unique value structure, emphasizing accumulation of skills and technological innovation, and

(4) finally, as an external condition, craftsmanship can flourish only in a society which provides economic and social rewards for skill and technical improvement among individuals.

In most developed countries, craftsmanship arose in the form of artisan guilds and similar organizations during the feudal period, and the emphasis on technological innovation and small-scale family-based production was frequently strengthened by subsequent social movements aimed at removing traditional constraints and at improving awareness of local autonomy. This is not to say, however, that development of such craftsmanship was limited to societies which passed through such pre-modern stages. In fact, such societies are more the exception than the rule, and the roots of craftsmanship can be found in virtually all societies. The decisive difference lies in how a society as a whole accords value to craftsmanship.

In some societies, manual work and the artisans themselves are ranked low in terms of human value. There is thus little appreciation for the aesthetic or functional value of their products. This kind of society as a whole generally has a poor understanding of 'skills', and skilled workers are accorded a low status. The conviction that a skilled worker is nothing more than a worker with long years of experience or service still remains deeply embedded in many societies, especially in developing countries. These societies appear heavily resistant to the development of highly sophisticated craftsmen as a strong driving force in support of industrialization (Takeuchi, J. 1992*a,b*). This observation contrasts significantly with the Lewisian hypothesis which suggests that economies can develop in their early stages regardless of the level of skill in the work-force.

The attitude of a society towards craftsmanship was a vital factor in the early stages of industrialization. To run a successful and internationally competitive industry, modern society needs various kinds of skilled people with the abilities to organize, to maintain and constantly strive towards increasing efficiency in the production process, to implement technological innovations, and to appreciate and thus constantly maintain and improve quality. The same attitudes and value system which are rooted in this type of craftsmanship are also required of modern industry managers, plant supervisors, foremen, and even of the workers themselves (Wada 1969). Moreover, they are essential for proper quality control (QC) and continual improvement awareness (Takeuchi, J. 1990).

These attitudes and norms would easily be found among American workers of the nineteenth century. In the USA, the moral attitude of highly skilled workers was a means for them to climb the social ladder and to enter the mass-consumption society (Rodgers 1974; Nelson 1975). However, even though Japanese skilled workers underwent 'intensive training for the sake of training' and tried to maintain their 'skill for the sake of skill', their life-style was not substantially improved in the pre-war period (Furushima, Tchikawa, and Watanabe 1961). Utilizing the terminology of Myrdal, it can be said that craftsmanship in Japan was established in terms of 'attitude' but not in terms of 'institution' (Myrdal 1968).

Unfortunately however, human resources of this quality are nearly impossible to develop in certain societies which do not place a high value on craftsmanship. In pre-modern eras, élite status in the society was

determined primarily on the basis of political or military power, or religious or other customary privileges. In some societies, this basic value has
been carried over into the modern period, and stands as a powerful obstacle
to industrialization. The reason is that such societies neither recognize
people with the qualities mentioned above nor the quality of human work
itself, and, as a result, serious difficulties are encountered in developing the
'skilled' human resources necessary for internationally competitive production efficiency and product quality. We can easily identify these kinds of
societies by the poverty of their vocabularies for expressing appreciation of
sophisticated skill, and by the rapid decline of traditional skills and products when modern products and materials were introduced from outside
(Myrdal 1954). This tendency has been strong in Asia until recently, and it
would not be difficult to conclude that a number of Asian countries still em-
brace such pre-modern value systems. There is also a surprisingly common
pattern of fraudulent behaviour in market transactions and other regular
economic aspects of the daily lives of ordinary people, which makes it difficult to diffuse a value system of industriousness.

In spite of the above, it should not be overlooked that there are some
exceptionally sophisticated and very traditional industries in various parts
of Asian societies. These industries are typically run by certain groups of
craftsmen who essentially stand independently from general social values
and prefer to maintain their own autonomous value systems. In such manufacturing areas, the workshops are usually kept clean and neat, the work is
all honest and free from authoritative restrictions, while there is greater than
average respect for the traditional norms of their own society. Although
their value system and behavioural patterns have potential to be a core factor in the reorganization of their social system and advancement towards
industrialization, there are typically too few of these people to effectively
realize this potential. A decisive constraint on development in these societies is that the élite class is generally indifferent to these artisans and their
works.

Conclusion

Generally speaking, economists have preferred to categorize industrial
sectors as either capital- or labour-intensive, and they have stated that the
change of sectors from labour-intensive to capital-intensive is the very turning point of development. However, it can be seen that there are alternative
routes, even within individual sectors, and that the choice of route can
define the results of long-term economic development. Also, there are
cases where the efficiency of labour-intensive sectors is higher than that of

capital-intensive ones, and such socio-economic conditions are strong factors in arranging effective (but painful) catch-up strategies.

In particular, the assumption of the Lewisian model is not appropriate for all late-starting countries, especially in certain notable cases of catching-up. Lewisians state that an abundant supply of cheap manual labour is the key factor in achieving the turning point. However, economies which have used a large supply of cheap labour have not been able to develop efficiently and have often stagnated. These economies neglected the necessity to develop skills, norms, and other human factors. The consequence was 'universal' stagnation within the course of capital-intensive production, which in turn resulted in a higher-cost economy without corresponding productivity improvement. Whether or not the Japanese experience can be applied to other cases of development, differences in initial conditions must be clearly identified prior to any 'universal' analysis, and this task has often been neglected by economists.

NOTES

1. Arisawa and Takahashi were essentially modernist in their thinking, but decidedly pessimistic concerning the expansion of SMEs. Although current analysis of contemporary macro-economic data suggests that the 1930s was a period of economic expansion and growing prosperity, these economists stressed that such data tended not only to conceal declines in actual living standards but also to mask various socio-economic problems such as the exploitation of small business and the continuation of restrictive paternalism in human relations.
2. For the features of Japanese agricultural systems and their impact on society, refer to Nojiri (1942); Sumiya (1955); Smith (1959); and Dore (1965).
3. Myrdal (1957) criticized this point already in the 1960s.
4. The Tohoku district (i.e. northern Japan below Hokkaido) featured a tradition of labour-extensive management and there were consequent difficulties in developing not only manufacturing SMEs but also extra-agricultural employment systems (Toya 1949; Takeuchi, J. 1991). The initial conditions and development processes of this district would be relevant to investigations of the industrial conditions of NIEs.
5. For activities of community merchants in Meiwa period (1759–68), refer to Tsuda (1961).

REFERENCES

Abe, Takeshi (1989), *Nihon ni okeru Sanchi Menorimonogyo no Tenkai* [*Regional Development of Cotton-Weaving in Japan*]. Tokyo: University of Tokyo Press.

—— (1996), 'Hujimoto Shotaro: Sakai Dantugyo no Sosiki-sha' ['Hujimoto Shotaro: An Organizer of Sakai Carpet Manufacturing'], in Takeuchi, Abe, and Sawai (eds.), *Kindai Nihon ni okeru Kigyoka no Shokeihu*.

Arisawa, Hiromi (1940), *Nihon Kogyo Toseiron* [*On Japanese Industrial Regulation*]. Tokyo: Yuhikaku.

Dore, R. P. (1965), *Education in Tokugawa Japan*. London: Routledge & Kegan Paul.

Endo, Motoo (1985), *Shokunin to Seikatsu Bunka* [*Artisans and Life Culture*]. Tokyo: Yuzankaku Shuppan.

Fucini, J. and Ficini, S. (1990), *Working for the Japanese*. New York: Free Press.

Furushima, Toshio, Ichikawa, T., and Watanabe, N. (1961), *Hoken Kaitaiki no Koyo Rodo* [*Employed Labour during the Dissolution Period of Feudal Society*]. Tokyo: Aoki Shoten.

Hang, Wang-Soung (1992), *Nihon Chusho Toshikogyoshi Kenkyu* [*A Study of Japanese Small- and Medium-Scale Urban Industries*]. Kyoto: Rinsen Shobo.

Hosoi, Wakizou (1925), *Jyoko Aishi* [*An Elegy of Female Operatives*]. Tokyo: Kaizosha.

Kagotani, Naoto (1989), 'Nishimikawa Chiho ni okeru Momen Nakagaisho no Doko' ['Cotton Goods Dealers in Nishimikawashima District']. *Okazakishishi-kenkyu* [*Study of the History of Okazaki-city*]. Okazaki: Okazaki City Hall.

—— (1990), '1880nendai no Ajia karano Shougeki to Nihon no Hanno' ['Asian Impact and Japanese Reaction in the 1880s']. *Rekishigaku Kenkyu* [*Historical Study*], 608.

Kajinishi, Mitsuhaya, Iwao, H., Kobayashi, Y., and Ito, T. (1960) (eds.), *Koza Chush-okigyo* [*Lectures on Small- and Medium-Scale Enterprises*]. Tokyo: Yuhikaku.

Kiyokawa, Yukihiko (1995), *Nihon no Keizaihatten to Gijyutsuhukyu* [*Japanese Economic Development and Technological Diffusion*]. Tokyo: Toyo Keizai Shinposha.

Kiyonari, Tadao (1972), *Gendai Chushokigyo no Shintenkai* [*New Trends of Modern Small- and Medium-Scale Businesses*]. Tokyo: Nihon Keizai Shinbunsha.

Lockwood, W. W. (1955), *The Economic Development of Japan*. Oxford: Oxford University Press.

Matsumura, Satoshi (1992), *Senkanki Nihon Sanshigyoushi Kenkyuu* [*A Study of the Japanese Silk Industry between the Two World Wars*]. Tokyo: University of Tokyo Press.

Miyamoto, Matarou and Abe, T. (1996) (eds.), *Nihon Keieishi 2: Keieikakushin to Kogyoka* [*Japanese Business History 2: Business Innovation and Industrialization*]. Tokyo: Iwanami Shoten.

Morikawa, Hidemasa (1981), *Nihonkeieishi* [*The History of Japanese Business*], Tokyo: Nihon Keizai Shinbunsha.

Myrdal, Gunnar (1957), *Economic Theory and Underdeveloped Regions*. London: Duckworth.

—— (1968), *Asian Drama: An Inquiry into the Poverty of Nations*. New York: Pantheon.

Nakamura, Hideichirou (1976), *Chuken Kigyo Ron* [*On Middle-sized Businesses*], rev. edn. Tokyo: Toyo Keizai Shinposha.

Nakamura, Satoshi (1968), *Meiji Ishin no Kisokozo* [*Basic Structure of Meiji Restoration*]. Tokyo: Miraisha.

Nakamura, Takahusa (1976), 'Zairai Sangyo no Kibo to Kosei' ['Scale and Structure of Conventional Manufacturing'], in Mataji Umemura, S. Nishikawa, T. Hayami, and H. Shinbo (eds.), *Suuryo Keizaishi Ronshu* [*Journal of Quantitative Economic History*], 1. Tokyo: Nihon Keizai Shinbunsha.

Nelson, Daniel (1975), *Managers and Workers: Origins of the New Factory System in the United States 1880–1920*. Madison, Wis.: University of Wisconsin Press.

Nojiri, Shigeo (1942), *Nomin Rison no Jisshoteki Kenkyu* [*An Empirical Study of Migrating Peasants*]. Tokyo: Iwanami Shoten.

Odaka, Kounosuke (1993), *Shokunin no Sekai, Kojyo no Sekai* [*The World of Craftsmen and the World of Factories*]. Tokyo: Libroboat.

Ohmori, Kazuhiro (1997), 'Kaigaigijyutu no Donyu to Jyoho Kodo' ['Transfer of Foreign Technology and Information Behaviour'], in S. Sasaki and N. Fujii (eds.), *Jyoho to Keiei Kakushin* [*Information and Managerial Innovation*]. Tokyo: Dobunkan.

Osaka Municipal Office (OMO) (1931), *Osaka no Burashi Kogyo* [*Brush Industry in Osaka*]. Osaka: Municipal Office.

—— (1933), *Meiji Taisho Osakashishi* [*The History of Osaka in the Meiji and Taisho Eras*]. Osaka: Municipal Office.

Rodgers, Daniel (1974), *The Work Ethic in Industrial America, 1850–1920*. Chicago: Chicago University Press.

Saitoh, Osamu (1985), *Purotokohgyoka no Jidai: Seiou to Nihon no Hikakushi* [*The Days of Proto-Industrialization: Comparative History of Europe and Japan*] Tokyo: Nihon Hyoronsha.

Sawai, Minoru (1987), '1910nendai ni okeru Yushutsuzakkakogyo no Tenkai' ['The Development of Export-oriented Miscellaneous Industry in the 1910s'], *Hokuseironshu*, 24.

—— (1990*a*), 'Kikaikogyo' ['Machine Industry'], in S. Nishikawa and T. Abe (eds.), *Nihon Keizaishi*, iv: *Sangyoka no Jidai* [*Japanese Economic History*, iv: *The Age of Industrialization*]. Tokyo: Iwanami Shoten.

—— (1990*b*), 'Kosakukikai' ['Machinery'] in Yonekawa, Shimokawa, and Yamasaki (eds.), *Sengo Nihon Keieishi* [*The History of Japanese Management after the Second World War*], ii. Tokyo: Toyo Keizai Shinposha.

—— (1993), 'Senzen Senchuki Nihon niokeru Kousakukikaikigyo no Gijyutu to Keiei' ['Technology and Management of Machine-tool Firms in Pre-War and War Time'] in T. Takeoka, H. Takahashi, and T. Nakaoka (eds.), *Singijyutu no Donyu: Kindai Kikaikogyo no Hatten* [*The Introduction of New Technology: The Development of Modern Machine Industry*]. Tokyo: Doubunkan.

—— (1996), 'Noda Shouichi: Kousakukikaikigyou Rokurokushouten no Keiei' ['Noda Shouichi: The Management of Rokurokushouten as a Machine-Dealer and Manufacturer'], in Takeuchi, Abe, and Sawai (eds.), *Kindai Nihon Ni Okeru Kigyoka no Shokeihu*.

Shinobu, Seizaburo (1942), *Kindai Nihon Sangyoshi Jyosetsu* [*Introduction to the History of Modern Industry of Japan*]. Tokyo: Nihon Hyoronsha.

Smith, T. C. (1959), *The Agrarian Origins of Modern Japan*. Stanford, Calif.: Stanford University Press.

Sumiya, Mikio (1955), *Nihon Chinrodoshi Ron* [*A Study of the History of Wage Labour in Japan*]. Tokyo: University of Tokyo Press.

Suzuki, Jun (1996), *Meiji no Kikaikogyo* [*Machine Industry in the Meiji Era*]. Kyoto: Minerva Shobo.

Takahashi, Kamekichi (1936), *Gendai Chusho Shokogyo Ron* [*On Modern Small- and Medium-Businesses*]. Tokyo: Chikura Shobo.

Takechi, Kyozo (1990), *Nihonshihonshugi to Jibashihon: Kansai no Jibasangyoushi-kennkyu* [*Japanese Capitalism and Regional Capital: A Study of Regional Industries in Kansai*]. Tokyo: Yuzankaku Shuppan.

Takeuchi, Johzen (1987), 'Machine-Dyeing and Weaving', in T. Toyoda (ed.), *Vocational Education in the Industrialization of Japan*. Tokyo: University of Tokyo Press.

—— (1988), 'Kaiso Kousei' ['Social Stratification'], in Socio-Economic History Society (ed.), *1930 nendai no Nihon Keizai [Japanese Economy in the 1930s]*. Tokyo: University of Tokyo Press.

—— (1990), 'The Role of Small- and Medium-Scale Enterprises in Japanese Industrialization', in Tamas Csato (ed.), *Small and Medium-Sized Enterprises in the Economy of the Latecomers Since the Industrial Revolution*. Budapest: Aula Kiando.

—— (1991), *The Role of Labour-Intensive Sectors in Japanese Industrialization*. Tokyo: United Nations University (UNU).

—— (1992*a*), 'Development of Rural Industries and its Implications for Policy Formation in Japan', in Asian Productivity Organization (APO) (ed.), *Policies and Programmes for Rural Employment Generation in Asia*. Tokyo: APO.

—— (1992*b*), 'Biruma Sangyo no Tokusei to Kadai' ['Some Characteristics of Burmese Industries' in IDE (ed.), *Kunibetu Keizai Kyoryoku Hokokusho: Biruma [An Analysis of Economic Development Aid Project: Burma]*. Tokyo: IDE.

——, Abe, T., and Sawai, M. (1996) (eds.), *Kindai Nihon niokeru Kigyouka no Shokeihu [Certain Types of Entrepreneurs in Modern Japan]*. Osaka: Osaka University Press.

Takeuchi, Yoshimi (1934), 'Sanson ni okeru Hokonin' ['Servants in Mountain Villages'], *Shakai Keizaisi Gaku [Journal of Socio-Economic History]*, 4/5.

Tanimoto, Masayuki (1987), 'Bakumatsu Meijiki Menpu Kokunaishijyo no Tenkai' ('The Development of Domestic Cotton-Cloth Market in the Bakumatsu Meiji Era'), *Tochiseidoshigaku*, 11/5.

—— (1990), 'Choshi Shoyu Jyozogyo no Keiei Doko: Zairai Sangyo to Chiho Shisanka' ['The Economic Trend of Soy Manufacturing in Choshi: Traditional Industry and the Regional Property Class'] in R. Hayashi (ed.), *Shoyu Jyozogyo no Kenkyu [Studies of Soy Manufacturing]*. Tokyo: Yoshikawa Kobunkan.

—— (1992), 'Chiikikeizai no Hatten to Suitai: 19seiki Shinkawamomen to Izumimomen no Hikaku wo tujite' ['The Rise and Fall of Regional Economy: A Comparative Study of Shinkawa and Izumi'], in Kindainihonkenkyukai, *Nenpo Kindainihon Kenkyu 14 Meiji Ishin no Kakushin to Renzoku [Annual Report of the Study on Modern Japan, 14: Innovation and Consistency of Meiji Restoration]*. Tokyo: Yamakawashuppan.

—— (1996), 'Sekiguchi Hachibei & Naotaro: Shoyu Jyozo to Chihokigyoka-Meiboka' ['Sekiguchi Hachibei & Naotaro: Soy-Sauce Manufacturers and Regional Entrepreneurs'] in Takeuchi, Abe, and Sawai (eds.), *Kindai Nihon niokeru Kigyouka no Shokeihu*.

Toya, Toshiyuki (1949), *Kinsei Nogyo Keieisi Ron [A Study of Agricultural Management in the Pre-Modern Era]*. Tokyo: Nihon Hyoronsha.

Toyoda, Toshio (1989) (ed.), *Vocational Education in the Industrialization of Japan*. Tokyo: UNU.

Tsuda, Hideo (1961), *Hoken Keizai Seisaku no Tenkai to Shijyo Kozo [Feudal Economic Policy and Market Structure]*. Tokyo: Ochanomizu Shobo.

Ueda, Hiroshi (1989), 'Senjitoseikeizai to Shitaukesei no Tenkai' ['Wartime Economic Regulations and the Development of the Subcontracting System'], Kindainihonkenkyukai, *Nenpokindainihonkenkyuu 9 Senjikeizai [Annual Report on Modern Japan, 9: Wartime Economy]*. Tokyo: Yamakawa Shuppan.

Wada, Hide (1969), *Tomioka Nikki* [*Diary at Tomioka*]. Tokyo: Tokyo Horei Shuppan (repr.).

Yamada, Katsuhisa (1995), 'Meijizenki Tojikisanti niokeru Kikaidonyu' ['The Introduction of the Machine System in Regional Pottery Production in the First Half of the Meiji Era'], *Osakadaigaku Keizaigaku* (Osaka University Economics). Osaka: Osaka University.

Yamashiro, Tomoe (1956), *Niguruma no Uta* [*An Elegy of a Cart*]. Tokyo: Chikuma Shobo.

Yanagi, Numeyoshi (1958), *Mingei 40nen* [*Forty Years of Mingei*]. Tokyo: Hobunkan.

Yokoyama, Gennosuke (1899), *Nihon no Kasoshakai* [*The Lower Society of Japan*]. Tokyo: Kyobunkan.

9

The Development of the Putting-out System in Modern Japan: The Case of the Cotton-Weaving Industry

TAKESHI ABE

One of the most important features of the rapid economic growth of modern Japan was dualistic industrial development. Nevertheless, scholars tend to emphasize only the growth of big businesses such as the *zaibatsu* (Mitsui, Mitsubishi, etc.) and a few cotton-spinning companies (Tôyôbô, Kanebô, etc.) in consideration of Japanese economic and business history. The indigenous, rural, small- and medium-sized industries, most of which had already developed during the pre-modern era (the Edo period), should also be examined. In early modern Japan, there were innumerable indigenous industries such as weaving, silk-reeling, brewing, ceramics, and paper manufacturing, and they often managed to survive side by side with the growth of modern big businesses. In addition, many indigenous industries even developed along with the modern sectors until the First World War (1914–18). The lower tier of the dual structure was generally composed of industries of this type.[1]

These indigenous industries, usually given less fiscal aid than more modern industries, often experienced healthy development. Yet entrepreneurs could not always grow by themselves; they were often backed by institutions such as the putting-out system. The purpose of this chapter is to show the genesis of the putting-out system, its influence on industrial development, and its metamorphosis in pre-war Japan.

The indigenous industry chosen here is the *sanchi* [producing-centre] cotton-weaving industry. The Japanese indigenous cotton industry had been highly developed since the Edo period (1603–1868), but after the beginning of foreign trade in 1859 it came to suffer from the tremendous inflows of cotton yarn and cloth from Lancashire in the UK and later of yarn from India. Although the Meiji government tried to transplant modern spinning-mills based on Lancashire technology, it was not until the mid-1880s that such mills took off, no longer depending on governmental policies. As shown in Table 9.1, the newly established spinning-mills remarkably expanded their production thereafter. They achieved import substitution and rapidly began to increase exports of yarn around 1890, with yarn exports surpassing imports in terms of volume in 1897. During and after the First World War, although the Japanese cotton industry lost its competitive advantage in yarn, the industry continued to develop through the expansion of the production and sale of cloth. In fact, Japanese exports of cotton cloth surpassed those of the UK in volume in 1933.[2]

It is noteworthy here that the main market for yarn was consistently composed of the domestic cotton weavers in the *sanchi* producing centres, as shown in Table 9.1. The Japanese cotton-weaving industry is divided into two large business groups, the first of which combines spinning and weaving and the second specializes in weaving only. It is the second group which formed the *sanchi* cotton-weaving industry, while the first group, which started to develop in the 1890s, consisted of large-scale factories equipped from the start with power looms, and was keen on adopting the latest mechanized technology. The traditional cotton weavers, in contrast, boasted of a history dating back to the Edo period. Although the creation of 'manufactories' (a small factory without machinery), to which Karl Marx paid great attention, proceeded in a few regions from the late Edo period, the overwhelming majority of weavers were, at least until about the time of the Russo-Japanese War (1904–5), part of a cottage industry in the putting-out system. They were members of farming households, using hand looms and working in their spare time, weaving cotton cloth to be collected by merchants. It was also common for large numbers of cotton-cloth producers, merchants, and processors to concentrate within relatively small areas known as *sanchi*, as illustrated by Map 9.1.[3]

The Establishment of the Putting-out System in the 1880s

From Kaufsystem to Putting-out System

Before the emergence of the factory system after the Russo-Japanese War, the prevailing form of business organization in the Japanese *sanchi* cotton-weaving industry was the putting-out system—a system similar to the European parallel as postulated by the theory of proto-industrialization.[4]

Table 9.1. *Supply and demand of cotton yarn in Japan (1858–1933) (1,000 pounds)*

Year	Supply				Demand			
	Japanese hand-spun yarn	Imported machine-spun yarn	Japanese machine-spun yarn	Total	Sanchi	Integrated weaving and spinning factories	Export	Total
1858	37,500	—	—	37,500	37,500	—	—	37,500
	100.0%	0.0%	0.0%	100.0%	100.0%	0.0%	0.0%	100.0%
1868	23,095	5,331	661	29,087	29,087	—	—	29,087
	79.4%	18.3%	2.3%	100.0%	100.0%	0.0%	0.0%	100.0%
1878	22,500	39,854	966	63,320	63,320	—	—	63,320
	35.5%	62.9%	1.5%	100.0%	100.0%	0.0%	0.0%	100.0%
1888	35,873	69,021	14,021	118,915	118,915	—	—	118,915
	30.2%	58.0%	11.8%	100.0%	100.0%	0.0%	0.0%	100.0%
1898	n.a.	23,175	281,336	304,511	203,373	—	100,159	303,532
	n.a.	7.6%	92.4%	100.0%	67.0%	0.0%	33.0%	100.0%
1908	—	1,821	351,428	353,249	238,436	47,676	67,137	353,249
	0.0%	0.5%	99.5%	100.0%	67.5%	13.5%	19.0%	100.0%
1913	—	506	607,193	607,699	309,045	111,160	187,494	607,699
	0.0%	0.1%	99.9%	100.0%	50.9%	18.3%	30.9%	100.0%
1923	—	2,533	868,461	870,994	531,084	240,980	98,930	870,994
	0.0%	0.3%	99.7%	100.0%	61.0%	27.7%	11.4%	100.0%
1933	—	23,586	1,239,943	1,263,529	881,905	362,301	19,323	1,263,529
	0.0%	1.9%	98.1%	100.0%	69.8%	28.7%	1.5%	100.0%

Note: Data on imported cloth are excluded. There may be a statistical discontinuity between the data in 1898 and those in 1908.

Sources: Nakamura (1968: App. Table 3); Dai Nihon Bōseki Rengō-kai (1908–33).

SANCHI	DISTRICTS (GUN) AND CITIES (SHI) (1937)
1 Sano	Tochigi Pref.: Aso-gun; Shimotsuga-gun; Tochigi-shi; Ashikaga-gun; Ashikaga-shi
2 Kita-Saitama	Saitama Pref.: Kita-Saitama-gun
3 Kita-Adachi	Saitama Pref.: Kita-Adachi-gun; Kawaguchi-shi; Urawa-shi
4 Tokorozawa	Saitama Pref.: Iruma-gun; Kawagoe-shi
5 Enshū	Shizuoka Pref.: Hamamatsu-shi; Hamana-gun; Inasa-gun; Iwata-gun; Shūchi-gun
6 Higashi-Mikawa	Aichi Pref.: Hoi-gun
7 Hazu	Aichi Pref.: Hazu-gun
8 Sanshū	Aichi Pref.: Nukada-gun; Okazaki-shi; Hekikai-gun; Higashi-Kamo-gun; Nishi-Kamo-gun
9 Bishū	Aichi Pref.: Niwa-gun; Haguri-gun
10 Bisai	Aichi Pref.: Ichinomiya-shi; Nakajima-gun
11 Nagoya	Aichi Pref.: Nagoya-shi; Aichi-gun; Nishi-Kasugai-gun
12 Chita	Aichi Pref.: Chita-gun; Handa-shi
13 Ise	Mie Pref.: Kawage-gun; Anō-gun; Tsu-shi; Suzuka-gun
14 Matsuzaka	Mie Pref.: Matsuzakashi; Iinan-gun; Ichishi-gun; Taki-gun
15 Naka-; Kita-Kawachi	Osaka Pref.: Naka-Kawachi-gun; Kita-Kawachi-gun; Fuse-shi
16 Minami-Kawachi	Osaka Pref.: Minami-Kawachi-gun
17 Senboku	Osaka Pref.: Senboku-gun
18 Sen'nan	Osaka Pref.: Sen'nan-gun; Kishiwada-shi
19 Wakayama	Wakayama Pref.: Wakayama-shi; Kaisō-gun; Kainan-shi
20 Banshū	Hyōgo Pref.: Taka-gun; Katō-gun; Kasai-gun
21 Kojima	Okayama Pref.: Kojima-gun
22 Ibara	Okayama Pref.: Shitsuki-gun; Oda-gun
23 Bingo	Hiroshima Pref.: Numakuma-gun; Ashina-gun; Fukayasu-gun; Fukuyama-shi
24 Imabari	Ehime Pref.: Imabari-shi; Ochi-gun; Shūsō-gun; Nii-gun
25 Matsuyama	Ehime Pref.: Matsuyama-shi; Onsen-gun; Iyo-gun
26 Yawatahama	Ehime Pref.: Yawatahama-shi; Nishi-Uwa-gun
27 Kurume	Fukuoka Pref.: Kurume-shi; Ukeha-gun; Mii-gun; Mitsuma-gun; Yame-gun; Asakura-gun

Map 9.1. *Principal cotton-textile sanchi (producing centres). This map shows main sanchi in 1937, by which time Mitsuke and Yamato, previously renowned for cotton weaving, ceased to be a major sanch.*

Source: Abe (1992: 10–11).

Map 9.2. *Sen'nan-gun: geographical distribution of Obitani's out-weavers around the time of the Russo-Japanese war.*

According to Table 9.2, among the 448,609 weaving households of Japan in 1905, 35 per cent were 'independent establishments', and 65 per cent were 'out-weavers'. 'Independent establishments' consisted of the following three categories: 'factory' (workshop or a factory with more than 10 workers), 'cottage industry' (an independent household in which the family members and fewer than 10 workers weave), and 'putting-out master' (a person who lends material yarn mainly to his/her out-weavers, having them weave cloth in exchange for wages) with their shares at 1, 31, and 3 per cent respectively. These data suggest that the out-weavers (*chimbata* or *chin'ori*) who borrowed material yarn and/or looms from a few putting-out masters and delivered cloth to them were quite numerous in many cotton-weaving *sanchi* around the time of the Russo-Japanese War. Even though similar nation-wide data were unavailable before 1904, many Japanese scholars recognize that the putting-out system was predominant in Japanese cotton-weaving *sanchi*, at least around the period from the mid-1880s to the Russo-Japanese War.

This system was found even in the Edo period, but became increasingly important as markets grew. First of all, let us review the features of representative cotton-weaving *sanchi* in the Edo period.[5] Although complete information is not available for every *sanchi*, the *watagae* system was identified in eight *shiromomen* (narrow white cotton cloth)[6] *sanchi* such as Chita (now in Aichi Prefecture) and Imabari (in Ehime Prefecture). Under this system, local merchants supplied ginned cotton to farm households and then collected the finished cloth; the wage was usually paid in kind, as part of the ginned cotton. Meanwhile, six *shimamomen* (narrow cotton stripe cloth) *sanchi* like Mitsuke (in Niigata Prefecture) and Bisai (in Aichi Prefecture) developed the *dashibata* (or *debata*) system, under which the merchants provided not only hand-spun yarn but also hand looms (usually known as *takabata*) to farm households and collected the woven cotton cloth in exchange for wages. The *dashibata* system is thought to have appeared after the adoption of improved looms, and was probably created in *shimamomen* *sanchi* when local merchants lent farm households the dyed or bleached hand-spun yarn and the *takabata* looms indispensable for *shimamomen* weaving, in order to collect more cloth later. In the *shiromomen sanchi*, however, the local merchants could obtain cloth merely by providing ginned cotton to the farm households, as hand-spun yarn and cloth could easily be made from ginned cotton using simple spinning wheels and looms. Although the *dashibata* system is a typical putting-out arrangement, the production of cloth by farm households in the *watagae* system was often for home consumption rather than for the market.[7]

These two systems were found in the newly emerging *sanchi*, but in the older *sanchi*, such as Kawachi and Senshû (both in present-day Osaka Prefecture), which began to develop in the sixteenth and seventeenth centuries, the local merchants generally provided neither material yarn nor

Table 9.2. *Looms and workers in Japan by type of work organization (independent establishments) (1903–1921)*

Year	Number	Power Looms	Hand Looms	Workers	Females
Factory[a]					
1903	—	—	—	—	—
1904	—	—	—	—	—
1905	3,097	13,887	60,681	91,279	80,753
1906	2,878	18,455	66,548	97,118	85,214
1907	3,701	25,298	67,713	95,199	84,837
1908	4,088	33,156	71,057	103,892	92,954
1909	4,944	46,579	74,018	113,522	101,770
1910	4,997	61,988	64,853	117,376	105,043
1911	4,894	75,300	61,539	122,842	110,644
1912	5,159	100,506	60,349	148,093	133,023
1913	4,598	101,713	55,249	143,983	128,710
1914	4,755	109,562	51,481	149,331	134,079
1915	3,967	116,591	41,403	153,805	132,643
1916	4,452	136,884	53,939	178,816	154,314
1917	5,053	156,551	52,050	208,033	177,182
1918	5,643	175,119	56,561	237,642	199,167
1919	6,834	208,529	52,244	279,050	232,017
1920	6,110	225,919	41,078	242,546	201,309
1921	6,893	249,713	37,849	263,808	217,145
Cottage Industry[b]					
1903	—	—	—	—	—
1904	—	—	—	—	—
1905	138,833	2,146	213,285	229,446	219,572
1906	175,379	1,260	259,140	274,484	262,821
1907	139,677	1,551	226,511	238,510	224,460
1908	149,846	2,931	228,462	243,436	230,324
1909	146,130	3,070	223,129	240,464	227,634
1910	139,583	3,421	214,778	229,827	217,249
1911	145,201	6,686	212,151	240,307	225,543
1912	134,771	4,668	211,191	216,266	205,276
1913	128,553	4,127	186,904	199,343	189,158
1914	119,626	5,333	165,923	178,062	169,697
1915	190,646	6,880	228,795	248,848	239,702
1916	252,485	7,540	282,148	319,683	308,947
1917	293,495	9,348	328,019	363,805	352,456
1918	275,003	10,654	308,800	339,764	327,140
1919	277,079	25,244	309,258	359,901	344,884
1920	259,046	26,185	292,332	339,011	323,338
1921	242,392	31,875	280,911	320,530	301,570

Putting-out master[c]

1903	—	—	—	—	—
1904	—	—	—	—	—
1905	14,370	89	57,611	58,591	52,379
1906	17,316	171	62,671	69,292	61,528
1907	17,440	145	47,925	38,736	35,786
1908	15,857	526	43,588	41,272	37,307
1909	13,596	325	30,293	40,293	36,636
1910	11,851	845	28,617	32,606	30,114
1911	10,690	308	17,100	21,834	19,092
1912	11,385	1,176	21,545	20,738	18,638
1913	9,202	1,438	17,373	17,182	15,705
1914	7,785	440	13,723	14,017	12,601
1915	10,291	2,128	17,896	24,482	20,926
1916	9,395	1,928	10,785	18,766	14,190
1917	10,865	1,850	13,617	21,433	16,783
1918	12,579	2,119	16,700	23,780	19,311
1919	14,898	4,783	19,365	31,892	25,117
1920	14,111	5,173	14,321	28,240	21,138
1921	15,731	10,534	15,983	37,531	28,946

Out-weaver[d]

1903	241,384	—	—	—	—
1904	240,168	—	—	—	—
1905	292,309	2,298	384,178	388,107	378,601
1906	267,592	771	327,812	351,597	342,042
1907	329,108	2,162	412,300	386,060	381,149
1908	337,660	1,017	402,418	369,679	365,267
1909	322,266	1,211	392,311	391,859	386,879
1910	294,137	2,339	375,448	381,500	373,635
1911	283,733	2,958	343,959	348,052	338,799
1912	276,321	5,306	328,298	312,601	304,019
1913	253,798	6,257	299,367	307,435	297,350
1914	220,227	7,495	268,142	269,367	259,420
1915	212,976	3,990	251,874	266,271	259,063
1916	223,189	3,092	264,856	282,069	272,172
1917	232,084	4,799	271,861	284,029	273,894
1918	246,803	9,952	298,221	321,984	308,307
1919	256,914	39,145	293,864	349,772	327,929
1920	227,190	23,866	284,396	321,127	304,347
1921	223,232	26,885	270,194	321,021	293,429

All figures relate to production of cotton, silk, hemp, and miscellaneous cloths.

[a] A workshop or a factory with more than 10 workers.

[b] *Kanai Kogyo* in Japanese. An independent household in which the family members and fewer than ten workers weave. This category would probably denote a non-factory establishment working on own loom(s).

[c] A person who lends material yarn mainly to his/her out-weavers, letting them weave cloth in exchange for wage.

[d] *chimbata* or *chin' ori* in Japanese. A person who borrows material yarn and/or loom(s) from a few putting-out masters and delivers cloth to them.

Source: Nôshômushô (1903–21).

looms to the farm households. The farmers bought yarn themselves and freely sold cloth to the merchants, i.e. the Kaufsystem.

Generally speaking, in the Edo period the organizers in cotton-weaving *sanchi* were local merchants. However, not all the *sanchi* incorporated the putting-out system, as some *sanchi* adopted the *watagae* system and others were organized according to the typical Kaufsystem.

The case of Sen'nan district, in the southern part of the present-day Osaka Prefecture, can be traced in some detail (see Map 9.2). Sen'nan was one of the most important *shiromomen sanchi* in Japan, and with extensive cultivation of cotton since the early Edo period, farm households in the district began to engage in producing ginned cotton, hand-spun yarn, and *shiromomen* as their only sideline occupation. *Shiromomen* was at first produced only for home consumption and nearby markets, but the commercialization of its surplus was greatly expanded in the Kanbun years (1661–73) by local merchants known as *watagai*. These merchants supplied part of the collected ginned cotton to certain farm households, took hand-spun yarn or cotton cloth in return, and sold the rest of the ginned cotton to the cotton merchants of Kyoto and Osaka.[8] With machine-spun cotton yarn being adopted in cotton-cloth weaving, the production of hand-spun yarn decreased in the Meiji Period (1868–1912), and the *watagai* also declined, seemingly to have died cut by 1892.[9] Around the early Meiji period in the Sen'nan and Senboku districts (i.e. Senshû) merchants called *momenya, momengai,* or *nakagai* appeared. They bought cotton cloth from farm households but without advancing them material yarn until about 1887.[10] However, their relationship with the *watagai* remains unclear.

In Sen'nan, after about 1887, a newer form of merchant appeared who lent Japanese machine-spun cotton yarn, and probably hand looms as well, to the farm households in the area, collected the woven cotton cloth in exchange for wages, and sold the cloth to the merchants in the city of Osaka. The larger merchants were known as *nakagai*, and the small- and medium-sized ones were called *dashibataya*, who were further classified into those dependent on the *nakagai* and those independent from them. In any case, such new merchants were typical putting-out masters, and the putting-out system was referred to as the *dashibata* (or *debata*) system in Sen'nan.

Around the period from 1884 to 1887, just before the diffusion of the putting-out system, one-third of the farm households in the district were engaged in cotton weaving in one form or another, and by the early 1890s well over 80 per cent (some persons say almost 100 per cent) had become out-weavers termed *chimbata*.[11]

The case of Sen'nan suggests that the putting-out system in many cotton weaving *sanchi* in the Meiji period was not a simple continuation of the legacy of the Edo period, but instead that many were newly formed. Let us briefly consider the cases of other *sanchi*, and generalize the above-mentioned hypothesis.

Mitsuke

This *sanchi* in Niigata Prefecture was well-known for silk weaving, but also produced *shimamomen* after the end of the Edo period. In 1900, it succeeded in producing a new cloth, *shin-fushiori*, made of a combination of cotton yarn and *sakusan* [a wild silkworm] pongee yarn from Manchuria known for being both beautiful and inexpensive. Mitsuke then began to develop as a *sanchi* of the silk-cotton yarn mixture, and the product change was accompanied by the diffusion of the putting-out system. The merchants there lent not only material yarn but also most of the looms (*takabata*) needed by *chimbata* weavers.[12]

Tokorozawa

In this district of Saitama Prefecture, one of the newly emerging *sanchi* at the end of Edo period, cloth-weaving farm households purchased hand-spun and imported yarn from the local yarn merchants, then selling to them the resulting *shimamomen* prior to being delivered to the local dyers for finish. Here at first the Kaufsystem was found, but around the time of the Matsukata deflation (1881–4) the cloth merchants appeared to become putting-out masters.[13]

Higashi-Mikawa

This *sanchi* in Aichi Prefecture had seen remarkable development since the early Meiji period as a *shimamomen sanchi*. Although manufacturers with improved hand looms existed in the early Meiji years, a putting-out system soon appeared. Especially about 1887, this system became prevalent along with the decline of raw cotton production due to foreign imports and the replacement of hand-spun yarn by machine-spun yarn. By about 1897, there were only 40–50 putting-out masters and about 1,000 out-weaving farm households around Gamagôri, the centre of Higashi-Mikawa. However, by 1902–3 the putting-out system of Higashi-Mikawa extended to the adjacent Hazu district.[14]

Sanshû

This *sanchi* around Okazaki in Aichi Prefecture had been famous for the production of *shiromomen* since the seventeenth century. Up until the early

Meiji years, the farm households grew raw cotton in the summer, spun yarn by hand, and wove *shiromomen* with hand looms in the winter. The output was usually sold to small cloth merchants (*momen nakatsugi*), and were finally collected by the large local cloth merchants (*kaitsugi-donya*) in a typical Kaufsystem. However, with the adoption of *garabô*, the new water-powered spinning equipment invented by Tacchi Gaun in 1873, the increasing labour productivity, and the introduction of the batten (flying shuttle) in this district in the 1880s, the putting-out system emerged and developed. The putting-out masters were new merchants who appeared at the end of the Edo period, and who often lent new hand looms to farm households.[15]

Bisai

This district in Aichi Prefecture had been a famous *shimamomen sanchi* since the latter half of the Edo period, with 'manufactories' developing especially during the Bunka and Tempo period (1818–43). After the opening of the ports in 1859, Bisai diversified the use of raw material in *shimamomen* by buying imported yarn. In addition, the district began to produce silk-cotton mixtures around 1875, the value of which surpassed that of cotton cloth after the Russo-Japanese War when Japanese machine-spun yarn was used. Although the 'manufactories' drove development in the beginning, they started to decline during the Matsukata deflation, while the putting-out system became prevalent. The putting-out masters in Bisai could be classified into two groups: those who had originally administered their factories as 'manufactories', later adopting and enlarging the putting-out system, finally abandoning the factories, and those who started out as yarn and cloth merchants, subsequently becoming putting-out masters.[16]

Yamato

This district in Nara Prefecture was a famous cotton weaving *sanchi* from the mid-17th century, and the Kaufsystem seems to have prevailed there. Although we had very little information on Yamato around the period of the Meiji Restoration, the putting-out system can be clearly identified from the mid-1880s, becoming the standard form of business organization before the First World War.[17]

Imabari

This *sanchi* in Ehime Prefecture had been well-known for the production of *shiromomen* from the latter half of the Edo period, operating under the typical *watagae* system. However, in 1888 certain merchants began to lend the newly introduced machine-spun yarn to farm households, and, in the following year, they organized Iyo Momen Kabushiki Kaisha (the Iyo Cotton Cloth Company), through which the merchants developed the putting-out system and lent not only yarn but also new hand looms to the *chimbata*.[18] The details of this organization's activity will be explained later.

From those cases, it can be seen that many cotton-weaving *sanchi* first adopted the putting-out system around the mid-1880s. This system of providing cotton yarn and looms is essentially the same as the *dashibata* system in the *shimamomen sanchi* in the Edo period, with the only difference being that not only *shimamomen* but also *shiromomen* was woven under the new putting-out system. On the other hand, the *watagae* system was no longer adopted after the Meiji Restoration.

Factors Accounting for the Establishment of the Putting-out System

Why did the putting-out system become prevalent in so many cotton-weaving *sanchi* in the 1880s? M. Tanimoto has suggested that this diffusion of the putting-out system was the result of 'the reorganization of the *sanchi* to changes in market conditions', that is, the rapid reduction of the domestic cotton cloth market during the Matsukata deflation.[19] This is a very interesting point, which is deserving of further consideration.

First, in some *sanchi* such as Sen'nan, Higashi-Mikawa, and Imabari, the emergence of the putting-out system was more pronounced during the boom after the Matsukata deflation. Tanimoto considered the reduction of the product market in the depression as the trigger for the diffusion of the putting-out system. The system certainly developed in a number of the above-mentioned *sanchi* such as Mitsuke, Tokorozawa, and Bisai in the depression, but there were actually several *sanchi* which promoted the putting-out system in order to secure more product for market enlargement during the boom.

Next, in Sen'nan, a kind of batten (*chonkobata*) came to be widely adopted after 1877, and 80 per cent were produced by the *chimbata* farm households. It is notable that, after the invention of the improved *chonkobata* (the *taikobata*) around 1892, the *dashibata* system of lending hand looms to farm households seems to have rapidly diffused since it was impossible for farm households to produce *taikobata* themselves.[20] Although the newly improved loom was superior to the old one in terms of the quality of cloth, productivity remained unchanged.[21] From this case it can be inferred that another factor in the diffusion of the putting-out system was the introduction of new-type of looms. As for other *sanchi* where the lending of looms was accompanied by the diffusion of the putting-out system, there are at least three: Mitsuke, Sanshû, and Imabari. New looms were often adopted for the improvement of the quality of the cloth in order to meet the fierce competition among the various cotton weaving *sanchi* under rapidly changing market conditions. Undeniably, the introduction of the putting-out system by the local merchants evolved out of the demand of farm households to borrow the expensive looms that they could not make or purchase. The term of *dashibata* (or *debata*), which means 'lending looms' in Japanese, is a testimony to this fact.

Thirdly, the substitution of Japanese machine-spun cotton yarn for hand-spun and imported machine-spun yarn is also important. The basic determinant of the remarkable development of the modern cotton-spinning industry in Japan since the mid-1880s had been successful sales of its yarn to the domestic cotton-weaving *sanchi*. The adoption of machine-spun yarn in many *sanchi* inevitably led to the reorganization of the traditional distribution system of Japanese cotton yarn and cloth, and it was just such a re-organization that enabled a few big merchants (*sanchi-donya*) in the *sanchi* to monopolize the distribution of the yarn. In the case of Sen'nan, data can be obtained for twenty-four clothiers established before 1894 whose adoption of Japanese machine-spun cotton yarn is indicated in Figure 9.1. The adoption was remarkable there after the mid-1880s, especially in 1887 and 1894. On the other hand, the newly established merchants known as *nakagai*, whose number was about ten, had controlled the supply of cotton yarn to the weavers as well as the collection of cotton cloth at least since around 1900.[22] Thus, the case of Sen'nan suggests that the introduction of Japanese machine-spun cotton yarn was realized through the limited channels of local yarn merchants, which seems to be another factor in the diffusion of the putting-out system.

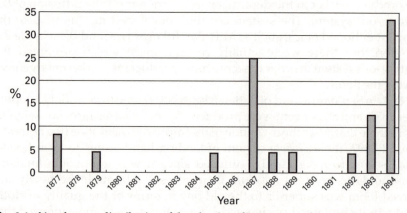

Fig. 9.1. *Year-by-year distribution of the adoption of Japanese machine-spun cotton yarn by the clothiers in Sen'nan. Numbers of clothiers who adopted Japanese machine-spun cotton yarn each year shown as percentage of total for the whole period from 1877 to 1894.*
Source: Osaka-fu (c.1904).

Local Trade Associations and the Putting-out System

Local Trade Associations in Modern Japan

The local trade associations in modern Japan[23] were an important force in propelling the formation of the putting-out system. In the latter half of the Edo period there were many trade associations similar to the guilds in Western medieval cities, termed *kabunakama* in the cities and *nakama* in the local areas, both of which were organized by merchants and artisans. They performed the four socio-economic functions of monopoly, privilege protection, regulation, and credit endorsement.[24] 'In other words, we could say that Japanese guilds in the Tokugawa [Edo] period played the role of commercial law in a capitalistic society to a certain degree.'[25] The early Meiji government pursued the policy of dissolving such associations on the principle of freedom of trade, with actual execution carried out by the local governments. In addition, modern commercial law was not completely enacted until 1899. As the commercial rules supported by the guild system were destroyed and disorder in trade became predominant in the early Meiji years, the traditional merchants and artisans soon became keen on reviving the former guild-like associations.

Both the merchants' strong desire and the Meiji government's intention of promoting export industries produced legislations related to new trade associations, of which the Jûyô Bussan Dôgyô Kumiai Hô (the Important Commodities Local Trade Association Law) enacted in 1900 was the most important. Although two functions of the *kabunakama* and *nakama*, monopoly and privilege protection, were still denied under the governmental principle of freedom of trade, regulation and endorsement of credit were taken on by the new associations, *Dôgyô Kumiai*. Another important difference between the guilds in the Edo period and the *Dôgyô Kumiai* was that the latter were organized mainly in local industries such as the traditional weaving industry. Before the establishment of the *Dôgyô Kumiai*, merchants and artisans often tried to re-establish commercial order by themselves, and the 'company system' diffused in the Meiji period was seen as a good way to accomplish their purpose.

The Kaisha *and the Putting-out System*

Although it took many years for Japanese businessmen to thoroughly understand the functions of the Western company system,[26] the number of *kaisha* (companies) increased annually during the Meiji Period. *Kaisha* were established in both urban and rural areas, and two cases are presented here.

Sen'nan

During the first half of the 1880s the cotton-weaving industry in Sen'nan suffered from overproduction of inferior articles, fierce competition from certain *shiromomen sanchi*, and the Matsukata deflation. During this period the merchants often organized loose associations (see Table 9.3), the most notable of which was named Kyôdô Kaisha (Co-operative Company) established in 1888. This company was a joint stock company with a capital of 15,000 yen and, according to Table 9.4 section (1), most of its executives were wealthy and of high social status. The column headed 'Occupation' in the same table shows that seven out of eight members were *nakagai*, three of whom were not only merchants but also manufacturers. Two members seem to have had their own factories, suggesting that they were typical putting-out masters, while six of them continued weaving in 1904, meaning that they were probably the larger merchants who survived after the Matsukata deflation.

As No. 20 count machine-spun cotton yarn became dominant in the cotton-weaving industry in Sen'nan after 1883, Kyôdô Kaisha encouraged the industry to produce *shiromomen* using Japanese machine-spun yarn for both warp and weft (i.e. *marutô momen*) and monopolized the distribution. In addition, after the invention of the new *taikobata* hand loom by Yonezô Matsunami in Sen'nan, Kyôdô Kaisha soon achieved significant quality improvement, and made efforts to diffuse the new technology. In consequence, *taikobata* looms were quickly adopted throughout most of the Sen'nan district. As the establishment of Kyôdô Kaisha coincided with a prosperous period of the Japanese economy, it is somewhat difficult to judge this achievement properly. Nevertheless, the production of cotton cloth in Sen'nan doubled from 3,000,000 *tan* in 1888 to 6,000,000 *tan* in 1894, but Kyôdô Kaisha was said to have ended because of internal troubles in 1898.[27]

Imabari

Imabari's production of *shiromomen* reached 400,000 *tan* in 1877, but dropped to 18,451 *tan* by 1885 because of intense inter-*sanchi* competition around 1882, the intense efforts of Senshû (Southern Osaka Prefecture) and Banshû in Hyôgo Prefecture, and the pressure from imported shirting. In 1888 Saburô Yanase, Shunjirô Yanase, Kamesaburô Tasaka, Kumatarô Murakami, and others began to supply weavers with machine-spun cotton yarn in order

Table 9.3. *Trade associations relating to the cotton-weaving industry in Sen'nan*

Year	Events
1885	*Junsoku Kumiai*, which controlled Mimami-gun and Hine-gun, both of which would later become Sen'nan-gun, were established on Osaka-fu Dôgyô Kumiai Jyunsoku promulgated in the same year. The president was Jihei Tabata in Kaizuka-chô. Nevertheless, this association seems to have been soon wound up because of the discord among members.
1888	Kabushiki Kaisha Kyôdô Kaisha was established in Kishiwada-sakai-cho with capital of 15,000 yen. President was Kusutarô Kakuno in Kishiwada-chô.
1895	Kyôdô Kaisha increased the capital to 300,000 yen.
1898	Kyôdô Kaisha was wound up.
1898	The application of establishment of the association which would control the cotton-weaving industry in Sen'nan was submitted to Osaka Prefecture under Jûyô Yushutsuhin Dôgyô Kumiai Hô [Important Export Products Local Trade Association Law] promulgated in the previous year.
1899	The above-mentioned application was admitted by Nôshômushô [Ministry of Agriculture and Commerce], and Sen'nan-gun Momen Dôgyô Kumiai was established in Numano-mura. President was Hironojyô Kusumoto in Yamadai-shimo-mura.
1900	Sen'nan-gun Momen Dôgyô Kumiai was wound up because of internal troubles.
1901	The persons who had *taikobata* submitted to the authorities the application of establishment of Izumi Momen Taikobata Dôgyô Kumiai controlling the former Hine-gun, but failed.
1902	A private association, Momen Kaseito-shô Kumiai, was established in Kishiwada by *nakagai* and yarn merchants.
1902	The application of re-establishment of Sen'nan-gun Momen Dôgyô Kumiai was submitted to Osaka Prefecture under Jûyô Bussan Dôgyô Kumiai Hô [Important Commodities Local Trade Association Law] promulgated in 1900.
1903	Nôshômushô rejected the above-mentioned application, but Sen'nan-gun and Osaka Prefecture continued to insist on the necessity of the re-establishment of the association to the ministry.
1905	Sen'nan-gun Momen Dôgyô Kumiai was re-established in Kishiwada. President was Kusutarô Kakuno. This association soon changed its name to Sen'nan-gun Orimono Dôgyô Kumiai.

Note: According to Aizawa (1938: 14–15), the persons submitting the application to Osaka Prefecture in 1902 overlapped the members of Momen Kaseito-shô Kumiai.

Sources: Sen'nan-gun Orimono Dôgyô Kumiai (*c*.1907); Takeuchi (1979: 59–119).

to overcome the crisis. This attempt succeeded, and in the same year Imabari recorded a production of 82,930 *tan*. Based on this experience, Seizaburô Yanase and nine others raised investments in stocks at the end of 1889, and established Iyo Momen Kabushiki Kaisha with a capital of 50,000 yen. This

Table 9.4. *Leaders of the associations relating to the cotton-weaving industry in Sen'nan (1888–1905)*

Name	Address	Position	Occupation	Occupation (July 1904)	Establishment	Place of production	Tax (c.1903)†	Land Tax (c.1903)†	Rank (1904)	Notes
(1) Kyōdō Kaisha (1888)										
Kusutarō Kakuno*	Kishiwada-chō	President	Cotton-cloth merchant	Manufacturing	By his father	—	366.753	120.593	Upper class	Member of chō assembly
Tokubei Kishimura*	Kishiwada-chō	Director	Cotton-cloth manufacturing and selling	Selling and manufacturing	—	—	—	—	—	—
Jiemon Okada*	Kishiwada-chō	Director	—	—	—	—	—	—	—	
Kanbei Kose*	Kishiwada-chō	Director	—	—	—	—	—	—	—	
Kyūkichi Kakuno*	Kishiwada-chō	Director	Cotton-cloth manufacturing and selling	Manufacturing and selling	In 1882	One-storey house in 500 tsubo**	49.880	—	Middle class	Began *dashibata* in 1895; younger brother of Kusutarō Kakuno; member of chō assembly
Shōshichi Sasajima	Numano-chō	Director	—	Manufacturing	—	—	—	—	—	—
Kichibei Fujii*	Kishiwada-chō	Director	Cotton-cloth manufacturing and selling	Selling and manufacturing	—	—	215.618	17.078	Nearly upper class	
Ihei Okada*	Kishiwada-chō	Manager	Cotton-cloth selling	Selling and manufacturing	—	—	275.540	—	Upper class	Member of gun assembly; mura chief
(2) Sen'nan-gun Momen Dōgyō Kumiai (1899)										
Hironojō Kusumoto	Yamadai-shimo-mura	President	—	—	—	—	—	—	—	—
Jinzaburō Kitagawa	Kumatori-mura	Vice-president	Cotton-cloth merchant	—	In 1896	—	—	—	—	Member of fu assembly
Heizō Shimizu	Yamadai-shimo-mura	Councillor	Agriculture, cotton-cloth manufacturing and selling	Manufacturing	By his ancestor	—	37.486	23.834	Middle class	Member of mura assembly

Name	Mura	Role	Business	Selling/manufacturing	Year	Location detail			Class	Notes
Kōgi Takimoto	Yagi-mura	Councillor	Cotton-cloth nakagai	—	In 1875	—	—	—	—	Member of mura assembly
Ichitarō Fujii	—	Councillor	Cotton-cloth merchant	Selling and manufacturing	By his father	—	—	—	—	Son of Kichibei Fujii in (1), whose name he succeeded to later
Yaozō Akasaka	Kita-nakadōri-mura	Councillor	Cotton-cloth merchant	Manufacturing	In 1894	Dashibata to two mura	—	—	—	—
Kiyomo Matsunami***	Kita-nakadōri-mura	Councillor	Cotton-cloth merchant	Manufacturing	In 1886	Dashibata to nine mura	—	—	—	Member of mura assembly
Tsunetarō Meshino**	Sano-mura	Councillor	Tile and cotton-cloth manufacturing	—	In 1897	—	—	—	—	—
Yahei Uenoyama**	Tajiri-mura	Councillor	Cotton cloth	Manufacturing	In 1877	One-storey house in 100 tubo Dashibata	—	—	—	Member of mura assembly
Kazō Kawaguchi**	Uenogō-mura	Councillor	Cotton cloth	Manufacturing	In 1880	—	—	—	—	Member of mura assembly
Yoshimatsu Shindō***	Hineno-mura	Councillor	Cotton cloth	Manufacturing	In 1888	—	—	—	—	—
Kusutarō Kakuno**	Kishiwada-chō	Councillor	For the following cols see (1)							

(3) Sen'nan-gun Momen Dōgyō Kumiai (1905)

Name	Mura	Role	Business	Selling/manufacturing	Year	Location detail			Class	Notes
Kusutarō Kakuno**	Kishiwada-chō	President	For the following cols see (1)							
Shinbei Muranaka*	Sano-mura	Vice-president	Cotton-cloth nakagai and manufacturing	—	—	—	86.788	—	Middle or upper class	—
Tokutarō Kawasaki*	Numano-mura	Councillor	Cotton-cloth manufacturing and selling	—	—	—	45.114	2.054	Middle class	Member of mura assembly
Isaburō Kakuno*	Numano-mura	Councillor	Cotton-cloth manufacturing and selling	—	—	—	25.397	0.377	Middle class	Member of mura assembly

Table 9.4. (cont.)

Name	Address	Position	Occupation	Occupation (July 1904)	Establish-ment	Place of production	Tax (c.1903)†	Land Tax (c.1903)†	Rank (1904)	Notes
Gihei Terada*	Kishiwada-hama-chō	Councillor	Cotton-cloth manufacturing	—	—	—	112.960	0.000	Upper class	Rice merchant; member of *chō* assembly
Hikoe Maekawa*	Yagi-mura	Councillor	Cotton-cloth selling	—	—	—	78.101	38.781	Nearly upper class	Member of *mura* assembly
Kakutarō Kakuhara	Yagi-mura	Councillor	Cotton-cloth manufacturing	—	—	—	6.348	2.468	Nearly middle class	—
Kōsuke Obitani	Kaizuka-chō	Councillor	—	—	—	—	—	—	—	*Dashibata* merchant
Jirokichi Mizohata	Kaizuka-chō	Councillor	—	—	In 1884	—	—	—	—	*Dashibata* merchant
Sakunoshin Shindō	Hineno-mura	Councillor	—	—	—	—	—	—	—	*Dashibata* merchant
Jisaburō Hara**	Tajiri-mura	Councillor	—	—	In 1882	One-storey house in 40 *tubo*	—	—	—	—
Toyokichi Kanazawa	Tarui-mura	Councillor								
Tokubei Kishimura	Kishiwada-chō	Councillor	For the following col. see (1)							
Kyūkichi Kakuno	Kishiwada-chō	Councillor	For the following col. see (1)							
Yaozō Akasaka	Kita-nakadōri-mura	Councillor	For the following col. see (2)							
Kiyomo Matsunami	Kita-nakadōri-mura	Councillor	For the following col. see (2)							
Kazō Kawaguchi	Uenogō-mura	Councillor	For the following col. see (2)							

* Person who seems to have been *nakagai*.

** Person who had *taikobata*.

† Yen.

Note: *Tubo* is Japanese unit of area. One *tubo* equals about 3.3 square metres.

Sources: Sen'nan-gun Orimono Dōgyō Kumiai (c.1907); Maekawa (1968: tables 1 and 2); the paper on establishment of Sen'nan-gun Momen Dōgyō Kumiai, July 1904 (Osaka City University Archives); Takeuchi (1979; 59–119). For the columns on address, occupation, and notes, also see Aizawa (1938); Taniguchi (1950).

'company' supplied the weavers with imported yarn and paid them wages in return for the cotton cloth produced. In 1891, Iyo Momen Kabushiki Kaisha, trying to increase production, opened branches in the Ochi, Shûsô, and Nii areas to invite weavers to work for them. If the weavers had no hand looms, reeds, or shuttles, the company would procure and sell such items to them, the payment for which could be made monthly from the weavers' wages.

Problems occurred when Iyo Momen Kabushiki Kaisha left all production including the preparatory process to the weavers, who were embezzling yarn, and the quality of the cloth deteriorated. The company subsequently made the following radical reforms: (1) it supplied the weavers with pre-set warp to cut costs and increase production; (2) it substituted Japanese machine-spun cotton yarn for imported yarn; and (3) it let the weavers adopt *takabata* (advanced hand looms) and new reeds. These strategies succeeded in improving the quality of the cloth, while the Sino-Japanese War (1894–5) increased demand for *shiromomen* from Imabari for bandages, with production in 1895 reaching 4,996,136 *tan*. Iyo Momen Kabushiki Kaisha overwhelmed the *sanchi* of Senshû, Banshû, and Yamato. Its *shiromomen* with the trademark picture of a peony tree was used by the Imperial Household, and won over thirty first prizes at national and local industrial expositions. However, the company was hit by the depression after the Sino-Japanese War, and was wound up in 1903.[28]

These cases demonstrate that in some cotton weaving *sanchi*, *de facto* local trade associations that adopted the company system were founded in the boom after the Matsukata deflation to cope with overproduction of inferior articles and intense competition with other *sanchi* and foreign countries. Despite their capital investments, however, the 'companies' were hardly modern organizations, with the merchants including the putting-out masters taking the leadership in organizing many small- and medium-sized weavers. The above-mentioned 'companies', for example, controlled the quality of products, made efforts to let the weavers use the new hand looms, and promoted the diffusion of Japanese machine-spun cotton yarn in the *sanchi*. In short, the 'companies', led by merchants, propelled the technological progress in the *sanchi* and contributed to the expansion of the market for the newly developing modern Japanese cotton-spinning industry. Nevertheless, they could not survive indefinitely, and would soon end in the depression occurring around the beginning of the twentieth century.

Dôgyô Kumiai *and the Local Merchants*

Although the careers of the leaders of Iyo Momen Kabushiki Kaisha are not known in detail, it can be verified that the executives of Kyôdô Kaisha in

Sen'nan were mainly local merchants including the putting-out masters. This feature was also found in the trade associations established there after the breakup of Kyôdô Kaisha in 1898 (see Table 9.3).

According to Table 9.4 section (2), in 1899 most of the leaders in the cotton-weaving industry in Sen'nan were merchants. The column 'Place of production' in 1902 suggests that Kyûkichi Kakuno, Yahei Uenoyama, and Jisaburô Hara had fairly large, centralized workshops (i.e. 'manufactories'), although their names cannot be found in *Kôjyô Tsûran* (the Directory of Japanese Factories) (1904) edited by Nôshômu-shô (Ministry of Agriculture and Commerce), which compiled the data at the end of 1902. Even if 'manufactories' were established, it may have been difficult for them to survive for long.[29] As shown in Table 9.4 section (2), two of the twelve executives founded their enterprises in the 1870s, three of them in the 1880s, and three of them in the 1890s. Many of them were relatively new entrants to the weaving industry, but eight of the members continued their businesses in the same industry in 1904. These facts suggest that the large merchants in Sen'nan were able to continue to deal in cotton yarn and/or cotton cloth. In addition, six of the twelve merchants had *taikobata*, and three of them were apparently *dashibata-ya*. Eight of them were listed as manufacturers, but only one (Uenoyama) had his own workshop and most seem to have been typical putting-out masters.

Referring to Table 9.4 section (3) for 1905, most of the leaders around the time of the Russo-Japanese War were wealthy men like those in the same section. Incidentally, in some cases the amount of land taxes and rates as a proportion of their total taxes are not particularly large except Maekawa, so it is difficult to determine whether or not they were keen on acquiring their own land. Judging from the column headed 'Occupation', commercial activities seemed to be the major interest for most of the executives in section (3), as was the case for the persons in sections (1) and (2) in the same table. Many Japanese scholars have emphasized that most Japanese clothiers were landowners,[30] and this author has argued that a merchant weaver in Banshû in Hyôgo Prefecture invested most of the profits earned from weaving in the accumulation of land instead of business expansion.[31] Accordingly, careful consideration should be taken as to what degree the case of Sen'nan can be generalized. However, it should not be ignored that most of the leaders of the cotton-weaving industry in Sen'nan in the latter half of the Meiji period were merchants rather than landowners.

Dôgyô Kumiai had many functions, clearly classified by T. Matsumoto[32] as: (1) inspections of manufactured goods;[33] (2) marketing research including foreign markets; (3) evaluation and public announcement: specifically, expositions, contests, competitions, etc.; (4) advertisement; (5) arrangements for infrastructure, particularly encouragement and establishment of industrial education institutes and industrial experimental stations; and (6) joint work relating to purchase of materials, sale of products, finance, and segments of the production process such as the finishing factory in Banshû.[34] Matsumoto insisted that those functions worked well during the inter-war period, but, as we shall see, the Japanese government abandoned efforts to foster *Dôgyô Kumiai* during the inter-war period, especially in the 1930s. Matsumoto's arguments were probably relevant for the period around the 1910s, but not during the inter-war period. It can be stated confidently, then, that *Dôgyô Kumiai* led by local merchants actively contributed to the development of Japanese indigenous industries such as the *sanchi* cotton-weaving industry around the 1910s.

Transformation of the Putting-out System

After the Russo-Japanese War the putting-out system was rapidly transformed into the mechanized factory system in several cotton-weaving *sanchi* including Sen'nan, Senboku, Banshû, Chita, and Enshû in Shizuoka Prefecture. The putting-out masters in Sen'nan were troubled by the 'scissors effect' consisting of stagnant cloth prices and rising yarn prices with the former problem probably a reflection of the growing intensity in inter-*sanchi* competition. In addition, the emergence of subcontractors from the ranks of the *chimbata* weavers, who were asking for high prices for their newly enhanced production capacity, annoyed the putting-out masters.

As Table 9.5 indicates, the power loom was introduced into Sen'nan in 1907 and the number of power looms driven by steam engines quintupled from 1908 to 1909. As a result, the 'factories' increased in number while those working on the rented hand looms started to decline. By 1910 'factories' outnumbered 'putting-out masters' and, by 1912, the number of power looms totalled nearly 10,000 while the traditional putting-out system had virtually disappeared. This chronology, together with the fact that the putting-out masters were facing the above-mentioned difficulties after about 1905, strongly suggests that the need to bring workers under tighter control and to save labour forced the putting-out masters to set up centralized, power-driven workshops.

At an initial stage when cheap labour could be easily found, especially around the depression of 1907–8, another alternative for putting-out masters was to make more use of the cheap labour of *chimbata* out-weavers. A putting-out master in Sen'nan, Obitani Shôten, did adopt that strategy at first, but sometime between late 1911 and early 1912, it too decided to abandon the traditional putting-out system and build a factory equipped with power looms. We are not sure why Obitani had to change its policy. It could be due to the difficulty of keeping a pool of cheap, agrarian labour located in close vicinity to the industrial city of Osaka, or that the decision was

Takeshi Abe

Table 9.5. *Looms and workers in Sen'nan by type of work organization (1906–1912)*

Year	Number	Power Looms	Hand Looms	Workers	Females
Factory					
1906	21	—	790	820	790
1907	35	400	668	1,096	1,040
1908	44	472	745	1,020	940
1909	67	2,319	753	2,161	1,948
1910	80	3,146	444	2,945	2,655
1911	124	6,782	681	4,312	3,919
1912	146	9,227	626	5,415	4,872
Cottage industry					
1906	3	—	10	10	10
1907	21	—	66	70	66
1908	40	—	176	179	176
1909	52	—	434	505	474
1910	49	—	479	502	449
1911	26	—	148	162	138
1912	14	—	156	135	135
Putting-out master					
1906	152	—	425	537	527
1907	136	—	545	577	548
1908	153	—	175	270	180
1909	154	[?]	[?]	[?]	[?]
1910	68	—	315	343	298
1911	36	—	—	—	—
1912	13	—	66	70	65
Out-weaver					
1906	[?]	—	11,711	11,780	11,780
1907	8,642	—	11,015	11,030	11,030
1908	8,208	—	9,399	9,406	9,406
1909	5,747	—	6,534	6,601	6,362
1910	3,258	—	3,699	4,069	4,007
1911	1,183	—	1,368	1,434	1,410
1912	654	—	833	843	819

Notes: See the notes to Table 9.2. '?' indicates a too high or too low figure.
Source: Osaka-fu (1906–12).

made under the guidance of the district's *Dôgyô Kumiai*. Still, it is worth noting that there were alternative responses at that juncture, such as to introduce a labour-saving method and a new organization suited to that method, or to stick to the conventional lines of the putting-out system, and/or to alter the product mix to make full use of *chimbata* out-workers.

Only a few *sanchi* including Sen'nan started to introduce power looms in the 1910s, while the rest, especially those producing cloth with traditional *kasuri* and *shimamomen* (splashed and striped patterns), appeared to have continued along traditional putting-out lines. However, we must not overlook the contemporary metamorphosis of the putting-out system in certain of the *sanchi*. Such a metamorphosis signified the increased sophistication rather than the decline of the putting-out system.[35]

In the case of Obitani,[36] for example, even after 1911–12 when it started factory operation, it continued to 'purchase' *shiromomen* from other producers to sell under its own brand name. In fact, Obitani put it out to them. One important difference from the traditional form of putting-out is that those who supplied products for Obitani were no longer hand-loom weavers, but other factory-owners (*chin'ori*). It was a new version of the putting-out system based on the factory system. There are several distinguishing features of the eleven *chin'ori* factories producing for Obitani at the end of 1916. Firstly, except for three factories, all other members were located in Kishiwada and in Kaizuka close to Obitani's factory in Sechigo near Kaizuka. Secondly, except for one factory founded during the First World War, all other factories were erected around 1910 like the Obitani factory. The scale of the *chin'ori* was generally smaller than the Obitani factory which had 260 power looms, although there were some larger ones such as the Sawa factory with 113 power looms. As far as can be ascertained, six factories had power looms made by two makers, Kitano and Hirano. Although all eleven factories were powered, nine *chin'ori* used gas, with none using electric power. According to the estimation of the author, six *chin'ori* delivered more than 50 per cent of their woven cloth to Obitani and, of particular note, three *chin'ori* seem to have delivered all of their products to Obitani. On the other hand, five factories seem to have been relatively independent of Obitani. In addition, six factories began dealing with Obitani before the First World War, the other five became Obitani's *chin'ori* around 1914. Finally, at least seven factories were founded by landowners. To sum up, during the boom of the First World War, Obitani organized a network of *chin'ori*-based powered factories with power looms set up mainly by the landowners in the area. Obitani had exclusive connections with about half of the *chin'ori*, but rather loose connections with the rest.

Why were many factories organized into Obitani's *chin'ori* network? Firstly, as many factories were short of capital, they could not deal directly with the cotton merchants in Osaka, the centre of cotton goods trading in Japan, particularly with those yarn merchants who dealt only in cash.[37] Probably they were unable to acquire yarn and to sell cloth without going through Obitani as a *nakagai* (a large cotton merchant in Sen'nan). Especially during the boom of the First World War, when the price of yarn rose to an extraordinarily high level, many factories appeared eager to become Obitani's *chin'ori*. Secondly, the *chin'ori* often lent long-term to their factories. When they became *chin'ori*, many of them received finance from Obitani in exchange for a written pledge agreeing to Obitani's proposal.

In 1920 Obitani had three of its own mills, which produced 42 per cent of all the cloth it collected. Obitani was a merchant rather than a manufacturer until the early 1920s, when it gave up merchant activities and devoted itself to administering its own mills.

Also in the case of Banshû, a *shimamomen sanchi*, small mills equipped with power looms were built after the Russo-Japanese War, but larger mills often dealt with *chin'ori* or *chimbata* until the early inter-war period. For example, Man'emon Maruyama established a factory in 1905, which had 112 Toyoda power looms at the end of 1916. As of August 1919, Maruyama had loose affiliations with six *chin'ori* and nine *chimbata*. Although the cases of the *chimbata* are not entirely clear, the features of seven *chin'ori* of Maruyama at the end of 1916 are summarized here. Firstly, except for one factory, all other members were located in the Taka district like the Maruyama factory, but not necessarily near it. All the factories were established after the Maruyama factory's foundation, and five of them were built in the 1910s. All the *chin'ori* were of smaller scale than the Maruyama factory, with six factories having about ten workers. Only two factories were powered, and, as far as is known, three factories had power looms. More than half of the *chin'ori* seemed to be 'manufactories' with hand looms or foot-pedal looms. Sources of power were not electricity but petroleum or gas. The power looms were made by two makers, Iketa (Toyoda) and Nakamura. In short, during the First World War boom Maruyama dealt with *chin'ori* factories or 'manufactories' established in the Taka district around 1910.[38]

Another example in Banshû is Gisaburô Okada.[39] In 1918, Okada had not only his own factory in Taka which was established in 1906 and equipped with 52 Toyoda power looms, but also relationships with three *chin'ori*. All were located far from the Okada factory and erected after its establishment. The scale of the three *chin'ori*, each employing thirteen workers, was smaller than the Okada factory with 43 workers, and, while two *chin'ori* had power looms, one *chin'ori* was a 'manufactory'. Several scholars have scrutinized the Okada factory and its *chin'ori*,[40] including J. Sasaki who found that during the boom of the First World War the Okada factory wove *tate-jima* involving an easy production process; the *chin'ori* with power looms supplemented the cloth, and a 'manufactory' and *chimbata* wove more elaborate *kôshijima*.[41] Okada implemented certain specialization and product differentiation among his own factory, *chin'ori*, and *chimbata*.

According to Table 9.2, the number of the 'cottage industry' establishments and 'out-weavers' increased in Japan around the First World War. It seems that the putting-out system was apparently once more revived. On the whole, however, the 1910s was a period of transformation and high development of the putting-out system.

Decline of the Putting-out System

The putting-out system in the cotton-weaving *sanchi* seems to have declined after the panic of 1920, and Table 9.2 shows the symptom of the collapse of this system through the decrease in 'cottage industry' establishments and 'out-weavers' in the early 1920s. Unfortunately, such nationwide data related to the putting-out system are not available after 1922, but the abandonment of the compilation of these statistics itself suggests that the authorities deemed the putting-out system as less important.

Proof of the decline of the putting-out system can be found for certain *sanchi*, as illustrated by the case of Obitani Shôten in Sen'nan.[42] After the Great Kantô Earthquake in 1923, Obitani gave up dealing in narrow *shiro-momen* for the domestic market and began mass production for export of wide grey cloth, mainly five shaft sateens, benefited by the yen depreciation. Around the mid-1920s, production became concentrated in the Obitani factories, and by the end of the 1920s, Obitani stopped dealing with the *chin'ori* completely.

Why did Obitani give up *nakagai* activities and devote itself to managing its own factories? Although documents are not available to provide a direct answer, it should be noted that Obitani's devotion to cotton-cloth production was concurrent with the conversion from narrow to wide cloth. Wide grey cotton cloth is a product that requires standardization and mass production and, probably because of this characteristic, Obitani stopped dealing with small-size factories which were often the cause of the lack of standardization, instead expanding its own factories and introducing mass-production methods.

In Banshû some larger weaving firms continued to have loose connections with the *chin'ori* after the First World War. Man'emon Maruyama appeared to cease his dealings with *chimbata* and 'manufactories' after the panic of 1920, but continued to deal with the *chin'ori* factories during the inter-war period. From April 1926 to March 1927, the volume of cloth collected from twenty-five *chin'ori* was almost the same as that made by Maruyama's two factories. The connection between Maruyama and the *chin'ori*, however, was not solid. Around the mid-1920s Maruyama dealt with *chin'ori*, which were small- and medium-sized, newly established factories with power looms, and on the whole, electrified. Even in the 1930s, Maruyama still had some *chin'ori*, which contributed 52.1 per cent of the total cloth collected by Maruyama during the period from 1933 to 1935, but it is noteworthy that the number of Maruyama's *chin'ori* decreased from twelve around 1930 to only three at the end of 1933. Through the Shôwa Panic (1930–1) Maruyama seems to have become selective in dealings with the *chin'ori*.[43]

However, the case of Maruyama is rather exceptional. Generally speaking, Banshû, stimulated by the devaluation of the yen after the Great Kantô Earthquake and throughout the rest of the 1920s, specialized in the production of wide cotton cloth for export, especially *shimamitsuaya* (striped drill). Smaller factories quickly adapted to this change, after which bigger factories slowly began to produce wide cloth in the latter half of the 1920s[44] when the putting-out system seems to have started its overall decline. Incidentally, Gisaburô Okada dealt with two *chin'ori* in the mid-1920s, which were not the same factories as the *chin'ori* in the First World War, but information is not available on the *chin'ori* of Okada after the late 1920s.[45]

In the 1920s, the retreat of the putting-out system was also notable in the other *sanchi*. The cases of two *sanchi* mentioned above strongly suggest that the standardization of products was an important factor in the decline of the putting-out system.

In addition, attention should be given to the fierce inter-*sanchi* competition. The 1920s was a period of successive depressions and hence, of stagnant cloth prices, while monetary wages remained sticky at least until the mid-1920s. Producers were obliged to install power looms to cut cost; meanwhile, the spread of electric power distribution, the fall in the relative prices of electric power to coal, and the diffusion of small-sized electromotors accelerated the change.[46] Many *sanchi* which could not adapt to mechanization drastically declined. The introduction of power looms in the 1920s was different from that after the Russo-Japanese War, since it developed nationwide and covered not only small- and medium-sized firms but also very small weavers like a few *chimbata* documented in Sano in Tochigi Prefecture. Small weavers such as the *chimbata* in Sano, in Kita-Saitama in Saitama Prefecture, in Matsuyama in Ehime Prefecture, or in Kurume in Fukuoka Prefecture, who found it difficult to install power looms for their traditional cloths for Japanese *kimono* woven with hand looms under the typical putting-out system, saw their *sanchi* ranking of production fall steeply.[47] Thus, the fierce competition among *sanchi* brought about by depressions and mechanization exerted severe strain on the putting-out system.

Finally, Shôkôshô (the Ministry of Commerce and Industry: MCI), which was newly established in 1925, and its predecessor, Nôshômushô (the Ministry of Agriculture and Commerce: MAC) played important roles in the decline of the putting-out system. Although MAC once admitted *Dôgyô Kumiai* led by local merchants, the ministry soon decided to weaken their influence because the officers saw local merchants as the oppressors of manufacturers.[48] MAC often issued notifications that forbade local trade associations from regulating and controlling prices, wages, and employment after 1909, of which the notification of 1916 was the most systematic and important. In the 1920s, backed by reports produced by MAC, namely, *Orimono oyobi Meriyasu ni kansuru Chôsa* (Report on the Weaving and Knitting Industry) (1925) and the Reports on the Dealings in Domestic

Important Commodities (1923–5), MAC/MCI determined that the traditional wholesale merchants including the putting-out masters like *nakagai* in Sen'nan exploited and oppressed small- and medium-sized producers. Hence, they enacted the Important Export Products Manufacturers' Association Law in 1925, the Manufacturers' Association Law in 1931 and the Merchants' Association Law in 1932. These three laws were aimed at the modernization of merchants and the development of pure producers, to the exclusion of the traditional merchants in the *Dôgyô Kumiai*. We must consider in the future whether such merchants did in fact sweat the producers harder in the 1920s than before, but at least in the cotton industry it is probable that many merchants involved in the speculative dealing in yarn during the boom of the First World War were violently hit by the panic of 1920 and thereafter intensified their exploitation of the producers.

The above-mentioned MAC/MCI policies were instrumental in weakening the *Dôgyô Kumiai* system. In the case of Banshû,[49] there were three *Dôgyô Kumiai*: Banshû Ori established in the Taka district in 1903, Kasai-gun Orimono established in the Kasai district in 1905, and Kandai Orimono established in the Katô district in 1911. These *Dôgyô Kumiai* seem to have made great contributions to Banshû's development in the 1920s. For example, Banshû Ori Dôgyô Kumiai, the largest association of the three, was particularly active in the employment of dyeing specialists, the provision of high-quality dyestuff, as well as in the encouragement of bleachers to use pressurized boiling kiers, the establishment of the first industrial association to run a proper sorting plant, and also the encouragement of weavers to adopt electrical power. Around 1930, however, several *Kôgyô Kumiai* (Manufacturers' Associations) were separated from them. In Kurodashô village in Taka, Banshû Ori Daiichi Kôgyô Kumiai with 14 weavers was authorized in July 1927, and in September 1928 Banshû Ori Kôgyô Kumiai was authorized with 127 weavers producing cloth in Taka (not including Kurodashô village) for export. After the establishment of this *Kôgyô Kumiai*, Banshû Ori Dôgyô Kumiai became the only member related to cloth for domestic market. In July 1931 Banshû Ori Noma Kôgyô Kumiai was authorized with 17 members in Nomadani village in Taka and became separate from Banshû Ori Kôgyô Kumiai. In Katô, discussion on the establishment of an export-products manufacturers' association was held at the general meeting of Kandai Orimono Dôgyô Kumiai in March 1928, and Kandai Ori Kôgyô Kumiai was authorized in November 1928. In Kasai, Kasai-gun Orimono Kôgyô Kumiai was authorized in October 1930.

As the case of Banshû indicates, *Kôgyô Kumiai* began to vigorously promote such activities as (1) strict inspection of products; (2) control over production and sale of certain types of cloth; and (3) joint work relating to purchase of materials, sale of products, finance, and certain segments of the production process. Meanwhile, the activities of *Dôgyô Kumiai* became generally dull and inactive, meaning that the basic foundation of traditional merchants came to a crisis. In 1943 the annulment of the law of 1900 on *Dôgyô Kumiai* marked the end of their historic role.

5 Concluding Remarks

In the *sanchi* cotton-weaving industry, a representative indigenous industry of modern Japan, the putting-out system was established in the 1880s. In Japan, the period from the 1880s to the early twentieth century is often called the Japanese Industrial Revolution, or the early stage of industrialization. Many scholars have concentrated solely on the growth of big business in those years, but, even in 1920, the work-force of the modern sector was no more than 28.8 per cent of all the people engaged in secondary and tertiary industries (who accounted for 44.3 per cent of the total working population).[50] Indigenous industries continued to hold a predominant share before the First World War, at least in the employment structure. The organizers of indigenous industries were generally local merchants, who developed the putting-out system both independently and through local associations like *Dôgyô Kumiai* in which they held important positions.

After the Russo-Japanese War, factories with power looms started up, while the number of *chimbata* began to decline in some *sanchi* near such large cities as Osaka, Nagoya, and Kobe. Those facts, however, did not immediately spell the collapse of the putting-out system. After the establishment of their own factories, some putting-out masters began to send yarn to other factories (*chin'ori*) and later collected cotton cloth in exchange for wages. In other words, a new factory-based version of the putting-out system appeared in Sen'nan around the 1910s and developed until the boom of the First World War.

It was not until the 1920s that the putting-out system in the *sanchi* cotton-weaving industry reached its declining stage. Mass production of wide cloth mainly for export and requiring standardization was the basic factor behind the decline of the putting-out system. Probably because of this characteristic of the new product, many putting-out masters stopped dealing with small-size *chin'ori* lacking in standardization, enlarged their own factories, and introduced mass production. The fierce inter-*sanchi* competition and the policies of weakening traditional merchants pursued by MAC and MCI in the inter-war period accelerated the decline of the putting-out system.

NOTES

1. Nakamura (1983); Abe (1989*a*).
2. Takamura (1971); Abe (1989*b*, 1990); Fletcher (1996).

3. Abe (1992: 23–47).
4. Abe and Saitô (1988: 143–57).
5. Abe (1988: 69–83).
6. For *shiromomen* and *shimamomen*, see Uchida (1988: 159–70).
7. Saitô and Tanimoto (1989: 263–4).
8. Aizawa (1938: 18–19).
9. Taniguchi (1950: 14–16).
10. Ibid. 22–3, 26–8.
11. Ibid. 19, 27–9, 32.
12. Ôshima (1984: 1–29).
13. Tanimoto (1986: 1–34). Iruma is another name of Tokorozawa.
14. Tsûshô Sangyô Daijin Kanbô Chôsa Tôkeibu (1952: 161).
15. Kagotani (1991: 581–97).
16. Shiozawa and Kondô (1985, 1. ch. 2).
17. Matsuzaki (1984: 33–47).
18. Sugawara (1951: 11–17).
19. Tanimoto (1987: 65).
20. Taniguchi (1950: 19, 27–9, 32).
21. Takamura (1971, i. 217).
22. Abe (1989*b*: 67, 70, 79–80, 132).
23. There are many books and articles on the history of Japanese trade associations. Above all, the following are important: Miyamoto (1938); Yui (1964); Fujita (1988, 1995).
24. Miyamoto (1938).
25. Fujita (1988: 88).
26. See Miyamoto and Abe (1995: 264–77); Takamura (1996).
27. On Kyôdô Kaisha, see Abe (1989*a*: 14–15).
28. On Iyo Momen Kabushiki Kaisha, see Sugawara (1951: 14–18).
29. Tanimoto and Abe (1995: 137–8).
30. For example, see Kandatsu (1974); Shiozawa and Kondô (1985).
31. Abe (1987: 83–111).
32. Matsumoto (1992/1993: 47–77).
33. On this point, also see Yasuoka (1989: 77–94, 1991: 166–83); Kiyokawa (1995: ch. 5).
34. Matsumoto did not refer to the co-operative production, but it seems very important. For the finishing factory in Banshû, see Abe (1992: 21).
35. On the above four paragraphs, see Abe and Saitô (1988).
36. Abe (1989*b*, ch. 3, 1994).
37. Taniguchi (1950: 82).
38. Abe (1989*b*, ch. 5).
39. Ibid.
40. Ibid; Kasai (1982: 95–145).
41. Sasaki (1991: *Keizaigaku Zasshi*, 91/5 and 91/6: 110–28; and 92/1: 53–68).
42. Abe (1989*b*, ch. 3, 1994).
43. Abe (1989*b*, ch. 5).
44. Ibid. 283–4.
45. Ibid., ch. 5.
46. Abe and Kikkawa (1987: 1–22).

47. Abe (1989*b*, ch. 1, 1992: 11–12).
48. Yui (1964, ch. 3); Fujita (1988, 1995).
49. Abe (1989*b*, ch. 5).
50. Nakamura (1983: 26).

REFERENCES

Abe, Takeshi (1987), 'Senzen-ki Nihon ni okeru Chihô Jigyô-ka no Shihon Chikuseki' ['Capital Accumulation of a Rural Entrepreneur in Pre-war Japan'], *Shakai Kagaku Kenkyû* [*Journal of Social Science*], 39/4 (Institute of Social Science, University of Tokyo).

—— (1988), 'Kinsei Nihon ni okeru Men Orimono Seisan-daka' ['The Production of Cotton Cloth in the Edo Period'] in Kônosuke Odaka and Yûzô Yamamoto (eds.), *Bakumatsu Meiji no Nihon Keizai* [*Japanese Economy from the End of the Edo Period to the Meiji Period*]. Tokyo: Nihon Keizai Shinbun-sha.

—— (1989*a*), 'Traditional Industries of Japan in Early Meiji Years: the Case of the Cotton Weaving Industry', Discussion Paper Series, 75, Faculty of Economics, Osaka University.

—— (1989*b*), *Nihon ni okeru Sanchi Men Orimono-gyô no Tenkai* [*The Development of the Producing-Centre Cotton Textile Industry in Japan*]. Tokyo: Tokyo Daigaku Shuppan-kai.

—— (1990), 'Men-kôgyô' ['Cotton Industry'] in Shunsaku Nishikawa and Takeshi Abe (eds.), *Nihon Keizai-shi 4: Sangyôka no Jidai, Jyô* [*Economic History of Japan, iv: The Age of Industrialization, 1*]. Tokyo: Iwanami Shoten.

—— (1992) 'The Development of the Producing-Centre Cotton Textile Industry in Japan between the Two World Wars', *Japanese Yearbook on Business History*, 9 (Japan Business History Institute), repr. (1995) in W. Lazonick and W. Mass (eds.) *Organizational Capability and Competitive Advantage*. Aldershot: Edward Elgar.

—— (1994), 'Obitani Shôten: The Strategy and Structure of a Cotton-Weaving Firm in the Sen'nan District of Osaka Prefecture', Discussion Papers in Economics and Business, 94–06, Faculty of Economics, Osaka University.

—— and Kikkawa, Takeo (1987), 'Nihon ni okeru Dôryoku Kakumei to Chûshô Kôgyô' ['Japan's Power Revolution and Small- and Medium-sized Industries'], *Shakai Keizai-shigaku* [*Socio-Economic History*], 53/2.

—— and Saitô, Osamu (1988), 'From Putting-out to the Factory: A Cotton-Weaving District in Late-Meiji Japan', *Textile History*, 19/2.

Aizawa, Masahiko (1938), *Sen'nan Shokufu Hattatsu-shi* [*The History of the Weaving Industry in Sen'nan*]. Kishiwada: Aizawa.

Dai Nihon Bôseki Rengô-kai (1908–33), *Menshi Bôseki Jijyô Sankô-sho* [*A Half-Year Report on the Cotton-spinning Industry*]. Osaka: Dai Nihon Bôseki Rengô-kai.

Fletcher, W. Miles (1996), 'The Japan Spinners Association: Creating Industrial Policy in Meiji Japan', *Journal of Japanese Studies*, 22/1.

Fujita, Teiichirô (1988), 'Local Trade Associations (*Dôgyô Kumiai*) in Prewar Japan', in Hiroaki Yamazaki and Matao Miyamoto (eds.), *The International Conference on*

Business History, xiv: *Trade Associations in Business History*. Tokyo: University of Tokyo Press.

—— (1995), *Kindai Nihon Dôgyô Kunmiai Shi-ron* [*The History of* Dôgyô Kumiai *in Modern Japan*]. Osaka: Seibun-dô.

Kagotani, Naoto (1991), 'Mengyô to Sanshigyô' ['The Cotton Industry and the Silk Industry'], in Okazaki-shi (ed.), *Shinpen Okazaki Shi-shi Kindai 4* [*New History of the City of Okazaki, 4*]. Okazaki: Okazaki-shi.

Kakutani, Tomakichi (1924) (ed.), *Taishô Meikan* [*Short Biographies of Famous Persons in Senshû in the Taishô Period*], Kishiwada: Kakutani.

Kandatsu, Haruki (1974), *Meiji-ki Nôson Orimono-gyô no Tenkai* [*The Development of the Weaving Industry in Farm Areas in the Meiji Period*]. Tokyo: Tokyo Daigaku Shuppan-kai.

Kasai, Yamato (1982), 'Men Orimono-gyô no Hatten to Nishiwaki Kôgyô Chitai no Keisei' ['The Development of the Cotton-Weaving Industry and the Formation of the Nishiwaki Industrial Area'], *Okayama Daigaku Bungaku-bu Kiyô* [*Journal of the Faculty of Letters, Okayama University*], 3.

Kiyokawa, Yukihiko (1995), *Nihon no Keizai Hatten to Gijyutsu Fukyû* [*Japan's Economic Development and Technological Diffusion*]. Tokyo: Tôyô Keizai Shinpô-sha.

Maekawa, Kyôichi (1968), 'Shitauke Seido no Rekishi-teki Kôsatsu' ['Historical Study of the Japanese Subcontract System'] in Shôtarô Takebayashi (ed.), *Chûshô Kigyô no Kenkyû* [Study of the Small- and Medium-sized Firms]. Kyoto: Mineruva Shobô.

Matsumoto, Takanori (1992/1993), 'Ryô-taisenkan-ki Nihon no Seizôgyô ni okeru Dôgyô Kumiai no Kinô' ['Functions of *Dôgyô Kumiai* and Manufacturing Industry in Inter-war Japan'], *Shakai Keizai-shigaku* [*Socio-Economic History*], 58/5.

Matsuzaki, Hisami (1984), 'Sangyô Kakumei-ki no Nara-ken Nôson Orimono-gyô to Nôson Rôdo-ryoku' ['The Rural Weaving Industry and Rural Labour in Nara Prefecture in the Period of the Industrial Revolution'], *Tochi Seido-shigaku* [*Journal of Agrarian History*], 104.

Miyamoto, Mataji (1938), *Kabunakama no Kenkyû* [*Study of* Kabunakama]. Tokyo: Yûhikaku.

Miyamoto, Matao and Abe, Takeshi (1995), 'Meiji no Shisan-ka to Kaisha Seido' ['Wealthy Persons and the Company System in the Meiji Period'], in M. Miyamoto and T. Abe (eds.), *Nihon Keiei-shi 2: Keiei Kakushin to Kôgyôka* [*Business History of Japan*, ii: *Innovation and Industrialization*]. Tokyo: Iwanami Shoten.

Nakamura, Satoru (1968), *Meiji Ishin no Kiso Kôzô* [*The Basic Structure of the Meiji Restoration*]. Tokyo: Mirai-sha.

Nakamura, Takafusa (1983), *Economic Growth in Pre-war Japan*, trans. R. A. Feldman, New Haven and London: Yale University Press.

Nôshômushô (1903–21), *Nôshômu Tôkei Hyô* [*Statistical Yearbook of Agriculture and Commerce*]. Tokyo: Nôshômushô.

Osaka-fu (c.1904), 'Dai Go Kai Naikoku Kangyô Hakurankai Shuppin Kaisetsu-sho Dai Ruku Bu: Men Orimono Rui' ['The Lists of Exhibits in the Fifth National Exhibition, vi: Cotton Cloth'], Osaka City University Archives.

——, *Osaka-fu Tôkei-sho* [*Statistical Yearbook of Osaka Prefecture*].

Ôshima, Eiko (1984), 'Ken-men Mazeorimono Sanchi no Keisei Katei' ['The Formation of a Silk- and Cotton-Weaving District'], *Shakai Keizai-shigaku* [*Socio-Economic History*], 50/5.

Saitô, Osamu and Tanimoto, Masayuki (1989), 'Zairai Sangyô no Saihensei' ['*Reorganization of the Indigenous Industries*'], in Mataji Umemura and Yûzô Yamamoto (eds.), *Nihon Keizai Shi 5: Kaikô to Ishin* [*Economic History of Japan*, v: *The Opening of the Ports and the Meiji Restoration*]. Tokyo: Iwanami Shoten.

Sasaki, Jun (1991), 'Sanchi Men Orimono-gyô ni okeru Rikishokki Dônyû-go no Tonya Seido' ['The Putting-out System after the Introduction of the Power Loom in the Producing Centers of the Cotton-Weaving Industry'], *Keizaigaku Zasshi* [*Journal of Economics*], 91/5, 91/6 and 92/1, The Economic Society of Osaka City University.

Shiozawa, Kimio and Kondô, Tetsuo (1985) (eds.), *Orimono-gyô no Hatten to Kisei Jinushi-sei* [*The Development of the Weaving Industry and the Landowner System in Bisai District in the Meiji Period*]. Tokyo: Ochanomizu Shobô.

Sen'nan-gun Orimono Dôgyô Kumiai (*c*.1907), *Sen'nan-gun Orimono Dôgyô Kumiai Enkaku-shi* [*The History of Sen'nan-gun Orimono Dôgyô Kumiai*]; repr. 1972 in *Izumi-shi*, vols. 48 and 49 (ed. Izumi Bunka Kenkyû-kai).

Sugawara, Toshiharu (1951), *Imabari Mengyô Hattatsu-shi* [*The History of the Development of the Cotton Industry of Imabari District*]. Imabari: Imabari Mengyô Kurabu.

Takamura, Naosuke (1971), *Nihon Boseki-gyô-shi Jyosetsu* [*The History of the Japanese Cotton-Spinning Industry*], 2 vols. Tokyo: Hanawa Shobô.

—— (1996), *Kaisha no Tanjyô* [*The Birth of the Company System*]. Tokyo: Yoshikawa Kôbun-kan.

Takeuchi, Ihori (1979), 'Meiji 30 Nendai ni okeru Sen'nan-gun Momen Dôgyô Kumiai' ['Sen'nan-gun Momen Dôgyô Kumiai from 1897 to 1907'], *Sen'nan-shi-shi Kiyô*, 7 (ed. Sen'nan Shi-yakusho).

Taniguchi, Yukio (1950), *Sen'nan-gun Men Orimono Hattatsu-shi* [*The History of Cotton-Weaving Industry in Sen'nan*]. Osaka: Taniguchi.

Tanimoto, Masayuki (1986), 'Bakumatsu Meiji Zenki Men Orimono-gyô no Tenkai' ['The Development of the Cotton-Weaving Industry in Iruma District of Saitama Prefecture from the End of the Edo Period to the Earlier Part of the Meiji Period'], *Shakai Keizai-shigaku* [*Socio-Economic History*], 52/2.

—— (1987), 'Bakumatsu Meiji-ki Menpu Kokunai Shijyô no Tenkai' ['The Development of the Domestic Market of Cotton Cloth from the End of the Edo Period to the Meiji Period'], *Tochi Seido-shigaku* [*Journal of Agrarian History*], 115.

—— and Abe, Takeshi (1995), 'Kigyô Bokkô to Kindai Keiei, Zairai Keiei' ['The Rise of Firms, and Modern Management and Indigenous Management'], in Miyamoto and Abe (eds.), *Nihon Keiei-shi 2: Keiei Kakushin to Kôgyôka*.

Tsûshô Sangyô Daijin Kanbô Chôsa Tôkeibu (1952) (ed.) (written by Mitsuhaya Kajinishi), *Jyûyô Shôhin no Ryûtsû Kikô Dai 4 shû: Men Orimono no Ryûtû Kikô* [*Distribution System of Important Commodities*, iv: *Cotton Cloth*]. Tokyo: Shôkô Kaikan Shuppan-bu.

Uchida, Hoshimi (1988), 'Narrow Cotton Stripes and their Substitutes: Fashion Change, Technological Progress, and Manufacturing Organizations in Japanese Popular Clothing', 1850–1920, *Textile History*, 19/2.

Yasuoka, Shigeaki (1989), 'Meiji-ki Osaka ni okeru Dôgyô Kumiai no Hinshitsu Kisei' ['Quality Control of *Dôgyô Kumiai* in Osaka in the Meiji Period'], *Hikone Ronsô*, 262 and 263, The Economic Society of Shiga University.

—— (1991), 'Shijyô no Kakudai to Dôgyo Kumiai no Hinshitsu Kisei' ['Expansion of

Market and Quality Control of *Dôgyô Kumiai'*], *Dôshisha Shôgaku* [*Doshisha Business Review*], 42/4 and 42/5, The Association of Commerce, Doshisha University, repr. in Masahiro Iwashita (1994) (ed.), *Shijyô, Shôhin Kaihatsu, Kigyô Kyôsô* [*Market, Development of Commodities, and Competition among Firms*]. Tokyo: Dôbun-kan.

Yui, Tsunehiko (1964), *Chûshô Kigyô Seisaku no Shiteki Kenkyû* [*Historical Study of Governmental Policies for Small- and Medium-sized Enterprises*]. Tokyo: Tôyô Keizai Shinpô-sha.

10

The Role of Technical Education and Public Research Institutes in the Development of Small and Medium Enterprises: The Case of Osaka Between the Wars

MINORU SAWAI

Introduction

Osaka Prefecture is one of the largest industrial centres in Japan, ranking third in 1994 in terms of its share of the value of Japan's manufactured goods shipments (MITI 1994). At 6.9 per cent, Osaka is just ahead of Tokyo (6.5 per cent), and is surpassed only by Aichi Prefecture (11.3 per cent) and Kanagawa Prefecture (8.0 per cent). In much of the pre-war period, however, Osaka was the undisputed king of Japanese industry, consistently contributing 16 to 17 per cent of the national value of production (see Table 10.1). It maintained its pre-eminent position until 1938, when the rising tide of war production carried Tokyo to the top position (MITI 1961). Osaka remained in second place through the first oil crisis, falling to third thereafter.

As shown in Table 10.1, Osaka's share of the total number of employees in Japan's manufacturing industries tended to decrease after 1965, as did its share of the value of shipments, and its 'decline' was viewed with much dismay by the local media. Meanwhile, however, it is important to note that Osaka's share of the nation's industrial base in terms of the number of manufacturing establishments did not undergo significant change from 1940 onward, when survey data began to include all factories and establishments, regardless of size. (1947 is an exception, due to the lingering effects of the air raids at the end of the war.) In fact, after the first oil crisis, Osaka actually boosted its share of manufacturing establishments.

Table 10.1. *Number of establishments and employees, and values of shipments, with percentage shares in Japanese manufacturing, Osaka prefecture, 1920–1985*

Year	Establishments		Employees		Value of shipments	
	No.	%	No. (000s)	%	m. yen	%
1920	6,022	13.2	227	12.9	995	16.8
1925	6,364	13.1	258	14.9	1,158	16.7
1930	7,878	12.8	206	12.3	996	16.7
1935	12,580	14.9	327	13.9	1.848	17.1
1940	52,559	7.6	580	11.7	4,042	13.8
1947	27,018	4.3	319	8.5	38,204	11.9
1950	23,877	6.8	425	10.0	287,478	12.1
1955	33,973	7.9	591	10.7	850,931	12.6
1960	40,793	8.4	934	11.4	2,095,783	13.5
1965	45,849	8.2	1,045	10.5	3,589,647	12.2
1970	56,954	8.7	1,126	9.6	7,834,291	11.3
1975	70,873	9.6	997	8.8	12,266,364	9.6
1980	71,914	9.7	931	8.5	19,051,977	8.9
1985	76,367	10.2	964	8.4	22,427,038	8.4

Notes: Surveys to 1935 cover factories with 5 employees or more, while surveys after 1940 include all factories and establishments. The figures of value of shipments to end-1947 are for value of production.

Source: Toyo Keizai Sinposha (1991) (ed.), *Kanketsu Showa Kokusei Soran* [*Overview of the State of the Nation in Showa Era*], i. 352–5.

Small and medium-sized enterprises (SMEs) have played a decisive role in the growth of the Osaka economy from the pre-war period through to the present. Table 10.2, which indicates the composition of manufacturing in Osaka by size of factory (number of workers), shows the small and medium-sized factories[1] as a percentage of the the total in 1920, 1925, 1930, and 1935, ranging from 95.3 to 97.5 per cent in terms of the number of factories, and from 41.3 to 59.1 per cent in terms of the number of operatives. The ratio of small and medium-sized establishments in the overall total then rose to 99.4 per cent in 1955 and 99.2 per cent in 1960, with the corresponding employee figures rising to 77.9 and 74.0 per cent. And in 1960 SMEs contributed 59.0 per cent of the value of shipments. The great majority of these Osaka factories and establishments were SMEs which had continued from the pre-war period.

The purpose of this chapter, then, is to focus attention on the role and significance of various kinds of technical education and the public research institutes in order to more cogently discuss the factors which supported the development of SMEs between the wars.

The industrial development of Osaka and the parallel development of its SMEs is surveyed in the first section, followed by a discussion in the second section of higher and secondary technical education and night school programmes. The third section traces the activities of the various public

Table 10.2. *Factories, operatives, and values of shipments of manufacturing in Osaka prefecture (1920–1960) (%)*

	No. of operatives						Totals (number)
	5–14	15–29	30–49	50–99	100–499	500+	
1920							
Factories	69.4	15.8	6.3	4.5	3.2	0.8	6,031
Operatives	16.4	10.2	7.4	9.7	20.4	35.9	190,815
1925							
Factories	65.6	16.8	7.9	5.1	3.6	1.1	6,369
Operatives	14.4	9.4	8.1	9.4	20.1	38.6	232,284
	5–29	30–99	100–199	200+			
1930							
Factories	84.3	12.4	1.6	1.7			7,889
Operatives	31.0	22.9	8.0	38.1			206,867
	1–14	15–29	30–49	50–99	100–499	500+	
1935a							
Factories	74.1	13.5	6.1	3.7	2.1	0.4	11,604
Operatives	22.8	13.1	11.1	12.1	19.4	21.5	242,699

Table 10.2. (cont.)

	1–3	4–9	4–29	10–29	30–99	30–299	100–299	300+	
1955									
Establishments	41.6		47.4			10.4		0.6	33,973
Employees	5.5		31.9			40.4		22.1	591,274
Shipments (bn. yen)	1.9		19.9			44.1		34.2	851
1960									
Establishments	34.3	22.6		28.3	11.3		2.7	0.8	40,793
Employees	3.6	6.5		20.5	24.8		18.4	26.0	934,114
Shipments (bn. yen)	1.1	2.9		12.5	21.0		21.4	41.0	2,096

^a Data is for the City of Osaka.

Sources: Ministry of Agriculture and Commerce (MAC); Ministry of Commerce and Industry (MCI); and Ministry of International Trade and Industry (MITI), *Kōjō Tōkei Hyo* [*Statistics on Factories*] and *Kōgyo Tokei Hyo* [*Statistics on Industry*], each year. Figures for 1935 are based on *Osaka Shi Tokeisho* [*Statistics on the City of Osaka*] edited by Osaka Municipal Government.

research institutes from the inter-war period through the war, their impact on SME development, and their legacy to the post-war period.

Overview of the Development of SMEs in Osaka

The nominal value of Osaka production and shipments expanded uninterruptedly with the single exception of 1930 (see Table 10.1); a breakdown by industry appears in Table 10.3. The most striking feature is the predominance of textiles during the inter-war period. Known for a time as 'the Manchester of the Orient', Osaka's position as the largest industrial centre in Japan rested in large measure on the development of the textile industry. In the depression year of 1930, however, the weight of textiles fell noticeably. It dropped again in 1935, just prior to the take-off of the war economy, and slid to about 10 per cent by 1940, when wartime economic controls were already in place. Although the textile industry recovered to its 1935 level by 1950, when the outbreak of the Korean War jump-started post-war reconstruction, the sector's importance again declined as Japan's high-growth economy started up from the mid-1950s.

In contrast to textiles, the metals and machinery sectors ascended rapidly during the 1930s, and the expansion of machinery during wartime was particularly striking. Accordingly, the share of what Japanese observers have dubbed 'heavy and chemical industries', composed of metals, machinery, and chemicals, accounted for 76 per cent of the 1940 output. Even so, war-related expansion of the machinery industry in Osaka was relatively small compared with Tokyo and Kanagawa, and it has been asserted that this was a primary determinant of Osaka's subsequent economic decline (Amakawa 1976). Nevertheless, it is also important to note that the wartime growth of Osaka's machinery industry was quite significant in absolute terms. Although the total share of heavy and chemical industries dipped below 60 per cent in 1950 due to the revival of textiles, the remarkable expansion of machinery continued in the era of high growth, even as the chemical industry retreated from its former position.

The Development of Technical Education

Educational Background of Entrepreneurs, Engineers, and Workers in SMEs

What were the sources for skilled SME workers, engineers, and entrepreneurs? According to a 1937 survey by the Osaka Municipal Government, of

Table 10.3. *Value of production and shipment of manufacturing in Osaka prefecture by industry (1920–1960) (%)*

	1920	1925	1930	1935	1940	1950	1955	1960
Textiles	43.7	41.8	29.5	25.8	10.5	24.0	20.1	15.2
Metals	11.6	12.0	14.5	23.1	27.8	21.7	24.5	24.1
Machinery	10.3	8.2	14.4	16.4	32.6	16.4	16.6	28.5
Ceramics	3.5	3.0	2.9	3.0	2.7	3.0	2.5	2.4
Chemicals	14.6	14.5	17.7	15.9	15.6	20.9	17.2	14.2
Wood and wood products	0.8	1.7	2.3	1.6	1.4	1.7	2.5	2.4
Printing and bookbinding	2.6	4.0	4.8	2.8	1.6	3.5	4.1	3.1
Food and beverages	6.8	8.8	8.6	5.6	4.9	6.5	9.7	6.9
Others	6.0	6.0	5.5	5.8	3.0	2.2	2.7	3.2

Note: After 1950 figures are for shipment only.

Sources: MAC, MCI, and MITI, *Kojo Tokei Hyo* [Statistics on Factories] and *Kogyo Tokei Hyo* [Statistics on Industry], each year.

the 4,979 factories in the metal industry in the City of Osaka, 4,386 were unincorporated (88.1 per cent) and 593 were organized in corporate form. In
the machinery industry, there were 7,461 unincorporated factories (90.2 per
cent), and 811 incorporated establishments among the total of 8,272 factories in machinery industry at the end of 1937. Of 11,847 entrepreneurs or
owners of these SMEs, by far the most popular professional path was 'independence from establishments in the same industry', at 67.9 per cent in
metals and 71.8 per cent in machinery. If 'succession to family business'
(16.5 and 11.2 per cent respectively) is added in, the total is well over 80 per
cent (Osaka Municipal Government 1940). Thus, in the pre-war metal and
machinery industries, the main route for SME entrepreneurs led from a job
as a worker following graduation from school, through the upgrading of
skills, the accumulation of start-up funds, and the expansion of the professional networks needed for the opening of independent operations.

However, before discussing the educational background of factory
workers and engineers, let us review the structure of the technical educational system in Japan between the wars (see Fig. 10.1). At first, compulsory
education was provided in lower elementary schools which offered six-year
schooling, and the term of compulsory education was extended from four
years to six years in 1908. There were also higher elementary schools with
two-year schooling which were not compulsory. On the other hand the higher
technical educational organizations were composed of technical colleges and
departments of engineering of the universities. Applicants for technical colleges were required to have completed middle schools with five-year school-

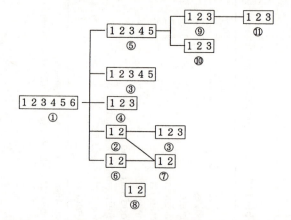

Fig. 10.1. *The system of technical education in Japan between the wars. 1 = lower
elementary schools; 2 = higher elementary schools; 3 = A-type technical schools;
4 = B-type technical schools; 5 = middle schools; 6 = technical or vocational continuation
schools (lower night schools); 7 = technical or vocational continuation schools (higher
night schools); 8 = private vocational schools; 9 = higher schools; 10 = technical colleges;
11 = universities. Numbers in rectangles indicate years of schooling.*

ing after lower elementary schools, and applicants for universities to have completed higher schools with three-year schooling after middle schools.

The system of secondary technical education was rather complicated. Secondary technical schools were divided into *Totei Gakko* (apprentice schools), *Kogyo Gakko* (technical schools), *Kogyo Hoshu Gakko* or *Shokko Hoshu Gakko* (technical or workers' continuation schools), and various kinds of *Kogyo Kakushu Gakko* (private vocational schools).[2]

Apprentice schools were established in accordance with legislation in 1894, and applicants were required to be at least 12 years old and to have completed compulsory lower elementary schools. The period of training was flexible from six months to four years. Meanwhile, technical schools based on the 1899 Vocational Schools Act required that applicants be at least 14 years old and have completed higher elementary school, with training courses lasting up to four years. Technical or workers' continuation schools in the form of night schools were established under the terms of legislation of 1893, and, as a result of an amendment made in 1902, they could be attached to various kinds of public vocational schools as well as elementary schools. Admission requirements stipulated an age of at least 10 years as well as graduation from lower elementary schools, with content ranging from special subjects of three or six months' duration to more general one-year courses. In addition to apprentice, technical, and technical continuation schools, there were various kinds of private vocational schools which offered secondary technical education, many of which were night schools providing practical courses over one to two years.

The secondary technical education as described above was largely modified by the 1920 amendment of the Vocational School Act and 1921 amendment of the terms governing technical schools. Apprentice schools, many of which related to manufacturing, were abolished by this amendment, and transferred to the technical schools. According to the new terms, lower elementary graduates were to undergo from three to five years of additional schooling, and higher elementary graduates were to receive two to three years. Subsequently, five-year technical schools for lower elementary graduates and two- or three-year schools for higher elementary graduates were known as 'A-type', while three-year programmes (or two-year and above from 1927) for lower elementary graduates were designated as 'B-type' (see Fig. 10.1).

The 1920 amendment of the Vocational School Act also modified the terms of technical or vocational continuation schools, providing a graded system of a first two-year course (for lower elementary graduates) and a second two-year course (for higher elementary and first course graduates). In addition, the establishment of higher-level courses was now permitted. Youth-training centres were initiated in 1926, and the Youth School Act, combining these centres with vocational/technical continuation schools, was announced in 1935.

As for the educational background of male factory workers, the first statistical survey on labour conditions in 1924, which covered factories with more than 30 operatives, indicated that 52.6 per cent had had at least some lower elementary schooling, 35.5 per cent had at least some higher elementary schooling, 4.4 per cent had at least some secondary education, 4.0 per cent had no formal education at all, 2.6 per cent had at least some vocational continuation schooling, and 0.2 per cent had at least some technical college education (Statistics Bureau of the Cabinet 1929). According to a survey of 59 major machinery factories by the Ministry of Education in 1930, 87.9 per cent of the operatives had at least graduated from elementary school (Sawai 1989). This suggests that the educational background of factory workers did not show a large differential according to factory scale.

Some workers in large enterprises, who were generally graduates of compulsory lower elementary schools or higher elementary two-year courses, could expect to eventually be promoted to the rank of foreman; it was rare for such workers to be promoted to engineering or management status. On the other hand, most university and technical college graduates were initially hired as assistant engineers, and promoted to the rank of engineer (a relatively senior position) after skill acquisition. The graduates of secondary vocational schools or technical schools stood in the middle in large companies like Hitachi Co., where corporate bureaucracy was already firmly in place, and where new graduates of A-type technical schools were hired to fill junior staff positions from the 1920s (Sugayama 1987).

Meanwhile, the stereotypical image of the pre-war SME owner/entrepreneur tends to be that of the man who opened his own factory after training as a worker, managed the entire operation himself, and who did not employ other engineers or managers with secondary education. This, however, is not necessarily correct. Table 10.4 shows the composition of employees in machinery and metal industries by size of factory, based on the previous survey by the Osaka Municipal Government. In small workshops having from 1 to 4 operatives, the workers were typically comprised of the owner, family members, and/or apprentices. There was no need for 'engineers', as the owners were also skilled workers and did the engineering work themselves. However, in factories with between 30 and 49 operatives in the metal industry and from 20 to 29 operatives in the machinery industry, one 'engineer' was employed on average, and the percentage of engineers who worked for SMEs with less than 100 operatives rose to about 50 per cent of the total number in metals and 45 per cent in machinery. Although the educational background of these 'engineers' is unknown, it is significant that around half of the engineers in the metal and machinery industries of Osaka in 1937 were employed in SMEs.

Assuming that, in both the metals and machinery industries, the larger the establishment the greater the likelihood of incorporation, the largest unincorporated factories could be expected to have had between 10 and 19

Table 10.4. Composition of employees in machinery and metal industries in the City of Osaka by size of factory (at end of 1937)

No. of operatives	No. of factories (1)	No. of engineers (2)	(2)/(1)	Clerks and others	Family workers	Apprentices	Employed workers[a]
Metal industries							
1–4	2,468	15	0.0	95	3,006	1,361	1,265
5–9	1,169	72	0.1	299	1,430	1,846	4,423
10–19	703	151	0.2	553	707	1,488	7,177
20–29	241	115	0.5	506	126	512	5,108
30–49	227	234	1.0	1,020	64	550	7,971
50–99	87	194	2.2	699	19	271	5,642
100–199	56	210	3.8	742	15	203	7,469
200–499	20	244	12.2	683		208	5,786
500–999	6	170	28.3	302			3,972
1000+	2	166	83.0	513		71	4,051
Totals	4,979	1,571	0.3	5,412	5,367	6,510	52,864
Machinery							
1–4	4,623	64	0.0	73	5,213	3,131	1,521
5–9	1,911	184	0.1	395	2,062	4,941	5,511
10–19	917	392	0.4	879	792	3,830	7,541
20–29	347	342	1.0	881	188	1,785	6,178
30–49	265	508	1.9	1,305	80	1,597	8,324
50–99	118	403	3.4	872	12	840	7,089
100–199	50	492	9.8	774	4	388	6,590
200–499	28	411	14.7	913		135	8,478
500–999	9	354	39.3	569			5,949
1000+	4	1,041	260.3	963		1	16,100
Totals	8,272	4,191	0.5	7,624	8,351	16,648	73,281

[a] Employed workers are the total of permanent and temporary workers and day labourers.

Source: Osaka Municipal Government (1940), Osaka Shi Kogyo Keiei Chosasho: Kinzoku Kikai Kogyo Showa 12-nen [Survey on Industrial Management in the City of Osaka: Metals and Machinery in 1937].

workers. Thus, while the stereotypical lack of engineers in pre-war SMEs basically accounts for this size of unincorporated factory, it should also be kept in mind that each corporate SME above this size probably employed several engineers.

Graduates of Osaka Technical College

The only higher technical educational organization located in Osaka during the inter-war period was the National Osaka Technical College (OTC). It was established in May 1896 under the direct control of the Ministry of Education as the Osaka Technical School,[3] and changed its name to Osaka Technical College in May 1901, after producing its first graduating class in July 1900. The college embarked on a decade-long effort from 1919 to acquire university designation, and its name was again changed to Osaka Technical University in 1929. In 1933 it became the Department of Engineering of the Osaka Imperial University (initially established in April 1931 with two departments: Medicine and Science), then integrated into the current Osaka University in 1949 as a result of post-war educational reform (Osaka University 1985: 30–47, 81–7, 155–8, 258–65).

Table 10.5 shows that the total number of graduates from this institution from 1920 to 1935, regardless of its name or administrative status, was 2,399 persons. Let us consider, then, the relationships between these graduates and Osaka-based SMEs. During this period, the seven courses of study available were machinery, applied chemicals, brewing and fermentation, mining and metallurgy, shipbuilding, marine engines, and electricity, and each year saw a graduating class of from 160 to 170 who completed the three-year programme. According to a survey of the employment of graduates in September 1928 (OTC 1928), the total number of living graduates from 1900 onward was 3,614, of which 1,873 (51.8 per cent of the total) were 'engineers in companies', 581 (16.1 per cent) were 'engineers in governmental offices', 456 (12.6 per cent) were 'self-employed', and 226 (6.3 per cent) were 'school teachers'. While the 'self-employed' figure was certainly not negligible, 310 of these graduates were from the brewing and fermentation course, 43 from applied chemicals, 32 from machinery, and 25 from marine engines, with brewing thereby occupying an overwhelming share. The total number of brewing graduates was 649, meaning that around half were self-employed. Sake and soy sauce brewing had long been important indigenous industries, along with cotton textiles, ceramics, and other light crafts, forming well-known production centres throughout Japan.[4] In 1928 there were 20 national technical colleges in Japan, of which only Osaka Technical College offered a course in brewing and fermentation (Ministry of Education 1928).

Table 10.5. *Number of graduates of technical schools in Osaka (1920–1935)*

Year	1	2	3	4	5	6	7	8	9	10	11	12
1920	172	89	—	66	68	68	—	—	210	187	—	—
1921	165	86	—	82	81	58	—	—	211	207	—	—
1922	167	100	—	147	69	48	—	—	222	178	—	—
1923	153	91	22	105	86	68	—	—	190	279	59	—
1924	161	85	22	95	113	79	—	—	172	220	42	—
1925	168	90	46	98	125	85	—	—	165	184	206	26
1926	160	170	63	109	150	91	—	—	186	173	200	110
1927	150	210	90	87	178	71	53	—	172	192	239	100
1928	177	173	92	128	129	90	54	—	159	208	278	—
1929	175	186	107	128	92	81	64	—	171	204	285	97
1930	195	178	94	132	157	89	58	—	160	223	308	135
1931	105	179	100	131	161	96	62	84	160	208	257	179
1932	99	183	91	103	151	109	60	94	148	224	208	221
1933	127	169	113	122	169	87	61	94	126	188	195	219
1934	120	187	120	112	173	93	70	96	207	204	172	192
1935	105	171	118	147	280	—	67	87	283	217	92	—
TOTALS	2,399	2,347	1,078	1,792	2,182	1,213	549	455	2,942	3,296	2,541	1,729

Notes: 1: Osaka Technical College; 2: Osaka Municipal Technical School (regular course) [Miyakojima]; 3: Osaka Municipal Izuo Technical School (regular course); 4: Osaka Prefectural Nishinoda Technical School (regular course); 5: Osaka Prefectural Imamiya Technical School (regular course); 6 Osaka Prefectural Imamiya Technical School (night course); 7: Osaka Prefectural Sano Technical School (regular course); 8: Osaka Prefectural Joto Technical School (regular course) 9: Osaka Vocational School (secondary course); 10: Osaka Vocational School (higher course); 11: Kansai Vocational School (night, regular course); 12: Kansai Vocational School (day, regular course).

The figures for Osaka Technical College in 1929 and 1930 are for the vocational college attached to Osaka Technical University; figures for 1931 and 1932 are for Osaka Technical University; and figures for years after 1933 are for the Department of Engineering of Osaka Imperial University. The regular course of Nishinoda Technical School after 1923 and of Imamiya Technical School after 1924 include higher courses, and the regular course of Imamiya in 1935 includes the night course. The night course of Kansai Vocational School in 1935 covers only graduates in March, and the number of graduates of the day course in 1935 is unknown.

Source: Ministry of Education, *Monbu Sho Nempo [Yearbook of the Ministry of Education]*, each year; Osaka Municipal Government, *Osaka Shi Tokeisho [Statistics on the City of Osaka]*, each year; Nuizo Ui (1932) (ed.), *Kansai Kogaku Ichiran [Kansai Vocational School Handbook]*, 126; Koin Asanuma (1935) (ed.), *Kansai Kogaku Ichiran [Kansai Vocational School Handbook]*, 145–59; and Osaka Vocational School (1936), *20-nen Shi [A 20-year History]*, 122–3.

The college therefore played a great role in supplying engineers and entre-preneurs to SMEs all over Japan.

An important question, however, is the content of the category 'engin-eers in companies'. Of the total of 1,873, the largest share was occupied by the 602 graduates of the machinery course. Let us follow the movements of the 117 who graduated from 1917 to 1919 (the boom period during and after the First World War) from machinery for ten years after graduation.[5] As ini-tial places of employment after graduation, large private companies and naval shipyards occupied a predominant share. Large companies in the Osaka and Kobe area which employed many graduates were, for example, Mitsubishi Kobe Shipyard, Kawasaki Shipyard, Hatsudoki Seizo Co. (engine manufacturing), Kisha Seizo Co. (locomotive manufacturing), and various companies affiliated with the Sumitomo Zaibatsu. The number of graduates who were initially employed by SMEs is estimated to have been under 10 per cent, but many graduates changed employers over the decade, and about 10 of them had experience in SMEs, with 10 starting up their own operations.

It is clear then, that relationships between OTC machinery graduates and SMEs were relatively limited. The number of graduates who stayed with the same employer during the decade following graduation was 46 (39 per cent of the total including 6 at Mitsubishi Kobe Shipyard, 4 at Sumitomo Steel Works, and 3 at Hitachi Co.) This compares with a ratio 15 per cent re-sulting from a similar survey of 151 OTC graduates who finished from 1900 to 1905, tracking their careers over the period from 1905 to 1914 (Sawai 1995: 193). The career paths of OTC graduates were still somewhat diverse after the First World War, but there was already an increasing trend towards long-term employment.

The Development of Secondary Technical Education in Osaka

With the exception of brewing, relationships between OTC graduates and MSEs were relatively limited, and secondary technical educational organ-izations played much more important roles in the supply of engineers and workers to SMEs in Osaka.

The first public technical secondary schools were the Municipal Osaka Technical School (which later changed its name to Osaka Municipal Miyakojima Technical School, and is referred to simply as Miyakojima hereafter), which opened its doors in April 1908, with the Osaka Prefectural Technical School (which later also changed its name to Osaka Prefectural Nishinoda Technical School: Nishinoda hereafter) starting up at the same time. The former was established as a technical school, and the latter was first founded as an apprentice school.[6] A branch school of Nishinoda was then established in 1913, and this branch became the independent Osaka Prefectural Imamiya Technical School (Imamiya hereafter) in 1916.

The ensuing decade saw the opening of a number of other technical education facilities. Osaka Municipal Vocational School was established in 1919 with a three-year programme. Osaka Municipal Izuo Technical School was an A-type technical school established in 1922, and Osaka Municipal Industrial Arts School was another A-type technical school founded in 1925. Osaka Prefectural Sano Technical School was a B-type technical school also established in 1925, and the B-type Osaka Prefectural Joto Technical School was founded in 1929.

Miyakojima originally had two main departments (four-year programmes for higher elementary graduates), consisting of machinery and architecture. An analysis department added in 1910, and a new preparatory course (two-year programme for lower elementary graduates) was initiated in 1918 (Tanba 1952; Memorial Committee for the 70th Anniversary of Industrial Education in Osaka 1956; and Board of Education of Osaka Prefecture 1973). Miyakojima's expansion continued in the following years with the establishment of departments of electricity and civil engineering, and the conversion of the analysis programme to applied chemistry. In 1926 Miyakojima abolished the division of preparatory and regular courses, becoming an A-type technical school with six-year programmes.

Miyakojima was originally established as a technical school, but its unique six-year programme set it apart and made it one of the most famous technical schools in Japan, with great emphasis on scientific principles and experimentation. Miyakojima also exceeded the level of ordinary technical schools in terms of both its facilities and its teaching faculty,[7] and entrance to the school became quite competitive; the pass rate for prospective applicants was 30 to 40 per cent in the 1920s (Osaka Prefectural Government, various years). Based on this reputation, the Naniwa Industrial Association (i.e. the Miyakojima alumni association) began lobbying for the promotion of Miyakojima to technical college status with a seven-year programme. This stemmed partly from the competitive spirit generated by the upgrading of Osaka Technical College to Osaka Technical University in 1929, but the aims of the Association were never realized.

A technical continuation school was attached to Miyakojima in 1909. Two departments were available, general education and industrial education, and students could choose one or several subjects. The period of schooling was left to the discretion of the principal, and a three-term system was adopted. This continuation school made efforts not only for the education of workers but also for the training of teachers of other Osaka City technical continuation schools. The school set up a higher course in 1924, and the Osaka Municipal Miyakojima Second Technical School, which succeeded this continuation school, was established in 1935 with the inauguration of a youth school.

Nishinoda originally featured two sections, machinery and architecture, with the former composed of departments for wooden patterns, moulding, forging, and finishing, and the latter made up of departments for house-building and furniture. (Memorial Committee 1956; Board of Education 1973; Commemorative Book Committee 1977). The Attached Technical Continuation Night School (later abolished by the promulgation of the Youth School Act in 1935, with a special six-month course opened instead) was founded in December 1908, and was followed by the addition of a department of architectural aesthetics in 1914 and the initiation of a higher course of study in 1922. The higher course was a three-year programme following the second grade of the regular course, and Nishinoda thereby acquired courses of both three and five years; the regular three-year course was a B-type technical school, while the five-year course was an A-type.

Imamiya featured five departments upon its establishment (house-building, printing, electricity, moulding, and finishing), and the requirements for admission and the period of schooling were the same as those of Nishinoda (Memorial Committee 1956; Editorial Committee for the Commemorative Book 1964; Editorial Committee for the Commemorative Book 1968; and Board of Education 1973). The technical continuation night school (also abolished in 1935 and replaced with a special substitute course) was attached to Imamiya. Programmes at the night school were originally from four to six months.

A B-type vocational school night course was established in 1917, composed of departments for machinery, electricity, and architecture, and offering two-year programmes for higher elementary graduates. In 1918, departments for wood patterns and forging were added to the day curriculum, and in 1922 a three-year higher course was established along the lines of the programme at Nishinoda. Imamiya thus had both three-year (regular) and five-year courses, and a department of precision machinery was added as a regular day course in 1925.

Differing from Miyakojima, which was founded for the training of middle-class engineers and entrepreneurs, the goal of Nishinoda and Imamiya was the training of workers who were well-informed of technical principles, as clearly shown by the school constitution of Nishinoda. Article 1 of the constitution was 'Not to be a school-like school, but a factory-like school', and Article 2 was 'Not to be a pupil-like pupil, but a worker-like pupil'.[8] Moreover, Nishinoda and Imamiya featured free tuition until 1918, as the establishment of prefectural technical schools was a component of social policies aimed at preventing and combating poverty in working families (Kawamura 1992: 50).

Graduates of prefectural technical schools who finished three-year programmes in advanced facilities under the guidance of devoted instructors were almost certainly given preferential treatment as foreman candidates. There were even chances for promotion to the position of junior or middle-rank engineers in factories, and this resulted in the rising popularity of the technical schools (Kawamura 1992: 60–1). Although the numbers of applicants for admission were drastically reduced by the introduction of tuition fees in 1919,[9] they increased again after 1922, and the reputations of Nishinoda and Imamiya were firmly established with their upgrade to A-type technical schools resulting from the 1922 establishment of higher courses. The pass ratio of prospective applicants to the two schools dropped significantly with the A-type upgrade, and held at between 20 and 40 per cent until the beginning of the 1930s. This level was rather more competitive than at Osaka Prefectural Sano and Joto Technical Schools, which had pass rates of 40 to 70 per cent (Osaka Prefectural Government, various years).

As indicated in Table 10.5, the total number of graduates of the Miyakojima regular course in the years from 1920 to 1935 was about the same as that of Osaka Technical College, while the total number of graduates of the regular and higher courses at Nishinoda and Imamiya reached just under 4,000 total. Where, then, were the graduates of these three technical schools first employed, and what were their ensuing career paths?

For Miyakojima, the number of graduates by place of employment is known from the establishment of the school until 1928.[10] According to this data, employment was secured in 'industrial companies' (from 33.1 to 38.3 per cent of the total), in 'individual industrial workshops' and 'individual shops' (13.1 to 19.7 per cent), in 'governmental industrial workshops' and 'governmental offices' (11.5 to 16.2 per cent), and as 'self-employed' (9.8 to 10.7 per cent). 'Self-employed' included both the succession of family businesses and the opening of new businesses, and this category added to those of 'individual industrial workshops' and 'individual shops' accounted for from 23.4 to 29.9 per cent of the total. Most of the self-employed situations and unincorporated enterprises were SMEs, while 'industrial companies' also included a significant number of SMEs. The ratio of graduates of Miyakojima, therefore, who were employed in SMEs can be assumed to have been relatively high.

The job-search process undertaken by the graduates of Nishinoda in the latter half of the 1920s can be traced. First, those who were expected to graduate took field-trips to factories located in Osaka and Kobe and decided on prospective employers based on individual preferences and family situations. They then applied at the school. After collecting students' applications, Nishinoda requested each company and factory to employ students, either by means of posted letters or through the dispatch of teachers to factories in order to undertake discussions. In addition, some students found employment through family introductions, and Nishinoda sent letters of recommendation. According to a 1928 survey, Nishinoda stated that, 'We have had no difficulties in placing students using the aforementioned methods. In fact, there have occasionally been regrettable cases where we could not satisfy job offers from individual factories because there were no applications from students.' (Bureau of Central Employment Agency 1928: 6–7).

As noted above, the graduates of prefectural technical schools showed a marked preference for positions in 'industrial companies' rather than in small individual workshops, although many of them did not actually gain employment in such 'industrial companies'. Of the 1929 and 1930 graduates of Miyakojima, who would have been even more inclined toward 'industrial companies' than graduates of prefectural technical schools, 16 per cent were initially employed in 'individual industrial workshops' and 'individual shops', while about 10 per cent of them were 'self-employed' (Osaka Municipal Government 1929 and 1930). According to Table 10.6, which reflects the 1928 employment situation of graduates of four technical schools (Miyakojima, Nishinoda, Imamiya, and Osaka Municipal Izuo Technical School), the number of job offers exceeded the total number of graduates, and 292 of the 319 graduates who entered into immediate employment were hired through the introduction of the schools. The largest number of graduates entered 'companies' (37.0 per cent of the total) followed by those entering 'individual (unincorporated) stores and factories' (25.3 per cent), those who 'entered higher schools' (19.4 per cent), and those who became 'self-employed' (7.7 per cent). The monthly earnings received from 'companies' and 'unincorporated stores and factories' showed no large disparities 'on average'.

The career paths of 231 Imamiya graduates still living in 1968 are briefly introduced in *Imako-Kai 50-nen-shi* [*A 50-year History of the Imamiya Alumni Association*], and our interest is focused on the 61 machinery graduates (44 from regular and higher courses, and 17 from the night course) from 1917 to 1944 (Editorial Committee 1968: 233–49, 259–65). Of the 61 graduates, 37 eventually established and managed their own metal and machinery-related factories and related businesses (including 5 graduates who were employed in other places after the closing of their original businesses), 17 were employed only in companies and factories, 4 succeeded family businesses, and 3 were self-employed in other fields. Needless to say, these individual careers are not necessarily representative of Imamiya graduates; they are better seen as examples of 'success stories' who responded positively to the request of the alumni association to provide details of their careers. Nevertheless, they suggest a strong entrepreneurial streak among technical school graduates.

Of the 40 graduates with self-employment experience, 4 opened their own factories just after graduation, 12 were employed in only one company or factory between graduation and self employment, 15 had two employers, 5 had three employers, and 4 had four employers. Meanwhile, of the 17 graduates who were employed in companies and factories for their entire careers, only 2 graduates stayed in the same place, with the other 15 changing employers from one to four times. It was quite natural for Imamiya graduates

Table 10.6. *Employment of the graduates of A-type technical schools in Osaka prefecture (1928)*

	Graduates
Number of schools	4
Number of graduates	470
Number of job offers	543
Number of employment placements	470
Graduates employed	319
Employment placement by schools	292
Others	27
Self-employed	36
Entrance to higher schools	91
Graduates not yet employed	4
Others	20
Total of graduates employed:	319
Government officials	15
Schools	3
Companies	174
Press	6
Unincorporated stores and factories	119
Others	2
	Monthly earnings (yen)
Government Officials:	
Highest	55
Lowest	35
Average	45
Schools:	
Highest	50
Lowest	40
Average	50
Companies:	
Highest	80
Lowest	35
Average	43
Press:	
Highest	45
Lowest	45
Average	45
Unincorporated stores and factories:	
Highest	60
Lowest	30
Average	45

Note: Total of Osaka Municipal Miyakojima Technical School; Osaka Municipal Izuo Technical School; Osaka Prefectural Nishinoda Technical School; and Osaka Prefectural Imamiya Technical School.

Source: Bureau of Central Employment Agency (1928), *Shuyo Todofuken Koshu Jitsugyo Gakko Sotsugyosei Shushoku Jokyo Chosa* [*Survey on Employment of the Graduates of A-type Vocational Schools in Major Prefectures*] August.

to occasionally change jobs at that time, and there was a wide range of employers, from SMEs to large firms.

The large number of technical school graduates not only supported the technological development of SMEs via the contributions of skilled workers, foremen, and engineers, but also promoted an increase in the number of SMEs through the initiatives of graduates who became entrepreneurs and factory owners. The contribution of secondary technical education to the development of SMEs, however, was not limited to the supply of human resources. Each technical school was also closely connected with the activities of public research institutes, which will be discussed in the next section.

The Municipal Osaka Technical Research Institute (which changed its name to Osaka Municipal Technical Research Institute, or OMTRI, in 1921) started up in a new building on the campus of Municipal Osaka Technical School in September 1916. Sagoro Horii, the principal of the school, had been appointed acting head of the institute in August, and subsequently served as the first head from January 1918 to June 1920. Until its change of location and accompanying expansion in May 1923, OMTRI was able to promote research activities in spite of its relatively low budget because of access to the facilities of Municipal Osaka Technical School (OMTRI 1936*a*: 5; Horii 1936: 106). The Municipal Osaka Technical School had begun a project in 1913, in which it set up a 'question box' (as opposed to a 'suggestion box') in the library for the purpose of answering the questions of industrialists and factory owners on technical or work-related matters, and this question box was relocated to OMTRI upon its establishment. The technical school adopted industrial efficiency as a regular subject in 1922, which was based on a donation of 5,000 yen from Taichi Nakayama, a famous industrialist who was deeply interested in industrial efficiency and scientific management. The school subsequently made efforts to diffuse more widely knowledge concerning industrial efficiency, appointing Koichi Inoue as an adjunct faculty member to head up the new course of study. Inoue who was a member of the first graduating class of the school's machinery department, had became an engineer at the Osaka Prefectural Institute for Industrial Management (OPIIM) (Department of Industry of Osaka Prefectural Government 1924: 40–1; Tanba 1952: 23).

The activities of Hideya Sato, the third principal of Imamiya (from 1917 to 1933), were also noteworthy. In 1915 he was appointed as the head of Imamiya's machinery department following his experience as an engineer at the Kamesaki Ironworks (Aichi Prefecture) and Shibaura Engineering Works. Sato had also been a teacher at Tochigi Prefectural Technical School after his graduation from Tokyo Technical College's department of machinery in 1905, and he was an enthusiastic promoter of the limit-gauge system (Editorial Committee 1968: 106–8).

As one of the preconditions for the introduction of production involving interchangeable parts, the limit-gauge system was watched by engineers in public and private sectors with keen interest between the wars in Japan, although its initial application to manufacturing processes was limited mainly to the small number of naval shipyards and advanced private machine-building companies. A technical course on the limit-gauge system was accordingly sponsored by Imamiya and by the Department of Industry of the Osaka Prefectural Government in the auditorium of Imamiya in August 1923, and the Osaka Limit Gauge Association was established in June 1924 through the efforts of Sato, Shogo Hasegawa (president of locomotive manufacturer Kisha Seizo Co.), and a number of others (Kawamura 1990). Sato was appointed as a director of the association, and he thereafter served as a leader of activities aimed at increased diffusion of the limit-gauge system. He also made Imamiya the first technical school in Japan to feature a regular department of precision machinery with day courses, thereby further promoting efforts to train specialists not only in the limit-gauge system but in general industrial standardization. OPIIM, established in 1925, appointed Sato as an adjunct researcher, and promoted research activities on industrial efficiency in close co-operation with Imamiya, establishing a workshop there for machinery prototypes related to efficiency study. Moreover, Osaka Prefectural Industrial Research Institute (OPIRI), established in 1929, also appointed Sato as an adjunct researcher in March 1930, and a technical course on the limit-gauge system was offered by OPIRI the following November.

The prefectural/municipal technical schools and public research institutes established intimate relationships that supported the development of SMEs in Osaka, and men such as Horii and Sato played pivotal roles in the formation of social networks[11] that contributed to SME development and to the technological upgrading of SME products.

The Significance of Various Kinds of Vocational Schools

At the Attached Technical Continuation Night School of Nishinoda, just prior to its abolition as a result of the 1935 Youth School Act, eleven subjects such as machine design and drafting, experimental machinery engineering, and lathe practice were offered. The school year was divided into trimesters lasting for four months each (starting in January, May, and September of each year), and, from 1908, the cumulative number of trimesters in which courses had been offered totalled 80.[12] At Imamiya's continuation school, there were 87 trimesters in which courses were offered from 1914 through to the school's abolition in 1935, and graduates totalled around 21,000 (Editorial Committee 1964: 47).

In addition to public technical continuation schools, there were also many private vocational schools which offered much more advanced training than that provided by the continuation and continuation night schools.

The first private vocational school in Osaka was the Kansai School of Commerce and Industry established in 1902. Through 1912, the school produced 466 graduates from its machinery department, 30 from shipbuilding, 421 from civil engineering, and 404 from electricity (Koganei 1965: 59, 61). An increasing number of private vocational schools were founded after the First World War, including Sumitomo Private School for the Training of Workers in 1915, Osaka Technical School, and Osaka Vocational Night School (Osaka Vocational School from 1918) in 1916, Kansai Vocational Special School (Kansai Vocational School from 1928) in 1922, and the Electricity Association Training School for Workers in 1925.

Sumitomo Private School for the Training of Workers was established for the purpose of 'offering knowledge and skill suitable for workers to children of poor families around Osaka, and training them to be trustworthy and good workers by cultivating their character'; the entire budget for the school was donated by the Sumitomo family (Kyocho Kai 1936: 328–40; Iwauchi 1989: 112, 129–31). The school had a three-year programme for lower elementary graduates, and there was no obligation as to the subsequent place of employment. There were a large number of applicants to the school, which was free of charge, and the pass rate averaged 14.5 per cent in the years from 1929 to 1933. According to a survey in June 1933, 641 of the cumulative number of 888 graduates through 1933 were employed as factory workers, suggesting that the goal of the school was well-realized.

Osaka Vocational School (OVS) was the most famous of the private vocational schools in Osaka (Osaka Vocational School 1936: 69, 122–3, 130–4; Asada 1964: 133–45). This school was established mainly by the Osaka Industrial Association, supported by Gisho Yasunaga, the president of Osaka Technical College, and Kaoru Nagao, the principal of Nishinoda, who were named the first principal and vice-principal of the school respectively. In 1916 the OVS higher two-year course (with departments of machinery, electricity, applied chemistry, mining and metallurgy, and textiles), open to graduates of technical schools and middle schools, was established within Osaka Technical College. An OVS two-year secondary course (offering the same five subjects) for higher elementary graduates was then set up at Nishinoda the following year, and a special one-year course (with departments of machinery, electricity, and applied chemistry) was attached to the higher course in 1925. As a rule, the students of OVS were taught by teachers and professors from Nishinoda and Osaka Technical College.

From the outset, the target of the OVS higher course was the training of engineers. This is seen in the requirements for admission, as well as in an address made by principal Yasunaga at the opening ceremony of the school in May 1916, in which he stated that, 'Nowadays we see a large shortage of engineers and assistant engineers. This is a tremendous opportunity for all of you.' (Osaka Vocational School 1936: 20) Of the first 398 students enrolled, 341 were also working during the daytime. Of these, 133 were in 'companies and banks', 83 were 'public servants', and 79 were self-employed. The age of the students varied from 18 to 38 years old, with an average age of 25 (Osaka Vocational School 1936: 24). As shown in Table 10.5, OVS turned out a large number of graduates, and Table 10.7 shows the numbers of OVS higher course graduates by place of employment for 1936. Interestingly, only 27 per cent of the graduates were working in places of employment where more than 10 graduates were employed (e.g. large private enterprises and government facilities). It is difficult to estimate the share of SMEs in the total, but, if we assume that 'companies and factories which employ from 1 to 2 graduates', 'self-employed', and 'unknown' are SMEs, the ratio reaches 66 per cent.

Kansai Vocational School was established mainly by Kenichi Tagami, an Osaka Prefectural Government engineer with the support of other engineers of the Osaka municipal and prefectural governments (Ui 1932: 1–8; Asanuma 1935: 1–14). It opened as a night school offering preparatory, regular, and higher courses, with departments of civil engineering and architecture, but a day course was attached in 1923.

The Activities of the Public Research Institutes and their Significance

The Osaka Industrial Research Institute (OIRI)

Excluding the science and engineering departments and the Industrial Science Institute of Osaka Imperial University, the most important public research institutes located in Osaka from the inter-war period through the war were: the Osaka Industrial Research Institute (or OIRI, established in 1918, succeeding the Osaka Prefectural Industrial Research Institute which had been established in 1903) under the direct control of the Ministry of Commerce and Industry; the Osaka Municipal Technical Research Institute (OMTRI, established in 1916); the Osaka Prefectural Institute for Industrial Management (OPIIM 1925); and the Osaka Prefectural Industrial Research Institute (OPIRI 1929).

At the outset, OIRI was composed of one section (general affairs) and three departments. The first department was for analysis and testing, the second for general industrial chemistry (including subsections for soap, oils and fats, matches, leather, carbonization, insulating materials, fuels, electro-chemistry, and synthetic materials), and the third for ceramics (glass, enamel, and fire-resistant materials) (OIRI 1967: 1–11, 24–5). A fourth department for synthetic chemistry and a fifth for machinery, electricity,

Table 10.7. *Number of graduates of Osaka Vocational School (Higher Course) by place of employment (survey in October and November 1936)*

Place of employment	Graduates
Osaka Bureau of Japan National Railways	95
Bureau of Electricity of Osaka Municipal Government	89
Ujigawa Electric Power Co.	78
Osaka Army Arsenal	77
Nankai Railway Co.	46
Sumitomo Metal Industries, Ltd. (Steel works)	40
Osaka Bureau of Ministry of Posts & Telecommunications	38
Hanshin Electric Railway Co.	38
Sumitomo Cable Works, Ltd.	34
Daido Electric Power Co.	31
Kawasaki Shipyard Co.	28
Toyo Spinning Co.	27
Kisha Seizo (Locomotives) Co.	25
Osaka Gas Co.	25
Sumitomo Metal Industries, Ltd. (Steel-pipe works)	22
Keihan Electric Railway Co.	21
Kubota Ironworks	20
The Mint Bureau	20
Kobe Steel, Ltd.	19
Bureau of Water Supply of Osaka Municipal Government	17
Nihon Electric Power Co.	17
Department of Engineering of Osaka Imperial University	16
Osaka Industrial Research Institute of Ministry of Commerce and Industry	15
Sumitomo Metal Industries, Ltd. (Rolled-copper works)	14
Osaka Machinery Co.	14
Osaka Ironworks	14
Osaka Municipal Miyakojima Technical School	14
Fujinagata Shipyard Co.	14
Hanshin Kyuko Electric Railway Co.	13
Dainihon Spinning Co.	13
Toyoda Loom Co.	11
Nihon Elevator Co.	11
Kawanishi Aircraft Co.	10
Nihon Dyestuff Co.	10
SUBTOTAL	976
Companies and Factories employing 5–9 graduates (24 companies)	161
Companies and Factories employing 3–4 graduates (32 companies)	110
Companies and Factories employing 1–2 graduates	1,299
Self-employed	95
Unknown	1,024
TOTAL	3,665

Note: Auditors are excluded.

Sources: Osaka Vocational School (1936), *20-nen Shi* [*A 20-year History*], 127–9, and Tunashima Industrial Association of Osaka Vocation School (higher course), *Kaiin Meibo* [*List of Members*], 1937 edn.

and metallurgy were added in 1925, and a special laboratory under the direct control of the director of OIRI, involved in research on colloid chemistry, photographic chemistry, and optical instruments, was set up at the same time. An open laboratory system (having 89 laboratory rooms, with a monthly rental fee per room of 60 yen) where researchers from private companies could engage in research activities was adopted in 1927.

As Table 10.8 indicates, the number of OIRI staff exceeded 200 by the end of the 1920s, and, by about 1935, some 90 per cent of engineers and assistant engineers were university graduates. The institute's budget expanded along with the prosperity of wartime studies, after having stagnated in the early 1930s. Each OIRI department laboratory conducted research along a specific theme based on ordinary budget, but big projects like optical glass and synthetic rubber were permitted extra expenses as well.[13] Projects which proved promising by initial research were followed up with interim industrial experimentation, and many of these projects led to privately produced industrial products. While pursuing its own research agenda, the institute also responded to requests from private companies for analysis of organic and inorganic chemicals and the testing of materials and electrical instruments.

According to OIRI historical records (OIRI 1967: 605–6), in which former research staff and directors share their recollections,

Despite the fact that OIRI was derived from a former prefectural industrial research institute, the institute subsequently became inclined to the development of big projects connected with national policy aims under the leadership of Mr Shoji [OIRI's first director, from 1918 to 1938]. Reacting to this change in OIRI's aims and activities, the prefectural government decided to establish another institute [OPIRI]. A municipal institute had already been established as well, and SMEs began to maintain closer relationships with the prefectural and municipal institutes.

Although OIRI initially emphasized research related to sundry export goods which were also staple products of Osaka manufacturing,[14] the relationships between the institute and local SMEs declined in importance as the focal points of research activities shifted to national policy projects.

The Osaka Municipal Technical Research Institute (OMTRI)

Unlike the nationally administered OIRI, the primary aims of the prefectural and municipal institutes were consistently fixed on the development of Osaka SMEs and the technological upgrading of their products. In spite of its 1923 expansion, the size of the staff of OMTRI (see Table 10.8) remained at around half that of OIRI, with a comparatively smaller budget. In fact, it was reported by a local newspaper that Gisho Yasunaga, the president of

Table 10.8. *Number of staff, and value of budget and expenses settled for Osaka Industrial Research Institute of MCI, Osaka Municipal Technical Research Institute, Osaka Prefectural Institute for Industrial Management, and Osaka Prefectural Industrial Research Institute (1920–1944)*

Year	Osaka Industrial Research Institute of MCI					Osaka Municipal Technical Research Institute					Osaka Prefectural Institute for Industrial Management		Osaka Prefectural Industrial Research Institute	
	Staff[a]			Budget[b] (000 yen)	Number of Patents obtained	Staff[c]			Budget[d] (000 yen)	Number of patents obtained	Staff	Expenses settled (000 yen)	Staff[e]	Expenses[f] settled (000 yen)
	Engineers and assistant engineers	Others	Total			Engineers and assistant engineers	Others	Total						
1920	52	93	145	267	—	16	21	37	59	2	—	—	—	—
1921	52	94	146	902	—	15	21	36	225	7	—	—	—	—
1922	52	106	158	795	—	17	25	42	272	8	—	—	—	—
1923	61	106	167	415	—	19	31	50	257	1	—	—	—	—
1924	61	96	157	394	3	21	34	55	87	—	—	—	—	—
1925	61	111	172	486	—	30	54	84	86	1	10	54	—	—
1926	61	120	181	1,010	4	33	59	92	92	4	33	57	—	—
1927	66	126	192	631	5	35	58	93	96	9	33	56	—	—
1928	66	131	197	636	3	35	51	86	157	—	33	45	—	—
1929	81	131	212	630	3	35	51	86	154	5	33	22	—	500
1930	81	—	—	556	4	35	51	86	155	4	23	39	33	144
1931	71	—	—	525	5	35	51	86	159	8	22	32	29	121
1932	65	—	—	459	7	35	46	81	154	5	23	35	29	122
1933	65	—	—	459	1	35	46	81	153	10	24	37	38	150
1934	65	—	—	485	—	34	46	80	143	7	27	45	42	168
1935	65	—	—	485	2	36	45	81	144	2	33	55	38	170
1936	65	—	—	485	7	37	45	82	140	6	31	54	42	406
1937	69	—	—	593	—	34	35	69	194	6	30	55	49	531
1938	69	—	—	524	2	43	28	71	380	4	29	51	56	322
1939	69	—	—	1,520	3	41	33	74	562	3	27	51	66	327
1940	67	189	256	1,345	6	43	36	79	425	1	19	45	69	391
1941	72	235	307	805	1	51	56	107	400	4	22	59	69	329

Table 10.8. (cont.)

Year	Osaka Industrial Research Institute of MCI					Osaka Municipal Technical Research Institute					Osaka Prefectural Institute for Industrial Management		Osaka Prefectural Industrial Research Institute	
	Staff[a]			Budget[b] (000 yen)	Number of Patents obtained	Staff[c]			Budget[d] (000 yen)	Number of patents obtained	Staff	Expenses settled (000 yen)	Staff[e]	Expenses[f] settled (000 yen)
	Engineers and assistant engineers	Others	Total			Engineers and assistant engineers	Others	Total						
1942	85	268	353	1,553	3	62	44	106	557	7	34	109	—	312
1943	79	341	420	—	4	57	43	100	581	5	41	134	—	375
1944	71	369	440	—	8	57	43	100	557	6	45	141	—	260

[a] Dashes in Staff cols. of Osaka Industrial Research Institute of MCI (OIRI) indicate numbers are unknown, and 'Others' which include a quote based on budget, differ from the actual number.
[b] The budgets of OIRI in 1943 and 1944 are unknown.
[c] The staff of Osaka Municipal Technical Research Institute (OMTRI) represent a quota based on budget, which differ from the actual number.
[d] The budget of OMTRI after 1937 are expenses settled, while personnel expenses after 1942 are estimates. Years after 1928 include budget for the Institute for Promotion of Industries.
[e] Dashes in Staff col. of Osaka Prefectural Industrial Research Institute (OPIRI) indicate numbers are unknown.
[f] The expenses settled of OPIRI in 1929 and 1936 are budget.

Sources: OIRI (1967), *Osaka Kogyo Gijutsu Sikensho 50-nen Shi* [*A 50-year History of OIRI*], 36–7, 41–2, 550–2; *Osaka Shiritsu Kogyo Kenkyusho Soritsu 20-nen Shi* [*A 20-year History of OMTRI*], *Kagaku to Kogyo* [*Science and Industry*] 11/5 May 1936; OMTRI (1966), *Soritsu 50 Shunen Kinenshi* [*A 50-year History*], 58, 60, 193–6; Osaka Prefectural Institute for Industrial Management (OPIIM) (1976), *Noken 50-nen Shi* [*A 50-year History of OPIIM*], 176, 178; Osaka Prefectural Government, *Osaka Fu Tokeisho* [*Statistics on Osaka Prefecture*], each year; Osaka Prefectural Government, *Osaka Fu Sainyu Saishutsu Kessansho* [*Statement of Accounts on Revenue and Expenditure of Osaka Prefecture*], each year; and Osaka Prefectural Government, *Osaka Fu Sainyu Saishutsu Yosansho* [*Budget on Revenue and Expenditure of Osaka Prefecture*], each year.

Osaka Technical College, 'split his sides laughing' upon being informed of the OMTRI start-up budget of 24,204 yen and its initial annual operating budget (for August 1916 to March 1917) of 14,002 yen (OMTRI 1936*a*: 13–15; Horii 1936: 106). But OMTRI was successful in promoting various activities in support of Osaka SMEs despite its budget constraints. OMTRI's basic management policy, as expressed by Hitoshi Takaoka, the second director (1920–34), was that, 'The staff of the institute must serve the public, as the citizens are important customers.' (Kishida 1934: 28).

OMTRI was established with a general affairs department and a research department (investigating matters of organic, inorganic, and electric chemistry, machine efficiency, machinery structure and materials, and architectural and furniture materials). The Institute for the Promotion of Industries was attached in 1925, and OMTRI's expansion continued thereafter (OMTRI 1936*a*: 17, 85–7; OMTRI 1966: 59).

As shown in Table 10.9, OMTRI's activities were quite diverse. The amount of 'requested testing and research' (simple testing and technical guidance conducted free of charge as well as paid analysis and research), which had replaced Osaka Municipal Technical School's 'question box', grew significantly, and this system supported the technological upgrading of Osaka SMEs, which typically could not afford to maintain their own facilities for testing and experimentation. By way of analogy, OMTRI sought to be a 'family doctor' on technical matters for its 'patients', the SMEs of Osaka.

The amount of 'special research', which continued from 1921 to 1941, also became more significant from the mid-1920s. Under this system, OMTRI staff carried out research at the request of private companies, trade associations, and individuals, and, when necessary, outside researchers were permitted to use the facilities of the institute under the guidance of the staff. Thus, interim industrial experimentation was conducted at the institute before undertaking the manufacture of actual industrial goods based on the original research. This system was modelled on the method of the Mellon Institute of Industrial Research in Pittsburgh in the USA, and all expenses for research were borne by clients. In 1919 Hitoshi Takaoka carried out a detailed observation of the management of the Mellon Institute of Industrial Research as part of an extended visit to the USA and Europe, and he subsequently endeavoured to improve OMTRI's facilities and organization. Many of the clients were SMEs and individuals, and certain of the 'special research' projects undertaken at the behest of trade associations met with spectacular success (OMTRI 1936*a*: 21–2, 32–69; Horii, 1936: 107).

'Ordered testing and research' consisted of research executed by order of the director of the institute, supported by its own budget, and, as indicated in Table 10.9, this also became significant. The effectiveness of the institute's research activities are also reflected in the number of patents granted (see Table 10.8). Moreover, OMTRI's activities were not limited to the confines

Table 10.9. *Number of instances of testing, and research and factory guidance (outside the Institute) by Osaka Municipal Technical Research Institute (1920–1942)*

Year	Requested testing and research[a]	Special research[b]	Ordered testing and research[c]	Factory guidance	
				Number of factories	Total instances of guidance
1920	408	—	6	—	—
1921	391	4	6	—	—
1922	589	6	33	—	—
1923	989	7	57	9	23
1924	1,719	9	35	12	18
1925	1,821	9	35	24	91
1926	1,509	18	85	15	77
1927	1,632	16	46	32	156
1928	1,587	21	82	46	166
1929	1,840	25	89	41	177
1930	2,048	33	40	285	594
1931	2,243	22	20	220	466
1932	2,174	32	19	38	289
1933	2,152	37	9	58	446
1934	2,257	38	13	48	408
1935	3,150	46	6	62	231
1936	3,085	47	—	—	—
1937	2,701	42	1	—	—
1938	2,686	37	2	—	—
1939	2,138	37	13	—	—
1940	1,019	35	41	—	—
1941	1,707	15	38	—	—
1942	2,978	—	28	—	—

[a] 'Requested testing and research' is the total of testing, technical guidance, etc.
[b] 'Special Research' finishes in 1941.
[c] 'Ordered testing and research' is the research based on the budget of the institute, ordered by the director of the institute.
Note: Research over a number of years classified by the year of acceptance or start of the research.
Sources: OMTRI, *Osaka Shiritsu kogyo Kenkyusho Soritsu 20-nen Shi,* [*A 20-year History of OMTRI*], 20–4, and OMTRI, *Soritsu 50 Shunen Kinenshi* [*A 50-year History*], 66–76, 78–9.

of the institute itself. As reflected in Table 10.9, the staff eagerly carried out factory guidance/diagnosis outside the institute in order to 'reduce costs of production at SMEs by introducing scientific methods to workshops and upgrading production technology' (Takaoka 1936: 111), particularly during the years of the Great Depression. The provision from 1917 of facilities for the use of private companies and factories which could not afford to maintain their own facilities for industrial research was also quite popular, especially among SMEs, and some 218 clients were using the facilities to the end of 1935. The open laboratory set up at OIRI was actually modelled on the practices in OMTRI, following the recognition of the popularity of the OMTRI labs (Shono 1934: 11; OMTRI 1936a: 24).

In addition to these activities, OMTRI also began encouraging invention in 1925, when the Institute for Promotion of Industries was attached. It produced invention prototypes in order to promote the practical utilization of registered inventions, and it offered free guidance on application procedures for patents and utility models. OMTRI also frequently held in-house exhibitions, as well as displaying the results of its research at outside exhibitions. In addition it sponsored lectures and technical courses to promote the upgrading of industrial technology, the diffusion of knowledge concerning new inventions, and the training of technicians. The number of lectures held between 1925 and 1942 reached 69, while the number of technical courses between 1923 and 1942 was 50.[15]

The Osaka Industrial Research Association was established in conjunction with OMTRI in 1926. The association not only sponsored various kinds of lectures, technical courses, and tours, but also published a monthly bulletin entitled *Kagaku to Kogyo* (Science and Industry), greatly contributing to the dissemination of research results (OMTRI 1936*b*).

The Osaka Prefectural Industrial Research Institute (OPIRI)

In line with an official statement by the Osaka Prefectural Government made upon OPIRI's establishment in 1929 that, 'OPIRI is to be established as an organization for the guidance and assistance of SMEs, with the goal of industrial innovation' (OPIRI 1960: 98), the institute's focus was on fostering SME development.

OPIRI was established with a general affairs section and three departments for industrial promotion, invention, and textile testing. A department was added in 1932 for the promotion of craft industries, another in 1935 for machinery improvement and guidance, and another in 1936 for technical guidance concerning metal materials, with other departments added in the years following (OPIRI 1960: 98–114). As Table 10.8 indicates, OPIRI's staff increased year by year as its activities expanded from the mid-1930s, and its budget far surpassed that of the Osaka Prefectural Institute for Industrial Management, as will be subsequently discussed.

While OMTRI emphasized the development of chemical industries, OPIRI focused mainly on fostering MSEs in the fields of metals, machinery, textiles, and crafts. In the case of machinery, OPIRI's department for industrial promotion initially provided technical guidance on the use and improvement of machinery, and the main activities of the department for machinery improvement and guidance (established in 1935) were technical guidance for machinery improvement and capabilities testing, and diffusion of knowledge on jigs, fixtures, precision machinery, precision measurement, limit gauges, etc. In 1936, for example, the department responded to 204 technical queries (out of a total of 2,371 for OPIRI as a whole); conducted 152 (965) surveys such as a 'survey on electric welding'; provided 347 (597) instances of guidance, such as 'guidance concerning precision-machine processing methods'; undertook 48 (256) research and experimentation projects, such as the 'manufacturing of micrometers'; made 967 precision measurements; sponsored 5 (17) technical lectures and courses; and held 4 (19) conferences and symposiums (Department of Economic Affairs of the Osaka Prefectural Government 1937: 138–41, 167–72).

In November 1938 after the outbreak of the Sino-Japanese War, a special department of munitions was established to provide manufacturing guidance and to allot orders for munitions among SMEs. Also, in October 1940, a special department was established for machine-tool testing and inspection, with nearly 10,000 machines tested by 1944. The training of workers on gauges indispensable to precision-machine processing was also adopted as a priority task of the department during the Pacific War, and about 600 workers from private firms took three- or six-month OPIRI training courses. Furthermore, based on subsidies from the Ministry of Munitions established in November 1943, OPIRI engineers were dispatched to locations ranging from the Kanto region to the southernmost main island of Kyushu (including Osaka and Kobe, of course, as well as Tokyo and Kanagawa). At these locations, OPIRI engineers provided guidance relating to methods for setting machine tools, upgrading products, and the repair of second-hand machine tools and some 300 factories were the recipients of such technical advice (OPIRI 1944*a*; OPIRI 1944*c*; OPIRI, Division of Precision Machinery, n.d.; OPIRI 1960: 112–13). By the end of the war, OPIRI activities had become highly constrained by the drafting of many staff members into the military, but major efforts continued and as late as 1943 OPIRI responded to 1,702 technical queries, provided 949 instances of 'guidance', undertook 2,359 'testing and experimentation' projects, and conducted 547 'surveys, other research, etc.' (OPIRI 1944*b*).

The Osaka Prefectural Institute for Industrial Management (OPIIM)

The three above-mentioned public research institutes were specifically directed towards research activities and factory guidance related to the application of particular industrial technologies. In contrast, OPIIM was a unique institute having the primary goal of diffusing knowledge concerning industrial efficiency and scientific management. Established in April 1925, OPIIM was Japan's first public institute for industrial efficiency. It promoted not only research and surveys on scientific management, industrial psychology, labour physiology, standardization, and machinery, but also responded to requests for related guidance, testing, and inspection.

OPIIM also held lectures and training sessions on industrial/factory efficiency three or four times a year, regular lectures/training from 1926 for the
education of foremen, and regular lectures from 1932 for the training of
engineers in sales efficiency. 'Factory diagnosis', meaning inspection and
technical guidance based on the principles of scientific management, was
especially stressed in OPIIM activities, and the cumulative number of factory diagnoses between 1925 and 1937 reached 499, while the number of instances of 'guidance' for the partial application of scientific management
principles was 1,326 over the same period (OPIIM 1936a: 1–3; OPIIM 1976:
32–43).

Although OPIIM's budget was slashed in 1929, due partly to the establishment of OPIRI and compounded by serious financial difficulties for the
Osaka Prefectural Government, OPIIM began expanding again from 1933.
By 1942 OPIIM consisted of six departments: general affairs, management
guidance, skills, conveyance, motive power, and labour science (OPIIM
1936a: 3–4; OPIIM 1942: 2–3).

OPIIM's objectives were not limited to SMEs. However, despite the conventional wisdom that it would be impossible to completely introduce the
OPIIM-advocated modern methods of scientific management to SMEs, especially in the cases of small workshops, the institute approached this as a
practical issue to be addressed. With respect to the implementation of basic
ideas on scientific management at SMEs, the OPIIM policy (OPIIM 1936b:
19, 21) was that,

All effective methods for the achievement of the ultimate goal of increased profits,
whether related to material or non-material matters, should be understood as
methods for increased management efficiency. We should not assume a formula
such as 'mass production = reduced production costs = increased sales = prosperity' as a golden rule, but instead always promote *kaizen* [improvement] from an
original viewpoint in order to make good use of each feature [of the situation at
hand].

Accordingly, OPIIM eagerly promoted factory diagnosis and technical
guidance for SMEs manufacturing celluloid toothbrushes, knitted goods,
bicycles, textiles, and a host of other products, as well as conducting surveys on methods to increase efficiency in large enterprises until the war
(OPIIM 1936a: 219–20).

During the war, OPIIM tackled intensive factory diagnosis and guidance
together with OPIRI, taking part in the Osaka Prefectural Production Promotion Corps, which began its activities in January 1943 (Osaka Prefectural
Government 1943; OPIIM 1976: 68–70). The Corps was composed of staff
members from OPIIM and OPIRI, the former providing 92 members divided into five squads and the latter providing 36 members divided into
four squads (Osaka Prefectural Government, n.d.; OPIIM 1976: 68). The
main activities of the Corps was an eight- to ten-day intensive factory diagnosis conducted at major factories through OPIIM/OPIRI co-operation.

Ironically, economic conditions were too severe during the war for the Corps to achieve real success in increasing production. However, the hard-won experience accumulated during the war formed a pool of valuable know-how concerning factory diagnosis and guidance which would be successfully transferred to the post-war setting.

The Legacy of Wartime Activities by Public Research Institutes

Let us note two examples of the post-war impact of the various activities carried out by the public research institutes during the war. First is the case of Shigeru Yasutomi (1906–1982), an OPIRI engineer who personified OPIRI's highly capable factory diagnosis skills (interviews with Mr Yoshio Okada and Mr Yutaka Yasutomi). He was trained as a skilled worker in a small ironworks shop after finishing lower elementary school, and he later managed his own factory (which unfortunately failed when a relative in charge of accounting absconded with the money). He was employed by OPIRI from its establishment, where he remained until the middle of the post-war high-growth era.

According to Shintaro Hayashi, a prominent MITI bureaucrat who led machinery-related policy-making in the 1950s, Yasutomi was '. . . perhaps a genius in factory diagnosis and guidance. Just entering a workshop, he could see what the defect was at once . . .' (Ekonomisuto 1977: 65). His factory diagnosis covered all fields, from the setting of machinery to design and processing technology, and he could instruct engineers and workers in a range of subjects from processing methods to the necessity of machinery renewal. In post-war years, Yasutomi played an active role in many fields including factory diagnosis, the establishment of Japan Industrial Standards (JIS) guidelines (concerning screws, machine elements, tools, inspection of precision, etc.), instruction of inspectors of associations for export-goods inspection, and as the first director of a technical centre established in Taiwan (from August 1953 to June 1955).[16] His experience in SME factory diagnosis at OPIRI during the war period no doubt served as an important foundation for these activities.

A second example can be found in the fact that SME policies in the post-war period have been led by the Small and Medium Enterprise Agency, established in August 1948, with SME diagnosis serving as an important tool. Objectives were expanded from individual firm diagnosis (for particular factories, workshops, distributors, etc.) initially, to collective diagnosis (for entire shopping districts, webs of relations between parent companies and their suppliers, manufacturing districts, etc.) (MITI 1991: 94–7; MITI 1992: 639–40).

OPIIM made a major contribution to the application of this diagnosis system to SMEs. Riichi Sonoda, an OPIIM director (March 1939 to August 1948), and simultaneously a group leader in the Osaka Prefectural Production Promotion Corps, became chief of the Bureau of Guidance of the Small and Medium Enterprises Agency upon its establishment. Furthermore, OPIIM sponsored lectures to facilitate private companies' transition from munitions production to civilian demand as early as September 1945, and began industry diagnosis from April 1947. Supported by the high capability of diagnosis which was accumulated via experience in factory diagnosis from the inter-war period to just after the war, the staff of OPIIM participated in the making of the diagnosis outline (the fundamental policies on diagnostic methods and standards), used as a basis for the application of diagnosis to SMEs subsequently carried out by the Small and Medium Enterprise Agency. Thus, the know-how concerning factory diagnosis accumulated at OPIIM significantly contributed to the modernization of SMEs in Japan through the policies of the Small and Medium Enterprise Agency (OPIIM 1976: 78–81).

Conclusion

Osaka Prefecture has continued to be not only one of the largest industrial centres in Japan but virtually a 'Kingdom of SMEs'. This chapter has directed attention to the roles and significance of various kinds of technical education and the public research institutes in order to better consider the institutional factors which supported the development of SMEs in Osaka between the wars.

It should be noted that the world of SMEs was not necessarily excluded from the supply of human resources having more than secondary technical education, as illustrated by the 1937 Osaka Municipal Government survey showing that around the half of the engineers in metal and machinery industries in Osaka were employed in SMEs. Still, with the exception of the brewing course, relationships between the Osaka Technical College (as a higher educational organization) and SMEs were relatively limited, and the career paths of OTC graduates in the inter-war period increasingly tended towards long-term employment with the same company.

It was the secondary technical educational organizations, i.e. *Totei Gakko* (public apprentice schools), *Kogyo Gakko* (public technical schools), *Kogyo Hoshu Gakko* (public technical continuation schools, mostly night schools) and *Kogyo Kakushu Gakko* (private vocational schools, mostly night schools), that made major contributions to the supply of eligible workers, foreman candidates, and engineers to the vast number of SMEs. Among the secondary technical educational organizations in Osaka, the Miyakojima occupied the top place in terms of both its facilities and its teaching faculty. Meanwhile, prefectural apprentice schools like Nishinoda and Imamiya were established as a component of social policies aimed at preventing and combating poverty in working families. These institutions experienced rising popularity after the First World War, and their reputations were firmly established with their upgrade to A-type technical schools due to the establishment of higher courses. In this sense social policies also functioned as industrial policies in the development of Osaka SMEs.

The large number of graduates from secondary technical educational organizations supported the technological development of SMEs both through contributions made by skilled workers, foremen, and engineers, and through an increased number of SMEs brought about by the initiatives of graduates who became entrepreneurs and owners. Unlike those who completed higher education, it was quite natural for them to change jobs occasionally, and their career paths were diverse. Night schools, such as private vocational schools and public continuation schools, played a decisive role in fulfilling the technological aspirations of ambitious young workers trying to realize their 'Japanese Dream' of becoming engineers and entrepreneurs of SMEs. These schools paralleled public secondary technical schools in promoting the active new entry of needed skills into the world of SMEs.

At the same time, excluding Osaka Imperial University, the most important public technical research institutes were: the national Osaka Industrial Research Institute (OIRI); the Osaka Municipal Technical Research Institute (OMTRI); the Osaka Prefectural Institute for Industrial Management (OPIIM); and the Osaka Prefectural Industrial Research Institute (OPIRI). The relationships between OIRI and local SMEs declined in importance as the focal points of research activities shifted to national policy projects, although OIRI initially emphasized research related to the sundry export goods which were staple products of Osaka-based SMEs.

Unlike the nationally-administered OIRI, the primary aims of the prefectural and municipal institutes were consistently fixed on the development of Osaka SMEs and the technological upgrading of their products. While OMTRI emphasized the development of chemical industries, OPIRI focused mainly on fostering SMEs in the sectors of metals, machinery, textiles, and crafts. While they proceeded with diverse research topics, their activities were not limited to the confines of the institutes themselves. Staff members eagerly carried out factory guidance/diagnosis outside the institutes, even as they responded to the vast number of daily requested testing, technical queries, etc. OPIIM was Japan's first public institute for industrial efficiency, the primary goal of which was to diffuse knowledge concerning industrial efficiency and scientific management not only in large companies but also in SMEs which could not otherwise afford to introduce such methods. OPIIM also accumulated know-how concerning factory guidance/diagnosis through its experiences from the pre-war period through wartime, which would be successfully transferred to the post-war setting. In short, these three public institutes served as 'family doctors' on matters of factory management and technological upgrading for their SME 'patients' in Osaka.

It should be noted that the prefectural and municipal secondary technical schools and public research institutes established intimate relationships that supported the development of SMEs in pre-war Osaka. Men such as Sagoro Horii of Miyakojima and Hideya Sato of Imamiya played pivotal roles in the formation of social networks which continued to supply both human resources and technical and managerial information to SMEs for their ongoing development and technological upgrading.

Industrial policies aimed at small business were executed not only by the central government in modern Japan. There were many cases of highly successful applications of local industrial policy led by local governments as this chapter has demonstrated, and these results were sometimes transferred to other regions through the impetus of 'competition among local governments'.

NOTES

1. In Japan the definition of 'small and medium-sized enterprises' by *Chosho Kigyo Kihon Ho* (the Medium and Small Enterprises Law of 1963) extends only to enterprises with 300 employees or less, or a capital of 50 million yen (100 million yen in the amended act of 1973) in manufacturing. Here, enterprises with less than 100 employees are tentatively defined as SMEs in the pre-war period. The survey of the Osaka Municipal Government in 1937 classified enterprises into three groups: 'large', with 100 or more operatives; 'medium', with from 30 to 99; and 'small', with less than 30 (Osaka Municipal Government 1940, introductory remarks).
2. On the development of secondary technical educational organizations, see National Institute of Education 1973, ix. 54, 56–8, 67–71, x. 89–116, and Sato 1984. On the youth schools, see Takano 1992.
3. Tokyo Vocational School was established in Tokyo in 1881, changed its name to Tokyo Technical School in 1890, changing again to Tokyo Technical College in 1901, the same year of a similar change in the case of Osaka. This college was promoted to Tokyo Technical University in 1929, again the same as Osaka (Morikawa 1975: 13).
4. On the development of the brewing and soy sauce industries, see Tanimoto 1996.

5. The following statements are based on the lists of graduates included in OTC handbooks (OTC, various years). These lists specify the names of companies and other organizations that employed particular graduates each year.
6. On the development of secondary technical education in Osaka, see Memorial Committee on the 70th Anniversary of Industrial Education in Osaka 1956: 65–127, and Board of Education of Osaka Prefecture 1973: 515–22.
7. The first principal, Sagoro Horii (1907–18), for example, visited the UK to observe industrial education and experimental engineering for four months in 1910. Katsuzo Okamoto, head of the department of machinery, went to Germany and the UK in 1912, and studied at the University of Manchester for about four years. Minoru Sugita, the second principal (1918–32), also stayed in the USA and Europe for six months for general inspection in 1924 and 1925 (Tanba 1952: 5, 15–16, 21).
8. Kyocho Kai 1936: 286–7. The school constitution of Imamiya was mostly the same as Nishinoda (Editorial Committee for the Commemorative Book 1974: 24). Someone who graduated from the department of finishing of Imamiya in 1919 recalled that, 'At the entrance ceremony, the principal said to us, "You will be workers after graduation. Quit right now, if you don't want that" ' (Editorial Committee for the Commemorative Book 1968: 282).
9. Kawamura 1992: 53, 63. Tuition fees of prefectural technical schools in 1920 were 11 yen per year (Kawamura 1992: 57). Those for the preparatory course and regular course of Miyakojima were 18 yen and 24 yen respectively (for residents of the City of Osaka) (Osaka Municipal Government 1920 edn., 156).
10. Osaka Municipal Government, each year edition. The situations of employment of new graduates is known only for each year after 1929.
11. As an important work discussing the process of technological development of modern Japan from the viewpoint of 'social network of innovation', see Morris-Suzuki 1994.
12. Kyocho Kai 1936: 290. The schooling period of each subject around 1932 was a little more than three months, the total hours of each subject reaching from 60 to 90 (Iida 1932: 38).
13. Optical glass, synthetic rubber, and pictures can be cited as major achievements of OIRI from the inter-war period through wartime. OIRI developed the research and trial manufacturing of lenses to be used in periscopes and range-finders, and Toru Takamatsu, who headed up this research, won the major army prize in 1943. Research on synthetic rubber by OIRI was also well known. It succeeded in interim industrial experimentation in 1940, and Nihon Chemical Industries, Ltd., manufactured it (OIRI 1967: 168–77, 306–8; MITI 1957: 24–5).
14. For the situation of industries of sundry export goods, see Sawai 1990.
15. OMTRI, 1936*a*: 25, 27–30, and OMTRI 1966: 108, 110–11. For example, the number of instances of guidance on inventions and trademarks totalled 983 from 1928 to 1935 (OMTRI 1936*a*: 25).
16. This technical centre was established by Osaka Prefectural Government for the purpose of promoting export of machinery products made in Osaka. The centre made an effort to promote such exports through the execution of factory diagnosis and guidance for SMEs in Taiwan.

286   *Minoru Sawai*

REFERENCES

Amakawa, Y. (1976), 'Senji Keizai Ikoki no Osaka Keizai: Iwayuru Keizaiteki Jiban Chinka Mondai wo Chusinni' ['Manufacturing in Osaka in the Transition to War Economy Focused on the So-called "Economic Decline" Problem'], in Osaka Historical Society, *Kindai Osaka no Rekishiteki Tenkai* [*Historical Development of Modern Osaka*]. Tokyo: Yoshikawa Kobunkan.

Asada, T. (1964) (ed.), *Osaka Kogyo Kai 50-nen Shi* [*A 50-year History of the Osaka Industrial Association*]. Osaka: Osaka Kogyo Kai.

Asanuma, K. (1935) ed., *Kansai Kogaku Ichiran* [*Kansai Vocational School Handbook*]. Osaka: Kansai Kogaku.

Board of Education of Osaka Prefecture (1973), *Osaka Fu Kyoiku 100-nen Shi* [*A 100-year History of Education in Osaka Prefecture*], vol. 1.

Bureau of Central Employment Agency (1928), *Shuyo Todofuken Koshu Jitsugyo Gakko Sotsugyosei Shushoku Jokyo Chosa* [*Survey of Employment of Graduates of A-type Vocational Schools in Major Prefectures*] Tokyo: Chuo Shokugyo Shokai Jimu Kyoku.

Commemorative Book Committee (1977), *Soritsu 70 Shunen Kinenshi Nishinoda* [*A History of the First 70 Years: Nishinoda*]. Osaka Prefectural Nishinoda Technical High School.

Department of Economic Affairs of the Osaka Prefectural Government (1937), *Osaka Fu Kogyo Nenpo* [*Industrial Yearbook of Osaka Prefecture*].

Department of Industry of Osaka Prefectural Government (1924), *Osaka Fu Noritsu Zoshin Undo Enkaku oyobi Fuka Noritsu Kenkyu Jotai Chosa* [*The History of Movement for the Promotion of Efficiency and Researches on Efficiency in Osaka Prefecture*].

Editorial Committee for the Commemorative Book (1964), *50-nen no Ayumi* [*A 50-year History*]. Osaka Prefectural Imamiya Technical High School.

—— (1968), *Imako Kai 50-nen Shi* [*A 50-year History of Imako Kai* (alumni association)]. Osaka Imako Kai.

—— (1974), *Imako 60-nen Shi* [*A 60-year History of Imamiya Technical High School*]. Osaka Prefectural Imamiya Technical High School.

Ekonomisuto Henshubu (1977), *Sengo Sangyo Shi eno Shogen* [*Oral History of Post-war Industries*, i: *Industrial Policies*]. Tokyo: Mainichi Shinbunsha.

Horii, S. (1936), 'Osaka Shiritsu Kogyo Kenkyusho Soritsu Zengo no Koto' ['On the Establishment of Osaka Municipal Technical Research Institute'], *Kagaku to Kogyo*, 11/5 (May).

Iida, K. (1932), 'Yo no Keiken niyoru Shokucho Kyoiku' ['My Experience in Education for Foremen'], *Kosei* (Feb.).

Interview with Mr Yoshio Okada (former vice-director of Osaka Prefectural Industrial Research Institute), 3 June 1994; and with Mr Yutaka Yasutomi (son of Mr Shigeru Yasutomi), 6 Aug. 1994.

Iwauchi, R. (1989), *Nihon no Kogyoka to Jukuren Keisei* [*Industrialization in Japan and Skill Formation*]. Tokyo: Nihon Hyoronsha.

Kawamura, M. (1990), 'Ryotaisenkanki ni Okeru Osaka Chiho no Genkai Geji Hosiki no Fukyu Katudo ni Tsuite' ['Diffusion of Limit-Gauge System in Osaka Between the Wars'], *Chiho Shi Kenkyu*, 40/1 (Feb.).

—— (1992), 'Osaka Furitsu Shokko Gakko no Setsuritu Zengo no Jokyo ni Tsuite' ['On the establishment of Osaka Prefectural Technical School', *Hisutoria*, 136 (Sept.).

Kishida, K. (1934), 'Takaoka Shocho no Kadode ni Saishite' [*On the Departure of Takaoka, Former Head*], *Kagaku to Kogyo*, 9/2 (Feb.).

Koganei, Y. (1965), 'Kakushu Gakko no Rekishi 4' [*The History of Vocational Schools*, 4], *Kakushu Gakko Kyoiku*, 4 (Sept.).

Kyocho Kai (1936), (ed.), *Toteiseido to Gijutsu Kyoiku* [*Apprentice System and Technical Education*]. Tokyo: Kyocho Kai.

Memorial Committee for the 70th Anniversary of Industrial Education in Osaka (1956), *Osaka Fu Sangyo Kyoiku 70 Shunen Kinenshi* [*A 70-year History of Industrial Education in Osaka Prefecture*].

Ministry of Education (1928), *Monbu Sho Nenpo* [*Yearbook of the Ministry of Education*], vol. 1. Tokyo: Monbu Sho.

Ministry of International Trade and Industry [MITI] (1994), *Kogyo Tokei Hyo* [*Statistics on Industry*] Tokyo: Tsusho Sangyo Chosa Kai.

—— (1957), *Tsusho Sangyo Sho Kogyo Gijutsuin Shozoku Shiken Kenkyu Kikan no Enkaku to Gyoseki* [*The History and Performance of Research Institutes Belonging to the Agency of Industrial Science and Technology of MITI*]. Tokyo: Tsusho Sangyo Sho.

—— (1961), *Kogyo Tokei 50-nen Shi* [*A 50-year History of Statistics on Industry*]. Tokyo: Okura Sho Insatsu Kyoku.

—— (1991, 1992), *Tsusho Sangyo Seisakushi* [*The History of Industrial Policies*], vols. 3 and 7.

Morikawa, H. (1975), *Gijutsusha* [*Engineers*]. Tokyo: Nihon Keizai Shinbunsha.

Morris-Suzuki, T. (1994), *Technological Transformation of Japan: From the Seventeenth to the Twenty-first Century*. Cambridge: Cambridge University Press.

National Institute of Education (1973), *Nihon Kindai Kyoiku 100-nen Shi* [*A 100-year History of Education of Modern Japan*, ix: *Industrial Education*, 1 and x: *Industrial Education 2*]. Tokyo: Kokuritsu Kyoiku Kenkyusho.

Osaka Industrial Research Institute of MITI (OIRI) (1967), *Osaka Kogyo Gijutsu Shikensho 50-nen Shi* [*A 50-year History of OIRI*].

Osaka Municipal Government (each year edn.), *Osaka Shi Gakuji Tokei* [*Statistics on Educational Affairs of the City of Osaka*].

—— (1940), *Osaka Shi Kogyo Keiei Chosasho: Kinzoku Kikai Kogyo showa 12-nen*, [*Survey of Industrial Management in the City of Osaka: Metals* and Machinery in 1937].

Osaka Municipal Technical Research Institute (OMTRI) (1936*a*), 'Osaka Shiritsu Kogyo Kenkyusho Soritsu 20-nen Shi' ['A 20-year History of OMTRI'], *Kagaku to Kogyo*, 11/5 (May).

—— (1936*b*), 'Koken Kyokai-Kio 10-nen no jigyo gaikyo' ['The Activities of Osaka Industrial Research Association in the past ten years'], *Kagaku to Kogyo*, 11/5 (May).

—— (1966), *Soritsu 50 Shunen Kinenshi* [*A 50-year History*].

Osaka Prefectural Government (each year edn.), *Osaka Fu Tokeisho* [*Statistics on Osaka Prefecture*].

—— (1943), 'Osaka Fu Seisan Zokyo Suishintai Kitei' ['Rules of the Osaka Prefectural Production Promotion Corps'], Library of Kokugakuin University.

Osaka Prefectural Government (n.d.), 'Osaka Fu Seisan Zokyo Suishintai Henseihyo' ['Organization of the Osaka Prefectural Production Promotion Corps'].

Osaka Prefectural Industrial Research Institute (OPIRI) (1944*a*,*b*), *Osaka Fu Kogyo Shorei Kan Gaiyo* [*Outline of OPIRI*], May/Nov., Osaka Prefectural Archives.

—— (1944*c*), 'Kagaku Gijutsu no Senryokuka ni Kansuru Jiko' ['On the use of Science and Technology as War Potential'], Nov., Osaka Prefectural Archives.

—— (Division of Precision Machinery) (n.d.), 'Showa 20-nendo Keikaku Gaiyo' ['Outline of Plans of 1945'], Osaka Prefectural Archives.

—— (1960), *Nobiyuku Kogyo Shorei Kan- Soritsu 30 Shunen Kinen* [*Developing Industrial Research Institute—the 30th Anniversary*].

Osaka Prefectural Institute for Industrial Management (OPIIM) (1936*a*), *Man10 shunen Kinen-Sangyo Noritsu to Sido Jisseki* [*The 10th Anniversary—Industrial Efficiency and Performance of Guidance*].

—— (1936*b*), *Kojo Shindan: Fuka Jitensha Kojo* [*Factory Guidance: Bicycle Factories in Osaka Prefecture*], Report of OPIIM (Sept.).

—— (1942), *Gyomu Nenpo* [*Yearbook of Activities*].

—— (1976), *Noken 50-nen Shi* [*A 50-year History of OPIIM*].

Osaka Technical College (each year edn.), *Osaka Koto Kogyo Gakko Ichiran* [*Osaka Technical College Handbook*].

Osaka University (1985), *Osaka Daigaku 50-nen Shi* [*A 50-year History of Osaka University*], General History vol.

Osaka Vocational School (1936), *20-nen Shi* [*A 20-year History*].

Sato, M. (1984), 'Jitugyo Hoshu Gakko no Seiritsu to Tenkai-Wagakuni Jitsugyo Kyoiku ni Okeru Ichi to Yakuwari' ['The Establishment and Development of Vocational Continuation Schools: Its Position and Role in Vocational Education in Japan'], in T. Toyoda (ed.), *Wagakuni Sangyoka to Jitsugyo Kyoiku* [*Industrialization in Japan and Vocational Education*]. Tokyo: United Nations University.

Sawai, M. (1989), 'The Development of Machine Industries and the Evolution of Production and Labor Management', in T. Yui and K. Nakagawa (eds.), *Japanese Management in Historical Perspective*. Tokyo: University of Tokyo Press.

—— (1990), '1920 Nendai no Yushutsu Zakka Kogyo-Haburashi, Kai Botan, Horo Tekki' ['Sundries Industries for Export in the 1920s: Toothbrushes, Shell Buttons and Enamelled Ironware'], *Keizai Ronshu* (Hokkai-Gakuen University), 38/2 (Dec.).

—— (1995), 'Jukagaku Kogyoka to Gijutsusha' ['The Development of Heavy and Chemical Industries and Engineers'], in M. Miyamoto and T. Abe (eds.), *Nihon Keiei-shi 2: Keiei Kakushin to Kogyoka*, [*Business History of Japan*, ii: *Management Innovation and Industrialization*]. Tokyo: Iwanami Shoten.

Shono, T. (1934), 'Gakusha ha Kakuatte Hoshii' ['Should Scholars Be Like This'], *Kagaku to Kogyo*, 9/2 (Feb.).

Statistics Bureau of the Cabinet (1929), *Rodo Tokei Yoran* [*Handbook on Labour Statistics*]. Tokyo: Naikaku Tokei Kyoku.

Sugayama, S. (1987), '1920 Nendai Judenki Keiei no Kakyu Shokuinso-Hitachi Seisakusho no Jirei Bunseki' ['Employment Management of Junior Staff in the 1920s Electrical Machinery Industry: A Case-study of Hitachi Ltd.'] *Shakai Keizai Shigaku*, 53/5 (Dec.).

Takano, Y. (1992), *Seinen Gakko Shi* [*The History of Youth School*]. Tokyo: Sanichi Shobo.

Takaoka, H. (1936), 'Konnichi no Kogyo Kenkyusho wo Kaerimite', ['Review of Technical Research Institute'], *Kagaku to Kogyo*, 11/5 (May).

Tanba, K. (1952) (ed.), *45-nen Shi* (*A 45-year History*). Osaka Municipal Miyakojima Technical High School.

Tanimoto, M. (1996), 'Jozogyo' ['The Brewing Industry'], in S. Nishikawa, K. Odaka, and O. Saito (eds.), *Nihon Keizai no 200-nen* [*Two-hundred Years of the Japanese Economy*]. Tokyo: Nihon Hyoronsha.

Ui, N. (1932) (ed.), *Kansai Kogaku Ichiran* [*Handbook of Kansai Vocational School*]. Osaka: Kansai Kogaku.

11

Evaluating Japanese Industrial Policy: The Auto-Parts Industry Example

KONOSUKE ODAKA

To promote the development of small and medium-size companies in machinery manufacturing, the Japanese Diet passed legislation in 1956 to supply greatly needed cash flow to the smaller makers of specified kinds of basic machinery, including auto parts and components. This chapter considers this programme as an example of a Japanese industrial policy that was small-scale but contributed greatly to the success of an industry that now sets world standards. The implication might be that the national government and, more specifically, the Ministry of International Trade and Industry (MITI) are due some credit for the success of the auto industry, albeit indirectly, since the creation of a world-class (or even a significant) auto industry was neither a stated policy nor a 'stealth' one. However, even if one argues that the programme was a necessary condition for the auto-sector's success, it was only one of many factors. The larger concern is to understand the motivation and intellectual underpinnings of Japanese industrial policy and how to evaluate it.

Intellectual Underpinnings

The use of significant protection of infant industries while forcing participant domestic firms to move toward international competitiveness is one of the most widely touted features of Japanese industrial policy. In other words, the gains from protection collected by manufacturing firms in Japan for the most part were invested in making the industry more productive. Japan successfully did this in dozens of instances, to the consternation of foreign

The author expresses his appreciation for the editorial assistance rendered by Larry Meissner on an earlier version of this essay.

firms—especially those that, often cheaply, had provided technology. In these cases, Japan stands in sharp contrast to the usual outcome of protection and import substitution: inefficient industries and domestic prices higher than world prices. (Of course, in many other areas Japan has experienced the usual outcome. These, however, were not targets for rationalization.)

This strategy, often termed a successful variant of import substitution in order to avoid the even more pejorative connotations of protectionism, is seen as a model for contemporary developing economies. In the 1980s something like it was tried as a way of providing an opportunity for mature industries in industrialized economies to rationalize in the face of international (i.e. typically Japanese) competition. Part of what differentiates Japan's historical implementation from current versions, and which made it perhaps uniquely successful in economic terms, is the motivation and the purpose (as revealed by outcomes rather than rhetoric). Although for the still-cloistered areas of contemporary Japan's economy, protectionism is primarily about preserving the status quo. To MITI and the manufacturing sectors it was simply a means to allow the dynamic changes necessary to achieve an important end: self-sufficiency for the good of society at large.

This goal grew out of a set of similar, yet intellectually different, motivations. Most immediately, autarky was advocated by Marxist economists, who held the majority of positions in economics departments at the major Japanese state universities from just after the war until the late 1960s. They naturally inspired young students, some of whom joined the central bureaucracy, including MITI, where they practised, sometimes only unconsciously, what they had been taught. This was convergent with an older tradition: there has been an autarkic streak in Japan at least since Tokugawa Ieyasu closed the country in the seventeenth century. In the nineteenth century, this evolved into a quest for self-sufficiency as a means of protection against the depredations of Western colonial powers. This quest helped drive industrialization as well as the imperialist ventures of the 1930s.

After the Second World War, the cold war (and the hot war in Korea) saved Japan from vindictiveness by the victors and helped lay the foundations for subsequent growth, but Japanese policy-makers and business leaders recognized that Japan, as in the past, would have to rely on itself for its well-being. This is self-sufficiency in the true sense, rather than the confused sense of some intellectuals who equate the term with strict autarky and isolationism as opposed to taking responsibility for and care of oneself. Although, from the mid-nineteenth century on, the talk was of 'catching up' with the West, it was understood as a necessary condition for independence.

Shortly after the Second World War Japan experienced a major debate between advocates of protecting domestic industries and those calling for unrestricted international transactions (see, for instance, Kosai 1988). Openness overwhelmed protectionism in the intellectual debate, but MITI adhered to protectionism with rationalization. For MITI, rationalization (*gorika* in

Japanese) was the driving force of policy. In the vocabulary of MITI, it was synonymous with price reductions from higher labour productivity, which would be realized by adopting more capital-intensive technology. This was a complete reversal of the late nineteenth-century drive in Japan, seen today in the emphasis on 'appropriate technologies' in developing countries, of conserving the scarce resource—capital—to utilize the abundant one, labour.

Japan has often been accused of being mercantilist, and it can be fairly said that many of the same means used by mercantilists have been used by Japan, and that this was done in the context of a strong state that extensively involved itself in the economy. Motive is important, however, and it is therefore necessary to distinguish between the use of the means used by mercantilists and the concept of mercantilism. Especially in the 1950s and 1960s, when there was a balance of payments constraint on imports, Japan sought to export in order to import more, not to build foreign reserves (which would be the modern equivalent of mercantilist accumulation of bullion).

Another intellectual current that played a role in industrial policy formation is the fact that after the war, especially in the 1950s but even in the 1960s, the idea of a more capital-intensive (that is, more 'rationalized') machinery industry was emphasized in visions of the future of Japanese manufacturing. Here, one can feel the influence of Minoru Toyosaki, an economist at Kyoto University who became well-known in the 1930s and continued to be active into the 1950s.[1]

The *Kishinhō*

In the mid-1950s, Japanese auto-parts manufacturers—like much of Japanese manufacturing—had outdated yet under-utilized technologies, little skilled labour, abundant unskilled labour, and meagre financial resources. Drawing on previously unpublished material, this chapter examines the ways and the important extent to which the *Kishinhō* legislation and related industrial policy fostered the automobile industry, in spite of the fact that it was not a direct target and auto parts were the very last item on the list of items to be promoted by the law. This analysis will help clarify the socio-economic significance of a specific policy package introduced immediately before the high-growth era.

The legislation, formally titled *Kikai Kōgyō Shinkō Rinji Sochi Hō*, which translates as 'Provisional Law to Promote the Machinery Industry' and generally referred to simply as the *Kishinhō*, was originally limited to five years—although it was extended twice before finally expiring in March 1971. The original policy targets were basic machinery (especially machine tools) and standard machine parts (such as machine bearings), as shown in Table 11.1.

Table 11.1. *Subgroups within the machinery industry (in the order of initial priority under Kishinhō, 1955)*

Tempered iron mouldings
Die-castings
Products of powdered metallurgy (tungsten and molybdenum)
Bolts, nuts, small screws
Bearings
Gears
Metal-cutting tools
Electric welding machines
Electric tools
Metal dies
Cutting tools
Sewing-machine parts
Measuring devices for metals
Testing devices for metals
Clock and watch movements
Resistors and condensers
Auto parts

Note: The number of items increased to 39 in the 1961 revision of *Kishinhō*.

Precision machine tools are prerequisites for the mass manufacturing of other machinery, particularly motor vehicles. Nevertheless, machine tools, let alone auto parts or automobile assembly, were hardly major targets of government industrial policy. Still, the auto industry grew, and that helped the machine-tool industry to renovate and expand, improving quality and lowering prices, which helped the auto industry, and so on in one of the many virtuous circles that characterize Japan's high-growth era.[2] By the end of the 1970s domestic manufacturers could make machine tools as sophisticated and effective as any in the world, with a few notable exceptions (such as gear-cutters, which continue to be imported from the US-based Gleason Corp.).

As early as the mid-1970s, the Japanese auto industry had begun to have considerable impact on US–Japan relations. Because part of the industry's competitive edge came from the measurable, positive impact of the *Kishinhō* on the growth of the auto-parts industry, one might argue that much of the friction over automobiles goes back to a policy undertaken decades earlier.

Historical and Economic Environment

Neither machine tools nor auto parts had ever been specific targets of industrial policy until the enactment of the *Kishinhō*. However, it was not the first

instance of the Japanese government encouraging the general development of the machinery industry. In 1919, the Ministry of Commerce and
Industry (*Shōkō Shō*) under Shinji Yoshino, encouraged adoption of the
Japan Engineering Standard (JES). This indicated awareness on the part of
the central government of the need not only to enlarge the size of the national market but also to upgrade the quality of domestic machines. Especially noteworthy in this respect was the 1929 introduction from Germany
of the industrial rationalization movement.

Increasingly in the 1930s the government became more actively involved
in supporting military-related production facilities. Thus there were the
Automobile Manufacturing Law (1936), the Aeroplane Manufacturing Law
(1939), and the Machine-Tool Manufacturing Law (1940), all promoting domestic production at the expense of both imports and the use of foreign-
made machinery.[3]

The intention of the Army, which was behind the legislation, was to control both production technology and the market for war-related capital
goods. By the late 1930s, foreign firms had been forced out—including Ford
and General Motors, which had had extensive assembly operations in Japan.
Henry Ford was appalled, exclaiming the 'Japanese people are not that
stupid!' (NHK 1986: 119). This reflected his conviction that Japan needed
his company's technology at whatever cost. His assessment was in fact real-
istic. It was widely reported that Japanese soldiers driving trucks in China
(the war there having already begun) openly expressed joy when assigned
American vehicles because of their obviously superior field performance
(ibid.: 44, 49–50).

After the Second World War, 'cheap but poor quality' was a widely circulated, and not unfair, characterization of Japanese products. A story tells of
a newly built truck being driven over the mountains from the factory to
Tokyo—along with many minor problems, its main axle broke. This reflected the fact that production equipment was aged and inferior for most
kinds of durable goods. Repair shops were indispensable.

By the mid-1950s, just before the *Kishinhō* was enacted, the Japanese automobile industry was feeling that it had finally been assured of its survival,
thanks to the demand created by the Korean War. Still, the average unit
price of a domestically made car was as much as 60 per cent higher than a
comparable foreign one (tariffs kept foreign cars out of Japan).

Machine-building firms (especially the smaller ones) were hampered by
poor production conditions, which meant their products were not internationally competitive—'extraordinarily inferior' in the words of one
observer (Hayashi 1961, p. v). The firms were characteristically engaged in
small-lot manufacturing of a large variety of products using dilapidated
production equipment and outdated technology. They did not have the
financial capacity to upgrade. This situation is reflected in the reports of
several surveys done in the late 1950s, such as one conducted by the Japan

Auto Parts Industry Association (JAPIA) and the Japan Federation of Manufacturing Industries (see Nihon Jidōsha Buhin Kōgyō Kai and Nihon Kōgyō Rengō Kai 1957).

While keenly aware of the conditions that prevailed in the parts industry, assemblers were not in a position to help directly, as they were stretching their limited financial resources to upgrade their own facilities (see Odaka, Ono, and Adachi 1988, ch. 4). Moreover, the general business community was not optimistic about the future of the automobile industry, which was to face trade liberalization in 1960.

High-ranking MITI officials directly responsible for automobile policy at the time did not then expect what was to happen. One, Ken Hirayama, later observed that 'It was simply inconceivable for me to imagine the day would come when the annual level of production would hit 500,000' (Odaka 1996: 351). Another, Shigeru Harada, noted 'I was quite pessimistic about the possibility of automobile exports; I also thought that the export of machine tools was a mere dream' (ibid.).

It should be noted that MITI's senior officials had only very limited information on frontier production technology, and very few had technical education—a degree in law or economics was the most common qualification for the ministry's administrative staff. For industries that were targeted, a fairly clear idea of what the future was to look like was formed based on where the industrialized countries already were. For peripheral industries, such as automobiles, there was no clear image of the future. In this sense, MITI can hardly be termed an 'engine of growth'.

This was also a time when business-cycle expectation increased risk, as booms were not expected to last longer than five years without corrections. Under the circumstances, the automobile industry faced a significant risk premium when looking for capital. This was true across the board, even though it was obvious from a technological viewpoint that some parts-makers, especially those serving the after-market ('fast-moving' replacement parts such as sparking-plugs, filters, etc.), could realize economies of scale relatively easily both because of the size of the market and the relative standardization of the products.

Although MITI was not at all sure of the future of the automobile industry in Japan, there was a general perception that Japan could eventually be a large market for passenger automobiles, and it was naturally preferred that this potential be met by domestic production.

The Nature of the *Kishinhō*

Kishinhō decreed that low-interest loans would be made by the Japan Development Bank (JDB)[4] as well as (after 1961) the Small Business Finance

Corporation (SBFC)[5] using funds from the postal savings system. Ordinarily, industrial financing does not call for legislation. The *Kishinhō* was
unique at the time in that specific legislation was introduced in order for the
government to, in effect, allocate part of the country's limited foreign exchange for imports to support a specific industry. (Remember that in the
1950s, the balance of payments was a major constraint on Japanese growth.
Also, while the loans were not explicitly for or limited to imported machinery, the 'highly advanced, first-rank machinery' for which financing
was available generally meant, especially in the early phases of the programme, imported machine tools.) Still, this could have been done in other
ways. The law also provided for accelerated depreciation on equipment
acquired under the programme.

The law stipulated, in Article 10, that 'concerted actions' (*kyōdō kōi*) under
the *Kishinhō* were exempt from the restrictions of the Anti-Monopoly Law
(*Dokusen Kinshi Hō*). This meant that the parts-suppliers could mutually
agree to particular product specifications or quality, and to limit some
firms' areas of business activity.

MITI's original strategy for assisting in the development of the machinery
industry was to establish a semi-public agency that would engage in import-
ing advanced machine tools, which would be loaned to designated parts-
manufacturers to help them improve their production capabilities. (A similar
policy, codified in legislation, had been introduced in 1955 for the coal industry: *Sekitan Kōgyō Gōrika Rinji Sochi Hō*, or Temporary Law to Rationalize
the Coal Industry.)

Unfortunately, however, the strategy could not be implemented, as it was
rejected by the Ministry of Finance (MOF). According to a MITI official at
the time, MOF would not welcome an outsider (MITI) interfering with its
sacred field (banking institutions). Whether or not this fairly describes the
situation, MITI's original intention was saved at the last minute by the
Cabinet Legal Bureau (Naikaku Hosei Kyoku), which proposed special
temporary legislation for financing and for exemption from the restrictions
of the Anti-Monopoly Law regarding concerted actions. It should be pointed
out here, however, that no such legislation would ever be required for the
purposes of industrial subsidization and, furthermore, that of the sixteen
cases where the special exemption clause (Article 10) was invoked during
the life of the *Kishinhō*, only one item (bearings) was directly related to auto-
parts production (Nihon Kikai Kōgyō Rengō Kai 1983: 4–8, 28).

It is truly surprising, even in retrospect, that it took only six months for
the *Kishinhō* to be prepared, discussed, and enacted (with little opposition
and no revisions). The only substantive point raised in the Diet came from
the Socialist Party, which wished the Law's application to be restricted to
'genuinely small firms' by excluding those with equity capital of 100 million or more yen. The quick passage reflects the non-confrontational political atmosphere prevailing at the time—the so-called Era of 1955. The

Democratic and Liberal parties had merged in November 1955 to form a grand, united front, the Liberal Democratic Party (LDP) that was to dominate Japanese politics for more than thirty-five years. Even without the merger, the legislation would undoubtedly have passed, however, because the parties (socialist or otherwise) were keen on gaining support from medium- and small-business owners.

Government policy did more than provide credit. Although loan applicants were expected to be moving quickly toward international standards of quality and cost, there was no actual competition from foreign firms in Japan's domestic market, either directly in the form of imports or even from foreign operations in Japan. A certain amount of market discipline was imposed on firms, but without exposing them directly to the full force of competition.

How the *Kishinhō* Worked

The *Kishinhō* had a unique manner of operation. Its action programmes were drawn up by the Deliberation Council on the Machinery Industry, which was composed of 'government experts and learned scholars in the field of the machinery industry' (*Kishinhō*, Article 14), appointed by the Minister of International Trade and Industry. The Council was convened on a fairly regular basis to investigate, discuss, and decide which products to promote, and on what grounds, based on first-hand information concerning technological and production practices for specific parts. This intelligence came from detailed, in-depth field surveys as well as from material collected by MITI officials and industry engineers that indicated which machine-producing technologies deserved priority support, and what level of support they would need. The outcome of these activities was the drawing-up of an annual programme of rationalization for each of the sub-industries selected as targets for that year from within the machinery industry.

In drawing its conclusions, the Council reviewed such matters as the availability and quality of raw materials, the gap between currently used and available technologies, and the ranking of auto parts in terms of their need for upgrading. The Basic Program Guide was quite specific in spelling out auto parts targeted for public support, the kinds of machine tools to be procured by the programme, and the size of the budget. Applications were then screened by a committee of the Association for the Promotion of the Machinery Industry (*Kikai Kōgyō Shinkō Kyōkai*). This association was a semi-public organization set up by MITI as a clearing house for administering the *Kishinhō*. The screening was done on a competitive basis in the sense that applications were judged against each other rather than being automatically approved if specific criteria were met.

It is important to note that, in deciding which applications to accept, the Council was making explicit decisions about the allocation of investment not only within the machinery industry's subgroups, but also as to which specific firms were to be helped.

When the selections were made, a formal recommendation was made by MITI to the JDB that loans be extended to the designated companies for the specified amounts. After 1961, the SBFC also was involved in disbursing loans. These financial agencies were both independent of the executive branch and had full authority to review from their own perspective the quality of the applications forwarded by MITI. However, neither the JDB nor the SBFC ever reached a different conclusion than MITI regarding a loan.

These were the first loans by the JDB to medium and small firms, and were thus considered epoch-making. Some recipients, such as Meiki Manufacturing, a relatively small die-maker in central Tokyo, proudly printed on their brochures the fact their applications had been accepted, albeit in rather small type.

All the applications had to be accompanied with plans spelling out detailed intentions regarding investment in production equipment, how obtaining imported machine tools would help, production schedules of the auto part in question, and even drawings of the plant's layout. Obviously, preparation of the applications was a discouraging factor for small and medium companies (SMCs). Some found the procedure so cumbersome that they would have withdrawn their applications had government officials not been insistent on their perseverance. Even with help and encouragement, a few applicants failed during the initial stage of *Kishinhō* administration. There were, however, no reported failures after the first year of its operation. This suggests a measure of 'self-selection', perhaps with government help.

MITI was actively involved, especially in the early years, in offering advice on the selection of equipment and even in negotiating discounts on the amount of royalties in the case of technology licensing. In such cases, it was able to draw on better informed and more experienced personnel than the firm would have been able to. MITI's assistance was thus of great value to the firms.

Recipients of loans under the *Kishinhō* were often able to use their favoured designation to borrow from city banks. This is the well-known 'cowbell effect' that attached to government-subsidized credit programmes during the period, i.e. private banks felt successful applicants were already well screened, thus saving them considerable costs. In the case of *Kishinhō* auto-parts programmes during 1956–65, the city banks loaned as much as 6.6 yen for each yen loaned by the JDB. While the JDB and the SBFC were lending specifically for purchases of designated production equipment and related facilities, the banks extended credit for general capital formation purposes.[6]

The total loans advanced under the *Kishinhō* during its 16-year life was 115 billion yen, equivalent to 1.9 per cent of the credit extended to private production sectors under central government loan programmes.[7]

Auto Parts under the *Kishinhō*

The law's original targets were 'basic machinery' (machine tools in particular) and 'standard machine parts' (such as machine bearings). Indeed, auto parts were the very last item on the list, so that in the initial stages only a few firms participated in the programme and the industry received a relatively small part of the funds lent out. This was not only because greater priority was placed elsewhere but also because firms were in effect expected to reach a certain level of capability on their own.

The financing extended to auto parts subsequently increased at a phenomenal rate in terms of both total and per-company amounts (Figure 11.1). There is no hard evidence as to why this happened, but it can be interpreted as reflecting the Council's positive response to a conscious effort by parts-makers to modernize in anticipation of trade liberalization, scheduled for 1961, and capital liberalization (allowing foreign investment), set for 1966. In 1963–4 clear peaks were reached in the number of applying firms and in the items that were made eligible (Figures 11.2 and 11.3)

Note that the SBFC generally financed the smaller firms, and the JDB the larger ones. This probably explains why SBFC financing per firm did not increase much. Smaller, often family, firms probably had a narrow range of products and less capacity (and opportunity) to expand offerings. A few

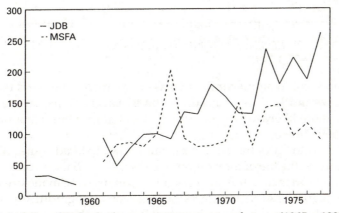

Fig. 11.1. *Index of* Kishinhō *loans per auto-parts manufacturer (1965 = 100). For administrative reasons, disbursements under* Kishinhō *did not take place for fiscal year 1960. Figures after 1971 indicate loans under* Kidenhō *(see note 2).*

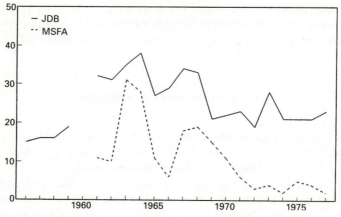

Fig. 11.2. *Number of* Kishinhō *applications submitted by auto-parts manufacturers.*

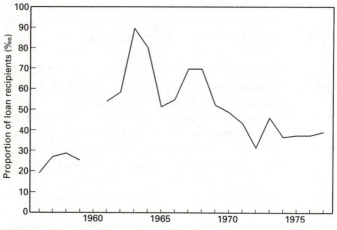

Fig. 11.3. *Distribution over time of the* Kishinhō *loan recipients (%) (total 1956–77: 1,149).*

new machines could significantly increase capacity for the parts the firm made. This would limit their need for funds. Larger firms, on the other hand, were more likely to be expanding not just output but the number of products they offered.

The Japan Auto Parts Industry Association (JAPIA) had some 330-plus members during the life of the programme (1956–71). Of these, only 161 received *Kishinhō* financing, but an average of 3.3 loans were made to each recipient (see Figure 11.4). This reflects the intention of upgrading 'relatively deficient' products quickly. For recipients of JDB loans, the financing covered about 23 per cent of their investment in production equipment, and as much as 40 per cent of purchases of 'advanced machinery' designated by

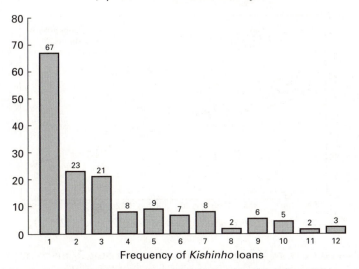

Fig. 11.4. Kishinhō *recipients in auto-parts industry as classified by frequency of loans (1956–70).*

the government. For SBFC borrowers, the numbers were 32 per cent and 32 per cent respectively.[8]

With access to better equipment, the quality of parts and labour productivity improved substantially. As shown in Figures 11.5 and 11.6, the prices of Japanese auto parts and components declined both in absolute terms and, despite an undervalued yen, relative to international levels. (In 1956, Japanese parts cost as much as 1.2 to 2.0 times international levels (Odaka, Ono, and Adachi 1988: 77–8).)

Complementing the *Kishinhō*, loosely affiliated production groups were formed which promoted an ongoing effort to simplify and standardize

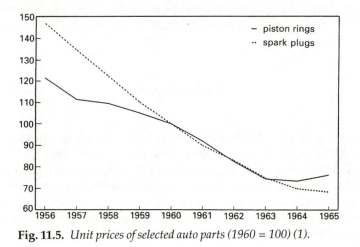

Fig. 11.5. *Unit prices of selected auto parts (1960 = 100) (1).*

Konosuke Odaka

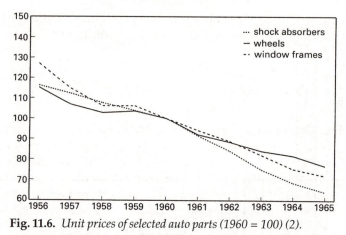

Fig. 11.6. *Unit prices of selected auto parts (1960 = 100) (2).*

products. There were 165 such groups, encompassing 27 machine products. In addition, ten joint production enterprises (*kyōdō jigyō kaisha*) were formed to encourage co-operation in production and to facilitate efficient use of equipment as well as labour (Nihon Kikai Kōgyō Rengō Kai 1983: 7–8).

The industry worked through JAPIA to form a unified position when dealing with those outside the industry, such as the assemblers and the government, and JAPIA served as a valuable forum for exchanging information. An example of this is the Deliberation Council, which consisted of administrators from government agencies related to auto parts, scholars, and other experts. Technical information was freely exchanged at its meetings and government officials had an opportunity to hear directly the real needs of the industry. These meetings also provided a sanctioned, monitored forum in which firms could exchange technical and engineering information to become collectively and individually more competitive. (Formal protection from the anti-trust laws notwithstanding, the government sought to increase competition among individual firms in the industry.)

The Outcome

The *Kishinhō* was extended twice. First, in 1961, when importation of passenger vehicles was to have been liberalized but was not. (That finally came about in October 1965.) Judging from the relative share of auto parts in total *Kishinhō* financing and from the share of that financing in auto-parts companies' investment, concerted effort by the industry and MITI to strengthen the competitiveness of Japanese auto production seems to have reached its peak around 1963.

The programme was extended again in 1966. By then, the policy objective of 'achieving international competitive power' in auto parts had been virtually achieved. So also had almost all the other policy targets of the Basic Rationalization Plans (*gōrika kihon keikaku*) which were formulated at the beginning of the policy-supported financing phase as a direct corollary to the 'Five-year Plan to Achieve Economic Independence' (*Keizai Jiritsu Gokanen Keikaku*) adopted by the government in 1955. It can be convincingly argued that the technological and managerial capabilities of the country were reflected in the fact that this was done in the short span of about a decade.

In January 1971 the lowering of barriers to foreign investment, originally scheduled for 1966, finally took place. Shortly thereafter, in March 1971, the law was allowed to expire. By then the parts-makers and assemblers had achieved price, quality, and design levels that, aided by the oil crisis and mistakes by their US competitors, allowed them by the mid-1980s to become world standard-setters in most categories of passenger vehicles. Virtually all *Kishinhō* financing was repaid, implying that the selection process properly identified firms with sufficient potential for successful growth.

From the evidence, it is fair to say that the rationalization process in the parts industry during the late 1950s and 1960s would have been at least substantially delayed, if not impossible. By extension, although the Japanese automobile assemblers would probably not have met the fate of the pessimists (the oil crisis and the sluggish performance of US auto-makers assured that), their international success would have been more difficult and more limited. The machine-tool industry, too, would have experienced slower growth without the *Kishinhō*, and this would have reduced the performance of the overall economy.

The success of the *Kishinhō* was predicated on two factors. First, there were international standards for what was being produced and the technology to achieve them was relatively stable at the time. Second, at least through the 1960s, the United States was a powerful forerunner and formidable competitor—a benchmark.

Evaluation

Several not necessarily inconsistent viewpoints exist for evaluating an industrial policy. This is a direct consequence of the difficulty in defining the 'effect' of a policy. The minimum condition for any policy to be judged successful is for its originally stated objectives to have been achieved. Even when success may have been realized irrespective of the policy, one can contend the policy was not a total failure. Policy-makers of course prefer cases where all positive outcomes are ascribable to the policy and its implementation. Sometimes goals are reached despite a policy, which should be termed a failure. (I ignore any unintended negative consequences of policies, which arguably must temper any claim for policy success made on the narrower grounds of its stated goals.)

Outcomes generally lie well within these extreme bounds. Even when a policy has attained its original targets, it is extremely unlikely that this can be attributed solely to the government's own doing because public policies in Japan are normally formed in close consultation with the private sector and executed with its co-operation. Indeed, Japanese industrial policy has never been possible without active support from the private sector. Sometimes the 'policies' have been little more than goals the government has little ability or interest in actively or directly furthering.

As an example, MITI's automobile division never had more than a handful of officers, not all of whom were wholly convinced of the bright future of the industry. It was the firms' self-help, especially through their industry association, that made the difference.

Thus, the fate of Japanese industrial policy hinged on the extent to which it ignited the investment activities of private entrepreneurs. To make a judgement on this point, one needs to know if it was at all possible for the private sector to have initiated, carried out, and achieved the same target by itself, without government inducement. This requires an exercise in alternative history, but it is still generally possible to make some inferences. This is especially true with the many Japanese policies that were aimed at clearing bottlenecks through technological upgrading and capacity expansion —as the *Kishinhō* was.

In the mid-1950s, the machinery industry generally, and parts in particular, needed better machines and more of them. This was not a situation where their existing equipment could be sufficiently 'tweaked' to achieve the goals of precision and output. The firms did not have sufficient collateral to borrow from the private financial system, which in any case faced tremendous demands on both its supply of loanable funds and on its capacity to assess loan applicants. Beyond that, the needed equipment had to be imported, meaning scarce foreign exchange was needed. In short, there is no obvious, plausible, alternative way that the Japanese auto-parts industry could have improved its economic efficiency in such a short time other than through a policy that addressed these barriers, and that is precisely what the *Kishinhō* did.

NOTES

1. The influence of Professor Toyosaki is apparent in, for instance, the writings of Shintaro Hayashi (see, for example, Hayashi 1961).

2. Another industry not (initially) targeted by MITI that enjoyed a virtuous circle did, like machine tools, have supportive legislation. An exact replica of *Kishinhō*, the *Denshinhō* (*Denshi Kōgyō Shinkō Rinji Sochi Hō*), was enacted in June 1957 to promote the electrical-machinery industry. It, too, expired in March 1971, but was followed by a series of laws supporting electronics (the *Kidenhō* (*Tokutei Denshi Kōgyō oyobi Tokutei Kikai Kōgyō Shinkō Rinji Sochi Hō*), April 1971 to March 1978) and information-related industries (the *Kijōhō* (*Tokutei Kikai Jōhō Sangyō Shinkō Rinji Sochi Hō*), July 1978). It was July 1985 when, in the face of intense US–Japan economic conflict, such legislation was finally terminated.

   General studies of the emergence of the auto industry in English include Cusumano 1985 and Odaka, Ono, and Adachi 1988, among others. Okimoto 1989 remains an important overview of the fact that MITI, whatever its vision and power, was only a part of the force driving Japan's incredible growth.

3. The formal titles of these laws are, respectively, *Jidōsha Seizō Jigyō Hō*, *Kōkūki Seizō Jigyō Hō*, and *Kōsaku Kikai Seizō Jigyō Hō*.

4. *Nihon Kaihatsu Ginkō*.

5. *Chūshō Kigyō Kinyū Kōko*.

6. During 1956–60, a total of 1.3 billion yen was lent by the JDB to *Kishinhō*-designated auto-parts producers. Total investment in production equipment by the same companies amounted to 14.8 billion yen, of which 8.6 billion was supplied by city banks. The remainder came from the companies' equity and retained earnings (MITI/JDB 1963: 169).

7. The figure is based on the loans extended by the following four financing organizations: JDB, SBFC, Export-Import Bank of Japan, and Agriculture, Forestry and Fisheries Finance Corporation. The figure is reduced to 0.8 per cent when one takes in the entire treasury investment financing programmes supported by the central government. The total budget under *Kishinhō* is from Nihon Kikai Kōgyō Rengō Kai 1983: 6, and the record of treasure programmes is from the Bank of Japan, *Keizai Tōkei Nempō* (*Economic Statistics Annual*), 1962 and 1968 editions.

8. The figures in this paragraph have been computed from JAPIA's annual reports (*Nihon Jidōsha Buhin Kōgyō Kai Jigyō Hōkokusho*), various years.

REFERENCES

Cusumano, Michael A. (1985), *The Japanese Automobile Industry, Technology and Management at Nissan and Toyota*. Cambridge, Mass.: Harvard University Press.

Hayashi, Shintarō (1961), *Nihon Kikai Yushutu Ron; Kakudai Hatten no Kozoteki Kiso* [*A Case for Machinery Export Promotion: The Structural Foundation for Expanding Economic Reproduction*]. Tokyo: Toyo Keizai Shimpō Sha.

Kosai, Yutaka (1988), 'The Reconstruction Period', in Ryutaro Komiya, Masahiro Okuno and Kotaro Suzumura (eds.), *Industrial Policy of Japan*. San Diego: Academic Press.

MITI/JDB (1963), *Tokutei Kikai Yūshi to sono Gōrika Kōka, Dai Ichiji Gōrika Kihon Keikaku Tassei Jōkyō* [*Financing Investment on Designated Machinery and Its Effects on Rationalization: A Review of the First Rationalization Plan*]. Tokyo: Kikai Kōgyō Shinkō Kyōkai.

NHK (Document Showa Shuzai Han) (1986), *Amerika Sha Jōriku o Soshi seyo* [*Stop the Landing of American Automobiles!*]. Tokyo: Kadokawa Shoten.

Nihon Jidōsha Buhin Kōgyō Kai [Japan Auto-Parts Industry Association, JAPIA] and Nihon Kōgyō Rengō Kai [Japan Federation of Manufacturing Industries] (1957), *Jidōsha Buhin Kōgyō no Jittai* [*A Report on the Survey of the Auto-Parts Industry*], 2 vols. Tokyo.

Nihon Kikai Kōgyō Rengō Kai [The Federation of the Machinery Industry in Japan] (1983), *Kikai Jōhō Sangyō ni kansuru Ichiren no Rippō Sochi no Gaiyō to Unyō* [*An Overview of the Working of the Law to Promote the Development of Machinery and Information Industries*]. Tokyo.

Odaka, Konosuke (1996), 'Kishinhō to Jidōsha Buhin—Kōdo Seichō ki Chokuzen ni okeru Sangyō Seisaku no Keizaiteki Kōka ni tsuite' ['The Provisional Act to Promote Machinery Industries (*Kishinhō*) and Auto-Parts Production in Post-war Japan—Economic Evaluation of an Industrial Policy'], *Keizai Kenkyu (Economic Review)*, 47/4 (Oct.).

——, Ono, Keinosuke and Adachi, Fumihiko (1988), *The Automobile Industry in Japan, A Study of Ancillary Firm Development*. Tokyo: Kinokuniya Bookstore and Oxford: Oxford University Press.

Okimoto, Daniel I. (1989), *Between MITI and the Market, Japanese Industrial Policy for High Technology*. Stanford, Calif.: Stanford University Press.

Epilogue:
Where Do We Go from Here?

KONOSUKE ODAKA and MINORU SAWAI

The present volume has presented a variety of experiences, both past and present, by different countries and relating to different aspects of SMCs. As pointed out in the introductory chapter, the definition of SMCs varies from one chapter to another, and, even within the same country, from one period to another. All the authors in the volume are united in one point, however, that one cannot possibly overlook the significance of SMCs in understanding the past and present of the economies dealt with in the respective chapters.

What about the future of SMCs? Clearly no one can be absolutely sure. On the basis of historical experience, as described in the present volume, it is fair to expect that SMCs will continue to play an important role in the future global economy. No doubt, the fields of their comparative advantage will shift from time to time, and they will continue to display relatively high rates of births and deaths. In the words of a well-known Japanese writer,

... the community-based [small] industries have the persistence of a weed; this is the quality which has enabled them to ride out crises they have confronted. In other words, it can be said that they have considerable flexibility for adaptation to change in the economic environment .... (Yamazaki 1980: 247)

The presence of economies of scale and of scope will hardly negate the *raison d'être* of the SMCs. In all likelihood both big and small firms will benefit from their coexistence, each supplementing and amplifying the functions of the other.

A crucial aspect missing from the present volume is the experiences of SMCs in contemporary developing economies. The follower countries in development have, in one way or another, faced the issue of 'dualism' between big and small, as in the case of Japan. As a possible next step of research, one might critically compare the rich content of the essays in the present volume with the situations of the follower countries. Utilizing the results of such comparisons, it will be the task of theoretically minded empirical economists to identify the conditions in which SMCs will make maximum contributions to the working of national and regional economies, thus enhancing the quality of people's living.

REFERENCES

Yamazaki, Mitsuru (1980), *Japan's Community-Based Industries: A Case-Study of Small Industry*. Tokyo: Asian Productivity Organization.

INDEX